T0259661

Design Patterns in C#

A Hands-on Guide with Real-world Examples

Second Edition

Vaskaran Sarcar
Foreword by Priya Shimanthoor

Apress®

Design Patterns in C#: A Hands-on Guide with Real-world Examples

Vaskaran Sarcar
Garia, Kolkata, West Bengal, India

ISBN-13 (pbk): 978-1-4842-6061-6   ISBN-13 (electronic): 978-1-4842-6062-3
https://doi.org/10.1007/978-1-4842-6062-3

Copyright © 2020 by Vaskaran Sarcar

This work is subject to copyright. All rights are reserved by the Publisher, whether the whole or part of the material is concerned, specifically the rights of translation, reprinting, reuse of illustrations, recitation, broadcasting, reproduction on microfilms or in any other physical way, and transmission or information storage and retrieval, electronic adaptation, computer software, or by similar or dissimilar methodology now known or hereafter developed.

Trademarked names, logos, and images may appear in this book. Rather than use a trademark symbol with every occurrence of a trademarked name, logo, or image we use the names, logos, and images only in an editorial fashion and to the benefit of the trademark owner, with no intention of infringement of the trademark.

The use in this publication of trade names, trademarks, service marks, and similar terms, even if they are not identified as such, is not to be taken as an expression of opinion as to whether or not they are subject to proprietary rights.

While the advice and information in this book are believed to be true and accurate at the date of publication, neither the authors nor the editors nor the publisher can accept any legal responsibility for any errors or omissions that may be made. The publisher makes no warranty, express or implied, with respect to the material contained herein.

Managing Director, Apress Media LLC: Welmoed Spahr
Acquisitions Editor: Smriti Srivastava
Development Editor: Laura Berendson
Coordinating Editor: Shrikant Vishwakarma

Cover designed by eStudioCalamar

Cover image designed by Freepik (www.freepik.com)

Distributed to the book trade worldwide by Springer Science+Business Media New York, 233 Spring Street, 6th Floor, New York, NY 10013. Phone 1-800-SPRINGER, fax (201) 348-4505, e-mail orders-ny@springer-sbm.com, or visit www.springeronline.com. Apress Media, LLC is a California LLC and the sole member (owner) is Springer Science + Business Media Finance Inc (SSBM Finance Inc). SSBM Finance Inc is a **Delaware** corporation.

For information on translations, please e-mail booktranslations@springernature.com; for reprint, paperback, or audio rights, please e-mail bookpermissions@springernature.com.

Apress titles may be purchased in bulk for academic, corporate, or promotional use. eBook versions and licenses are also available for most titles. For more information, reference our Print and eBook Bulk Sales web page at http://www.apress.com/bulk-sales.

Any source code or other supplementary material referenced by the author in this book is available to readers on GitHub via the book's product page, located at www.apress.com/978-1-4842-6061-6. For more detailed information, please visit http://www.apress.com/source-code.

Printed on acid-free paper

This book is dedicated to all the unsung heroes and volunteers who are continuously fighting at the frontlines of the COVID-19 battle to save humanity and this beautiful world.

Table of Contents

TABLE OF CONTENTS

About the Author

Vaskaran Sarcar obtained his master's degree in software engineering from Jadavpur University, Kolkata (India), and an MCA from Vidyasagar University, Midnapore (India). He was a National Gate Scholar (2007–2009), and he has more than 12 years of experience in education and the IT industry. Vaskaran devoted his early years (2005–2007) in teaching at various engineering colleges. Later, he joined HP India PPS R&D Hub Bangalore, where he worked until August 2019. At the time of his retirement from the IT industry, he was a Senior Software Engineer and Team Lead at HP. Following his passion, Vaskaran is now an independent full-time author. His books include the following:

- *Getting Started with Advanced C#* (Apress, 2020)
- *Interactive Object-Oriented Programming in Java Second Edition* (Apress, 2019)
- *Java Design Patterns Second Edition* (Apress, 2019)
- *Design Patterns in C#* (Apress, 2018)
- *Interactive C#* (Apress, 2017)
- *Interactive Object-Oriented Programming in Java* (Apress, 2016)
- *Java Design Patterns* (Apress, 2016)
- *C# Basics: Test Your Skills* (Createspace, 2015)
- *Operating System: Computer Science Interview Series* (Createspace, 2014)

About the Technical Reviewers

Carsten Thomsen is a back-end developer primarily but works with smaller front-end bits as well. He has authored and reviewed several books and has created numerous Microsoft Learning courses on software development. Carsten works as a freelancer/contractor in various countries in Europe; Azure, Visual Studio, Azure DevOps, and GitHub are some of his favorite tools. An exceptional troubleshooter, he asks the right questions, including the less logical ones, in the most logical to least logical fashion. He also enjoys working with architecture, research, analysis, development, testing, and bug fixing. Carsten is a communicator with skills in mentoring, team leadership, research, and presenting new material.

Shekhar Kumar Maravi is a lead engineer in design and development whose main interests are programming languages, algorithms, and data structures. He obtained his master's degree in computer science and engineering from the Indian Institute of Technology, Bombay. After graduation, he joined Hewlett-Packard's R&D Hub in India to work on printer firmware. Currently, he is a technical lead engineer at Siemens Healthcare's R&D division. He can be reached by email at shekhar.maravi@gmail.com or via LinkedIn at www.linkedin.com/in/shekharmaravi.

Foreword

Written programs need to be flexible, easily maintainable, and reusable. How do we know that a program is as elegant as it can be? The answer is that a successful programmer must use two primary tools: a good programming language (here it is C#) and design patterns.

When working on a problem, it is unusual to tackle it by inventing a new solution that is completely dissimilar from the existing ones. One often recalls a similar problem and reuses the essence of its solution to solve the new problem. This kind of thinking in problem-solving is common to many different domains, such as software engineering.

Design patterns are important building blocks for designing and modeling applications on all platforms. Design patterns help us understand, discuss, and reuse applications on a specific platform. The most common reasons for studying patterns are the reuse of solutions and the establishment of common terminology. By reusing established designs, a developer gets a headstart on the problem and avoids common mistakes. The benefit of learning from the experience of others' results is that the developer does not have to reinvent solutions for recurring problems. The other reason for using patterns is that common terminology brings a common base of vocabulary and viewpoint of the problem for developers. It provides a common point of reference during the analysis and design phase of a project.

Vaskaran Sarcar, who has worked with me for several years now, has been a Most Valuable Professional over the years in C#. He is enthusiastic, knowledgeable, talented, curious, analytical, and a teacher of others. He gets to the root of any problem he is trying to resolve in a well-defined and organized way. He is very committed and works hard until he gets to the solution. He gets involved and is deeply focused while working on any problem.

And that is also why I am excited about this book. The book brings the frequently complex world of design patterns into sharp focus with the approach used: the definition, the core concept, a real-life example, a computer-world example, and a sample program with output. In this edition, Vaskaran has provided asynchronous programming patterns usage using C#.

I look forward to seeing where developers can go with this easy approach and language, and the useful patterns they can build into the infrastructure of other languages.

—Priya Shimanthoor

Test Architect

Managed Print Services Team

Bangalore, India

June 3, 2020

Acknowledgments

First, I thank the Almighty. I sincerely believe that I could complete this book only with His blessings. I extend my deepest gratitude and thanks to the following people.

Ratanlal Sarkar and Manikuntala Sarkar: My dear parents, only with your blessings could I complete this work.

Indrani, my wife; **Ambika**, my daughter; **Aryaman**, my son: Sweethearts, once again, without your love, I could not proceed at all. I know that we need to limit many social gatherings and invitations to complete my books on time, and each time I promise you that I'll take a long break and spend more time with you.

Sambaran, my brother: Thank you for your constant encouragement.

Carsten: I know that whenever I was in need, your support was there. Thank you once more.

Sekhar: I know this time you helped only in the incremented version of the book, but thank you once more.

Ankit, my technical advisor in the first edition of this book: I always acknowledge your contribution and help. I know that your valuable comments were some of the key foundations for this enhanced edition.

Priya, my ex-colleague cum senior: A special thanks to you for investing your time to write the forewords for both editions of this book. When experts like you agree to write for me, I get the additional motivation to enhance the quality of my work.

Celestin, Laura, Smriti: Thanks for giving me another opportunity to work with you and Apress.

Shrikant: Thank you for your exceptional support to beautify my work.

The production team—Krishnan Sathyamurthy, Sherly, Ramraj, Selvakumar, and MathaRajamohan: Thank you guys; your efforts are extraordinary.

Lastly, I extend my deepest gratitude to my publisher, the editorial board members, and everyone who directly or indirectly supports this book.

Preface

Welcome to your journey through *Design Patterns in C# Second Edition*.

This book is an introductory guide to the design patterns that you want to use in C#. You probably know that the concept of design patterns became extremely popular with the Gang of Four's famous book *Design Patterns: Elements of Reusable Object-Oriented Software* (Addison-Wesley, 1994). That book was primarily focused on C++, but these concepts still apply in today's programming world.

C# had its first major release (C# 2.0) in 2005. Since then, it has become rich with new features and is now a popular programming language. In 2015, I wrote the book *Design Patterns in C#: Computer Science Interview Series*. In 2018, *Design Patterns in C#: A Hands-on Guide with Real-World Examples* was born. In these books, my core intention was to implement each of the 23 Gang of Four (GoF) design patterns with C# implementations. I wanted to present each pattern with simple examples. One thing was always on my mind when writing: I wanted to use the most basic constructs of C# so that the code would be compatible with both the upcoming version and the legacy version of C#. I have found this method helpful in the world of programming.

In the last few years, I got a lot of constructive feedback from my readers. This fully revised and updated version was created with that feedback in mind. I took the opportunity to update the formatting and correct some typos from the previous version of the book and add new content to this new edition. In this book, I focus on another important area; I call it the "doubt-clearing sessions." I knew that if I could add more information, such as alternative ways to write the implementations, the pros and cons of the patterns, when to choose one approach over another, and so on, readers would find this book even more helpful.

In this updated version of the original, the "Q&A Session" sections in each chapter are further enhanced. These sessions can help you learn about each pattern in more depth. In addition, you see more code explanations for all the programs, and in many cases, the programs are further simplified, and new programs are added for the patterns. *To learn about the most important enhancements in this edition, refer to* Appendix D at the end of this book.

How Is the Book Organized?

This book has three major parts.

Part I consists of the first 23 chapters, which discusses and implements all the GoF design patterns.

In the world of programming, there is no shortage of patterns, and each has its own significance. Part II discusses some additional design patterns (Simple Factory, Null Object, and MVC) that are equally important in today's world of programming. In this second edition, I dropped discussions of memory leaks, but I include several patterns from asynchronous programming. In modern applications, these patterns are very common.

Part III discusses the criticism of design patterns and overviews antipatterns, which are important when you implement the concepts of design patterns in your applications.

Each chapter is divided into six major parts: a definition (which is basically the intent in the GoF book), a core concept, a real-world example, a computer/coding–world example, a sample program with various output, and the "Q&A Session" section. These sections help you learn about each pattern in more depth.

Please remember that you have just started this journey. As you learn the concepts, try to write your own code; only then will you master an area.

You will be able to download all the book's source code from the Apress website. I plan to maintain the errata, and if necessary, I will also make updates and announcements there.

Prerequisite Knowledge

This book's target readers are those who are familiar with C# basic language constructs and pure object-oriented concepts, like polymorphism, inheritance, abstraction, encapsulation, and most importantly, how to compile or run a C# application in Visual Studio. This book does not invest time in easily available topics, such as how to install Visual Studio on your system, or how to write a "Hello World" program in C#, or how can you use an if-else statement or a while loop, and so forth. This book was written using the most basic features of C#, so for most of the programs in this book, you do not need to be familiar with C# advanced topics. The examples are simple and straightforward. I believe that the examples are written in such a way that even if you are familiar with another popular language, such as Java or C++, you can still easily grasp the concepts in this book.

Who Is This Book For?

In short, you want this book if your answer is "yes" to all of the following questions.

- Are you familiar with basic constructs in C# and object-oriented concepts like polymorphism, inheritance, abstraction, and encapsulation?

- Do you know how to set up your coding environment?

- Do you want to explore the design patterns in C# step by step?

- Do you want to explore GoF design patterns?

- Are you interested in learning about Simple Factory, Null Object, MVC, and asynchronous programming patterns?

- Do you want to know how the core constructs of C# work behind these patterns?

You probably don't want this book if the answer is "yes" to any of the following questions.

- Are you new to C#?

- Are you looking for advanced concepts in C#, excluding the topics mentioned previously?

- Are you interested in exploring a book where the focus is on GoF patterns (and the patterns listed in the previous section)?

- Do you dislike a book that uses Q&A sessions?

- "I do not like Windows, Visual Studio, and .NET Core. I want to learn and use C# without them." Is this statement true for you?

Guidelines for Using This Book

Here are some suggestions to help you use this book more effectively.

- I assume that you have some knowledge of GoF design patterns. If you are new to design patterns, I suggest you quickly go through Appendix A, which helps you become familiar with the basic concepts of design patterns.

- If you are confident with what Appendix A covers, you can start with any part of the book. But I suggest you go through the chapters sequentially. The reason is that some fundamental design techniques may have been discussed in the Q&A Session of a previous chapter, and I do not repeat those techniques in later chapters.

- There is only one exception to the previous suggestion. There are three factory patterns: Simple Factory, Factory Method, and Abstract Factory. These three patterns are closely related, but the Simple Factory pattern does not directly fall into the GoF design catalog, so it appears in Part II of the book. Therefore, of the three patterns, I suggest that you begin with the Simple Factory.

- Except for a few programs in Chapter 27, all programs were executed and tested in .NET Core 3.1. The remaining programs were executed in .NET Framework 4.7.2 because .NET Core doesn't support certain functionalities. The specific reasons are discussed in Chapter 27.

- I used Visual Studio Community edition 2019 (version 16.3.9) in a Windows 10 environment. This Community edition is free. If you do not use the Windows operating system, you can use Visual Studio Code, which is a source code editor developed by Microsoft to support Windows, Linux, or macOS operating systems. This multiplatform IDE is free. When I started writing this book, I used the latest versions of C# available. In this context, it is useful to know that the C# language version is automatically selected based on your project's target framework(s) so that you always have the highest compatible version by default. In the most recent versions, Visual Studio doesn't support the UI to change the value, but you can change it by editing the .csproj file. The Visual Studio 2019 compiler and the .NET Core 3.0 SDK follow this rule. Therefore, you can simply say that when your target framework is .NET Core 3.x (or newer), you'll get C# 8.0(and higher) by default. If you are interested in C# language versioning, go to `https://docs.microsoft.com/en-us/dotnet/csharp/language-reference/configure-language-version`.

- Version updates are continuous, but I strongly believe that
  the versions should not matter much to you because I use the
  fundamental constructs of C# in this book. The code should
  execute smoothly in the upcoming versions of C#/Visual Studio
  as well. Although I believe that the results should not vary in other
  environments, you know the nature of a software-it can be naughty.
  So, I recommend that if you want to see the same output, it is best to
  mimic the same environment.

- You can download and install Visual Studio IDE from `https://
  visualstudio.microsoft.com/downloads/`. You should see what's
  shown in Figure P-1.

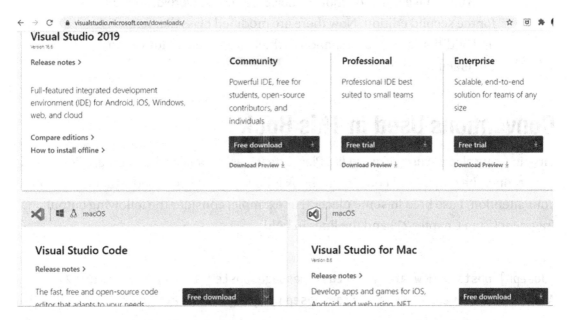

Figure P-1. *Download link for Visual Studio 2019 and Visual Studio Code*

Note   At the time of this writing, this link works fine, and the information is
correct. But the link and policies may change in the future.

- I installed the class designer component in Visual Studio 2019 to draw class diagrams for my programs. I needed to edit some of these diagrams for better readability (for example, to show composition, aggregation, etc.). I added some valuable notes to these diagrams so that you can better understand them. These additional efforts were required because UML designers are removed in Visual Studio 2017. For more information, visit https://blogs.msdn.microsoft.com/devops/2016/10/14/uml-designers-have-been-removed-layer-designer-now-supports-live-architectural-analysis/.

- In the first edition of this book, I drew a few directed graph documents (DAGs) using an older version of Visual Studio (Ultimate 2013). To make the book more concise, the DAGs were dropped for the second edition. Now there are modified class diagrams and additional code explanations, which are sufficient for you to understand the code.

Conventions Used in This Book

First, in many places, I use the word *his*. Please treat it as *his* or *her*, whichever applies to you.

Second, the output and code in this book follow the same font and structure. To draw your attention, I use bold in some places. For example, consider the following output fragment (from Chapter 21) and the lines in bold.

```
...
[Joseph] posts:  How are you? Last message posted 15-05-2020 11:30:52
Amit has received a message from Joseph saying:  How are you?

An outsider named Todd of [MediatorPatternModifiedDemo.Friend] is trying to
send a message to Joseph.

Amit, at this moment, you cannot send a message to Todd because he is
either not a registered user, or he is currently offline.

An outsider named Jack of [MediatorPatternModifiedDemo.Stranger] is trying
to send a message to Joseph.
Sohel is going offline now.
...
```

Final Words

You are showing interest in a subject that can assist you throughout your career. If you are a developer/programmer, you need these concepts. If you are an architect at a software company, you need these concepts. If you are a college student, you need these concepts, not only to score well on exams, but to enter the corporate world. Even if you are a tester who needs to take care of white-box testing, or needs to know the code paths of a product, knowing these concepts will help you. So, I suggest that you should not demotivate yourself, if in the first attempt, you do not understand everything in a particular chapter. It's perfectly natural. Based on your C# knowledge, you may find one pattern easier than other. In that case, move on to the next chapter, learn from it, gain confidence, and come back to the old chapter.

This book is designed to help you develop an adequate knowledge of design patterns in C#, and more importantly, help you learn how to go further. I hope that this book will help you and you will value the effort.

PART I

Gang of Four
Design Patterns

PART I.A

Creational Patterns

CHAPTER 1

Singleton Pattern

This chapter covers the Singleton pattern.

GoF Definition

Ensure a class has only one instance, and provide a global point of access to it.

Concept

Let's assume that you have a class called A, and you need to create an object from it. Normally, what would you do? You could simply use this line of code: A obA=new A();

But let's take a closer look. If you use the new keyword ten more times, you'll have ten more objects, right? But in a real-world scenario, unnecessary object creation is a big concern (particularly when constructor calls are truly expensive), so you need to restrict it. In a situation like this, the Singleton pattern comes in handy. It restricts the use of new and ensures that you do not have more than one instance of the class.

In short, this pattern says that a class should have only one instance. You can create an instance if it is not available; otherwise, you should use an existing instance to serve your needs. By following this approach, you can avoid creating unnecessary objects.

Real-World Example

Let's assume that you have a sports team that is participating in a tournament. Your team needs to play against multiple opponents throughout the tournament. At the beginning of each of the matches, as per the rules of the game, the two team captains must toss a coin. If your team does not have a captain, you need to elect someone to be the captain

5

© Vaskaran Sarcar 2020
V. Sarcar, *Design Patterns in C#*, https://doi.org/10.1007/978-1-4842-6062-3_1

for the duration of the tournament. Prior to each match and each coin toss, you may not repeat the process of electing a captain if you have already done so.

Computer-World Example

In some software systems, you may decide to maintain only one file system so that you can use it for the centralized management of resources. This approach helps you implement a caching mechanism effectively. Consider another example. You can also use this pattern to maintain a thread pool in a multithreading environment.

Implementation

A Singleton pattern can be implemented in many ways. Each approach has its own pros and cons. In the following demonstration, I show you a simple approach. Here the class is named Singleton, and it has the following characteristics. Before you proceed, you must go through them.

- I used a private parameterless constructor in this example. So, you cannot instantiate the type in a normal fashion (using new).

- This class is sealed. (For our upcoming demonstration, it is not required, but it can be beneficial if you make specific modifications to this Singleton class. This is discussed in the Q&A session).

- Since new is blocked, how do you get an instance? In a case like this, you can opt for a utility method or a property. In this example, I chose a property, and in my Singleton class, you see the following code:

```
public static Singleton GetInstance
{
    get
        {
            return Instance;
        }
}
```

- If you like to use an expression-bodied, read-only property (which came in C# v6), you can replace the code segment with the following line of code:

```
public static Singleton GetInstance => Instance;
```

- I used a static constructor inside the Singleton class. A static constructor must be parameterless. Per Microsoft, in C#, it initializes static data and performs a specific action only once. In addition, a static constructor is called automatically before you create the first instance, or you refer to any static class member. You can safely assume that I've taken full advantage of these specifications.

- Inside the Main() method, I use a simple check to ensure that I'm using the same and only available instance.

- You see the following line of code in the Singleton class:

```
private static readonly Singleton Instance;
```

The **public static** member ensures a global point of access. It confirms that the instantiation process will not start until you invoke the Instance property of the class (in other words, it supports lazy instantiation), and readonly ensures that the assignment process takes place in the static constructor only. A readonly field can't be assigned once you exit the constructor. By mistake, if you repeatedly try to assign this static readonly field, you'll encounter the CS0198 compile-time error, which says that a static readonly field cannot be assigned (except in a static constructor or a variable initializer).

- The Singleton class is also marked with the sealed keyword to prevent the further derivation of the class (so that its subclass cannot misuse it).

Note   I've kept the important comments to help you better understand. I'll do the same for most of the programs in this book; for example, when you download the code from the Apress website, you can see the usage of an expression-bodied, read-only property in the commented lines.

Class Diagram

Figure 1-1 is a class diagram for the illustration of the Singleton pattern.

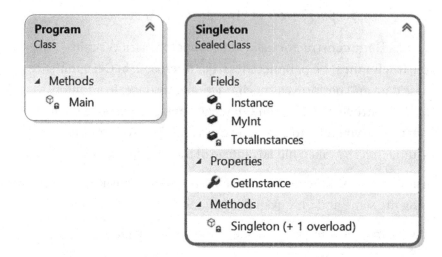

Figure 1-1. *Class diagram*

Solution Explorer View

Figure 1-2 shows the high-level structure of the program.

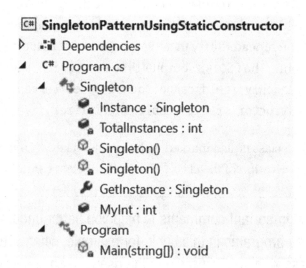

Figure 1-2. *Solution Explorer view*

Demonstration 1

Go through the following implementation, and use the supportive comments to help you better understand.

```
using System;

namespace SingletonPatternUsingStaticConstructor
{
    public sealed class Singleton
    {
        #region Singleton implementation using static constructor

        private static readonly Singleton Instance;
        private static int TotalInstances;
        /*
         * Private constructor is used to prevent
         * creation of instances with the 'new' keyword
         * outside this class.
         */
        private Singleton()
        {
            Console.WriteLine("--Private constructor is called.");
            Console.WriteLine("--Exit now from private constructor.");
        }

        /*
         * A static constructor is used for the following purposes:
         * 1. To initialize any static data
         * 2. To perform a specific action only once
         *
         * The static constructor will be called automatically before:
         * i. You create the first instance; or
         * ii.You refer to any static members in your code.
         *
         */
```

```csharp
        // Here is the static constructor
        static Singleton()
        {
            // Printing some messages before you create the instance
            Console.WriteLine("-Static constructor is called.");
            Instance = new Singleton();
            TotalInstances++;
            Console.WriteLine($"-Singleton instance is created.Number of
            instances:{ TotalInstances}");
            Console.WriteLine("-Exit from static constructor.");
        }
        public static Singleton GetInstance
        {
            get
            {
                return Instance;
            }
        }
    /*
      * If you like to use expression-bodied read-only
      * property, you can use the following line (C# v6.0 onwards).
      */
        // public static Singleton GetInstance => Instance;
        #endregion
        /* The following line is used to discuss
        the drawback of the approach. */
        public static int MyInt = 25;
    }
    class Program
    {
        static void Main(string[] args)
        {
            Console.WriteLine("***Singleton Pattern Demonstration.***\n");
            /* The following line is used to discuss
               the drawback of the approach. */
```

```
//Console.WriteLine($"The value of MyInt is :{Singleton.MyInt}");
// Private Constructor.So, you cannot use the 'new' keyword.
//Singleton s = new Singleton(); // error
Console.WriteLine("Trying to get a Singleton instance, called
firstInstance.");
Singleton firstInstance = Singleton.GetInstance;
Console.WriteLine("Trying to get another Singleton instance,
called secondInstance.");
Singleton secondInstance = Singleton.GetInstance;
if (firstInstance.Equals(secondInstance))
{
    Console.WriteLine("The firstInstance and secondInstance are
    the same.");
}
else
{
    Console.WriteLine("Different instances exist.");
}
Console.Read();
        }
    }
}
```

Output

Here is the output for this example.

```
***Singleton Pattern Demonstration.***

Trying to get a Singleton instance, called firstInstance.
-Static constructor is called.
--Private constructor is called.
--Exit now from private constructor.
-Singleton instance is created.Number of instances:1
-Exit from static constructor.
Trying to get another Singleton instance, called secondInstance.
The firstInstance and secondInstance are the same.
```

11

Note   Microsoft recommends Pascal naming conventions for static fields. I followed this in the previous demonstration.

Analysis

In this section, I discuss two important points regarding the previous demonstration. First, I show you how to shorten your code size, and then I discuss a potential drawback in the approach that I just followed. Let's start.

From the associated comments, you see that if you like to use expression-bodied, read-only properties, you can replace the following code segment

```
public static Singleton GetInstance
    {
        get
        {
            return Instance;
        }
    }
```

with the following line of code.

```
public static Singleton GetInstance => Instance;
```

Keeping the existing code, add the following code segment inside the Singleton class.

```
/* The following line is used to discuss
the drawback of the approach.*/
public static int MyInt = 25;
```

After this addition, the Singleton class is as follows.

```
public sealed class Singleton
    {
        #region Singleton implementation using static constructor
        // Keeping all existing code shown in the previous demonstration
```

```
    #endregion
    /* The following line is used to discuss
    the drawback of the approach.*/
    public static int MyInt = 25;
}
```

Now suppose that you use the following `Main()` method.

```
static void Main(string[] args)
    {
        Console.WriteLine("***Singleton Pattern Demonstration.***\n");
        Console.WriteLine($"The value of MyInt is :{Singleton.MyInt}");
        Console.Read();
    }
```

If you execute the program now, you see the following output.

```
***Singleton Pattern Demonstration.***

-Static constructor is called.
--Private constructor is called.
--Exit now from private constructor.
-Singleton instance is created.Number of instances:1
-Exit from static constructor.
The value of MyInt is :25
```

Although you were supposed to see only the last line of the output, you are getting all the instantiation details of the `Singleton` class, which illustrates the downside of this approach. Specifically, inside the `Main()` method, you tried to use the `MyInt` static variable, but your application still created an instance of the Singleton class. So, when you use this approach, you have less control over the instantiation process.

Apart from this issue, however, there is no significant drawback associated with it. You simply acknowledge that it is a one-time activity, and the initialization process will not be repeated. If you can tolerate this drawback, you can claim that you have implemented a simple, nice Singleton pattern. Here I'm repeating that each approach has its own pros and cons; no approach is 100% perfect. Based on your requirements, you may prefer one over the others.

Next, I present another common variant of this implementation. I could directly use the following line

```
private static readonly Singleton Instance = new Singleton();
```

and avoid printing the special messages in the console using a static constructor. The following code segment also demonstrates a Singleton pattern.

```
public sealed class Singleton
    {
        #region Using static initialization
        private static readonly Singleton Instance = new Singleton();

        private static int TotalInstances;
        /*
         * Private constructor is used to prevent
         * creation of instances with 'new' keyword
         * outside this class.
         */
        private Singleton()
        {
            Console.WriteLine("--Private constructor is called.");
            Console.WriteLine("--Exit now from private constructor.");
        }
        public static Singleton GetInstance
        {
            get
            {
                return Instance;
            }
        }

        #endregion
    }
```

This kind of coding is often called *static initialization*. I wanted to print custom messages in the console, so my preferred approach is shown in demonstration 1.

Q&A Session

1.1 Why are you complicating things? You could simply write your Singleton class as follows.

```
public class Singleton
    {
        private static Singleton instance;
        private Singleton() { }
        public static Singleton Instance
        {
            get
            {
                if (instance == null)
                {
                    instance = new Singleton();
                }
                return instance;
            }
        }
    }
```

Yes, this approach can work in a single-threaded environment, but consider a multithreaded environment where two (or more) threads may try to evaluate the following code at the same time.

```
if (instance == null)
```

If the instance has not been created yet, each thread will try to create a new instance. As a result, you may end up with multiple instances of the class.

1.2 Can you show an alternative approach for modeling the Singleton design pattern?

There are many approaches. Each of them has pros and cons.

The following code shows *double-checked locking*. The following code segment outlines this approach.

```
// Singleton implementation using double checked locking.
public sealed class Singleton
{
    /*
     * We are using volatile to ensure
     * that assignment to the instance variable finishes
     * before it's accessed.
     */
    private static volatile Singleton Instance;
    private static object lockObject = new Object();

    private Singleton() { }

    public static Singleton GetInstance
    {
        get
        {
            // First Check
            if (Instance == null)
            {
                lock (lockObject)
                {
                    // Second(Double) Check
                    if (Instance == null)
                        Instance = new Singleton();
                }
            }
            return Instance;
        }
    }
}
```

This approach can help you create instances when they are needed. But you must remember that, in general, the locking mechanism is expensive.

Instead of using double locks, you can also use a single lock, as follows.

```
//Singleton implementation using single lock
    public sealed class Singleton
    {
        /*
         * We are using volatile to ensure
         * that assignment to the instance variable finishes
         * before it's access.
         */
        private static volatile Singleton Instance;
        private static object lockObject = new Object();

        private Singleton() { }

        public static Singleton GetInstance
        {
            get
            {
                // Locking it first
                lock (lockObject)
                {
                    // Single check
                    if (Instance == null)
                    {
                        Instance = new Singleton();
                    }
                }
                return Instance;
            }
        }
    }
```

Although this approach may look simpler, it is not considered a better approach because you're acquiring the lock each time an instance of the Singleton instance is requested, which degrades the performance of your application.

At the end of this chapter, you see another approach to implement a Singleton pattern using built-in constructs in C#.

Note   When you keep the client code the same, you can simply replace the Singleton class using your preferred approach. I provide full demonstrations on this, which you can download from Apress's website.

1.3 Why are you marking the instance as volatile in the double-checked locking example?

Many developers believe that it is unnecessary for .NET 2.0 and above, but there is debate. To make it simple, let's look at what the C# specifications state: "The volatile keyword indicates that a field might be modified by multiple threads that are executing at the same time. The compiler, the runtime system, and even the hardware may rearrange reads and writes to a memory location for performance reasons. Fields that are declared volatile are not subject to these optimizations. Adding the volatile modifier ensures that all threads will observe volatile writes performed by any other thread in the order in which they were performed." This simply means that the volatile keyword helps provide a serialize access mechanism, so all threads observe the changes by any other thread as per their execution order. *It ensures that the most current value is always present in the field.* Thus, using the volatile modifier makes your code safer.

In this context, you should remember that the volatile keyword cannot be applied to all types, and there are certain restrictions. For example, you can apply it to class or struct fields, but not to local variables.

1.4 Why are multiple object creations a big concern?

Here are two important points to remember.

- Object creations can be costly if you are working with resource-intensive objects.

- In some applications, you may need to pass a common object to multiple places.

1.5 When should I use the Singleton pattern?

It depends. Here are some common use cases in which this pattern is useful.

- When working with a centralized system (for example a database)

- When maintaining a common log file

- When maintaining a thread pool in a multithreaded environment

- When implementing a caching mechanism or device drivers, and so forth

1.6 Why are you using the `sealed` keyword? The Singleton class has a private constructor that is sufficient for stopping the derivation process.

Good catch. It is not mandatory, but it is always best to clearly show your intentions. I use it to guard one special case: when you are tempted to use a derived nested class, and you prefer to initialize inside the private constructor itself. To better understand this, let's assume that you have the following class, which is not sealed. In this class, you do not use a static constructor; instead, you use a private constructor to track the number of instances. I formatted the key changes in bold.

```
public class Singleton
{
private static readonly Singleton Instance = new Singleton();
private static int TotalInstances;
/*
 * Private constructor is used to prevent
 * creation of instances with 'new' keyword
 * outside this class.
 */
private Singleton()
{
    Console.WriteLine("--Private constructor is called.");
    TotalInstances++;
    Console.WriteLine($"-Singleton instance is created. Number of
    instances:{ TotalInstances}");
    Console.WriteLine("--Exit now from private constructor.");
}
```

```
public static Singleton GetInstance
{
    get
    {
     return Instance;
    }
}

// The keyword "sealed" can guard this scenario.
// public class NestedDerived : Singleton { }

}
```

Inside the Main() method, let's make a small change to the first line of the console messages to differentiate the output from the original one, but let's keep the remaining part as it is. It now looks as follows.

```
class Program
    {
        static void Main(string[] args)
        {
            Console.WriteLine("***Singleton Pattern Q&A***\n");
            Console.WriteLine("Trying to get a Singleton instance, called
            firstInstance.");
            Singleton firstInstance = Singleton.GetInstance;
            Console.WriteLine("Trying to get another Singleton instance,
            called secondInstance.");
            Singleton secondInstance = Singleton.GetInstance;
            if (firstInstance.Equals(secondInstance))
            {
                Console.WriteLine("The firstInstance and secondInstance are
                same.");
            }
            else
            {
                Console.WriteLine("Different instances exist.");
            }
```

```
//Singleton.NestedDerived nestedClassObject1 = new Singleton.
NestedDerived();
//Singleton.NestedDerived nestedClassObject2 = new Singleton.
NestedDerived();
            Console.Read();
        }
}
```

If you run the program, you'll get the following output.

```
***Singleton Pattern Q&A***

Trying to get a Singleton instance, called firstInstance.

--Private constructor is called.
-Singleton instance is created. Number of instances:1
--Exit now from private constructor.

Trying to get another Singleton instance, called secondInstance.
The firstInstance and secondInstance are same.
```

This is straightforward and similar to the output from our original demonstration. Now uncomment the following line in the Singleton class.

```
//public class NestedDerived : Singleton { }
```

Then uncomment the following two lines of code inside the Main() method.

```
//Singleton.NestedDerived nestedClassObject1 = new Singleton.NestedDerived();
//Singleton.NestedDerived nestedClassObject2 = new Singleton.NestedDerived();
```

Run the application again. This time, you get the following output.

```
***Singleton Pattern Q&A***

Trying to get a Singleton instance, called firstInstance.
--Private constructor is called.
-Singleton instance is created.Number of instances:1
--Exit now from private constructor.
Trying to get another Singleton instance, called secondInstance.
The firstInstance and secondInstance are same.
```

--Private constructor is called.
-Singleton instance is created.Number of instances:2
--Exit now from private constructor.
--Private constructor is called.
-Singleton instance is created.Number of instances:3
--Exit now from private constructor.

Have you noticed that the total number of instances is increasing? Although in my original demonstration, I could exclude the use of sealed, I kept it to guard this type of situation, which may arise due to modifying the original implementation of the Singleton class.

Alternative Implementation

Now I'll show you another approach that uses built-in constructs in C#. In the previous edition of the book, I skipped this because to understand this code, you need to be familiar with generics, delegates, and lambda expressions. If you are not familiar with delegates, you can skip this section for now; otherwise, let's proceed.

In this example, I'm showing you three different ways to use the code effectively (using a custom delegate, using a built-in Func delegate, and finally, using a lambda expression). Let's look at the core code segment for the Singleton class with the associated comments, and then follow with the analysis.

```
// Singleton implementation using Lazy<T>
public sealed class Singleton
{
    // Custom delegate
    delegate Singleton SingletonDelegateWithNoParameter();
    static SingletonDelegateWithNoParameter myDel = MakeSingletonInstance;

    // Using built-in Func<out TResult> delegate
    static Func<Singleton> myFuncDelegate= MakeSingletonInstance;

    private static readonly Lazy<Singleton> Instance = new
    Lazy<Singleton>(
        //myDel()  // Also ok. Using a custom delegate
        myFuncDelegate()
```

```
        //() => new Singleton() // Using lambda expression
        );

    private static Singleton MakeSingletonInstance()
    {
        return new Singleton();
    }
    private Singleton() { }
    public static Singleton GetInstance
    {
        get
        {
            return Instance.Value;
        }
    }
}
```

Analysis

The most important part of this code is

```
private static readonly Lazy<Singleton> Instance = new Lazy<Singleton>(
        //myDel()  // Also ok. Using a custom delegate
        myFuncDelegate()
        //() => new Singleton()  // Using lambda expression
    );
```

Here myDel() is commented out; it can be used when you use the custom delegate. myFuncDelegate() is already executed where the built-in Func delegate is used. The final commented line can be used if you want to use a lambda expression instead of the delegates. In short, when you experiment with any of these approaches, the other two lines should be commented out.

If you hover your mouse on Lazy<Singleton>, you see that Lazy<T> supports lazy initialization; at the time of this writing, it has seven overloaded versions of constructor, and some of them can accept a Func delegate instance as a method parameter. Now you know why I used the Func delegate in this example. Figure 1-3 is a Visual Studio screenshot.

```
namespace System
{
    //
    // Summary:
    //      Provides support for lazy initialization.
    //
    // Type parameters:
    //   T:
    //      The type of object that is being lazily initialized.
    [NullableAttribute(0)]
    [NullableContextAttribute(1)]
    public class Lazy<[NullableAttribute(2)]
    T>
    {
        ...public Lazy();
        ...public Lazy(bool isThreadSafe);
        ...public Lazy(Func<T> valueFactory);
        ...public Lazy(LazyThreadSafetyMode mode);
        ...public Lazy(T value);
        ...public Lazy(Func<T> valueFactory, bool isThreadSafe);
        ...public Lazy(Func<T> valueFactory, LazyThreadSafetyMode mode);

        ...public bool IsValueCreated { get; }
        ...public T Value { get; }

        ...public override string? ToString();
    }
}
```

Figure 1-3. *Visual Studio screenshot for Lazy<T> class*

In this example, I used the following version.

```
public Lazy(Func<T> valueFactory);
```

Although the Func delegate has many overloaded versions, in this case, you can only use the following version.

```
public delegate TResult Func<[NullableAttribute(2)] out TResult>();
```

This Func version can point a method that accepts no parameter but returns a value of the type specified by the TResult parameter, which is why it can correctly point to the following method.

```
private static Singleton MakeSingletonInstance()
      {
          return new Singleton();
      }
```

If you want to use your own delegate, you can do so. The following code segment can be used for that purpose.

```
// Custom delegate
delegate Singleton SingletonDelegateWithNoParameter();
static SingletonDelegateWithNoParameter myDel = MakeSingletonInstance;
```

In such a case, you need to use myDel() instead of myFuncDelegate().

Finally, if you opt for a lambda expression, you do not need the MakeSingletonInstance() method, and you can directly use the following segment of code.

```
private static readonly Lazy<Singleton> Instance = new Lazy<Singleton>(

        () => new Singleton()  // Using lambda expression
    );
```

Note   In all the approaches to implementing a Singleton pattern, the Main() method is essentially the same. So, for brevity, I did not include this in the discussions.

Q&A Session

1.7 You used the term *lazy initialization*. What does it mean?

It's a technique that you use to delay the object creation process. The basic idea is that you should create the object only when it is truly required. This method is useful when object creation is a costly operation.

Hopefully, you have a better idea of the Singleton design pattern. Performance vs. laziness is always a concern in this pattern, and some developers always question those areas. But the truth is that this pattern is found in many applications in various forms.

Let's finish the chapter with an Erich Gamma (a Swiss computer scientist and one of the GoF authors) quote from an interview in 2009: "When discussing which patterns to drop, we found that we still love them all. Not really—I'm in favor of dropping Singleton. Its use is almost always a design smell." If you are interested to see the details of this interview,you can follow the link: `https://www.informit.com/articles/article.aspx?p=1404056`.

CHAPTER 2

Prototype Pattern

This chapter covers the Prototype pattern.

GoF Definition

Specify the kinds of objects to create using a prototypical instance, and create new objects by copying this prototype.

Concept

The Prototype pattern provides an alternative method for instantiating new objects by copying or cloning an instance of an existing object. You can avoid the expense of creating a new instance using this concept. If you look at the intent of the pattern (the GoF definition), you see that the core idea of this pattern is to create an object that is based on another object. This existing object acts as a template for the new object.

When you write code for this pattern, in general, you see there is an abstract class or interface that plays the role of an abstract prototype. This abstract prototype contains a cloning method that is implemented by concrete prototypes. A client can create a new object by asking a prototype to clone itself. In the upcoming program (demonstration 1) of this chapter, I follow the same approach.

Real-World Example

Suppose that you have a master copy of a valuable document. You need to incorporate some changes to it to analyze the effect of the changes. In this case, you can make a photocopy of the original document and edit the changes in the photocopied document.

27

© Vaskaran Sarcar 2020
V. Sarcar, *Design Patterns in C#*, https://doi.org/10.1007/978-1-4842-6062-3_2

Computer-World Example

Let's assume that you already have a stable application. In the future, you may want to modify the application with some small changes. You must start with a copy of your original application, make the changes, and then analyze it further. You do not want to start from scratch merely to make a change; this would cost you time and money.

In .NET, the ICloneable interface contains a Clone() method. In Visual Studio IDE, you can easily find the following details.

```
namespace System
{
    //
    // Summary:
    //      Supports cloning, which creates a new instance of a class with
    //      the same value as an existing instance.
    [NullableContextAttribute(1)]
    public interface ICloneable
    {
        //
        // Summary:
        //      Creates a new object that is a copy of the current instance.
        //
        // Returns:
        //      A new object that is a copy of this instance.
        object Clone();
    }
}
```

You can use this built-in construct when you implement the Prototype pattern, but in this example, I used my own Clone() method.

Implementation

In this example, I follow the structure shown in Figure 2-1.

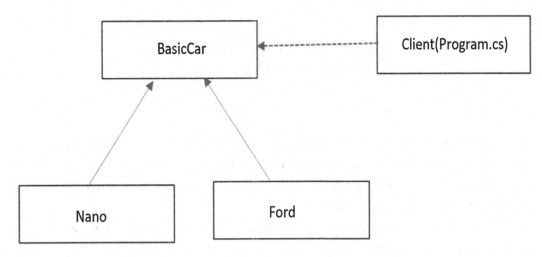

Figure 2-1. *Prototype example*

Here BasicCar is the prototype. It is an abstract class that has an abstract method called Clone(). Nano and Ford are the concrete classes (i.e., concrete prototypes), which inherit from BasicCar. Both concrete classes have implemented the Clone() method. In this example, initially, I created a BasicCar object with a default price. Later, I modified that price per model. Program.cs is the client in the implementation.

Inside the BasicCar class, there is a method named SetAdditionalPrice(). It generates a random value between 200,000(inclusive) and 500,000(exclusive). This value is added to the base price before I calculate the final onRoad price of a car. In this example, I mention the price of these cars in Indian currency (Rupee).

A car model's base price is set through the constructor of the concrete prototypes. So, you see the code segments like the following, where the concrete prototype (Nano) initializes the base price. Again, this class also overrides the Clone() method in BasicCar.

```
public class Nano : BasicCar
    {
        public Nano(string m)
        {
            ModelName = m;
```

```
        // Setting a basic price for Nano.
        basePrice = 100000;
    }
    public override BasicCar Clone()
    {
        // Creating a shallow copy and returning it.
        return this.MemberwiseClone() as Nano;
    }
}
```

Ford, another concrete prototype, has a similar structure. In this example, I used two concrete prototypes (Ford and Nano). To better understand the Prototype pattern, one concrete prototype is enough. So, if you want, you can simply drop either of these concrete prototypes to reduce the code size.

Lastly and most importantly, you see the MemberwiseClone() method in the upcoming examples. It is defined in the Object class and has the following description.

```
// Summary:
//      Creates a shallow copy of the current System.Object.
//
// Returns:
//      A shallow copy of the current System.Object.
[NullableContextAttribute(1)]
protected Object MemberwiseClone();
```

Note   You may be wondering about the term *shallow*. Actually, there are two types of cloning: shallow and deep. This chapter includes a discussion and a complete program to help you understand their differences. For now, you only need to know that in a shallow copy, the simple type fields of a class are copied to the cloned instance; but for reference type fields, only the references are copied. So, in this type of cloning, both the original and cloned instances point to the same reference, which may cause problems in some cases. To overcome this, you may need to employ a deep copy.

Class Diagram

Figure 2-2 shows the class diagram.

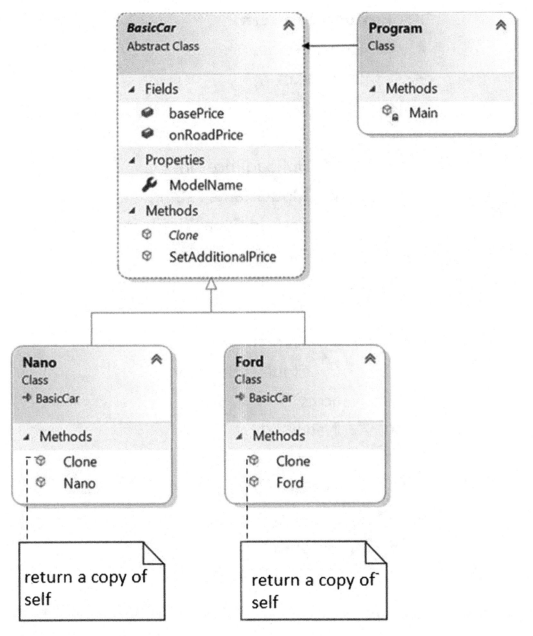

Figure 2-2. *Class diagram*

Solution Explorer View

Figure 2-3 shows the high-level structure of the parts of the program.

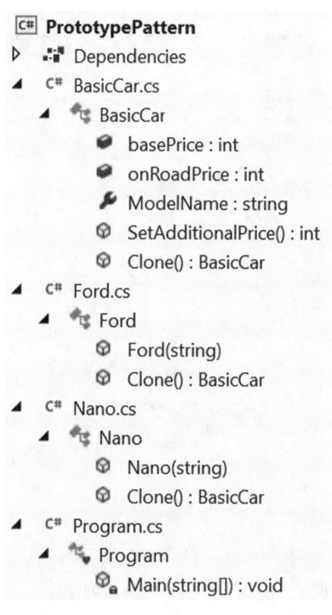

Figure 2-3. *Solution Explorer view*

Demonstration 1

Here's the implementation.

```
// BasicCar.cs

using System;

namespace PrototypePattern
{
    public abstract class BasicCar
    {
        public int basePrice = 0, onRoadPrice=0;
        public string ModelName { get; set; }

        /*
            We'll add this price before
            the final calculation of onRoadPrice.
        */
        public static int SetAdditionalPrice()
        {
            Random random = new Random();
            int additionalPrice = random.Next(200000, 500000);
            return additionalPrice;
        }
        public abstract BasicCar Clone();
    }
}

// Nano.cs

namespace PrototypePattern
{
    public class Nano : BasicCar
    {
        public Nano(string m)
        {
```

```csharp
            ModelName = m;
            // Setting a base price for Nano.
            basePrice = 100000;
        }
        public override BasicCar Clone()
        {
            // Creating a shallow copy and returning it.
            return this.MemberwiseClone() as Nano;
        }
    }
}
// Ford.cs

namespace PrototypePattern
{
    public class Ford : BasicCar
    {
        public Ford(string m)
        {
            ModelName = m;
            // Setting a basic price for Ford.
            basePrice = 500000;
        }

        public override BasicCar Clone()
        {
            // Creating a shallow copy and returning it.
            return this.MemberwiseClone() as Ford;
        }
    }
}
// Client
```

```csharp
using System;

namespace PrototypePattern
{
    class Program
    {
        static void Main(string[] args)
        {
            Console.WriteLine("***Prototype Pattern Demo***\n");
            // Base or Original Copy
            BasicCar nano = new Nano("Green Nano");
            BasicCar ford = new Ford("Ford Yellow");
            BasicCar basicCar;
            // Nano
            basicCar = nano.Clone();
            // Working on cloned copy
            basicCar.onRoadPrice = basicCar.basePrice + BasicCar.
            SetAdditionalPrice();
            Console.WriteLine($"Car is: {basicCar.ModelName}, and it's
            price is Rs. {basicCar.onRoadPrice}");

            // Ford
            basicCar = ford.Clone();
            // Working on cloned copy
            basicCar.onRoadPrice = basicCar.basePrice + BasicCar.
            SetAdditionalPrice();
            Console.WriteLine($"Car is: {basicCar.ModelName}, and it's
            price is Rs. {basicCar.onRoadPrice}");

            Console.ReadLine();
        }
    }
}
```

Output

The following is a possible output.

```
***Prototype Pattern Demo***

Car is: Green Nano, and it's price is Rs. 368104
Car is: Ford Yellow, and it's price is Rs. 878072
```

Note   You may see a different price in your system because I generated a random price in the `SetAdditionalPrice()` method inside the `BasicCar` class. But I ensured that the price of `Ford` is greater than `Nano`.

Modified Implementation

In demonstration 1, before making a clone, the client instantiated the objects as follows.

```
BasicCar nano = new Nano("Green Nano");
BasicCar ford = new Ford("Ford Yellow");
```

This is fine, but in some examples of the Prototype pattern, you may notice an additional participant creating the prototypes and supplying them to the client. Experts often like this approach because it hides the complexity of creating new instances from the client. Let's look at how to implement this in demonstration 2.

Class Diagram

Figure 2-4 shows the key changes in the modified class diagram.

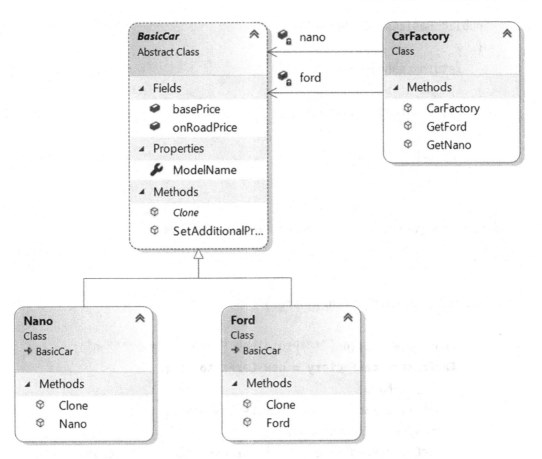

Figure 2-4. *Key changes in the class diagram for demonstration 2*

Demonstration 2

To demonstrate this, I added the following class, called CarFactory, to our previous demonstration.

```
class CarFactory
    {
        private readonly BasicCar nano, ford;

        public CarFactory()
        {
            nano = new Nano("Green Nano");
            ford = new Ford("Ford Yellow");
        }
```

```
      public BasicCar GetNano()
      {
         return  nano.Clone();
      }
      public BasicCar GetFord()
      {
          return ford.Clone();
      }
   }
```

With this class, your client code can be modified as follows.

```
class Program
   {
      static void Main(string[] args)
      {
         Console.WriteLine("***Prototype Pattern Demo2.***\n");
         CarFactory carFactory = new CarFactory();
         // Get a Nano
         BasicCar basicCar = carFactory.GetNano();
         //Working on cloned copy
         basicCar.onRoadPrice = basicCar.basePrice + BasicCar.
         SetAdditionalPrice();
         Console.WriteLine($"Car is: {basicCar.ModelName}, and it's
         price is Rs. {basicCar.onRoadPrice}");

         // Get a Ford now
         basicCar = carFactory.GetFord();
         // Working on cloned copy
         basicCar.onRoadPrice = basicCar.basePrice + BasicCar.
         SetAdditionalPrice();
         Console.WriteLine($"Car is: {basicCar.ModelName}, and it's
         price is Rs. {basicCar.onRoadPrice}");

         Console.ReadLine();
      }
   }
```

Output

The following is a possible output.

Prototype Pattern Demo2.

Car is: Green Nano, and it's price is Rs. 546365
Car is: Ford Yellow, and it's price is Rs. 828518

Analysis

This output is just like the previous output, and there is no magic. The CarFactory class serves our needs, but there is a potential drawback to it. I initialized the cars inside the constructor of CarFactory. As a result, it always creates instances of both car types when the class is initialized. So, if you want to implement a lazy initialization, you can modify the GetNano() method in the CarFactory class, as follows.

```
public BasicCar GetNano()
        {
            if (nano!=null)
            {
                // Nano was created earlier.
                // Returning a clone of it.
                return nano.Clone();
            }
            else
            {
                /*
                   Create a nano for the first
                   time and return it.
                */
                nano = new Nano("Green Nano");
                return nano;
            }
        }
```

You can modify the GetFord() method in the same way.

Note   When you implement these changes, do not forget to remove the read-only modifier to avoid a compile-time error.

Here is the modified class.

```
class CarFactory
    {
        private BasicCar nano,ford;
        public BasicCar GetNano()
        {
           if (nano!=null)
            {
                // Nano was created earlier.
                // Returning a clone of it.
                return nano.Clone();
            }
            else
            {
                /*
                   Create a nano for the first
                   time and return it.
                */
                nano = new Nano("Green Nano");
                return nano;
            }
        }
        public BasicCar GetFord()
        {
           if (ford != null)
            {
                // Ford was created earlier.
                // Returning a clone of it.
                return ford.Clone();
            }
            else
```

```
    {
        /*
          Create a nano for the first
          time and return it.
        */
        ford = new Ford("Ford Yellow");
        return ford;
    }
  }
}
```

Lastly, this is not the ultimate modification. In Chapter 1, you learned that in a multithreading environment, additional objects might be produced when you check the if-conditions. Since you learned possible solutions in Chapter 1, I do not focus on them in this discussion or upcoming discussions. I believe that you should now have a clear idea about the intent of this pattern.

Q&A Session

2.1 What are the advantages of using the prototype design pattern?
Here are some of the important usages.

- You do not want to modify the existing object and experiment on that.

- You can include or discard products at runtime.

- In some contexts, you can create new instances at a cheaper cost.

- You can focus on the key activities rather than focusing on complicated instance creation processes. For example, once you ignore the complex object creation processes, you can simply start with cloning or copying objects and implementing the remaining parts.

- You want to get a feel for the new object's behavior before you fully implement it.

2.2 What are the challenges associated with using the Prototype design pattern?
Here are some of the challenges.

- Each subclass needs to implement the cloning or copying mechanism.

- Implementing the cloning mechanism can be challenging if the objects under consideration do not support copying or if there are circular references.

In this example, I used the `MemberwiseClone()` member method, which provides a shallow copy. It is a very simple technique and can serve your basic needs. But if you need to provide a deep copy implementation for a complex object, it can be expensive because you not only need to copy the object, you also need to take care of all the references, which may form a very complicated graph.

2.3 Can you elaborate on the difference between a shallow copy and a deep copy in C#?
The following section explains their differences.

Shallow Copy vs. Deep Copy

A shallow copy creates a new object and then copies the nonstatic fields from the original object to the new object. If a value type field exists in the original object, a bit-by-bit copy is performed. But if the field is a reference type, this method copies the reference, not the actual object. Let's try to understand the mechanism with a simple diagram (see Figure 2-5). Suppose that you have an object, X1, and it has a reference to another object, Y1. Further, assume that object Y1 has a reference to object Z1.

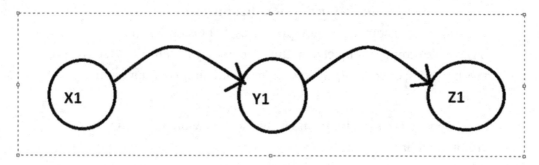

Figure 2-5. *Before the shallow copy of the references*

With a shallow copy of X1, a new object (say, X2) is created that also has a reference to Y1 (see Figure 2-6).

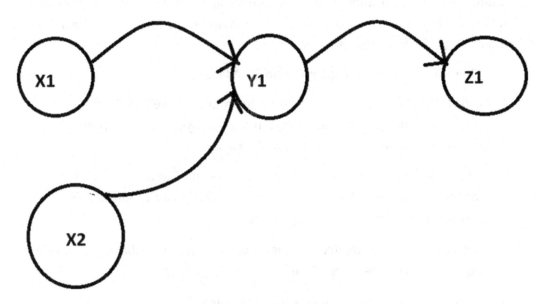

Figure 2-6. *After a shallow copy of the reference*

I used MemberwiseClone() in the implementation. It performs a shallow copy.

For a deep copy of X1, a new object (say, X3) is created, and X3 has a reference to the new object Y3 that is a copy of Y1. Also, Y3, in turn, has a reference to another new object, Z3, which is a copy of Z1 (see Figure 2-7).

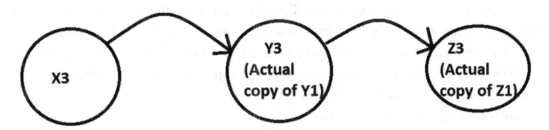

Figure 2-7. *After a deep copy of the reference*

Now consider the following demonstration to get a better understanding.

Demonstration 3

This simple demonstration shows you the difference between a shallow copy and a deep copy. It also shows you why a deep copy is important in certain situations. The following are the key characteristics of the program.

- There are two classes: Employee and EmpAddress.

- EmpAddress has only a single read-write property, called Address. It sets the address of an employee, but the Employee class has three read-write properties: Id, Name, and EmpAddress.

- To form an Employee object, you need to pass an ID and the name of the employee, and at the same time, you need to pass the address. So, you see code segments like the following.

```
EmpAddress initialAddress = new EmpAddress("21, abc Road, USA");
Employee emp = new Employee(1, "John", initialAddress);
```

- In the client code, first, you create an Employee object (emp), and then you create another object, empClone, through cloning. You see the following lines of code.

```
Console.WriteLine("Making a clone of emp1 now.");
Employee empClone = (Employee)emp.Clone();
```

- Later, you change the values inside empClone.

When you use a shallow copy, a side effect of this change is that the address of the emp object also changed, which is unwanted. (The Prototype pattern is straightforward; you should not change the original object when you work on a cloned copy of the object).

In the following example, the code for the deep copy is initially commented so that you can see the effect of the shallow copy only.

Now go through the demonstration.

```
using System;

namespace ShallowVsDeepCopy
{
    class EmpAddress
    {
```

```csharp
    public string Address { get; set; }

    public EmpAddress(string address)
    {
        this.Address = address;
    }

    public override string ToString()
    {
        return this.Address;
    }

    public object CloneAddress()
    {
        // Shallow Copy
        return this.MemberwiseClone();
    }
}
class Employee
{
    public int Id { get; set; }
    public string Name { get; set; }
    public EmpAddress EmpAddress { get; set; }

    public Employee(int id, string name, EmpAddress empAddress)
    {
        this.Id = id;
        this.Name = name;
        this.EmpAddress = empAddress;
    }

    public override string ToString()
    {
        return string.Format("Employee Id is : {0},Employee Name is
        : {1}, Employee Address is : {2}", this.Id,this.Name,this.
        EmpAddress);
    }
```

```csharp
    public object Clone()
    {
        // Shallow Copy
        return this.MemberwiseClone();

        #region For deep copy

        //Employee employee = (Employee)this.MemberwiseClone();
        //employee.EmpAddress = (EmpAddress)this.EmpAddress.
        //CloneAddress();

        /*
         * NOTE:
         * Error: MemberwiseClone() is protected, you cannot access
         it via a qualifier of type EmpAddress. The qualifier must be
         Employee or its derived type.
         */
        //employee.EmpAddress = (EmpAddress)this.EmpAddress.
        MemberwiseClone(); // error

        // return employee;
        #endregion

    }
}

class Program
{
    static void Main(string[] args)
    {
        Console.WriteLine("***Shallow vs Deep Copy Demo.***\n");
        EmpAddress initialAddress = new EmpAddress("21, abc Road, USA");
        Employee emp = new Employee(1, "John", initialAddress);

        Console.WriteLine("The original object is emp1 which is as
        follows:");
        Console.WriteLine(emp);

        Console.WriteLine("Making a clone of emp1 now.");
```

```csharp
        Employee empClone = (Employee)emp.Clone();
        Console.WriteLine("empClone object is as follows:");
        Console.WriteLine(empClone);

        Console.WriteLine("\n Now changing the name, id and address of
        the cloned object ");
        empClone.Id=10;
        empClone.Name="Sam";
        empClone.EmpAddress.Address= "221, xyz Road, Canada";

        Console.WriteLine("Now emp1 object is as follows:");
        Console.WriteLine(emp);
        Console.WriteLine("And emp1Clone object is as follows:");
        Console.WriteLine(empClone);
    }

  }
}
```

Output from a Shallow Copy

The following is the program's output.

```
***Shallow vs Deep Copy Demo.***

The original object is emp1 which is as follows:
Employee Id is : 1,Employee Name is : John, Employee Address is : 21, abc
Road, USA
Making a clone of emp1 now.
empClone object is as follows:
Employee Id is : 1,Employee Name is : John, Employee Address is : 21, abc
Road, USA

 Now changing the name, id and address of the cloned object
Now emp1 object is as follows:
Employee Id is : 1,Employee Name is : John, Employee Address is : 221, xyz
Road, Canada
```

And emp1Clone object is as follows:
Employee Id is : 10,Employee Name is : Sam, Employee Address is : **221, xyz Road, Canada**

Analysis

There is an unwanted side effect. In the previous output, the address of the original object (emp) is modified due to modifying the cloned object (empClone). It happened because both the original object and the cloned object pointed to the same address, and they are not 100% disjointed. Figure 2-8 depicts the scenario.

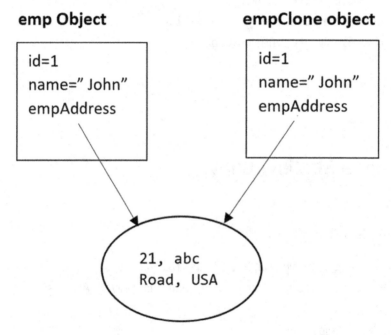

Figure 2-8. *Shallow copy*

Now let's experiment with a deep copy implementation. Let's modify the Clone method of the Employee class as follows. (I uncommented the code for the deep copy and commented out the code in the shallow copy.)

```
public Object Clone()
        {
            // Shallow Copy
            //return this.MemberwiseClone();
```

```
#region For deep copy

Employee employee = (Employee)this.MemberwiseClone();
employee.EmpAddress = (EmpAddress)this.EmpAddress.CloneAddress();

/*
 * NOTE:
 Error: MemberwiseClone() is protected, you cannot access it
 via a qualifier of type EmpAddress.The qualifier must be
 Employee or its derived type.
*/
//employee.EmpAddress = (EmpAddress)this.EmpAddress.
MemberwiseClone();//error

return employee;
#endregion

}
```

Output from Deep Copy

Here is the modified output.

```
***Shallow vs Deep Copy Demo***

The original object is emp1 which is as follows:
Employee Id is : 1,Employee Name is : John, Employee Address is : 21, abc
Road, USA
Making a clone of emp1 now.
empClone object is as follows:
Employee Id is : 1,Employee Name is : John, Employee Address is : 21, abc
Road, USA

Now changing the name, id and address of the cloned object
Now emp1 object is as follows:
Employee Id is : 1,Employee Name is : John, Employee Address is : 21, abc
Road, USA
And emp1Clone object is as follows:
Employee Id is : 10,Employee Name is : Sam, Employee Address is : 221, xyz
Road, Canada
```

Analysis

This time, you do not see the unwanted side effect due to the modification to the empClone object. This is because the original object and cloned object are different from and independent of each other. Figure 2-9 depicts the scenario.

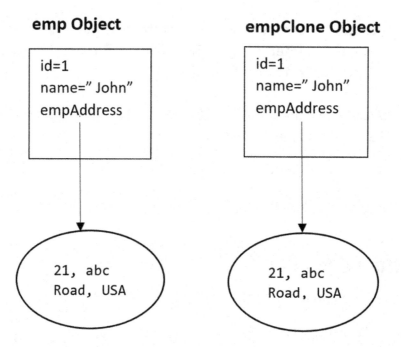

Figure 2-9. *Deep copy*

Q&A Session

2.4 When should you choose a shallow copy over a deep copy (and vice versa)?
Here are the key reasons.

- A shallow copy is faster and less expensive. It is always better to use if your target object has only the primitive fields.

- A deep copy is expensive and slow, but it is useful if your target object contains many fields that have references to other objects.

2.5 In C#, if I need to copy an object, I need to use the `MemberwiseClone()` method. Is this correct?

No, there are alternatives available. For example, you can opt for a serialization mechanism when you implement a deep copy, or you can write your own copy constructor, and so forth. Each approach has its pros and cons. So, in the end, it is the developer's call as to which approach best suits his needs. Many objects are very simple, and they do not contain references to other objects. So, to copy from those objects, a simple shallow copy mechanism is sufficient.

2.6 Can you show me an example that demonstrates the use of a copy constructor?

Since C# does not support a default copy constructor, you may need to write your own copy constructor. Demonstration 4 is for your reference.

Demonstration 4

In this example, the Employee and EmpAddress classes both have almost the same description as in demonstration 3. The only difference is that this time, instead of the Clone() method in the Employee class, you notice the presence of a copy constructor inside it. Let's proceed.

This time, using the following instance constructor,

```
// Instance Constructor
public Employee(int id, string name, EmpAddress empAddress)
{
        this.Id = id;
        this.Name = name;
        this.EmpAddress = empAddress;
}
```

you can create an object of Employee as follows.

```
EmpAddress initialAddress = new EmpAddress("21, abc Road, USA");
Employee emp = new Employee(1, "John",initialAddress);
```

In this Employee class, there is also a user-defined copy constructor, which is as follows.

```
// Copy Constructor
public Employee(Employee originalEmployee)
{
```

51

```
    this.Id = originalEmployee.Id;
    this.Name = originalEmployee.Name;
    //this.EmpAddress = (EmpAddress)this.EmpAddress.CloneAddress(); // ok
    this.EmpAddress = originalEmployee.EmpAddress.CloneAddress() as
    EmpAddress; // also ok
}
```

You can see that by using the copy constructor, I'm copying both the simple types (Id, Name) and the reference type (EmpAddress). So, once an Employee object like emp is created, you can create another empClone object from it using the following code.

```
Employee empClone= new Employee(emp);
```

As in the previous demonstration, once I created a copy (empClone) from the existing object (emp), I made changes to the copied object for verification purposes to make it easier to understand. Here is the complete code.

```
using System;
namespace UserdefinedCopyConstructorDemo
{
    class EmpAddress
    {
        public string Address { get; set; }
        public EmpAddress(string address)
        {
            this.Address = address;
        }
        public override string ToString()
        {
            return this.Address;
        }
        public object CloneAddress()
        {
            // Shallow Copy
            return this.MemberwiseClone();
```

```
        }
    }
    class Employee
    {
        public int Id { get; set; }
        public string Name { get; set; }
        public EmpAddress EmpAddress { get; set; }

        // Instance Constructor
        public Employee(int id, string name, EmpAddress empAddress)
        {
            this.Id = id;
            this.Name = name;
            this.EmpAddress = empAddress;
        }
        // Copy Constructor

        public Employee(Employee originalEmployee)
        {
            this.Id = originalEmployee.Id;
            this.Name = originalEmployee.Name;
            //this.EmpAddress = (EmpAddress)this.EmpAddress.CloneAddress();
            // ok
            this.EmpAddress = originalEmployee.EmpAddress.CloneAddress() as
            EmpAddress; // Also ok
        }
        public override string ToString()
        {
            return string.Format("Employee Id is : {0},Employee Name is
            : {1}, Employee Address is : {2}", this.Id, this.Name, this.
            EmpAddress);
        }
    }
    class Program
    {
        static void Main(string[] args)
```

```
        {
            Console.WriteLine("***A simple copy constructor demo***\n");
            EmpAddress initialAddress = new EmpAddress("21, abc Road, USA");
            Employee emp = new Employee(1, "John",initialAddress);
            Console.WriteLine("The details of emp is as follows:");
            Console.WriteLine(emp);
            Console.WriteLine("\n Copying from emp1 to empClone now.");
            Employee empClone= new Employee(emp);
            Console.WriteLine("The details of empClone is as follows:");
            Console.WriteLine(empClone);
            Console.WriteLine("\nNow changing the id,name and address of
            empClone.");
            empClone.Name = "Sam";
            empClone.Id = 2;
            empClone.EmpAddress.Address= "221, xyz Road, Canada";
            Console.WriteLine("The details of emp is as follows:");
            Console.WriteLine(emp);
            Console.WriteLine("The details of empClone is as follows:");
            Console.WriteLine(empClone);
            Console.ReadKey();
        }
    }
}
```

Output

Here is the sample output.

```
***A simple copy constructor demo***

The details of emp is as follows:
Employee Id is : 1,Employee Name is : John, Employee Address is : 21, abc
Road, USA

 Copying from emp1 to empClone now.
The details of empClone is as follows:
```

Employee Id is : 1,Employee Name is : John, Employee Address is : 21, abc Road, USA

Now changing the id,name and address of empClone.
The details of emp is as follows:
Employee Id is : 1,Employee Name is : John, Employee Address is : 21, abc Road, USA
The details of empClone is as follows:
Employee Id is : 2,Employee Name is : Sam, Employee Address is : 221, xyz Road, Canada

Analysis

Note the final portion of the output. It reflects that the changes were properly made to the copied object only.

This chapter showed you multiple implementations of prototype design patterns and discussed the difference between a shallow copy and a deep copy. You also learned about a user-defined copy constructor. Now you can move to the next chapter and learn about the Builder pattern.

CHAPTER 3

Builder Pattern

This chapter covers the Builder pattern.

GoF Definition

Separate the construction of a complex object from its representation so that the same construction processes can create different representations.

Concept

The Builder pattern is useful for creating complex objects that have multiple parts. The object creation process should be independent of these parts; in other words, the construction process does not care how these parts are assembled. In addition, as per the definition, you should be able to use the same construction process to create different representations of the objects.

According to the GoF, four different players are involved in this pattern, and they have the relationship shown in Figure 3-1.

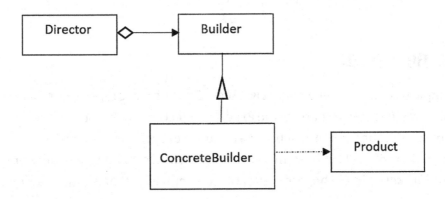

Figure 3-1. *Builder pattern example*

© Vaskaran Sarcar 2020
V. Sarcar, *Design Patterns in C#*, https://doi.org/10.1007/978-1-4842-6062-3_3

Here, Product is the complex object under consideration, and it is the final output. Builder is an interface, which contains the methods to build parts of the final product. ConcreteBuilder implements the Builder interface and assembles different parts of a Product object. The ConcreteBuilder object builds the internal representations of the Product instance, and it has a method that can be called to get this Product instance. Director is responsible for creating the final object using the Builder interface. It is important to note that Director is the class/object that decides the sequence of steps to build the product. So, you can safely assume that a Director object can be used to vary the sequence to make different products.

In demonstration 1, IBuilder denotes the Builder interface; Car and Motorcycle are each ConcreteBuilders. Product and Director classes have their usual meaning.

Real-World Example

To order a computer, different hardware parts are assembled based on the customer's preferences. For example, a customer can opt for a 500 GB hard disk with an Intel processor, and another customer can choose a 250 GB hard disk with an AMD processor. Here the computer is the final product, the customer plays the role of the director, and the seller/assembler plays the role of the concrete builder.

Computer-World Example

You can use this pattern when you want to convert one text format to another text format, such as converting from RTF to ASCII.

Implementation

This example has the following parts: IBuilder, Car, MotorCycle, Product, and Director. IBuilder creates parts of the Product object, where Product represents the complex object under construction. Car and MotorCycle are the concrete implementations of the IBuilder interface. (Yes, IVehicle could be a better naming instead of IBuilder, but I chose the latter one to emphasize that it's a builder interface.) They implement the IBuilder interface, which has the following representation.

CHAPTER 3   BUILDER PATTERN

```
interface IBuilder
{
    void StartUpOperations();
    void BuildBody();
    void InsertWheels();
    void AddHeadlights();
    void EndOperations();
    Product GetVehicle();
}
```

That's why `Car` and `Motorcycle` need to supply the body for the following methods: `StartUpOperations()`, `BuildBody()`, `InsertWheels()`, `AddHeadlights()`, `EndOperations()`, and `GetVehicle()`. The first five methods are straightforward; they perform various operations at the beginning, build the body of the vehicle, add wheels and headlights, and perform an operation at the end. (Let's say that the manufacturer wants to add a logo or polish the vehicle, and so forth. In the upcoming example, I make the operation very simple by drawing a simple line for motorcycles and a dashed line for cars.) The `GetVehicle()` method returns the ultimate product. The `Product` class is very easy to understand, and although I used the LinkedList data structure in it, you can use any of your preferred data structures for a similar purpose.

Finally, the `Director` class is responsible for constructing the final parts of these products using the `IBuilder` interface. (See the structure defined by the GoF in Figure 3-1.) Therefore, in our code, the `Director` class looks as follows.

```
class Director
{
    IBuilder builder;
    /*
     * A series of steps.In real life, these steps
     * can be much more complex.
     */
    public void Construct(IBuilder builder)
    {
        this.builder = builder;
        builder.StartUpOperations();
        builder.BuildBody();
```

```
        builder.InsertWheels();
        builder.AddHeadlights();
        builder.EndOperations();
    }
}
```

A Director object calls this Construct() method to create different types of vehicles. Now let's go through the code to see how different parts are assembled for this pattern.

Class Diagram

Figure 3-2 shows the class diagram.

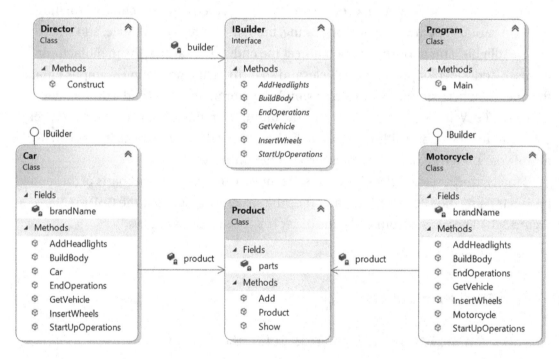

Figure 3-2. *Class diagram*

Solution Explorer View

Figure 3-3 shows the high-level structure of the program.

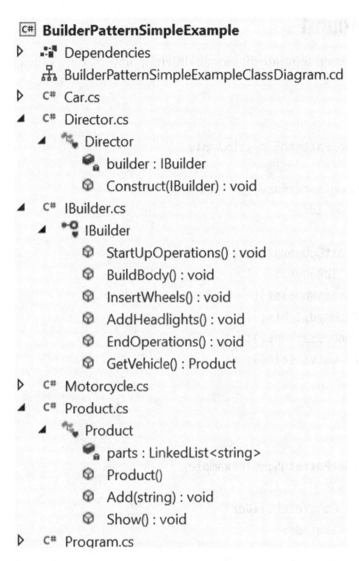

Figure 3-3. *Solution Explorer view*

Note   To keep it short, I did not extend the Car and Motorcycle classes. These classes implement IBuilder and are easy to understand. You can also refer to the class diagram (see Figure 3-2) if you need them. I followed the same mechanism for some other screenshots of the book; that is, when a screenshot is really big, I show only the important parts.

Demonstration 1

In this example, I used separate files for all different players. Here's the complete implementation.

// IBuilder.cs

```
namespace BuilderPatternSimpleExample
{
    // The common interface
    interface IBuilder
    {
        void StartUpOperations();
        void BuildBody();
        void InsertWheels();
        void AddHeadlights();
        void EndOperations();
        Product GetVehicle();
    }
}
```

// Car.cs

```
namespace BuilderPatternSimpleExample
{
    // Car is a ConcreteBuilder
    class Car : IBuilder
    {
        private string brandName;
        private Product product;
        public Car(string brand)
        {
            product = new Product();
            this.brandName = brand;
        }
```

```csharp
        public void StartUpOperations()
        {    // Starting with brandname
            product.Add("-----------");
            product.Add($"Car model name :{this.brandName}");
        }
        public void BuildBody()
        {
            product.Add("This is a body of a Car");
        }
        public void InsertWheels()
        {
            product.Add("4 wheels are added");
        }

        public void AddHeadlights()
        {
            product.Add("2 Headlights are added");
        }
        public void EndOperations()
        {
            product.Add("-----------");
        }
        public Product GetVehicle()
        {
            return product;
        }
    }
}

// Motorcycle.cs

namespace BuilderPatternSimpleExample
{
    // Motorcycle is another ConcreteBuilder
    class Motorcycle : IBuilder
    {
        private string brandName;
```

```
        private Product product;
        public Motorcycle(string brand)
        {
            product = new Product();
            this.brandName = brand;
        }
        public void StartUpOperations()
        {
            product.Add("_____");
        }

        public void BuildBody()
        {
            product.Add("This is a body of a Motorcycle");
        }

        public void InsertWheels()
        {
            product.Add("2 wheels are added");
        }

        public void AddHeadlights()
        {
            product.Add("1 Headlights are added");
        }
        public void EndOperations()
        {
            // Finishing up with brandname
            product.Add($"Motorcycle model name :{this.brandName}");
            product.Add("_____");
        }
        public Product GetVehicle()
        {
            return product;
        }
    }
}
```

// Product.cs

```
using System;
using System.Collections.Generic; // For LinkedList

namespace BuilderPatternSimpleExample
{
    // "Product"
    class Product
    {
        /*
        You can use any data structure that you prefer    e.g.List<string> etc.
        */
        private LinkedList<string> parts;
        public Product()
        {
            parts = new LinkedList<string>();
        }

        public void Add(string part)
        {
            // Adding parts
            parts.AddLast(part);
        }

        public void Show()
        {
            Console.WriteLine("\nProduct completed as below :");
            foreach (string part in parts)
                Console.WriteLine(part);
        }
    }
}
```

// Director.cs

```
namespace BuilderPatternSimpleExample
{
```

```
    // "Director"
    class Director
    {
        private IBuilder builder;
        /*
         * A series of steps.In real life, these steps
         * can be much more complex.
         */
        public void Construct(IBuilder builder)
        {
            this.builder = builder;
            builder.StartUpOperations();
            builder.BuildBody();
            builder.InsertWheels();
            builder.AddHeadlights();
            builder.EndOperations();
        }
    }
}
```

// Client (Program.cs)

```
using System;
namespace BuilderPatternSimpleExample
{
    class Program
    {
        static void Main(string[] args)
        {
            Console.WriteLine("***Builder Pattern Demo.***");
            Director director = new Director();

            IBuilder b1 = new Car("Ford");
            IBuilder b2 = new Motorcycle("Honda");
            // Making Car
            director.Construct(b1);
            Product p1 = b1.GetVehicle();
```

```
        p1.Show();

        // Making Motorcycle
        director.Construct(b2);
        Product p2 = b2.GetVehicle();
        p2.Show();

        Console.ReadLine();
    }
  }
}
```

Output

Here's the output.

```
***Builder Pattern Demo.***

Product completed as below :
-----------
Car model name :Ford
This is a body of a Car
4 wheels are added
2 Headlights are added
-----------

Product completed as below :
_____
This is a body of a Motorcycle
2 wheels are added
1 Headlights are added
Motorcycle model name :Honda

_____
```

Analysis

Inside `Main()`, one `Director` instance has created two different products because I passed two different builders in the `Construct()` method, which simply invokes the `StartUpOperations()`, `BuildBody()`, `InsertWheels()`, `AddHeadlights()`, and `EndOperations()` methods sequentially. Also, different builders have different implementations for these methods.

Q&A Session

3.1 What are the advantages of using the Builder pattern?

Here are some of the advantages.

- You direct the builder to build the objects step-by-step, and you promote encapsulation by hiding the details of the complex construction process. The director can retrieve the final product from the builder when the whole construction process is over. In general, at a high level, you seem to have only one method that makes the complete product, but other internal methods are involved in the creation process. So, you have finer control over the construction process.

- Using this pattern, the same construction process can produce different products.

- You can also vary the internal representation of products.

3.2 What are the drawbacks associated with the Builder pattern?

Here are some of the drawbacks.

- It is not suitable if you want to deal with mutable objects (which can be modified later).

- You may need to duplicate some portion of the code. These duplications may have a significant impact in some contexts.

- To create different types of products, you need to create different types of concrete builders.

3.3 Could you use an abstract class instead of the interface in the illustration of this pattern?

Yes. You could use an abstract class instead of an interface in this example.

3.4 How do you decide whether to use an abstract class or an interface in an application?

If you want centralized or default behaviors, an abstract class is a better choice. In those cases, you can provide some default implementation. On the other hand, the interface implementation starts from scratch and indicates rules/contracts such as what is to be done, but it does not enforce the "how" part upon you. Also, interfaces are preferred when you are trying to implement the concept of multiple inheritance.

Remember that if you need to add a new method in an interface, then you need to track down all the implementations of that interface, and you need to put the concrete implementation for that method in all those places. In such a case, an abstract class is a better choice because you can add a new method in an abstract class with a default implementation, and the existing code can run smoothly. But C# v8 in .NET Core 3.0 introduced the concept of default interface methods also. So, the last few lines of the suggestion are best if you work with a legacy version, which is beyond C# v8.0.

Here are some important suggestions from the MSDN community.

- When you have multiple versions of components, use an abstract class. Once you update the base class, all derived classes are updated automatically. The interface, on the other hand, should not be changed once created.

- When the functionalities are widespread among dissimilar/unrelated objects, use an interface. Abstract classes should be used for closely related objects which share common functionalities.

- Abstract classes allow you to partially implement your class, whereas interfaces contain no implementation for any members (ignoring the default interface methods in C# v8.0).

3.5 In the cars example, the model names were added at the beginning, but for motorcycles, the model names were added at the end. Was this intentional?

Yes. I did this to demonstrate the fact that each of the concrete builders can decide how it wants to produce individual parts of the final product. They have this freedom.

3.6 Why are you using a separate class for the director? You could use the client code to play the role of the director.

No one constrains you from doing that. In the preceding implementation, I wanted to separate this role from the client code in the implementation. But in the upcoming demonstration, I use the client as a director.

3.7 What do you mean by *client code*?

The class that contains the `Main()` method is the client code.

3.8 Several times you mentioned varying steps. Can you demonstrate an implementation where the final product is created with different variations and steps?

Good catch. You are asking me to demonstrate the real power of the Builder pattern. Let's consider another example, which is discussed next.

An Alternative Implementation

Let's consider an alternative implementation. It gives you more flexibility. Here are the key characteristics of the modified implementation.

- To focus on the core design, in this implementation, let's consider cars as the final products.

- The client code itself is playing the role of a director in this implementation.

- Like the previous example, `IBuilder` represents the builder interface, but instead of the `GetVehicle()` method, this time, I renamed it `ConstructCar()`.

- As in demonstration 1, the `Car` class has implemented all the methods defined in the interface, which is defined as follows:

```
interface IBuilder
    {
        /*
         * All these methods return type is IBuilder.
         * This will help us to apply method chaining.
         * I'm also providing values for default arguments.
         */
```

```
        IBuilder StartUpOperations(string optionalStartUpMessage =
        " Making a car for you.");
        IBuilder BuildBody(string optionalBodyType = "Steel");
        IBuilder InsertWheels(int optionalNoOfWheels = 4);
        IBuilder AddHeadlights(int optionalNoOfHeadLights = 2);
        IBuilder EndOperations(string optionalEndMessage = "Car
        construction is completed.");
        /*Combine the parts and make the final product.*/
        Product ConstructCar();
    }
```

Notice that these methods are similar to those in the previous demonstration, but there are two major changes: their return type is IBuilder, and they accept the optional parameters. This gives you flexibility—you can either pass arguments to them, or you can simply omit them. But most importantly, since the return type is IBuilder, now you can apply *method chaining*, which is why you see code segments like the following inside Main().

```
Product customCar2 = new Car("Sedan")
.InsertWheels(7)
.AddHeadlights(6)
.StartUpOperations("Sedan creation in progress")
.BuildBody()
.EndOperations()//will take default end message
.ConstructCar();
customCar2.Show();
```

- In the previous segment, I did not pass any argument to the EndOperations method. Also, before I call the StartUpOperations method, I called the InsertWheels and AddHeadlights methods. This gives freedom to the client object (who is the director in this case), how he wants to create the final product.

- Finally, the Product class is as follows.

```
sealed class Product
    {
```

```
/*
 * You can use any data structure that you prefer
 * e.g. List<string> etc.
 */
private LinkedList<string> parts;
public Product()
{
  parts = new LinkedList<string>();
}

public void Add(string part)
{
  // Adding parts
  parts.AddLast(part);
}

public void Show()
{
  Console.WriteLine("\nProduct completed as below :");
  foreach (string part in parts)
        Console.WriteLine(part);
}
}
```

- I made the Product class sealed this time because I wanted to prevent inheritance. Like the previous demonstration, the parts attribute is private, and there is no setter method inside the class. All these constructs can help you to promote immutability (this is optional in the upcoming demonstration), which is often required when you work with the Builder pattern. You could even exclude the private modifier from the parts declaration because the class member has private access by default.

- You can note another point. Inside the client code, I used customCar and CustomCar2 to make cars. These are Product class instances. The first one is a static field, and the second one is a non-static field. I kept both to show you the variations of usage of Product class inside Main().

Class Diagram

Figure 3-4 shows the modified class diagram for the alternative implementation in demonstration 2.

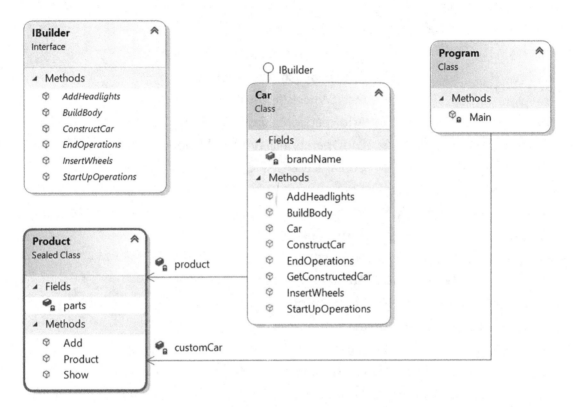

Figure 3-4.   *Class diagram for alternative implementation*

Solution Explorer View

Figure 3-5 shows the new Solution Explorer view.

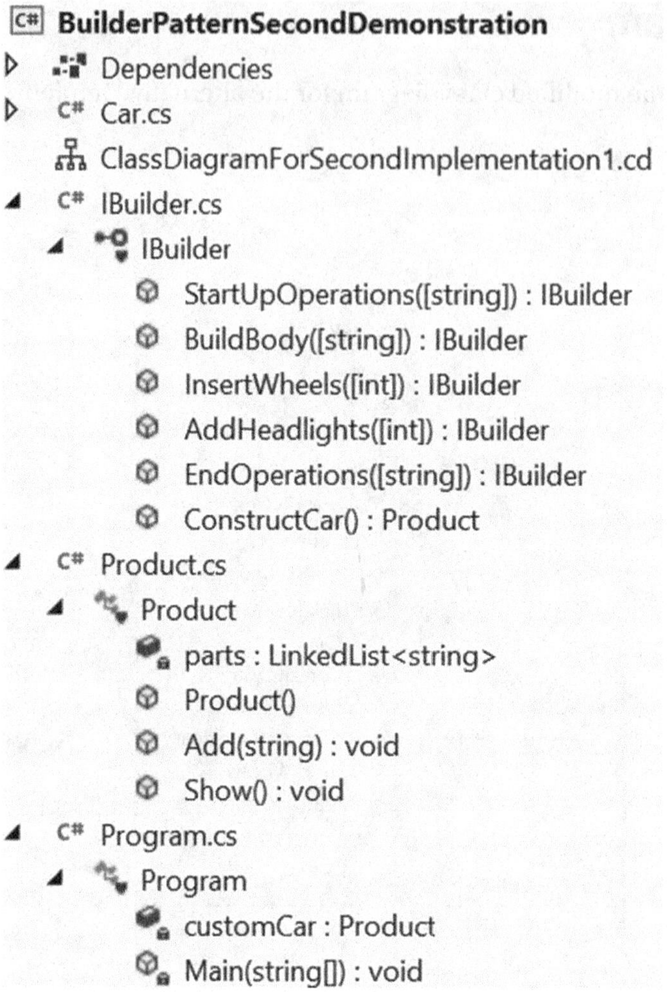

C# **BuilderPatternSecondDemonstration**

▷　⣿ Dependencies

▷　C# Car.cs

　　⫞ ClassDiagramForSecondImplementation1.cd

◢　C# IBuilder.cs

　◢　•⬢ IBuilder

　　　　⬡ StartUpOperations([string]) : IBuilder

　　　　⬡ BuildBody([string]) : IBuilder

　　　　⬡ InsertWheels([int]) : IBuilder

　　　　⬡ AddHeadlights([int]) : IBuilder

　　　　⬡ EndOperations([string]) : IBuilder

　　　　⬡ ConstructCar() : Product

◢　C# Product.cs

　◢　⬥ Product

　　　　⬤ parts : LinkedList<string>

　　　　⬡ Product()

　　　　⬡ Add(string) : void

　　　　⬡ Show() : void

◢　C# Program.cs

　◢　⬥ Program

　　　　⬤ customCar : Product

　　　　⬤ Main(string[]) : void

Figure 3-5. *Solution Explorer view*

Demonstration 2

Here is an alternative implementation for the Builder pattern.

```
using System;
using System.Collections.Generic;

namespace BuilderPatternSecondDemonstration
{
    // The common interface
    interface IBuilder
```

```
{
    /*
     * All these methods return types are IBuilder.
     * This will help us to apply method chaining.
     * I'm also providing values for default arguments.
     */
    IBuilder StartUpOperations(string optionalStartUpMessage = "Making
    a car for you.");
    IBuilder BuildBody(string optionalBodyType = "Steel");
    IBuilder InsertWheels(int optionalNoOfWheels = 4);
    IBuilder AddHeadlights(int optionalNoOfHeadLights = 2);
    IBuilder EndOperations(string optionalEndMessage = "Car
    construction is complete.");
    // Combine the parts and make the final product.
    Product ConstructCar();
}

// Car class
class Car : IBuilder
{
    Product product;

    private string brandName;
    public Car(string brand)
    {
        product = new Product();
        this.brandName = brand;
    }
    public IBuilder StartUpOperations(string optionalStartUpMessage = "
    Making a car for you.")
    {   // Starting with brandname
        product.Add(optionalStartUpMessage);
        product.Add($"Car model name :{this.brandName}");
        return this;
    }
```

```
    public IBuilder BuildBody(string optionalBodyType = "Steel")
    {

        product.Add(($"Body type:{optionalBodyType}"));
        return this;
    }

    public IBuilder InsertWheels(int optionalNoOfWheels = 4)
    {

        product.Add(($"Wheels:{optionalNoOfWheels.ToString()}"));
        return this;
    }

    public IBuilder AddHeadlights(int optionalNoOfHeadLights = 2)
    {

        product.Add(($"Headlights:{optionalNoOfHeadLights.ToString()}"));
        return this;
    }

    public IBuilder EndOperations(string optionalEndMessage = "Car
    construction is completed.")
    {

        product.Add(optionalEndMessage);
        return this;
    }
    public Product ConstructCar()
    {

        return product;
    }

}

// Product class
/*
 * Making the class sealed. The attributes are also private and
 * there is no setter methods. These are used to promote immutability.
 */
```

```
sealed class Product
{
    /* You can use any data structure that you prefer e.g.List<string> etc.*/
    private LinkedList<string> parts;
    public Product()
    {
        parts = new LinkedList<string>();
    }

    public void Add(string part)
    {
        // Adding parts
        parts.AddLast(part);
    }

    public void Show()
    {
        Console.WriteLine("\nProduct completed as below :");
        foreach (string part in parts)
            Console.WriteLine(part);

    }

}
// Director class (Client Code)
class Program
{
    static Product customCar;
    static void Main(string[] args)
    {
        Console.WriteLine("***Builder Pattern alternative
        implementation.***");
        /* Making a custom car (through builder)
            Note the steps:
            Step1:Get a builder object with required parameters
            Step2:Setter like methods are used.They will set the
            optional fields also.
            Step3:Invoke the ConstructCar() method to get the final car.
        */
```

```
        customCar = new Car("Suzuki Swift").StartUpOperations()
        //will take default message
                .AddHeadlights(6)
                .InsertWheels()//Will consider default value
                .BuildBody("Plastic")
                .EndOperations("Suzuki construction Completed.")
                .ConstructCar();

    customCar.Show();
     /*
     Making another custom car (through builder) with a different
     sequence and steps.
     */
    // Directly using the Product class now.
    // (Just for a variation of usage)
    Product customCar2 = new Car("Sedan")
                .InsertWheels(7)
                .AddHeadlights(6)
                .StartUpOperations("Sedan creation in progress")
                .BuildBody()
                .EndOperations() // will take default end message
                .ConstructCar();
    customCar2.Show();
        }
    }

}
```

Output

Here's the new output. The lines in bold are to draw your attention to the differences in the output.

```
***Builder Pattern alternative implementation.***
```

```
Product completed as below :
```
Making a car for you.
```
Car model name :Suzuki Swift
```

```
Headlights:6
Wheels:4
Body type:Plastic
Suzuki construction Completed.

Product completed as below :
Wheels:7
Headlights:6
Sedan creation in progress
Car model name :Sedan
Body type:Steel
Car construction is completed.
```

Analysis

Look at the Main() method closely. You can see that the director (client) could create two different products using the builder, and each time it followed a different sequence of steps. This makes your application very flexible.

Q&A Session

3.9 You are trying to promote immutability. What is the key benefit associated with immutable objects?

Once constructed, they can be safely shared, and most importantly, they are thread safe, and you save synchronization costs in a multithreaded environment.

3.10 When should I consider using the Builder pattern?

If you need to make a complex object that involves various steps of the construction process, and at the same time, the products need to be immutable, the Builder pattern is a good choice.

CHAPTER 4

Factory Method Pattern

This chapter covers the Factory Method pattern.

Note   To better understand this pattern, I suggest you first read Chapter 24, which covers the Simple Factory pattern. The Simple Factory pattern does not fall directly into the Gang of Four design patterns, so it appears in Part II of the book; however, the Factory Method pattern will make more sense if you first understand the pros and cons of the Simple Factory pattern.

GoF Definition

Define an interface for creating an object, but let subclasses decide which class to instantiate. Factory Method lets a class defer instantiation to subclasses.

Concept

Here you start with an abstract creator class that defines the basic structure of an application, and the subclasses (that derive from this abstract class) take the responsibility of doing the actual instantiation process. This concept will make sense to you when you analyze the following examples.

Real-World Example

The example from a Simple Factory pattern also applies here. For instance, in a restaurant, depending on customer preferences, a chef can add more (or less) spice, oil, and so forth during the preparation of the final product.

81

© Vaskaran Sarcar 2020
V. Sarcar, *Design Patterns in C#*, https://doi.org/10.1007/978-1-4842-6062-3_4

Let's look at another example. Consider a car manufacturing company that produces different models of a car every year. Depending on their market survey, they decide a model and start manufacturing. Based on the model of the car, different parts are built and assembled. A company should always be prepared for changes in which a customer can opt for a better model in the future. If the company needs to create an entirely new setup for a new model that demands only a few new features, that can hugely impact the company's profit margin. So, the company should set up the factory in such a way that it can easily produce parts for the upcoming models.

Computer-World Example

In database programming, you may need to support different database users. For example, one user may use SQL Server, and the other may opt for Oracle. When you need to insert data into your database, you first create a connection object, such as SqlConnection or OracleConnection, and then can you proceed. If you put the code into an if-else block (or switch statements), you may need to repeat lots of similar code, which isn't easily maintainable. Also, whenever you decide to start supporting a new type of connection, you need to reopen your code and make some modifications. This type of problem can be resolved using the Factory Method pattern.

Implementation

The upcoming example provides an abstract creator class called AnimalFactory to define the basic structure. According to the definition, the instantiation process is carried out through the subclasses that derive from this abstract class. There are many small classes in this example. I could make separate files for each of these classes, and this approach is often encouraged by many developers. But these classes are very short, simple, and straightforward. So, I placed them in a single file. I follow the same principle for similar examples in this book.

Class Diagram

Figure 4-1 shows the class diagram.

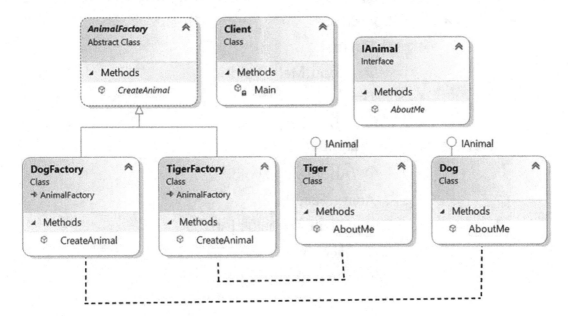

Figure 4-1. *Class diagram*

Solution Explorer View

Figure 4-2 shows the high-level structure of the program.

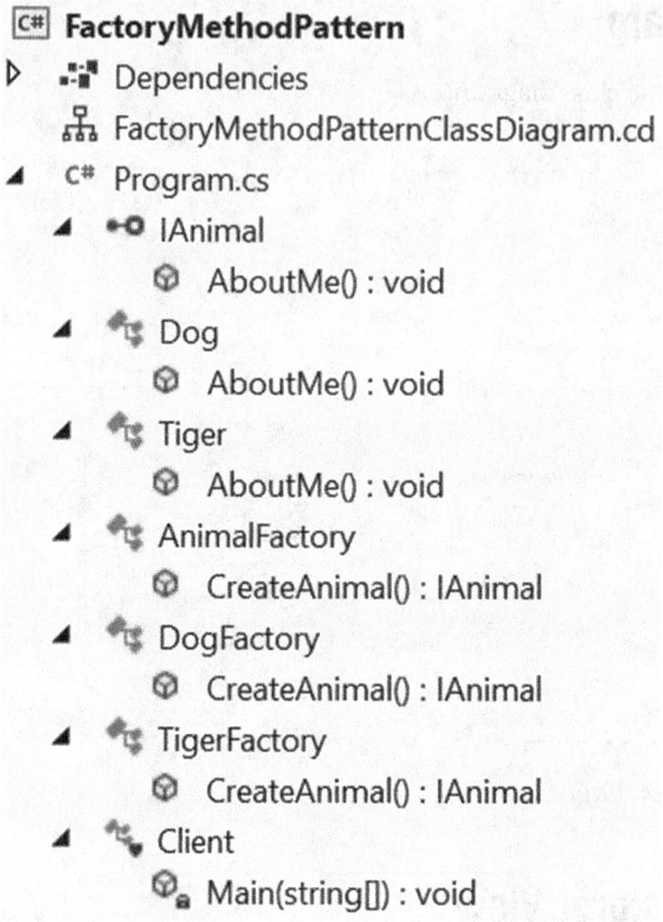

C# **FactoryMethodPattern**

▷   ⚏ Dependencies

      ⛬ FactoryMethodPatternClassDiagram.cd

◢   C# Program.cs

  ◢   •○ IAnimal

          ⬡ AboutMe() : void

  ◢   ⬥ Dog

          ⬡ AboutMe() : void

  ◢   ⬥ Tiger

          ⬡ AboutMe() : void

  ◢   ⬥ AnimalFactory

          ⬡ CreateAnimal() : IAnimal

  ◢   ⬥ DogFactory

          ⬡ CreateAnimal() : IAnimal

  ◢   ⬥ TigerFactory

          ⬡ CreateAnimal() : IAnimal

  ◢   ⬥ Client

          ⬡ Main(string[]) : void

Figure 4-2. *Solution Explorer view*

Demonstration 1

Here is the implementation. Similar to the Simple Factory pattern in Chapter 24, I use the same inheritance hierarchy; that is, this time, you see that both the Dog and Tiger classes implement the AboutMe() method of their parent interface IAnimal. So, you see the following code segment at the beginning of the example.

```
public interface IAnimal
    {
        void AboutMe();
    }
```

```
public class Dog : IAnimal
{
    public void AboutMe()
    {
        Console.WriteLine("The dog says: Bow-Wow. I prefer barking.");
    }
}
public class Tiger : IAnimal
{
    public void AboutMe()
    {
        Console.WriteLine("The tiger says: Halum. I prefer hunting.");
    }
}
```

You see another inheritance hierarchy where two concrete classes—called DogFactory and TigerFactory—create dog and tiger objects. Each of them inherits from an abstract class AnimalFactory. These two concrete classes defer the instantiation process. I include supportive comments to help you better understand. The following code segment describes it.

```
public abstract class AnimalFactory
    {
        /*
        Remember the GoF definition which says
        "....Factory method lets a class defer instantiation
        to subclasses." The following method will create a tiger or a dog
        object, but at this point it does not know whether it will get a
        dog or a tiger. It will be decided by
        the subclasses i.e. DogFactory or TigerFactory.
        So, the following method is acting like a factory
        (of creation).
        */
        public abstract IAnimal CreateAnimal();
    }
// DogFactory is used to create dog
public class DogFactory : AnimalFactory
```

```csharp
    {
        public override IAnimal CreateAnimal()
        {
            // Creating a Dog
            return new Dog();
        }
    }
    // TigerFactory is used to create tigers
    public class TigerFactory : AnimalFactory
    {
        public override IAnimal CreateAnimal()
        {
            // Creating a Tiger
            return new Tiger();
        }
    }
```

Here is the complete demonstration.

```csharp
using System;

namespace FactoryMethodPattern
{
    #region Animal Hierarchy
    /*
     * Both the Dog and Tiger classes will
     * implement the IAnimal interface method.
     */
    public interface IAnimal
    {
        void AboutMe();
    }
    // Dog class
    public class Dog : IAnimal
    {
        public void AboutMe()
        {
```

```
        Console.WriteLine("The dog says: Bow-Wow. I prefer barking.");
    }
}
//Tiger class
public class Tiger : IAnimal
{
    public void AboutMe()
    {
        Console.WriteLine("The tiger says: Halum. I prefer hunting.");
    }
}
#endregion

#region Factory Hierarchy

// Both DogFactory and TigerFactory will use this.
public abstract class AnimalFactory
{
    /*
    Remember the GoF definition which says
    "....Factory method lets a class defer instantiation
    to subclasses." The following method will create a Tiger
    or a Dog, but at this point it does not know whether
    it will get a dog or a tiger. It will be decided by
    the subclasses i.e. DogFactory or TigerFactory.
    So, the following method is acting like a factory
    (of creation).
    */
    public abstract IAnimal CreateAnimal();
}
// DogFactory is used to create dog
public class DogFactory : AnimalFactory
{
    public override IAnimal CreateAnimal()
    {
        // Creating a Dog
```

```csharp
                return new Dog();
        }
    }
    // TigerFactory is used to create tigers
    public class TigerFactory : AnimalFactory
    {
        public override IAnimal CreateAnimal()
        {
            // Creating a Tiger
            return new Tiger();
        }
    }
    #endregion
    class Client
    {
        static void Main(string[] args)
        {
            Console.WriteLine("***Factory Pattern Demo.***\n");
            // Creating a Tiger Factory
            AnimalFactory tigerFactory = new TigerFactory();
            // Creating a tiger using the Factory Method
            IAnimal tiger = tigerFactory.CreateAnimal();
            tiger.AboutMe();

            // Creating a DogFactory
            AnimalFactory dogFactory = new DogFactory();
            // Creating a dog using the Factory Method
            IAnimal dog = dogFactory.CreateAnimal();
            dog.AboutMe();

            Console.ReadKey();
        }
    }
}
```

Output

The following is the output from running the program.

```
***Factory Pattern Demo.***

The tiger says: Halum. I prefer hunting.
The dog says: Bow-Wow. I prefer barking.
```

Modified Implementation 1

Now let's look at two important modifications that you can make to demonstration 1.

In the first modified implementation, more flexibilities are added to our earlier implementation. Note that the AnimalFactory class is an abstract class, so you can take advantage of using it. Suppose you want a subclass to follow a rule that can be imposed from its parent (or base) class. For simplicity, let's impose the rule through a console message which is shown in the following demonstration.

Partial Demonstration 1

In the modified implementation, I introduce a new method called MakeAnimal() in the AnimalFactory class.

```
// Modifying the AnimalFactory class.
public abstract class AnimalFactory
    {
    public IAnimal MakeAnimal()
        {
            Console.WriteLine("AnimalFactory.MakeAnimal()-You cannot
            ignore parent rules.");
            IAnimal animal = CreateAnimal();
            animal.AboutMe();
            return animal;
        }
    /*
    Remember the GoF definition which says
    "....Factory method lets a class defer instantiation
```

```
        to subclasses." Following method will create a Tiger
        or a Dog class, but at this point it does not know whether
        it will get a dog or a tiger. It will be decided by
        the subclasses i.e.DogFactory or TigerFactory.
        So, the following method is acting like a factory
        (of creation).
        */
        public abstract IAnimal CreateAnimal();
    }
```

The client code has adopted these changes; that is, instead of calling CreateAnimal() and then using AboutMe(). I simply invoke MakeAnimal() inside the following code segment. The old code is commented for your reference and to compare to the new code.

```
class Client
    {
        static void Main(string[] args)
        {
            Console.WriteLine("***Factory Pattern Modified Demo.***\n");
            // Creating a Tiger Factory
            AnimalFactory tigerFactory = new TigerFactory();
            // Creating a tiger using the Factory Method
            //IAnimal tiger = tigerFactory.CreateAnimal();
            //tiger.AboutMe();
            IAnimal tiger = tigerFactory.MakeAnimal();

            // Creating a DogFactory
            AnimalFactory dogFactory = new DogFactory();
            // Creating a dog using the Factory Method
            //IAnimal dog = dogFactory.CreateAnimal();
            //dog.AboutMe();
            IAnimal dog = dogFactory.MakeAnimal();

            Console.ReadKey();
        }
    }
```

Output

Here is the modified output.

```
***Factory Pattern Modified Demo.***

AnimalFactory.MakeAnimal()-You cannot ignore parent rules.
The tiger says: Halum. I prefer hunting.

AnimalFactory.MakeAnimal()-You cannot ignore parent rules.
The dog says: Bow-Wow. I prefer barking.
```

Analysis

Now in each case, you see the following warning: "...You cannot ignore parent rules." It is an enhancement to the demonstration 1.

Q&A Session

4.1 Why have you separated the CreateAnimal() method from the client code?

I did it for one purpose. I wanted the subclasses to create specialized objects. If you look carefully, you see that only this "creational part" varies across the products. I discuss this in detail in the "Q&A Session" section of Chapter 24.

4.2 What are the advantages of using a factory like this?

Here are some of the key advantages.

- You are separating the code that varies from the code that does not vary (in other words, the advantages of using the Simple Factory pattern are still present), which helps you easily maintain the code.

- The code is not tightly coupled, so you can add new classes such as Lion, Bear, and so on, at any time in the system without modifying the existing architecture. In other words, I followed the "closed for modification but open for extension" principle.

4.3 What are the challenges of using a factory like this?

If you need to deal with many different types of objects, then the overall performance of the system can be affected.

4.4 The Factory Method pattern supports two parallel hierarchies. Is this correct?

Good catch. Yes, from the class diagram, it is evident that this pattern supports parallel class hierarchies (see Figure 4-3).

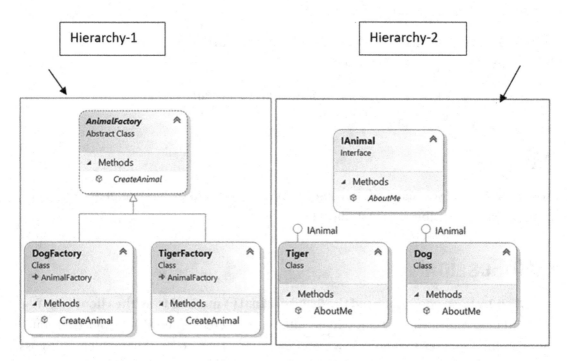

Figure 4-3. *The two class hierarchies in this example*

In this example, `AnimalFactory`, `DogFactory`, and `TigerFactory` are placed in one hierarchy, and `IAnimal`, `Dog`, and `Tiger` are placed in another hierarchy. So, you can see that the creators and their creations/products are the two hierarchies that are running in parallel.

4.5 You should always mark the factory method with an abstract keyword so that subclasses can complete them. Is this correct?

No. You may be interested in a default factory method when the creator has no subclasses. In that case, you cannot mark the factory method with an `abstract` keyword.

However, to see the real power of the Factory Method pattern, you may need to follow the design that is implemented here in most cases.

4.6 It appears that the Factory Method pattern is not that much different from the Simple Factory pattern. Is this correct?

If you look at the subclasses in the examples in both chapters, you may find some similarities. But you should not forget the key aim of the Factory Method pattern; it is supplying you with the framework through which different subclasses can make different products. In the Simple Factory pattern, you cannot vary the products in a similar manner. You can think of the Simple Factory pattern as a one-time deal, but most importantly, your creational part will not be closed for modification. Whenever you want to add something new, you need to add an `if-else` block or a `switch` statement in the factory class of your Simple Factory pattern.

In this context, always keep in mind the GoF definition, which says, "The Factory Method pattern lets a class defer instantiation to subclasses." Look at the modified implementation closely. You can see that `CreateAnimal()` creates a dog or a tiger by appropriate subclasses of `AnimalFactory`. So, `CreateAnimal()` is the factory method that is abstract in this design. When `MakeAnimal()` uses `CreateAnimal()` inside its body, it has no clue whether it is going to work on a dog or a tiger. The subclasses of `AnimalFactory` only know to create the concrete implementations (a dog or a tiger) for this application.

Note   In the `System.Web.WebRequest` class, you can see the `Create` method, which has two overloads. In this method, you can pass a Uniform Resource Identifier (URI). This method determines the appropriate protocol for a request and returns the appropriate subclass, for example, HttpWebRequest (if the URI starts with http:// or https://), FtpWebRequest (if the URI starts with ftp://), and so forth. If the URI changes from HTTP to FTP, the underlying code does not need to be changed, and the caller does not need to worry about detailed specifics of the protocol. This architecture promotes the use of factory patterns, but HttpWebRequest is not recommended for new development. Microsoft suggests that you use System.Net.Http.HttpClient class instead.

Modified Implementation 2

This chapter ends with an additional update to our initial implementation. Now let's update demonstration 1 by using method parameters. Let's proceed. You can get the full implementation when you download the code from the Apress website. For brevity, only the partial demonstration is presented here.

Partial Demonstration 2

This code segment shows that you can make the original implementation even better if you use method parameters inside CreateAnimal(). And this approach offers a benefit. Instead of creating DogFactory, TigerFactory, and so forth, you can make only one concrete factory class, as follows.

```
#region Factory Hierarchy

    // Both DogFactory and TigerFactory will use this.
    public abstract class AnimalFactory
    {
        /*
        Remember the GoF definition which says
        "....Factory method lets a class defer instantiation
        to subclasses." Following method will create a Tiger
        or a Dog, but at this point it does not know whether
        it will get a dog or a tiger. It will be decided by
        the subclasses i.e.DogFactory or TigerFactory.
        So, the following method is acting like a factory
        (of creation).
        */
        public abstract IAnimal CreateAnimal(string animalType);
    }
    /*
     * ConcreteAnimalFactory is used to create dogs or tigers
     * based on method parameter of CreateAnimal() method.
     */
    public class ConcreteAnimalFactory : AnimalFactory
    {
        public override IAnimal CreateAnimal(string animalType)
        {
            if (animalType.Contains("dog"))
            {
                // Creating a Dog
                return new Dog();
            }
```

```
        else
        if (animalType.Contains("tiger"))
        {
            // Creating a Dog
            return new Tiger();
        }
        else
        {

            throw new ArgumentException("You need to pass either a dog
            or a tiger as an argument.");
        }
    }
}

#endregion
```

Now you can pass either a "dog" string or a "tiger" string inside the CreateAnimal(...) method to create a Dog or a Tiger instance. To accommodate these changes, you can update the client code as follows. (This time, animalFactory creates both the Dog and Tiger instances. Everyone knows that "programming to interfaces" has this kind of benefit.)

```
class Client
    {
        static void Main(string[] args)
        {
            Console.WriteLine("***Factory Pattern Demo.***");
            Console.WriteLine("***It's a modified version using method
            parameter(s).***\n");
            // Creating a factory that can produce animals
            AnimalFactory animalFactory = new ConcreteAnimalFactory();
            // Creating a tiger using the Factory Method
            IAnimal tiger = animalFactory.CreateAnimal("tiger");
            tiger.AboutMe();
            // Now creating a dog.
            IAnimal dog = animalFactory.CreateAnimal("dog");
            dog.AboutMe();
```

```
        Console.ReadKey();
    }
  }
```

Output

Now if you execute this program, you can get the following output.

```
***Factory Pattern Demo.***
***It's a modified version using method parameter(s).***

The tiger says: Halum. I prefer hunting.
The dog says: Bow-Wow. I prefer barking.
```

I hope that you now have a better understanding of how to implement the Factory Method pattern. The two modified implementations are provided as a reference. (Full implementations are provided on the Apress website.). It is up to you whether you want to use either (or both) of these modifications in your program. But you should keep in mind that the factory method should create the appropriate object for the client behind the scene, and it's the ultimate motto of the pattern.

CHAPTER 5

Abstract Factory Pattern

This chapter covers the Abstract Factory pattern.

GoF Definition

Provide an interface for creating families of related or dependent objects without specifying their concrete classes.

Note   The Abstract Factory pattern will make more sense to you if you understand the Simple Factory pattern (Chapter 24) and the Factory Method pattern (Chapter 4). The Simple Factory pattern does not fall directly into the Gang of Four design patterns, so the discussion of that pattern appears in Part II of the book. I suggest that you read Chapters 4 and 24 before jumping into this one.

Concept

An abstract factory is often referred to as a *factory of factories*. This pattern provides a way to encapsulate a group of individual factories that have a common theme. In this process, you do not instantiate a class directly; instead, you instantiate a concrete factory and, after that, create products using the factory.

In our upcoming example, a factory instance (`animalFactory`) is instantiated. By using this factory instance, I create dog and tiger instances (dogs and tigers are the final products), which is why you see the following segment inside the client code.

```
// Making a wild dog and wild tiger through WildAnimalFactory
IAnimalFactory animalFactory = FactoryProvider.GetAnimalFactory("wild");
IDog dog = animalFactory.GetDog();
```

97

© Vaskaran Sarcar 2020
V. Sarcar, *Design Patterns in C#*, https://doi.org/10.1007/978-1-4842-6062-3_5

```
ITiger tiger = animalFactory.GetTiger();
dog.AboutMe();
tiger.AboutMe();
```

This pattern suits best when products are similar, but the product families are different (for example, a domestic dog is quite different from a wild dog). This pattern helps you to interchange specific implementations without changing the code that uses them, even at runtime. However, it may result in unnecessary complexity and extra work. Even debugging becomes tough in some cases.

Real-World Example

Suppose that you are decorating your room with two different types of tables; one is made of wood and the other one of steel. For the wooden type, you need to visit a carpenter, and for the other type, you may need to go to a metal shop. All of these are table factories. So, based on demand, you decide what kind of factory you need.

Computer-World Example

ADO.NET implements similar concepts to establish a connection to a database.

Implementation

Wikipedia describes a typical structure of this pattern, which is similar to what is shown in Figure 5-1 (see `https://en.wikipedia.org/wiki/Abstract_factory_pattern`).

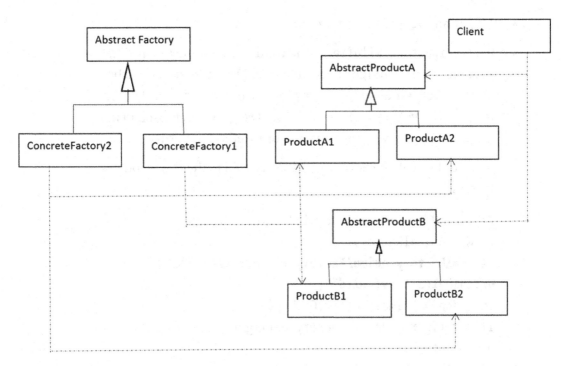

Figure 5-1. *Abstract Factory pattern*

I follow a similar structure in this chapter's implementation. In this example, there are two types of animals: pet animals and wild animals. Program.cs is the client who is looking for some animals (which are wild dogs, pet dogs, wild tigers, and pet tigers in this case). You explore the construction processes of both pet animals and wild animals in this implementation.

IAnimalFactory is an abstract factory. Two concrete factories called WildAnimalFactory and PetAnimalFactory inherits from this abstract factory. You can see that these concrete factories are responsible for creating the concrete products of dogs and tigers. As their names suggest, WildAnimalFactory creates wild animals (wild dogs and wild tigers), and PetAnimalFactory creates pet animals (pet dogs and pet tigers). The following summarizes the participants and their roles.

- IAnimalFactory: Abstract factory

- WildAnimalFactory: A concrete factory that implements IAnimalFactory; it creates wild dogs and wild tigers

- PetAnimalFactory: A concrete factory that implements IAnimalFactory, but this factory creates pet dogs and pet tigers

- ITiger and IDog: Abstract products

- PetTiger, PetDog, WildTiger, and WildDog: The concrete products.
  PetTiger and WildTiger implement the ITiger interface. PetDog
  and WildDog implement the IDog interface. The IDog and ITiger
  interfaces have only one method, AboutMe(), which is used in both
  the Simple Factory pattern and Factory Method pattern.

- A static class called FactoryProvider is used in the client code as
  follows:

  ```
  // Making a wild dog and wild tiger through
  // WildAnimalFactory
  IAnimalFactory animalFactory = FactoryProvider.
  GetAnimalFactory("wild");
  IDog dog = animalFactory.GetDog();
  ITiger tiger = animalFactory.GetTiger();
  dog.AboutMe();
  tiger.AboutMe();
  ```

- From the bold line in the previous code segment, you can see that
  I'm *not* directly instantiating the factory instance; instead, I'm
  using the FactoryProvider static class to get the factory instance.
  (This class has a similar structure as to when you used the concrete
  factories in the Factory Method pattern.) FactoryProvider provides
  the appropriate factory based on the parameter passed inside
  GetAnimalFactory(...) method.

Class Diagram

Figure 5-2 shows the class diagram.

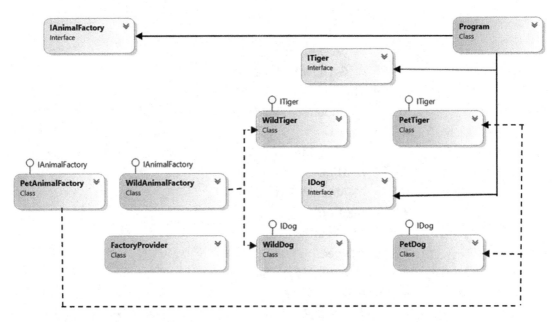

Figure 5-2. *Class diagram*

Solution Explorer View

Figure 5-3 shows the high-level structure of the program.

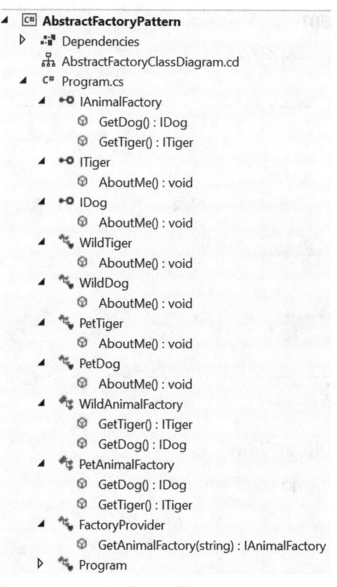

Figure 5-3. *Solution Explorer view*

Demonstration 1

Here's the complete program.

```
using System;

namespace AbstractFactoryPattern
{
```

```
// Abstract Factory
public interface IAnimalFactory
{
    IDog GetDog();
    ITiger GetTiger();
}

// Abstract Product-1
public interface ITiger
{
    void AboutMe();
}
// Abstract Product-2
public interface IDog
{
    void AboutMe();
}

// Concrete product-A1(WildTiger)
class WildTiger : ITiger
{
    public void AboutMe()
    {
        Console.WriteLine("Wild tiger says: I prefer hunting in
        jungles. Halum.");
    }
}
// Concrete product-B1(WildDog)
class WildDog : IDog
{
    public void AboutMe()
    {
        Console.WriteLine("Wild dog says: I prefer to roam freely in
        jungles. Bow-Wow.");
    }
}
```

```csharp
// Concrete product-A2(PetTiger)
class PetTiger : ITiger
{
    public void AboutMe()
    {
        Console.WriteLine("Pet tiger says: Halum. I play in an animal
        circus.");
    }
}

// Concrete product-B2(PetDog)
class PetDog : IDog
{
    public void AboutMe()
    {
        Console.WriteLine("Pet dog says: Bow-Wow. I prefer to stay at
        home.");
    }
}
// Concrete Factory 1-Wild Animal Factory
public class WildAnimalFactory : IAnimalFactory
{

    public ITiger GetTiger()
    {
        return new WildTiger();
    }
    public IDog GetDog()
    {
        return new WildDog();
    }
}
// Concrete Factory 2-Pet Animal Factory
public class PetAnimalFactory : IAnimalFactory
{
    public IDog GetDog()
```

```
    {
        return new PetDog();
    }

    public ITiger GetTiger()
    {
        return new PetTiger();
    }
}
// Factory provider
class FactoryProvider
{
    public static IAnimalFactory GetAnimalFactory(string factoryType)
    {
        if (factoryType.Contains("wild"))
        {
            // Returning a WildAnimalFactory
            return new WildAnimalFactory();
        }
        else
        if (factoryType.Contains("pet"))
        {
            // Returning a PetAnimalFactory
            return new PetAnimalFactory();
        }
        else
        {
            throw new ArgumentException("You need to pass either wild
            or pet as argument.");
        }
    }
}

// Client
class Program
{
```

```
static void Main(string[] args)
{
    Console.WriteLine("***Abstract Factory Pattern Demo.***\n");
    // Making a wild dog and wild tiger through WildAnimalFactory
    IAnimalFactory animalFactory = FactoryProvider.
    GetAnimalFactory("wild");
    IDog dog = animalFactory.GetDog();
    ITiger tiger = animalFactory.GetTiger();
    dog.AboutMe();
    tiger.AboutMe();

    Console.WriteLine("*****************");

    // Making a pet dog and pet tiger through PetAnimalFactory now.
    animalFactory = FactoryProvider.GetAnimalFactory("pet");
    dog = animalFactory.GetDog();
    tiger = animalFactory.GetTiger();
    dog.AboutMe();
    tiger.AboutMe();

    Console.ReadLine();
    }
  }
}
```

Output

Here's the output.

```
***Abstract Factory Pattern Demo.***

Wild dog says: I prefer to roam freely in jungles. Bow-Wow.
Wild tiger says: I prefer hunting in jungles. Halum.
*****************
Pet dog says: Bow-Wow.I prefer to stay at home.
Pet tiger says: Halum.I play in an animal circus.
```

Q&A Session

5.1   Both the IDog and ITiger interfaces contain methods that have the same names. For example, both interfaces contain the AboutMe() method. Is that mandatory?

No. You can use different names for your methods. Also, the number of methods can be different in these interfaces. However, in Chapter 24, I cover the Simple Factory pattern, and in Chapter 4, I cover the Factory Method pattern. In this chapter, I continued the examples, which is why I kept the same method.

5.2   What are the challenges of using an abstract factory like this?

Any change in the abstract factory forces you to propagate the modification to the concrete factories. Standard design philosophy suggests you to program to an interface, but not to an implementation. This is one of the key principles that developers should always keep in mind. In most scenarios, developers do not want to change their abstract factories.

Also, the overall architecture is complex, which is why debugging is very challenging in some cases.

5.3   How do you distinguish a Simple Factory pattern from a Factory Method pattern or an Abstract Factory pattern?

I discuss the differences between a Simple Factory pattern and a Factory Method pattern in the "Q&A Session" section in Chapter 4.

Let's revise how the client code uses these factories, as shown in the following diagrams. Here's a code snippet from the Simple Factory pattern.

```
IAnimal preferredType = null;
SimpleFactory simpleFactory = new SimpleFactory();
#region The code region that can vary based on users preference
/*
* Since this part may vary, we're moving the
* part to CreateAnimal() in SimpleFactory class.
*/
preferredType = simpleFactory.CreateAnimal();
#endregion

#region The codes that do not change frequently.
preferredType.AboutMe();
#endregion
```

Figure 5-4 shows the Simple Factory pattern.

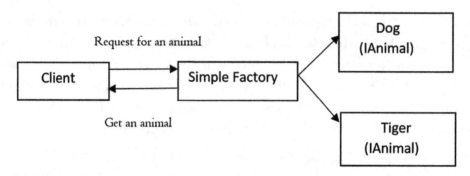

Figure 5-4. *Simple Factory pattern*

Here's the code snippet from the Factory Method pattern.

```
// Creating a Tiger Factory
AnimalFactory tigerFactory = new TigerFactory();
// Creating a tiger using the Factory Method
IAnimal tiger = tigerFactory.CreateAnimal();
tiger.AboutMe();

// Creating a DogFactory
AnimalFactory dogFactory = new DogFactory();
// Creating a dog using the Factory Method
IAnimal dog = dogFactory.CreateAnimal();
dog.AboutMe();
```

Figure 5-5 shows the Factory Method pattern.

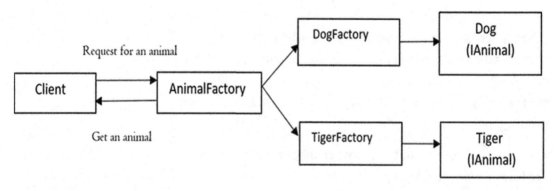

Figure 5-5. *Factory Method pattern*

Here's the code snippet from Abstract Factory pattern.

```
// Making a wild dog and wild tiger through WildAnimalFactory
IAnimalFactory animalFactory = FactoryProvider.GetAnimalFactory("wild");
IDog dog = animalFactory.GetDog();
ITiger tiger = animalFactory.GetTiger();
dog.AboutMe();
tiger.AboutMe();

Console.WriteLine("*****************");

// Making a pet dog and pet tiger through PetAnimalFactory now.
animalFactory = FactoryProvider.GetAnimalFactory("pet");
dog = animalFactory.GetDog();
tiger = animalFactory.GetTiger();
dog.AboutMe();
tiger.AboutMe();
```

Figure 5-6 shows the Abstract Factory pattern.

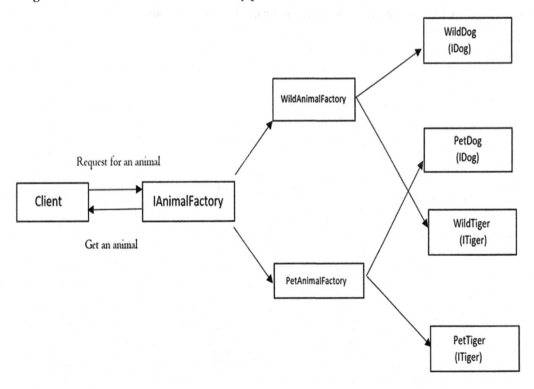

Figure 5-6. *Abstract Factory pattern*

In short, with the Simple Factory pattern, you can separate the code that varies from the rest of the code (basically, you decouple the client code). This approach helps you to manage the code more easily. Another key advantage of this approach is that the client is unaware of how the objects are created. So, it promotes both security and abstraction.

However, this approach can violate the open-closed principle. You can overcome this drawback using the Factory Method pattern, which allows subclasses to decide how the instantiation process is completed. Put simply, you delegate the object creation to the subclasses that implement the factory method to create objects.

The abstract factory is basically a factory of factories. It creates a family of related objects, but it does not depend on the concrete classes. In this pattern, you encapsulate a group of individual factories that have a common theme. In this process, you do not instantiate a class directly; instead, you get a concrete factory (I used a provider for that) and, after that, create products using the factory.

Lastly, I tried to keep the examples simple. A factory method promotes inheritance, and its subclasses need to implement the factory method to create objects. The Abstract Factory pattern can promote object composition by creating related objects using the methods that are exposed in a factory interface. In the end, all the factories promote loose coupling by reducing the dependencies on concrete classes.

PART I.B

Structural Patterns

CHAPTER 6

Proxy Pattern

This chapter covers the Proxy pattern.

GoF Definition

Provide a surrogate or placeholder for another object to control access to it.

Concept

You need to support this kind of design because, in many situations, direct communication with an original object is not always possible. This is due to many factors, including security and performance issues, resource constraints, the final product is in the development phase, and so forth. Proxies can be of different types, but fundamentally it is a substitute (or a placeholder) for an original object. As a result, when a client interacts with a proxy object, it appears that it is directly talking to the actual object. So, using this pattern, you may want to use a class that can perform as an interface to the original one.

Real-World Example

In a classroom, when one student is absent, his best friend may try to mimic his voice during roll call to get the teacher to think his friend is there. Apart from this example, you can consider the example from a different domain, for instance, ATMs. An ATM implementation can hold proxy objects for bank information that can exist on a remote server.

© Vaskaran Sarcar 2020
V. Sarcar, *Design Patterns in C#*, https://doi.org/10.1007/978-1-4842-6062-3_6

Computer-World Example

In the real programming world, creating multiple instances of a complex object can be costly because you may need resources that are not easily available or allocatable. In such a situation, you can create multiple proxy objects that can point to the original object. This mechanism can help you to save the computer/system memory and improve the performance of your application.

Another very common use of a proxy is seen when a user doesn't want to disclose the true IP address of his/her machine and make it anonymous.

In WCF applications, you may notice WCF client proxies, which a client application uses to communicate with the service. You can also configure a REST API to work behind a proxy server to promote an authorized communication.

Implementation

In this program, Subject is an abstract class with an abstract method called DoSomeWork(). It looks like the following.

```
public abstract class Subject
    {
        public abstract void DoSomeWork();
    }
```

ConcreteSubject is a concrete class that inherits from Subject and completes the DoSomeWork() method. So, it looks like the following.

```
public class ConcreteSubject : Subject
    {
        public override void DoSomeWork()
        {
            Console.WriteLine("I've processed your request.");
        }
    }
```

Let's assume you want to restrict the client from directly invoking the method in
ConcreteSubject. (Consider the cases discussed in the computer-world examples
for some reasons behind this.) So, you make a proxy class called Proxy. In our
implementation, the Proxy class also contains a method called DoSomeWork(), and a
client can use this method using a Proxy instance. When a client calls the DoSomeWork()
method of the proxy object that, in turn, this call is propagated to the DoSomeWork()
method in the ConcreteSubject object. This lets the clients feel as if they have invoked
the method from ConcreteSubject directly, which is why the Proxy class looks like the
following.

```
public class Proxy : Subject
    {
        Subject subject;

        public override void DoSomeWork()
        {
            Console.WriteLine("Welcome, my client.");
            /*
            Lazy initialization:We'll not instantiate until
            the method is called.
            */
            if (subject == null)
            {
                subject = new ConcreteSubject();
            }
            subject.DoSomeWork();
        }
    }
```

Class Diagram

Figure 6-1 shows the class diagram.

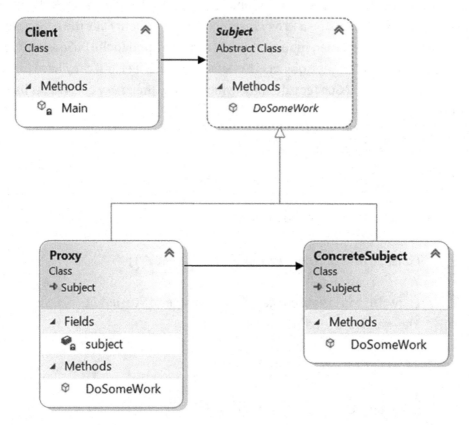

Figure 6-1. *Class diagram*

Solution Explorer View

Figure 6-2 shows the high-level structure of the program. (Note that you could separate the proxy class into a different file, but since the parts are small in this example, I put everything in a single file. The same comment applies to other programs in this book.)

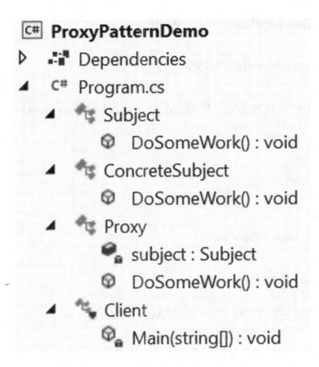

Figure 6-2. *Solution Explorer view*

Demonstration 1

Here's the complete implementation.

```
using System;

namespace ProxyPatternDemo
{
    /// <summary>
    /// Abstract class Subject
    /// </summary>
    public abstract class Subject
    {
        public abstract void DoSomeWork();
    }
    /// <summary>
    /// ConcreteSubject class
    /// </summary>
```

117

```csharp
public class ConcreteSubject : Subject
{
    public override void DoSomeWork()
    {
        Console.WriteLine("I've processed your request.");
    }
}
/// <summary>
/// Proxy class
/// </summary>
public class Proxy : Subject
{
    Subject subject;

    public override void DoSomeWork()
    {
        Console.WriteLine("Welcome, my client.");
        /*
         Lazy initialization:We'll not instantiate the object until the
         method is called.
        */
        if (subject == null)
        {
            subject = new ConcreteSubject();
        }
        subject.DoSomeWork();
    }
}
/// <summary>
/// Client class
/// </summary>

class Client
{
    static void Main(string[] args)
    {
```

```
        Console.WriteLine("***Proxy Pattern Demo.***\n");
        Subject proxy = new Proxy();
        proxy.DoSomeWork();
        Console.ReadKey();
    }
  }
}
```

Output

Here's the output.

```
***Proxy Pattern Demo.***

Welcome, my client.
I've processed your request.
```

Q&A Session

6.1 What are the different types of proxies?

These are the common types of proxies.

- *Remote proxies*: These proxies can hide an object that sits in a different address space.

- *Virtual proxies*: These proxies perform optimization techniques, such as creating a heavy object on an on-demand basis.

- *Protection proxies*: These proxies generally deal with different access rights.

- *Smart reference*: Performs additional housekeeping when a client accesses an object. A typical operation may include counting the number of references to an object at a certain moment in time.

6.2 You could create the `ConcreteSubject` instance in the proxy class constructor as shown here.

```
/// <summary>
/// Proxy class
/// </summary>
public class Proxy : Subject
        {
        Subject subject;
        public Proxy()
        {
                // Instantiating inside the constructor
                subject = new ConcreteSubject();
        }
        public override void DoSomeWork()
        {
                Console.WriteLine("Proxy call happening now..");
                cs.DoSomeWork();
        }
}
}
```

Is this correct?

Yes, you could do that. But do not forget that a proxy class can have additional methods that may not rely on `ConcreteSubject`. So, if you need these methods from the Proxy class, and you follow your proposed design, whenever you instantiate a proxy object, you instantiate an object of the `ConcreteSubject` class also. So, this may end up creating unnecessary objects.

6.3 Using this lazy instantiation process, you may create unnecessary objects in a multithreaded application. Is this correct?

Yes. It is a simple illustration to give you the core idea behind the actual pattern. In the discussions of the Singleton pattern in Chapter 1, we analyzed some alternative approaches which tell you how to work in a multithreaded environment. You can always refer to those discussions in situations like this. (For example, in this scenario, you could implement a smart proxy to ensure that an object is locked before you grant access to the object).

6.4 Can you give an example of a remote proxy?

Suppose you want to call a method of an object, but the object is running in a different address space (for example, in a different location or on a different computer). How do you proceed? With the help of remote proxies, you can call the method on the proxy object, which in turn forwards the call to the actual object that is running on the remote machine. (Demonstration 1 is an example of this category in this context if the actual method exists on a different computer and you connect to it via a proxy object over a network.) This type of need can be realized through different well-known mechanisms such as ASP.NET, CORBA, COM/DCOM, or Java's RMI. In C# applications, you can exercise a similar mechanism with WCF (.NET Framework version 3.0 and onward) or .NET web services/remoting (mainly used in earlier versions). It is useful to note that .NET remoting is *not* supported by .NET Core, and Microsoft doesn't plan to add this support in the future (see `https://docs.microsoft.com/en-us/dotnet/core/ porting/net-framework-tech-unavailable#:~:text=NET%20Remoting%20isn't%20 supported,IO`).

Figure 6-3 shows a simple remote proxy structure.

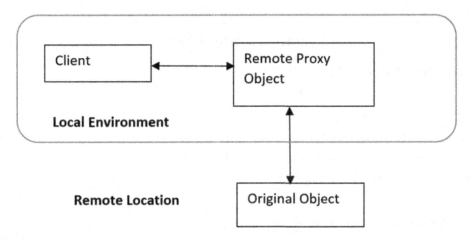

Figure 6-3. *A simple remote proxy diagram*

6.5 When do you use a virtual proxy?

A virtual proxy preserves memory from being allocated to an object. If the actual object creation is an expensive operation, you can create a light copy of the intended object with the most important details and supply it to the user. The expensive object is created only when it is truly needed. For example, you can use the concept to avoid loading an extremely large image unnecessarily for better application performance.

6.6 When do you use a protection proxy?

In an organization, the security team can implement a protection proxy to block Internet access to specific web sites.

Consider the following example, which is a modified version of the Proxy pattern implementation described earlier. For simplicity, let's assume you have only three registered users who can exercise the DoSomeWork() proxy method. If an unwanted user (named Robin) tries to invoke the method, the system rejects his access requests. When the system rejects this kind of unwanted access, there is no point in making a proxy object. In the upcoming example, these registered users are initialized in the proxy class constructor, but I avoid the instantiation of a ConcreteSubject object inside it. It helps me to avoid creating an unnecessary object creation for an unauthorized user.

Now let's go through the modified implementation.

Demonstration 2

Here's the modified implementation.

```
using System;
using System.Linq; // For Contains() method below

namespace ProxyPatternQAs
{
    /// <summary>
    /// Abstract class Subject
    /// </summary>
    public abstract class Subject
    {
        public abstract void DoSomeWork();
    }
    /// <summary>
    /// ConcreteSubject class
    /// </summary>
    public class ConcreteSubject : Subject
    {
        public override void DoSomeWork()
        {
```

```csharp
        Console.WriteLine("I've processed your request.\n");
    }
}
/// <summary>
/// Proxy class
/// </summary>
public class Proxy : Subject
{
    Subject subject;
    string[] registeredUsers;
    string currentUser;
    public Proxy(string currentUser)
    {
        /*
         * Avoiding to instantiate ConcreteSubject
         * inside the Proxy class constructor.
         */
        //subject = new ConcreteSubject();

        // Registered users
        registeredUsers = new string[] { "Admin", "Rohit", "Sam" };
        this.currentUser = currentUser;
    }
    public override void DoSomeWork()
    {
        Console.WriteLine($"{currentUser} wants to access into the system.");
        if (registeredUsers.Contains(currentUser))
        {
            Console.WriteLine($"Welcome, {currentUser}.");
            /* Lazy initialization: We'll not instantiate until the
            method is called through an authorized user. *.
            if (subject == null)
            {
                subject = new ConcreteSubject();
            }
```

```
            subject.DoSomeWork();
        }
        else
        {
            Console.WriteLine($"Sorry {currentUser}, you do not have
            access into the system.");
        }
    }
}
/// <summary>
/// Client
/// </summary>

class Client
{
    static void Main(string[] args)
    {
        Console.WriteLine("***Proxy Pattern Demo2.***\n");
        // Authorized user-Admin
        Subject proxy = new Proxy("Admin");
        proxy.DoSomeWork();
        // Authorized user-Sam
        proxy = new Proxy("Sam");
        proxy.DoSomeWork();
        // Unauthorized User-Robin
        proxy = new Proxy("Robin");
        proxy.DoSomeWork();
        Console.ReadKey();
    }
}
}
```

Output

Here's the modified output.

```
***Proxy Pattern Demo2.***

Admin wants to access into the system.
Welcome, Admin.
I've processed your request.

Sam wants to access into the system.
Welcome, Sam.
I've processed your request.

Robin wants to access into the system.
Sorry Robin, you do not have access into the system.
```

6.7 It looks as if proxies act like decorators (see Chapter 7). Is this correct?

Sometimes a proxy implementation can have some similarities to a decorator, but you should not forget the true intent of a proxy. Decorators focus on adding responsibilities, whereas proxies focus on controlling access to an object. So, if you remember their purpose, in most cases, you can distinguish proxies from decorators.

6.8 When should I consider designing a proxy?

The following are some important use cases where proxies can help you.

- You are writing test cases for a scenario that is still in the development phase or very hard to reproduce. For example, when you want to evaluate behavior in an application that can be seen in a customer environment only, but you also recognize that when the application is running, the probability of getting the behavior is very low. In such a case, you can mimic the customer environment behavior in your proxy object and execute your test cases to evaluate the correctness of this behavior. You do not want your client to talk directly to the target object.

- You want to hide the complexity and enhance the security of the system.

6.9 What are the cons associated with proxies?

Here are some factors that you should keep in mind while using this pattern.

- The overall response time can be an issue because you are not directly talking to the actual object.

- You need to maintain additional layers for the proxies.

- A proxy can hide the actual responses from objects, which may create confusion in some scenarios.

CHAPTER 7

Decorator Pattern

This chapter covers the Decorator pattern.

GoF Definition

Attach additional responsibilities to an object dynamically. Decorators provide a flexible alternative to subclassing for extending functionality.

Concept

From the GoF definition, it is evident that this pattern uses an alternative to subclassing (i.e., inheritance). If inheritance is not allowed, how do you proceed? Yes, you guessed it right. It prescribes you to use composition instead of inheritance.

By following the SOLID principle, this pattern promotes the concept where your class is closed for modification but open for extension. (If you want to learn more about SOLID principles, go to `https://en.wikipedia.org/wiki/SOLID_(object-oriented_design)`.) Using this pattern, you can add special functionality to a specific object without altering the underlying class.

A decorator is just like a wrapper (or topping) that surrounds the original object and adds additional functionality to it. This is why the Decorator pattern is also called a Wrapper pattern. This pattern is most effective when you add decorators dynamically. Since decorators are often added dynamically, it's perfectly fine if you do not want them in a later phase of development, because the original object may still work.

© Vaskaran Sarcar 2020
V. Sarcar, *Design Patterns in C#*, https://doi.org/10.1007/978-1-4842-6062-3_7

Real-World Example

Suppose that you own a single-story house, and you decide to build an additional floor on top of it. You may not want to change the architecture of the ground floor, but you may want to employ a new design for the newly added floor that can fit on top of the existing architecture.

Figures 7-1, 7-2, and 7-3 illustrate this concept.

Figure 7-1. *Original house*

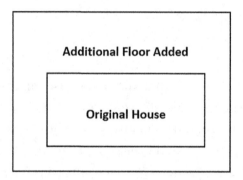

Figure 7-2. *Original house with a decorator (the additional floor is built on top of original structure)*

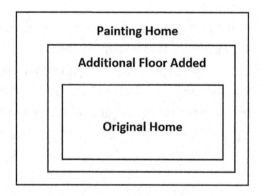

Figure 7-3. *Applying an additional decorator on top of the existing decorator and modifying the house (now painting the house)*

Note   The case shown in Figure 7-3 is optional. You can use an existing decorator object to enhance the behavior, or you can create a new decorator object and add the new behavior to it. In step 2, you could also directly paint the original house. You don't need to start painting once the new floor is added.

Computer-World Example

Suppose that you want to add border properties to a GUI-based toolkit. You could do this using inheritance, but that cannot be treated as an ultimate solution because you may not have absolute control over everything since the beginning. So, this technique is static by nature.

In this context, decorators can offer you a flexible approach. They promote the concept of dynamic choices. For example, you can wrap the component in another object (similar to Figures 7-2 and 7-3). The enclosing object is called a decorator, and it must conform to the interface of the component that it decorates. It forwards the requests to the original component and can perform additional operations before or after those requests. In fact, this concept allows you to add an unlimited number of responsibilities.

Implementation

In this example, five players are involved: `AbstractHome`, `ConcreteHome`, `AbstractDecorator`, `FloorDecorator`, and `PaintDecorator`.

`AbstractHome` is defined as follows.

```
abstract class AbstractHome
{
    public double AdditionalPrice { get; set; }
    public abstract void MakeHome();
}
```

A concrete implementor of AbstractHome must implement the MakeHome() method. In addition to this, you can set a price by using the AdditionalPrice property. This is why a concrete class called ConcreteHome inherits from AbstractHome, completes the original structure, and looks like the following (I assume that once the home is built, there is no immediate modification needed; so, AdditionalPrice is initially set to 0).

```
class ConcreteHome : AbstractHome
{
    public ConcreteHome()
    {
        AdditionalPrice = 0;
    }
    public override void MakeHome()
    {
        Console.WriteLine($"Original House is constructed.Price for
        this 10000$");
    }
}
```

At this moment, you can opt for an additional floor to this existing home, or you may want to paint the home or you may want to do both. So, FloorDecorator and PaintDecorator both come into the picture. Though it was not strictly needed, to share the common code, both decorators inherit from AbstractDecorator, which has the following structure.

```
abstract class AbstractDecorator : AbstractHome
{
    protected AbstractHome home;
    public AbstractDecorator(AbstractHome home)
    {
        this.home = home;
        this.AdditionalPrice = 0;
    }
    public override void MakeHome()
    {
        home.MakeHome();
    }
}
```

Notice that AbstractDecorator holds a reference to AbstractHome. So, the concrete decorators (FloorDecorator or PaintDecorator in this example) are decorating an instance of AbstractHome.

Now let's look at the structure of a concrete decorator, FloorDecorator, which is as follows.

```
// Floor Decorator used to add a floor
class FloorDecorator : AbstractDecorator
{
    public FloorDecorator(AbstractHome home) : base(home)
    {

        this.AdditionalPrice = 2500;
    }
    public override void MakeHome()
    {
        base.MakeHome();
        // Adding a floor on top of original house.
        AddFloor();
    }
    private void AddFloor()
    {

        Console.WriteLine($"-Additional Floor added.Pay additional
        {AdditionalPrice}$ for it .");
    }
}
```

You can see that FloorDecorator can add a floor (using the AddFloor() method), and when you use it, you must pay an additional $2500 for the additional construction. More importantly, before adding a floor, it calls the MakeHome() method of the AbstractHome class, which in turn calls the MakeHome() method from a concrete implementation of AbstractHome (i.e., ConcreteHome).

PaintDecorator acts similarly, but you have to pay more for it. (Yes, I assume that you are using luxurious paints for your home.)

Class Diagram

Figure 7-4 shows the most important parts of the class diagram.

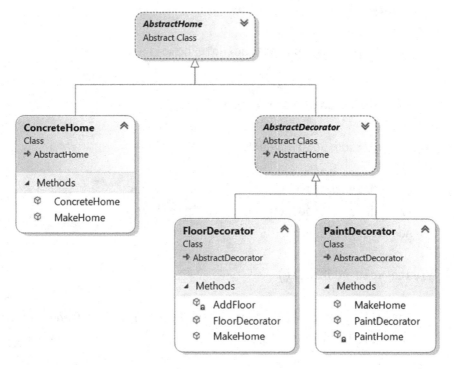

Figure 7-4. *Class diagram. Client class is not shown here.*

Solution Explorer View

Figure 7-5 shows the high-level structure of the program.

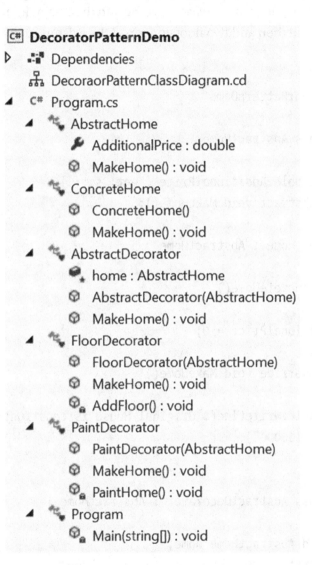

Figure 7-5. *Solution Explorer view*

Demonstration

Here's the complete implementation, which tested two scenarios (marked with #region). In scenario 1, I add one floor to the existing home and then paint it. In scenario 2, I paint the original home and then add two floors on top of the existing architecture.

```
using System;

namespace DecoratorPatternDemo
{
    abstract class AbstractHome
    {
        public double AdditionalPrice { get; set; }
        public abstract void MakeHome();
    }
    class ConcreteHome : AbstractHome
    {
        public ConcreteHome()
        {
            AdditionalPrice = 0;
        }
        public override void MakeHome()
        {
            Console.WriteLine($"Original House is constructed.Price for
            this $10000");
        }
    }
    abstract class AbstractDecorator : AbstractHome
    {
        protected AbstractHome home;
        public AbstractDecorator(AbstractHome home)
        {
            this.home = home;
            this.AdditionalPrice = 0;
        }
        public override void MakeHome()
        {
```

```
        home.MakeHome();//Delegating task
    }
}

// Floor Decorator is used to add a floor

class FloorDecorator : AbstractDecorator
{
    public FloorDecorator(AbstractHome home) : base(home)
    {
        //this.home = home;
        this.AdditionalPrice = 2500;
    }
    public override void MakeHome()
    {
        base.MakeHome();
        // Adding a floor on top of original house.
        AddFloor();
    }
    private void AddFloor()
    {
        Console.WriteLine($"-Additional Floor added.Pay additional
        ${AdditionalPrice} for it .");
    }
}

// Paint Decorator used to paint the home.

class PaintDecorator : AbstractDecorator
{
    public PaintDecorator(AbstractHome home):base(home)
    {
        //this.home = home;
        this.AdditionalPrice = 5000;
    }
```

```
    public override void MakeHome()
    {
        base.MakeHome();
        // Painting home.
        PaintHome();
    }
    private void PaintHome()
    {
        Console.WriteLine($"--Painting done.Pay additional
        ${AdditionalPrice} for it .");
    }
}
class Program
{
    static void Main(string[] args)
    {
        Console.WriteLine("***Decorator pattern Demo***\n");

        #region Scenario-1
        Console.WriteLine("\n**Scenario-1:");
        Console.WriteLine("**Building home.Adding floor and then
        painting it.**");

        AbstractHome home = new ConcreteHome();
        Console.WriteLine("Current bill breakups are as follows:");
        home.MakeHome();

        // Applying a decorator
        // Adding a floor
        home = new FloorDecorator(home);
        Console.WriteLine("\nFloor added.Current bill breakups are as
        follows:");
        home.MakeHome();

        // Working on top of the previous decorator.
        // Painting the home
        home = new PaintDecorator(home);
```

```csharp
Console.WriteLine("\nPaint applied.Current bill breakups are as
follows:");
home.MakeHome();
#endregion

#region Scenario-2
Console.WriteLine("\n**Scenario-2:");
Console.WriteLine("**Building home,painting it and then adding
two additional floors on top of it.**");
// Fresh start once again.
home = new ConcreteHome();
Console.WriteLine("\nGoing back to original home.Current bill
breakups are as follows:");
home.MakeHome();

// Applying paint on original home.
home = new PaintDecorator(home);
Console.WriteLine("\nPaint applied.Current bill breakups are as
follows:");
home.MakeHome();

// Adding a floor on the painted home.
home = new FloorDecorator(home);
Console.WriteLine("\nFloor added.Current bill breakups are as
follows:");
home.MakeHome();

// Adding another floor on the current home.
home = new FloorDecorator(home);
Console.WriteLine("\nFloor added.Current bill breakups are as
follows:");
home.MakeHome();
#endregion

Console.ReadKey();
        }
    }
}
```

Output

Decorator pattern Demo

Scenario-1:
Building home. Adding floor and then painting it.
Current bill breakups are as follows:
Original House is constructed. Price for this $10000

Floor added. Current bill breakups are as follows:
Original House is constructed.Price for this $10000
-Additional Floor added.Pay additional $2500 for it.

Paint applied. Current bill breakups are as follows:
Original House is constructed.Price for this $10000
-Additional Floor added. Pay additional $2500 for it.
--Painting done. Pay additional $5000 for it.

Scenario-2:
Building home, painting it and then adding two additional floors on top of it.

Going back to original home. Current bill breakups are as follows:
Original House is constructed. Price for this $10000

Paint applied. Current bill breakups are as follows:
Original House is constructed. Price for this $10000
--Painting done. Pay additional $5000 for it.

Floor added.Current bill breakups are as follows:
Original House is constructed.Price for this $10000
--Painting done.Pay additional $5000 for it.
-Additional Floor added. Pay additional $2500 for it.

Floor added.Current bill breakups are as follows:
Original House is constructed. Price for this $10000
--Painting done.Pay additional $5000 for it.
-Additional Floor added.Pay additional $2500 for it.
-Additional Floor added.Pay additional $2500 for it.

Q&A Session

7.1 Can you explain how composition promotes a dynamic behavior that inheritance cannot?

When a derived class inherits from a base class, it inherits the behavior of the base class at that time only. Though different subclasses can extend the base or parent class in different ways, this type of binding is known at compile time. So, the method is static. But by using the concept of composition, as in the previous example, you get dynamic behavior.

When you design a parent class, you may not have enough visibility about what kind of additional responsibilities your clients may want in some later phase. Since the constraint is that you cannot modify the existing code, in this case, object composition not only outclasses inheritance, but it also ensures that you are not introducing bugs in the old architecture.

Lastly, in this context, you must try to remember a key design principle that says *classes should be open for extension but closed for modification.*

7.2 What are the key advantages of using a decorator?

Here are some of the key advantages.

- The existing structure is untouched, so you cannot introduce bugs there.

- New functionalities can be easily added to an existing object.

- You can not only add a behavior to an interface, but you can alter the behavior too.

- You do not need to predict/implement all the supported functionalities at once (for example, in the initial design phase). You can develop incrementally. For example, you can add decorator objects one by one to support your needs. You must acknowledge that if you make a complex class first and then want to extend the functionalities, it will be a tedious process.

7.3 How is the overall design pattern different from inheritance?

You can add, alter, or remove responsibilities by simply attaching or detaching decorators. But with simple inheritance techniques, you need to create new classes for new responsibilities. So, you may end up with a complex system.

Consider the example again. Suppose that you want to add a new floor, paint the house, and do some extra work. To fulfill this need, you can start with `FloorDecorator` because it is already providing the support to add a floor, and then use `PaintDecorator` to paint the house. Then you need to add a simple wrapper to complete those additional responsibilities.

But if you start with inheritance, and then you may have multiple subclasses; for example, one for adding a floor and one for painting the house, as shown in Figure 7-6 (a hierarchical inheritance).

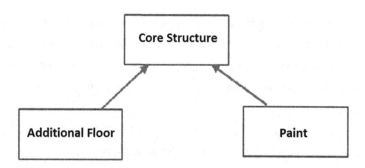

Figure 7-6. *A hierarchical inheritance*

So, if you need an additional painted floor with some extra features, you may need to end up with a design like in Figure 7-7.

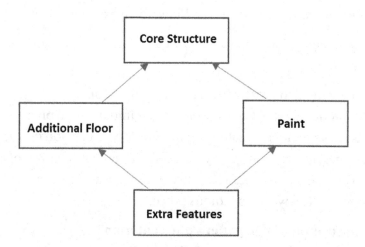

Figure 7-7. *A class (Extra Features) needs to inherit from multiple base classes*

Now you feel the heat of the "diamond effect" because in many programming languages, including C#, multiple base classes are not allowed.

You also discover that the inheritance mechanism is not only much more challenging and time-consuming compared to the Decorator pattern, but it may promote duplicate code in your application. Lastly, do not forget that inheritance promotes only compile-time binding (not dynamic binding).

7.4 Why are you creating a class with a single responsibility? You could make a subclass that can simply add a floor and then paint. In that case, you may end up with fewer subclasses. Is this correct?

If you are familiar with the SOLID principles, you know that there is a principle called *single responsibility*. The idea behind this principle is that each class should have responsibility for a single part of the functionality provided in the software. The Decorator pattern is effective when you use the single responsibility principle because you can simply add or remove responsibilities dynamically.

7.5 What are the disadvantages associated with this pattern?

I believe that if you are careful, there are no significant disadvantages. But if you create too many decorators in the system, it will be hard to maintain and debug. So, in that case, they can create unnecessary confusion.

7.6 In the example, the AbstractDecorator class is abstract, but there is no abstract method in it. How is this possible?

In C#, a class can be abstract without containing an abstract method, but the reverse is not true. In other words, if a class contains at least one abstract method, it means that the class is incomplete, and you are forced to mark it with the abstract keyword.

Also, if you read the comment in Figure 7-8, you are delegating the task to a concrete decorator, in this case, because you want to use and instantiate the concrete decorators only.

```
abstract class AbstractDecorator : AbstractHome
{
    protected AbstractHome home;
    2 references
    public AbstractDecorator(AbstractHome home)
    {
        this.home = home;
        this.AdditionalPrice = 0;
    }
    14 references
    public override void MakeHome()
    {
        home.MakeHome();//Delegating task
    }
}
```

Figure 7-8. *An abstract class: AbstractDecorator*

So, in this example, you cannot simply instantiate an AbstractDecorator instance, because it is marked with the abstract keyword.

The following line creates a compilation error.

AbstractDecorator abstractDecorator = new AbstractDecorator();
saying *"CS0144   Cannot create an instance of the abstract class or interface 'AbstractDecorator'"*

7.7 Are decorators used for dynamic binding only?

No. You can use the concept for both static and dynamic binding. But dynamic binding is its strength, so I concentrated on that here. The GoF definition also focuses on dynamic binding only.

Note   The I/O streams implementations in the .NET Framework, .NET Core, and Java use the Decorator pattern. For example, the BufferedStream class inherits from the Stream class. Note the presence of two overloaded constructors in this class; each of them takes a Stream (Parent class) as a parameter (just like demonstration 1). When you see this kind of construct, there is a possibility that you are seeing an example of the Decorator pattern. BufferedStream is acting like a decorator in .NET.

CHAPTER 8

Adapter Pattern

This chapter covers the Adapter pattern.

GoF Definition

Convert the interface of a class into another interface client's expect. Adapter lets classes work together that otherwise could not because of incompatible interfaces.

Concept

From the GoF definition, you can guess that this pattern deals with at least two incompatible inheritance hierarchies. In a domain-specific system, the clients are habituated on how to invoke methods in software. Those methods can follow an inheritance hierarchy. Now assume that you need to upgrade your system and need to implement a new inheritance hierarchy. When you do that, you do not want to force your clients to learn the new way to access the software. So, what can you do? The solution is simple: you write an adapter that accepts client requests and translates these requests in a form that the methods in the new hierarchy can understand. As a result, clients can enjoy the updated software without any hassle.

The following examples can also help you better understand the patterns.

Real-World Example

A common use of this pattern is when you use an electrical outlet adapter/AC power adapter on international travels. These adapters can act as middlemen so that an electronic device, such as a laptop that accepts a US power supply, can be plugged into a European power outlet.

© Vaskaran Sarcar 2020
V. Sarcar, *Design Patterns in C#*, https://doi.org/10.1007/978-1-4842-6062-3_8

Consider another example. Suppose that you need to charge your mobile phone. But you see that the electrical outlet is not compatible with your charger. In this case, you may need to use an adapter. Even a translator who is converting one language to another follows this pattern in real life.

Let's consider a situation where you have two different shapes (e.g., Shape1 and Shape2), neither of which is a rectangle, and they look like Figure 8-1.

Figure 8-1. *Before using an adapter*

Let's further assume that combining these two different shapes, you need to form a rectangle. How do you proceed? One simple solution is to bring another bounded X-shaped figure (filled with color), as shown in Figure 8-2.

Figure 8-2. *An adapter*

Then attach the three shapes, as shown in Figure 8-3.

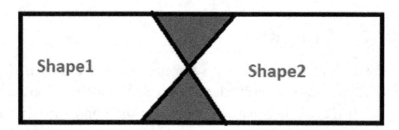

Figure 8-3. *After using an adapter*

In programming, you can think of Shape1 and Shape2 as two different interfaces that can't work together unless you combine them to form a rectangle using this X-shaped figure. The X-shaped figure is playing the role of an adapter in this scenario.

Computer-World Example

Suppose that you have an application that can be broadly classified into two parts: the user interface (UI or the front end) and the database (the back end). Through the user interface, clients can pass some specific type of data or objects. Your database is compatible with those objects and can store them smoothly. Over time, you may realize that you need to upgrade your software to make your clients happy. So, you may want to allow some other type of object also to pass through the UI. But in this case, the first issue comes from your database because it cannot store these new types of objects. In such a situation, you can use an adapter that takes care of the conversion of these new objects to a compatible form that your existing database can accept and store.

Implementation

In the upcoming example, there are two hierarchies: one for Rectangle and one for Triangle. IRectangle interface has two methods called CalculateArea() and AboutMe(). The Rectangle class implements the IRectangle interface and form the first hierarchy as follows.

```
class Rectangle : IRectangle
    {
        double length;
        public double width;
        public Rectangle(double length, double width)
        {
            this.length = length;
            this.width = width;
        }
```

```
    public double CalculateArea()
    {
        return length * width;
    }

    public void AboutMe()
    {
        Console.WriteLine("Actually, I am a Rectangle");
    }
}
```

The ITriangle interface has two methods: CalculateAreaOfTriangle() and AboutTriangle(). The Triangle class implements the ITriangle interface and forms another hierarchy, as follows.

```
class Triangle : ITriangle
    {
        double baseLength; // base
        double height; // height
        public Triangle(double length, double height)
        {
            this.baseLength = length;
            this.height = height;
        }
        public double CalculateAreaOfTriangle()
        {
            return 0.5 * baseLength * height;
        }
        public void AboutTriangle()
        {
            Console.WriteLine("Actually, I am a Triangle.");
        }
    }
```

These two hierarchies are easy to understand. Now, let's look at a problem in which you need to calculate the area of a triangle using the Rectangle hierarchy.

How do you proceed? You can use an adapter to solve this problem, as shown in the following example.

```
/*
 * RectangleAdapter is implementing IRectangle.
 * So, it needs to implement all the methods
 * defined in the target interface.
 */
class RectangleAdapter : IRectangle
{
        ITriangle triangle;
        public RectangleAdapter(ITriangle triangle)
        {
                this.triangle = triangle;
        }

        public void AboutMe()
        {
                triangle.AboutTriangle();
        }

        public double CalculateArea()
        {
                return triangle.CalculateAreaOfTriangle();
        }
}
```

Notice the beauty of using the adapter. You are not making any changes to any hierarchy, and at a high level, it appears that by using the IRectangle methods, you can calculate the area of a triangle. This is because you are using the AboutMe() and CalculateArea() methods of the IRectangle interface at a high level, but inside those methods, you are invoking the ITriangle methods.

Apart from this advantage, you can also extend the benefit of using an adapter. For example, suppose that you need to have a large number of rectangles in an application, but there is a constraint on the number of rectangles you create. (For simplicity, let's assume that in an application, you are allowed to create a maximum of five rectangles and ten triangles, but when the application runs, in certain scenarios, you may need to supply ten rectangles.) In those cases, using this pattern, you can use some of the triangle objects that can behave like rectangle objects. How? Well, when using the adapter, you are calling CalculateArea(), but it is invoking CalculateAreaOfTriangle(). So, you can modify the method body as you need. For example, in your application, let's assume that each rectangle object has a length of 20 units and a width of 10 units, whereas each triangle object has a base of 20 units and a height of 10 units. So, each rectangle object has an area of 20*10=200 square units, and each triangle object has an area of 0.5*20*10=100 square units. So, you can simply multiply each triangle area by 2 to get an equivalent rectangle area and substitute (or use) it where a rectangle area is needed. I hope that this makes sense to you.

Finally, you need to keep in mind that this technique suits best when you deal with objects that are not exactly the same but very similar.

Note   In the context of the previous point, you should not try to convert a circle area to a rectangle area (or do a similar type of conversion), because they are different shapes. In this example, I talk about triangles and rectangles because they have similarities.

Class Diagram

Figure 8-4 shows a class diagram of the important parts of the program.

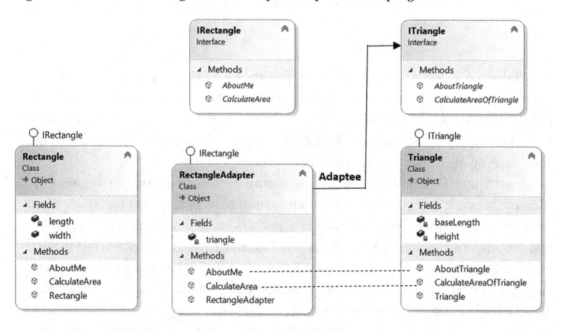

Figure 8-4. *Class diagram. Client class is not shown here.*

Solution Explorer View

Figure 8-5 shows a high-level structure of the program.

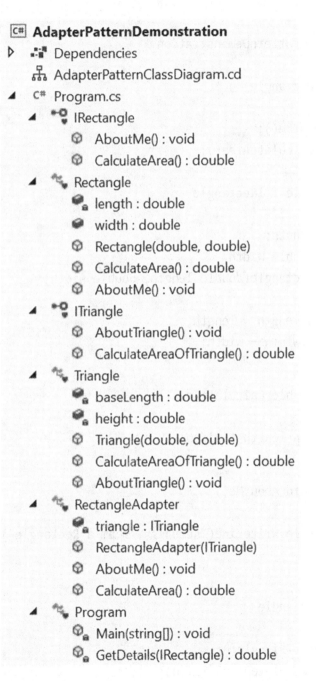

Figure 8-5. *Solution Explorer view*

Demonstration 1

Here's the implementation.

```
using System;

namespace AdapterPatternDemonstration
{
    interface IRectangle
    {
        void AboutMe();
        double CalculateArea();
    }
    class Rectangle : IRectangle
    {
        double length;
        public double width;
        public Rectangle(double length, double width)
        {
            this.length = length;
            this.width = width;
        }

        public double CalculateArea()
        {
            return length * width;
        }

        public void AboutMe()
        {
            Console.WriteLine("Actually, I am a Rectangle");
        }
    }

    interface ITriangle
    {
        void AboutTriangle();
        double CalculateAreaOfTriangle();
    }
```

```
class Triangle : ITriangle
{
    double baseLength; // base
    double height; // height
    public Triangle(double length, double height)
    {
        this.baseLength = length;
        this.height = height;
    }
    public double CalculateAreaOfTriangle()
    {
        return 0.5 * baseLength * height;
    }
    public void AboutTriangle()
    {
        Console.WriteLine("Actually, I am a Triangle.");
    }
}

/*
 * RectangleAdapter is implementing IRectangle.
 * So, it needs to implement all the methods
 * defined in the target interface.
 */
class RectangleAdapter : IRectangle
{
    ITriangle triangle;
    public RectangleAdapter(ITriangle triangle)
    {
        this.triangle = triangle;
    }

    public void AboutMe()
    {
        triangle.AboutTriangle();
    }
```

```
    public double CalculateArea()
    {
        return triangle.CalculateAreaOfTriangle();
    }
}

class Program
{
    static void Main(string[] args)
    {
        Console.WriteLine("***Adapter Pattern  Demo***\n");
        IRectangle rectangle = new Rectangle(20, 10);
        Console.WriteLine("For initial verification purposes, printing
        the areas of both shapes.");
        Console.WriteLine("Rectangle area is:{0} Square unit",
        rectangle.CalculateArea());
        ITriangle triangle = new Triangle(20, 10);
        Console.WriteLine("Triangle area is:{0} Square unit", triangle.
        CalculateAreaOfTriangle());

        Console.WriteLine("\nNow using the adapter.");
        IRectangle adapter = new RectangleAdapter(triangle);
        Console.Write("True fact : ");
        adapter.AboutMe();
        Console.WriteLine($" and my area is : {adapter.CalculateArea()}
        square unit.");

        // Alternative way:
        Console.WriteLine("\nUsing the adapter in a different way now.");
        // Passing a Triangle instead of a Rectangle
        Console.WriteLine($"Area of the triangle using the adapter is
        :{GetDetails(adapter)} square unit.");
        Console.ReadKey();
    }
```

```
/*
 * The following method does not know
 * that through the adapter, it can
 * actually process a
 * Triangle instead of a Rectangle.
 */
static double GetDetails(IRectangle rectangle)
{
    rectangle.AboutMe();
    return rectangle.CalculateArea();
}
    }
}
```

Output

Here's the output.

```
***Adapter Pattern  Demo***
```

```
For initial verification purposes, printing the areas of both shapes.
Rectangle area is:200 Square unit
Triangle area is:100 Square unit
```

Now using the adapter.
```
True fact : Actually, I am a Triangle.
 and my area is : 100 square unit.
```

Using the adapter in a different way now.
```
Actually, I am a Triangle.
Area of the triangle using the adapter is :100 square unit.
```

Analysis

Note the following code segment with comments inside the Main() method, as follows.

```
/*
 * The following method does not know
 * that through the adapter, it can
 * actually process a
 * Triangle instead of a Rectangle.
 */
static double GetDetails(IRectangle rectangle)
{
        rectangle.AboutMe();
        return rectangle.CalculateArea();
}
```

This segment is optional. I kept it to show you where you can invoke both adaptee methods in one call.

Types of Adapters

The GoF described two types of adapters: class adapters and object adapters.

Object Adapters

Object adapters adapt through object composition, as shown in Figure 8-6. So, the adapter discussed so far is an example of an object adapter.

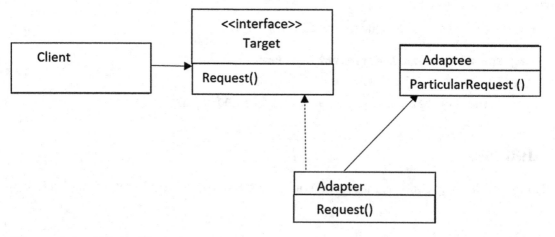

Figure 8-6. *Object adapter*

In our example, RectangleAdapter is the adapter that implements IRectangle (Target interface). ITriangle is the Adaptee interface. The adapter holds the adaptee instance.

Class Adapters

Class adapters adapt through subclassing and support multiple inheritance. But you know that in C#, multiple inheritance through classes is not supported. (You need interfaces to implement the concept of multiple inheritance.)

Figure 8-7 shows the typical class diagram for class adapters, which support multiple inheritance.

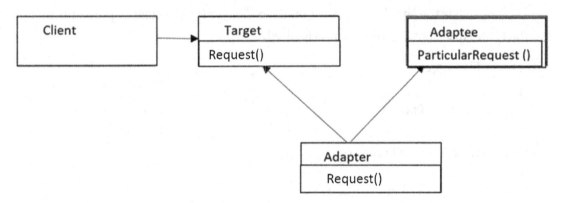

Figure 8-7. *Class adapter*

Q&A Session

8.1 How do you implement a class adapter design pattern in C#?

You can subclass an existing class and implement the desired interface. Demonstration 2 shows you a complete example with output.

Demonstration 2

This demonstration shows a class adapter. To make the example short and simple, I made the IRectangle and ITriangle interfaces with only one method. IRectangle has only the AboutMe() method, and the Rectangle class implements the IRectangle interface, and thus the following hierarchy is formed.

```
interface IRectangle
    {
        void AboutMe();
    }
    class Rectangle : IRectangle
    {
        public void AboutMe()
        {
            Console.WriteLine("Actually, I am a Rectangle");
        }
    }
```

ITriangle has the AboutTriangle() method. The Triangle class implements this interface, and the following hierarchy is formed.

```
interface ITriangle
    {
        void AboutTriangle();
    }
    class Triangle : ITriangle
    {
        public void AboutTriangle()
        {
            Console.WriteLine("Actually, I am a Triangle");
        }
    }
```

Now comes our class adapter, which uses the concept of multiple inheritance using a concrete class and an interface. The attached comments help you better understand the code.

```
    /*
     * RectangleAdapter is implementing IRectangle.
     * So, it needs to implement all the methods
     * defined in the target interface.
     */
    class RectangleAdapter : Triangle, IRectangle
```

```
    {
        public void AboutMe()
        {
            // Invoking the adaptee method
            AboutTriangle();
        }
    }
```

Now you can go through the complete demonstration, which is as follows.

```
using System;
namespace AdapterPatternAlternativeImplementationDemo
{
    interface IRectangle
    {
        void AboutMe();
    }
    class Rectangle : IRectangle
    {
        public void AboutMe()
        {
            Console.WriteLine("Actually, I am a Rectangle");
        }
    }

    interface ITriangle
    {
        void AboutTriangle();
    }
    class Triangle : ITriangle
    {
        public void AboutTriangle()
        {
            Console.WriteLine("Actually, I am a Triangle");
        }
    }
```

```
/*
 * RectangleAdapter is implementing IRectangle.
 * So, it needs to implement all the methods
 * defined in the target interface.
 */
class RectangleAdapter : Triangle, IRectangle
{
    public void AboutMe()
    {
        // Invoking the adaptee method
        AboutTriangle();
    }
}

class Program
{
    static void Main(string[] args)
    {
        Console.WriteLine("***Adapter Pattern Alternative
        Implementation Technique Demo.***\n");
        IRectangle rectangle = new Rectangle();
        Console.WriteLine("For initial verification purposes, printing
        the details from of both shapes.");
        Console.WriteLine("The rectangle.AboutMe() says:");
        rectangle.AboutMe();
        ITriangle triangle = new Triangle();
        Console.WriteLine("The triangle.AboutTriangle() says:");
        triangle.AboutTriangle();

        Console.WriteLine("\nNow using the adapter.");
        IRectangle adapter = new RectangleAdapter();
        Console.Write("True fact : ");
        adapter.AboutMe();
    }
}
```

```
***Adapter Pattern Alternative Implementation Technique Demo.***

For initial verification purposes, printing the details from of both shapes.
The rectangle.AboutTriangle() says:
Actually, I am a Rectangle.
The triangle.AboutTriangle() says:
Actually, I am a Triangle.

Now using the adapter.
True fact : Actually, I am a Triangle.
```

Analysis

This approach may not be suitable in all scenarios. For example, you may need to adapt a method that is not specified in a C# interface. In those cases, object adapters are better.

Q&A Session

8.2 Which do you prefer—class adapters or object adapters?

In most cases, I prefer compositions over inheritance. Object adapters use compositions and are more flexible. In many cases, it is challenging to implement a true class adapter when you need to adapt a specific method from adaptee interface, but there is no close match for that in the target interface. Apart from this, if the adaptee class (Triangle in our example) is sealed, then you cannot inherit from it.

8.3 You said, "...it is challenging to implement a true class adapter when you need to adapt a specific method from an adaptee interface, but there is no close match for that in the target interface." Can you please elaborate?

In my examples, the target interface methods and adaptee interface methods were similar. For example, in IRectangle, there is AboutMe() method, and in ITriangle, there is the AboutTriangle() method. What do they do? They state whether it is a rectangle or a triangle.

Now suppose that there is no such method called AboutMe() in IRectangle, but AboutTriangle() still exists in ITriangle. So, in a case like this, if you need to adapt the AboutTriangle() method, you need to analyze how to proceed. In our example, AboutTriangle() is a simple method, but in real-world programming, the method is much more complex, and there can be dependency associated with it. So, when you do not have a corresponding target method, you may find challenges to adapt the method from an adaptee.

8.4 I understand that clients should not know that they are using adapters. Is this correct?

Correct. I made this implementation to show you that clients *do not* need to know that their requests are translated through an adapter to the adaptee. If you want them to show any message, you could simply add a console message in your adapter in demonstration 2, as shown next.

```
class RectangleAdapter : Triangle, IRectangle
{
        public void AboutMe()
        {
                // Invoking the adaptee method
                // For Q&A
                Console.WriteLine("You are using an adapter now.");
                AboutTriangle();
        }
}
```

8.5 What happens if the target interface and adaptee interface method signature differ?

Not a problem at all. If an adapter method has a few parameters, you can invoke the adaptee method with some additional dummy parameters. In the Builder pattern (demonstration 2 in Chapter 3), you saw optional parameters. You can use the same concept here.

In the reverse scenario (if the adapter method has more parameters than the adaptee method), by using those additional parameters, you can add functionality before you transfer the call to the adaptee method.

Lastly, if the method parameters are incompatible, you may need to do casting (if possible).

8.6 What are the drawbacks associated with this pattern?

I do not see any major challenges. I believe that an adapter's job is simple and straightforward, but you need to write some additional code. However, the payoff is great, particularly for those legacy systems that cannot be changed, but you still want to use them for their stability and simplicity.

CHAPTER 9

Facade Pattern

This chapter covers the Facade pattern.

GoF Definition

Provide a unified interface to a set of interfaces in a subsystem. Facade defines a higher-level interface that makes the subsystem easier to use.

Concept

This pattern supports loose coupling. Using this pattern, you can emphasize on the abstraction and hide the complex details by exposing a simple interface.

Consider a simple case. Let's say that in an application, there are multiple classes, and each of them consists of multiple methods. A client can make a product using a combination of methods from these classes, but he needs to remember which classes to pick and which methods to use with the calling sequence of these constructs. It's okay, but it makes the client's life difficult if there are lots of variations among these products.

To overcome this, the Facade pattern is useful. It offers the client a user-friendly interface because all the inner complexities are hidden. As a result, the client can simply concentrate on what he needs to.

Real-World Example

Suppose that you are going to host a birthday party with 300 guests. Nowadays, you can hire a party organizer and let them know the key information such as the party type, date and time of the party, the number of attendees, and so on. The organizer does the rest for you. You do not need to think about how they decorate the party room, how they manage the food, and so on.

© Vaskaran Sarcar 2020
V. Sarcar, *Design Patterns in C#*, https://doi.org/10.1007/978-1-4842-6062-3_9

Consider another example. Suppose that a customer requests a loan from a bank. In this case, the customer is only interested in knowing whether the loan can be approved or not; he does not care about the inner background verification processes that are conducted at the back end.

Computer-World Example

Think about when you use a method from a library (in the context of a programming language). It doesn't matter how the method is implemented in the library, you just call the method for its easy usage. The following example makes this clearer.

Implementation

In this example, a client can request to get different kinds of robots with his preferred color. To serve this purpose, there are only two classes. The first one is RobotBody, which makes the body of a robot. The second class is RobotColor, which colors the robot.

RobotBody has a parameterized constructor, and there are two methods called MakeRobotBody and DestroyRobotBody. These methods are responsible for making a robot and destroying a robot. I use a counter to keep track of the number of robots. If there is no robot in the system, the destroy request is ignored. If you want, you can ignore the counter and focus fully on the parts that describe the important aspects of this pattern. Now let's look at the RobotBody class.

```
class RobotBody
  {
      string robotType;
      /*
      * To keep a count of number of robots.
      * This operation is optional for you.
      */
      static int count = 0;
      public RobotBody(string robotType)
      {
          this.robotType = robotType;
      }
```

```
public void MakeRobotBody()
{
  Console.WriteLine($"Constructing one {robotType} robot.");
  Console.WriteLine("Robot creation finished.");
  Console.WriteLine($"Total number of robot created at this
  moment={++count}");
}
public void DestroyRobotBody()
{
    if (count > 0)
    {
        --count;
        Console.WriteLine("Robot's destruction process is over.");
    }
    else
    {
        Console.WriteLine("All robots are destroyed.");
        Console.WriteLine("Color removal operation will not
        continue.");
    }
  }
}
```

RobotColor is very easy to understand. It has a parameterized constructor and two methods—SetColor() and RemoveColor()—to color a robot or remove the paint from the robot. The following code segment is for RobotColor.

```
public class RobotColor
{
    string color;
    public RobotColor(string color)
    {
        this.color = color;
    }
    public void SetColor()
    {
```

```
            if (color == "steel")
            {
                Console.WriteLine($"The default color {color} is set for
                the robot.");
            }
            else
            {
                Console.WriteLine($"Painting the robot with your favourite
                {color} color.");
            }
        }
        public void RemoveColor()
        {
            Console.WriteLine("Attempting to remove the colors from the
            robot.");
        }
    }
```

Now comes the most important part. You can see that a client can make a robot by supplying the required string argument to an object of RobotBody, invoke the MakeRobotBody(), and then paint the robot using SetColor() of the RobotColor class. As a result, the following lines can be used.

```
// Without Facade pattern
RobotBody robotBody = new RobotBody("Milano");
robotBody.MakeRobotBody();
RobotColor robotColor = new RobotColor("green");
robotColor.SetColor();
```

But what happens if a client has a single class called RobotFacade and makes calls like the following?

```
RobotFacade facade = new RobotFacade("Milano","green");
facade.ConstructRobot();
```

Or, you allow him to make calls like the following (by providing a default color)?

```
// Making a robonaut robot with default steel color.
facade = new RobotFacade("Robonaut");
facade.ConstructRobot();
```

You know the answer: the client will be happy; in these cases, he doesn't need to remember the steps to create a robot. For simplicity, only two classes are used in the example, but in the real world, you may need to use a large number of classes and methods to make a product like this. In such cases, the Facade pattern is even more powerful. You can tell your client to use the RobotFacade class to create and destroy robots instead of calling each class, like RobotBody and RobotColor.

Let's look at the RobotFacade now. I composed RobotBody and RobotColor into it and delegated the task to the corresponding component when I use ConstructRobot() and DestroyRobot() method of this class. From now on, RobotBody and RobotColor can be called *subsystem classes* in this example.

Here is the facade class.

```
class RobotFacade
    {
        RobotBody robotBody;
        RobotColor robotColor;
        public RobotFacade(string robotType, string color = "steel")
        {
            robotBody = new RobotBody(robotType);
            robotColor = new RobotColor(color);
        }
        public void ConstructRobot()
        {
            Console.WriteLine("Robot creation through facade starts...");
            robotBody.MakeRobotBody();
            robotColor.SetColor();
            Console.WriteLine();
        }
```

```
    public void DestroyRobot()
    {
        Console.WriteLine("Making an attempt to destroy one robot
        using  the facade now.");
        robotColor.RemoveColor();
        robotBody.DestroyRobotBody();
        Console.WriteLine();
    }
}
```

Class Diagram

Figure 9-1 shows the class diagram.

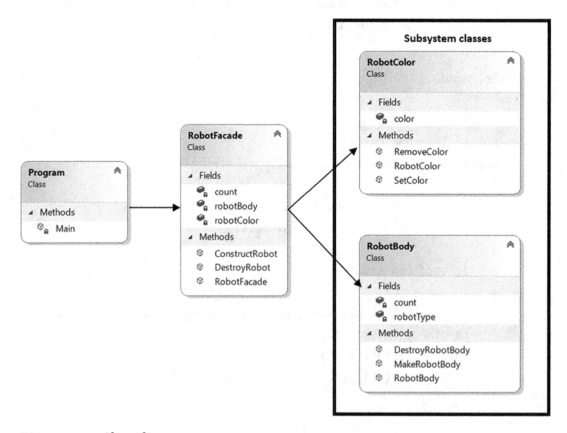

Figure 9-1. *Class diagram*

Solution Explorer View

Figure 9-2 shows the high-level structure of the program. From Solution Explorer, you can see that at a high level, I segregated the subsystem classes from the facade class and the client code. The subsystem classes are placed inside the RobotParts folder.

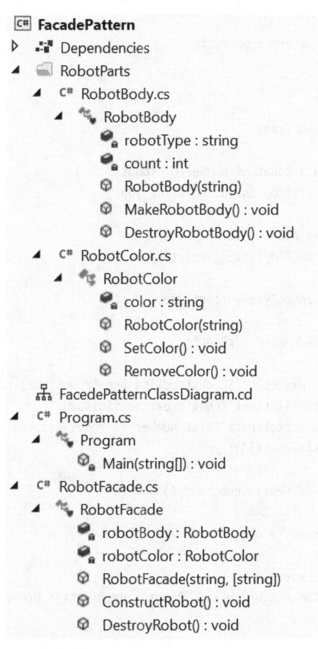

Figure 9-2. Solution Explorer view

Demonstration

Here's the full implementation.

// RobotBody.cs

```
using System;

namespace FacadePattern.RobotParts
{
    class RobotBody
    {
        string robotType;
        /*
        * To keep a count of number of robots.
        * This operation is optional for you.
        */
        static int count = 0;
        public RobotBody(string robotType)
        {
            this.robotType = robotType;
        }
        public void MakeRobotBody()
        {
          Console.WriteLine($"Constructing one {robotType} robot.");
          Console.WriteLine("Robot creation finished.");
          Console.WriteLine($"Total number of robot created at this
          moment={++count}");
        }
        public void DestroyRobotBody()
        {
            if (count > 0)
            {
                --count;
                Console.WriteLine("Robot's destruction process is over.");
            }
            else
```

```
        {
            Console.WriteLine("All robots are destroyed.");
            Console.WriteLine("Color removal operation will not
            continue.");
        }
      }
    }
}

// RobotColor.cs

using System;

namespace FacadePattern.RobotParts
{
    public class RobotColor
    {
        string color;
        public RobotColor(string color)
        {
            this.color = color;
        }
        public void SetColor()
        {
            if (color == "steel")
            {
                Console.WriteLine($"The default color {color} is set for
                the robot.");
            }
            else
            {
                Console.WriteLine($"Painting the robot with your favourite
                {color} color.");
            }
        }
        public void RemoveColor()
        {
```

171

```
            Console.WriteLine("Attempting to remove the colors from the
            robot.");
        }
    }
}
```

// RobotFacade.cs

```csharp
using System;

namespace FacadePattern.RobotParts
{
    class RobotFacade
    {
        RobotBody robotBody;
        RobotColor robotColor;
        public RobotFacade(string robotType, string color = "steel")
        {
            robotBody = new RobotBody(robotType);
            robotColor = new RobotColor(color);
        }
        public void ConstructRobot()
        {
            Console.WriteLine("Robot creation through facade starts...");
            robotBody.MakeRobotBody();
            robotColor.SetColor();
            Console.WriteLine();
        }

        public void DestroyRobot()
        {
            Console.WriteLine("Making an attempt to destroy one robot using
            the facade now.");
            robotColor.RemoveColor();
            robotBody.DestroyRobotBody();
            Console.WriteLine();
        }
```

```
        }
    }

    // Program.cs

using System;
using FacadePattern.RobotParts;

namespace FacadePattern
{
    class Program
    {
        static void Main(string[] args)
        {
            Console.WriteLine("***Facade Pattern Demo.***\n");
            // Making a Milano robot with green color.
            RobotFacade facade = new RobotFacade("Milano","green");
            facade.ConstructRobot();
            // Making a robonaut robot with default steel color.
            facade = new RobotFacade("Robonaut");
            facade.ConstructRobot();
            // Destroying one robot
            facade.DestroyRobot();
            // Destroying another robot
            facade.DestroyRobot();
            // This destrcution attempt should fail.
            facade.DestroyRobot();
            Console.ReadLine();

        }
    }
}
```

```
***Facade Pattern Demo.***

Robot creation through facade starts...
Constructing one Milano robot.
Robot creation finished.
Total number of robot created at this moment=1
Painting the robot with your favourite green color.

Robot creation through facade starts...
Constructing one Robonaut robot.
Robot creation finished.
Total number of robot created at this moment=2
The default color steel is set for the robot.

Making an attempt to destroy one robot using the facade now.
Attempting to remove the colors from the robot.
Robot's destruction process is over.

Making an attempt to destroy one robot using the facade now.
Attempting to remove the colors from the robot.
Robot's destruction process is over.

Making an attempt to destroy one robot using the facade now.
Attempting to remove the colors from the robot.
All robots are destroyed.
Color removal operation will not continue.
```

Q&A Session

9.1 What are the key advantages of using the Facade pattern?

Here are some advantages.

- If your system consists of many subsystems, managing those subsystems becomes tough, and clients find it difficult to communicate separately with each of these subsystems. In this scenario, Facade patterns are handy. Instead of presenting complex subsystems, you present one simplified interface to clients. This approach also supports weak coupling by separating the client code from the subsystems.

- It can also help reduce the number of objects that a client needs to deal with.

9.2 The facade class is using compositions in this example. Is this necessary?

Yes. With this approach, you can access the intended methods in each subsystem. I delegated the task to the corresponding component when I used the `ConstructRobot()` and `DestroyRobot()` methods of this class.

9.3 Can you now access each of the subsystems directly?

Yes, you can. The Facade pattern does not restrict you from doing this. I showed you this before I introduced the facade class. But in that case, the code may look dirty, and you may lose the benefits associated with the Facade pattern. In this context, you can note that since the client can directly access the subsystem, it is called a transparent facade. But when you restrict that usage and force them to create robots only through RobotFacade, you can call the facade as an opaque facade.

9.4 How is Facade different from the Adapter design pattern?

In the Adapter pattern, you are trying to alter an interface so that your clients do not see any difference between the interfaces. By contrast, the Facade pattern simplifies the interface. It presents the client with a simple interface to interact with (instead of a complex subsystem).

9.5 There should be only one facade for a complex subsystem. Is this correct?

Not at all. You can create any number of facades for a specific subsystem.

9.6 Can you add new things or additional code with a facade?

Yes, you can. You saw that I used the following line inside `ConstructRobot()` of the `RobotFacade` class before I delegated the call to actual components.

```
Console.WriteLine("Robot creation through facade starts...");
```

In the same way, `DestroyRobot()` has the following line before it tries to destroy a robot.

```
Console.WriteLine("Making an attempt to destroy one robot using  the facade now.");
```

9.7 What are the challenges associated with the Facade pattern?

Here are some challenges.

- Subsystems are connected to the facade layer. So, you need to take care of an additional layer of coding (increasing your codebase).

- When the internal structure of a subsystem changes, you need to incorporate the changes in the facade layer also.

- Some developers may need to learn about this new layer, but some of them know how to use the subsystems/APIs efficiently.

9.8 Can I make the facade class static?

In many examples, there is only one facade, and you may not need to initialize the facade class. In those cases, it makes sense if you make the facade class static.

CHAPTER 10

Flyweight Pattern

This chapter covers the Flyweight pattern.

GoF Definition

Use sharing to support large numbers of fine-grained objects efficiently.

Concept

This pattern may look simple, but if you do not identify the core concepts, the implementations may appear to be complex. Let's start with a basic but detailed explanation before you implement this pattern.

Sometimes you need to handle lots of objects that are very similar but not exactly the same. The constraint is that you cannot create all of them to lessen resource and memory usage. The Flyweight pattern is made to handle these scenarios.

Now the question is how to do that? To understand this, let's quickly revisit the fundamentals of object-oriented programming. A class is a template or blueprint, and an object is an instance of that. An object can have states and behaviors. For example, if you are familiar with the game of football (or *soccer*, as it's known in the United States), you can say that Ronaldo or Beckham are objects from the Footballer class. You may notice that they have states like "playing state" or "non-playing state." In the playing state, they can show different skills (or behaviors)—they can run, they can kick, they can pass the ball, and so forth. To begin with object-oriented programming, you can ask the following questions.

- What are the possible states of my objects?

- What are the different functions (behaviors) that they can perform in those states?

177

Once you get the answers to these questions, you are ready to proceed. Now come back to the Flyweight pattern. Here your job is to identify.

- What are the states of my objects?

- Which part of these states can be changed?

Once you identify the answers, you break the states into two parts, called intrinsic (which does not vary) and extrinsic (which can vary). Now you understand that if you make objects with intrinsic states that can be shared among all objects. For the extrinsic part, the user or client needs to pass the information. So, whenever you need to have an object, you can get the object with intrinsic states, and then you can configure the object on the fly by passing the extrinsic states. Following this technique, you can reduce unnecessary object creations and memory usage.

Now let's verify your knowledge in the following paragraph, which is extremely important. Let's look at what the GoF said about flyweights.

> *A flyweight is a shared object that can be used in multiple contexts simulta-neously. The flyweight acts as an independent object in each context—it's indistinguishable from an instance of the object that's not shared. Flyweights cannot make assumptions about the context in which they operate. The key concept here is the distinction between intrinsic and extrinsic state. The intrinsic state is stored in the flyweight; it consists of information that's independent of the flyweight's context, thereby making it sharable. The extrinsic state depends on and varies with the flyweight's context and, there-fore, can't be shared. Client objects are responsible for passing the extrinsic state to the flyweight when it needs it.*

Real-World Example

Suppose you have a pen. You can use different ink refills to write with different colors. So, the pen without the refill can be considered the flyweight with intrinsic data, and the refills can be considered the extrinsic data in this example.

Computer-World Example

Suppose that in a computer game, you have a large number of participants whose core structures are the same, but their appearances vary (for example, they may have different states, colors, weapons, and so on). Therefore, if you want to store all the objects with all the variations/states, the memory requirement will be huge. So, instead of storing all the objects, you can design the application in such a way that you create one of these instances with the states that don't vary among objects, and your client can maintain remaining variations/states. If you can successfully implement the concept in the design phase, then you have followed the Flyweight pattern in the application.

Consider another example. Suppose a company needs to print business cards for its employees. In this case, what is the starting point? The business can create a common template where the company logo, address, and so on, is already printed (intrinsic), and later the company places a particular employee's information (extrinsic) on a card.

Another common use of this pattern is seen in the graphical representation of characters in a word processor or when you deal with string interning in your application.

Implementation

The following example shows the usage of three different types of vehicles: Car, Bus, and FutureVehicle (I assume that it will be used in 2050). In this application, I assume that a client may want to use a large number of objects from these classes with different colors that they like. I also assume that the basic structure of a car (or bus, etc.) does not vary.

When a client requests a particular vehicle, the application does not create an object from scratch, if it previously created an instance of that type of vehicle earlier; instead, it'll prepare the existing one (without color) to serve his needs. Just before delivering the product, it'll paint the vehicle with the color that the client prefers. Now let's look at the implementation strategies.

First, you create an interface for flyweights. This interface is made to provide common methods that accept extrinsic states of flyweights. In our example, color is supplied by clients; so, this is treated as an extrinsic state, which is why you see the following code segment.

```
/// <summary>
/// The 'Flyweight' interface
/// </summary>
interface IVehicle
    {
```

```
        /*
         * Client will supply the color.
         * It is extrinsic state.
         */
        void AboutMe(string color);
    }
```

Most often, you see a factory that supplies the flyweights to the client. This factory caches flyweights and provides methods to get them. In a shared flyweight object, you add intrinsic states and implement methods, if necessary. You can have unshared flyweights too. In those cases, you can ignore the extrinsic states which are passed by a client.

In an upcoming example, VehicleFactory is the factory that supplies the flyweights with intrinsic states. A Dictionary object stores the key/value pairs to store vehicles with a specific type. Initially, there are no objects inside the factory, but once it starts receiving requests for vehicles, it creates the vehicles and caches those for future use. Notice that "One car is created," "One bus is created," and "Vehicle 2050 is created" are supplied by the factory inside the flyweight objects during the object-creation phase. These are intrinsic state of these vehicles and doesn't vary across among the products. The following code segment shows this factory class.

```
/// <summary>
/// The factory class for flyweights.
/// </summary>
class VehicleFactory
{
    private Dictionary<string, IVehicle> vehicles = new Dictionary<string,
    IVehicle>();
    public int TotalObjectsCreated
    {
        get { return vehicles.Count; }
    }

    public IVehicle GetVehicleFromVehicleFactory(string vehicleType)
    {
        IVehicle vehicleCategory = null;
        if (vehicles.ContainsKey(vehicleType))
        {
```

```
        vehicleCategory = vehicles[vehicleType];

    }
    else
    {
        switch (vehicleType)
        {
            case "car":
                vehicleCategory = new Car("One car is created");
                vehicles.Add("car", vehicleCategory);
                break;
            case "bus":
                vehicleCategory = new Bus("One bus is created");
                vehicles.Add("bus", vehicleCategory);
                break;
            case "future":
                vehicleCategory = new FutureVehicle("Vehicle 2050
                is created");
                vehicles.Add("future", vehicleCategory);
                break;
            default:
                throw new Exception("Vehicle Factory can give you
                cars and buses only.");
        }

    }
    return vehicleCategory;
    }
}
```

Let's see a concrete flyweight class now. Here is one of these classes (others are similar). The associated comments help you understand how the AboutMe() method contains both the intrinsic state and the extrinsic state of the vehicle.

```
/// <summary>
/// A 'ConcreteFlyweight' class called Car
/// </summary>
```

```
class Car : IVehicle
{
    /*
     * It is intrinsic state and
     * it is independent of flyweight context.
     * this can be shared.So, our factory method will supply
     * this value inside the flyweight object.
     */
    private string description;
    /*
     * Flyweight factory will supply this
     * inside the flyweight object.
     */
    public Car(string description)
    {
        this.description = description;
    }
    // Client will supply the color
    public void AboutMe(string color)
    {
        Console.WriteLine($"{description} with {color} color.");
    }
}
```

From this code segment, you can see that the description is supplied during the object creation process (the Flyweight factory does this), but color is supplied by the clients. In this example, I draw colors at random using a method called GetRandomColor(). So, inside Main(), you see the following code:

```
vehicle.AboutMe(GetRandomColor());
```

The read-only TotalObjectsCreated property counts different types of vehicles at any given moment; it is very easy to understand the following code in the factory class.

```
public int TotalObjectsCreated
{
    get
```

```
    {
        return vehicles.Count;
    }
}
```

Lastly, FutureVehicle is considered an unshared flyweight in this example. So, in this class, AboutMe(...) method ignores the string argument. As a result, it always produces vehicles that are blue and ignores the client's preferences.

```
// Client cannot choose color for FutureVehicle
//since it's unshared flyweight,ignoring client's input
    public void AboutMe(string color)
    {
        Console.WriteLine($"{description} with blue color.");
    }
```

Class Diagram

Figure 10-1 shows the class diagram.

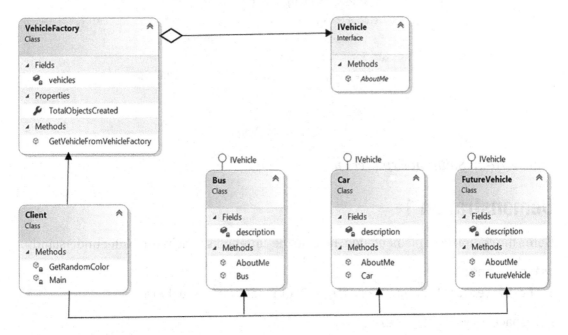

Figure 10-1. *Class diagram*

Solution Explorer View

Figure 10-2 shows the high-level structure of the parts of the program.

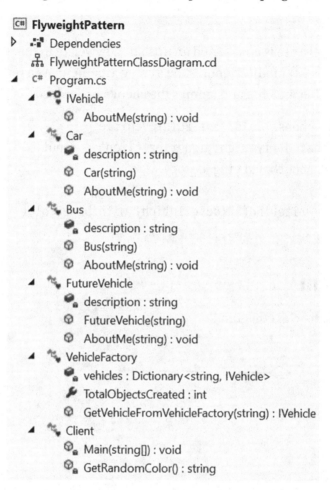

Figure 10-2. *Solution Explorer view*

Demonstration 1

Here's the complete implementation. Refer to the comments to help you better understand.

```
using System;
using System.Collections.Generic;//Dictionary is used here

namespace FlyweightPattern
{
```

```
/// <summary>
/// The 'Flyweight' interface
/// </summary>
interface IVehicle
{
    /*
     * Client will supply the color.
     * It is extrinsic state.
     */
    void AboutMe(string color);
}
/// <summary>
/// A 'ConcreteFlyweight' class called Car
/// </summary>
class Car : IVehicle
{
    /*
     * It is intrinsic state and
     * it is independent of flyweight context.
     * this can be shared.So, our factory method will supply
     * this value inside the flyweight object.
     */
    private string description;
    /*
     * Flyweight factory will supply this
     * inside the flyweight object.
     */
    public Car(string description)
    {
        this.description = description;
    }
    // Client will supply the color
    public void AboutMe(string color)
    {
        Console.WriteLine($"{description} with {color} color.");
    }
}
```

```csharp
/// <summary>
/// A 'ConcreteFlyweight' class called Bus
/// </summary>
class Bus : IVehicle
{
    /*
     * It is intrinsic state and
     * it is independent of flyweight context.
     * this can be shared.So, our factory method will supply
     * this value inside the flyweight object.
     */
    private string description;
    public Bus(string description)
    {
        this.description = description;
    }
    // Client will supply the color
    public void AboutMe(string color)
    {
        Console.WriteLine($"{description} with {color} color.");
    }
}
/// <summary>
/// A 'ConcreteFlyweight' class called FutureVehicle
/// </summary>
class FutureVehicle : IVehicle
{
    /*
     * It is intrinsic state and
     * it is independent of flyweight context.
     * this can be shared.So, our factory method will supply
     * this value inside the flyweight object.
     */
    private string description;
    public FutureVehicle(string description)
```

```csharp
    {
        this.description = description;
    }
    // Client cannot choose color for FutureVehicle
    // since it's unshared flyweight,ignoring client's input
    public void AboutMe(string color)
    {
        Console.WriteLine($"{description} with blue color.");
    }
}

/// <summary>
/// The factory class for flyweights.
/// </summary>
class VehicleFactory
{
    private Dictionary<string, IVehicle> vehicles = new
    Dictionary<string, IVehicle>();
    /*
     * To count different types of vehicles
     * in a given moment.
     */
    public int TotalObjectsCreated
    {
        get
        {
            return vehicles.Count;
        }
    }
    public IVehicle GetVehicleFromVehicleFactory(string vehicleType)
    {
        IVehicle vehicleCategory = null;
        if (vehicles.ContainsKey(vehicleType))
        {
            vehicleCategory = vehicles[vehicleType];
        }
```

```csharp
            else
            {
                switch (vehicleType)
                {
                    case "car":
                        vehicleCategory = new Car("One car is created");
                        vehicles.Add("car", vehicleCategory);
                        break;
                    case "bus":
                        vehicleCategory = new Bus("One bus is created");
                        vehicles.Add("bus", vehicleCategory);
                        break;
                    case "future":
                        vehicleCategory = new FutureVehicle("Vehicle 2050
                        is created");
                        vehicles.Add("future", vehicleCategory);
                        break;
                    default:
                        throw new Exception("Vehicle Factory can give you
                        cars and buses only.");
                }
            }
            return vehicleCategory;
        }
    }

    class Client
    {
        static void Main(string[] args)
        {
            Console.WriteLine("***Flyweight Pattern Demo.***\n");
            VehicleFactory vehiclefactory = new VehicleFactory();
            IVehicle vehicle;
            /*
            * Now we are trying to get the 3 cars. Note that:we need not create
            additional cars if we have already created one of this category.
            */
```

```
for (int i = 0; i < 3; i++)
{
    vehicle = vehiclefactory.GetVehicleFromVehicleFactory("car");
    vehicle.AboutMe(GetRandomColor());
}
int numOfDistinctRobots = vehiclefactory.TotalObjectsCreated;
Console.WriteLine($"\n Now, total numbers of distinct vehicle
object(s) is = {numOfDistinctRobots}\n");
/*
Here we are trying to get the 5 more buses.Note that: we need
not create additional buses if we have already created one of
this category.
*/

for (int i = 0; i < 5; i++)
{
    vehicle = vehiclefactory.GetVehicleFromVehicleFactory("bus");
    vehicle.AboutMe(GetRandomColor());
}
numOfDistinctRobots = vehiclefactory.TotalObjectsCreated;
Console.WriteLine($"\n Now, total numbers of distinct vehicle
object(s) is = {numOfDistinctRobots}\n");
/*
 Here we are trying to get the 2 future vehicles.Note that: we
 need not create additional future vehicle if we have already
 created one of this category.
 */
for (int i = 0; i < 2; i++)
{
    vehicle = vehiclefactory.GetVehicleFromVehicleFactory("future");
    vehicle.AboutMe(GetRandomColor());
}
numOfDistinctRobots = vehiclefactory.TotalObjectsCreated;
Console.WriteLine($"\n Now, total numbers of distinct vehicle
object(s) is = {numOfDistinctRobots}\n");
```

```
        Console.ReadKey();
    }

    private static string GetRandomColor()
    {
        Random r = new Random();
        /*
         You can supply any number of your choice in nextInt argument.
         we are simply checking the random number generated is an even
         number or an odd number. And based on that we are choosing the
         color. For simplicity, we'll use only two colors-red and green.
        */
        int random = r.Next(100);
        if (random % 2 == 0)
        {
            return "red";
        }
        else
        {
            return "green";
        }
    }
}
}
```

Output

The following is a possible output (because color is generated at random). It is from the
first run on my machine.

```
***Flyweight Pattern Demo.***

One car is created with green color.
One car is created with red color.
One car is created with green color.

 Now, total numbers of distinct vehicle object(s) is = 1
```

```
One bus is created with green color.
One bus is created with red color.
One bus is created with green color.
One bus is created with red color.
One bus is created with red color.

 Now, total numbers of distinct vehicle object(s) is = 2

Vehicle 2050 is created with blue color.
Vehicle 2050 is created with blue color.

 Now, total numbers of distinct vehicle object(s) is = 3
```

Here's another probable output. It is from the second run on my machine.

```
***Flyweight Pattern Demo.***

One car is created with red color.
One car is created with red color.
One car is created with red color.

 Now, total numbers of distinct vehicle object(s) is = 1

One bus is created with red color.
One bus is created with green color.
One bus is created with red color.
One bus is created with green color.
One bus is created with red color.

 Now, total numbers of distinct vehicle object(s) is = 2

Vehicle 2050 is created with blue color.
Vehicle 2050 is created with blue color.

 Now, total numbers of distinct vehicle object(s) is = 3
```

Note   The output varies because I chose colors randomly in this example.

Analysis

The application is creating an object if and only if the object is not available at that moment. Henceforth, it is caching the object for future reuse.

Q&A Session

10.1   Can you highlight the key differences between a Singleton pattern and a Flyweight pattern?

Singleton helps you to maintain at most one object that is required in the system. In other words, once the required object is created, you cannot create more of that. You need to reuse the existing object.

The Flyweight pattern generally concerns with heavy but similar objects (in which the states are not the same) because they may occupy big blocks of memory. So, you try to create a smaller set of template objects that can be configured on the fly to make these heavy objects. These smaller and configurable objects are called flyweights. You can reuse them in your application when you deal with many large objects. This approach helps you reduce the consumption of big chunks of memory. Basically, flyweights make *one look like many*, which is why the GoF states: "A flyweight is a shared object that can be used in multiple contexts simultaneously. The flyweight acts as an independent object in each context—it's indistinguishable from an instance of the object that's not shared."

Figure 10-3 shows you how to visualize the core concepts of the Flyweight pattern before using flyweights.

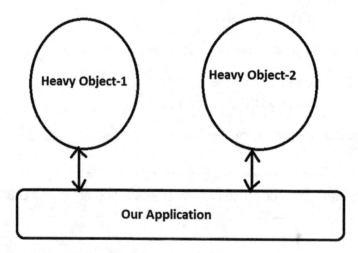

Figure 10-3. *Before using flyweights*

Figure 10-4 shows the design after using flyweights.

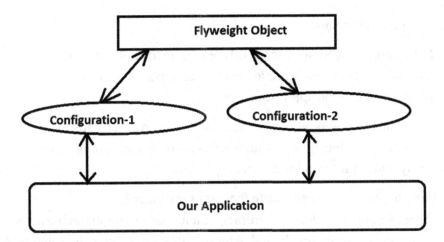

Figure 10-4. *After using flyweights*

So, from Figure 10-4, you can see Heavy-Object1 is created when we apply Configuration-1 to the Flyweight Object, and similarly, Heavy-Object2 is created when we apply Configuration-2 to the Flyweight Object. You can see that instance-specific contents (like color in our demonstration 1) can be passed to the flyweights to make these heavy objects. In this example, the flyweight object is acting like a common template that can be configured as needed.

10.2 What is the impact of multithreading?

If you are creating objects with a new operator, in a multithreaded environment, you may end up creating multiple unwanted objects. This is similar to the Singleton pattern, and the remedy is also similar.

10.3 What are the advantages of using the Flyweight design pattern?

Here are some advantages.

- You can reduce memory consumptions of heavy objects that can be controlled identically.

- You can reduce the total number of objects in the system.

- You can maintain centralized states of many "virtual" objects.

10.4 What are the challenges associated with using the Flyweight design pattern?

Here are some challenges.

- In this pattern, you need to spend some time to configure these flyweights. These configuration times can impact the overall performance of the application.

- To create flyweights, you are extracting a common template class from existing objects. This additional layer of programming can be tricky and sometimes hard to debug and maintain.

10.5 Can you have a nonshareable flyweight interface?

Yes, a flyweight interface does not enforce that it needs to be shareable always. So, in some cases, you may have nonshareable flyweights with concrete flyweight objects as children. In demonstration 1, FutureVehicle is made for that. You can see that it always consists of a blue color, and for this vehicle, it doesn't matter whatever color (red or green) a client supply to it as an extrinsic state.

10.6 Since the intrinsic data of flyweights is the same, you can try to share them. Is this correct?

Yes. Notice that "One car is created," "One bus is created," and "Vehicle 2050 is created," are supplied by the factory inside the flyweights during the flyweight (with the intrinsic state) object creation phase.

10.7 How do clients handle these flyweights' extrinsic data?

They need to pass that information (the states) to the flyweights when they need to use this concept.

10.8 Extrinsic data is not shareable. Is this correct?

Yes. It's very important to understand this pattern before you implement it.

10.9 What is the role of VehicleFactory in this implementation?

It caches flyweights and provides a method to get them. In this example, there are multiple objects with an intrinsic state that can be shared. So, storing them in a central place is always a good idea.

10.10 Can I implement the factory class as a singleton?

Yes, you can. In fact, in many applications, you may see this. Demonstration 2 describes it.

Demonstration 2

In this example, the VehicleFactory factory class is implemented as a singleton. So, you can replace the factory class in demonstration 1 with the following code.

```
/// <summary>
/// The factory class for flyweights implemented as singleton.
/// </summary>
class VehicleFactory
{
    private static readonly VehicleFactory Instance = new VehicleFactory();
        private Dictionary<string, IVehicle> vehicles = new
        Dictionary<string, IVehicle>();

        private VehicleFactory()
        {
          vehicles.Add("car", new Car("One car is created"));
          vehicles.Add("bus", new Bus("One bus is created"));
          vehicles.Add("future", new FutureVehicle("Vehicle 2050 is created"));
        }
        public static VehicleFactory GetInstance
        {
            get
            {
                return Instance;
            }
        }
        /*
        * To count different types of vehicles
        * in a given moment.
        */
        public int TotalObjectsCreated
        {
            get
            {
```

```
            return vehicles.Count;
        }
    }

    public IVehicle GetVehicleFromVehicleFactory(string vehicleType)
    {
        IVehicle vehicleCategory = null;
        if (vehicles.ContainsKey(vehicleType))
        {
            vehicleCategory = vehicles[vehicleType];
            return vehicleCategory;
        }
        else
        {
            throw new Exception("Currently, the vehicle factory can have
            cars and buses only.");
        }
    }
}
```

And now, inside the client code, instead of using the following line (which is commented out), you need to use a new line of code to adapt the previous changes.

```
//VehicleFactory vehiclefactory = new VehicleFactory();
VehicleFactory vehiclefactory = VehicleFactory.GetInstance;
```

Output

When you run the application using these new code segments, you may get (because the color is generated at random) output like the following.

```
***Flyweight Pattern Demo.***

One car is created with red color.
One car is created  with red color.
One car is created with red color.
```

Now, total numbers of distinct vehicle object(s) is = 3

One bus is created with green color.
One bus is created with green color.
One bus is created with green color.
One bus is created with red color.
One bus is created with red color.

Now, total numbers of distinct vehicle object(s) is = 3

Vehicle 2050 is created with blue color.
Vehicle 2050 is created with blue color.

Now, total numbers of distinct vehicle object(s) is = 3

Analysis

Notice that in this implementation, I initialized all different types of vehicles at the beginning, inside the constructor. As a result, I started with three distinct vehicle objects at the beginning. So, if I do not need any bus, car, or Vehicle2050, I waste the memory for the objects. On the contrary, in demonstration 1, if any of these objects is not available, the factory class creates it and caches it for future use. So, my vote is for demonstration 1 unless you modify demonstration 2, keeping this potential drawback in mind. In short, whenever you use this pattern, you create an object, fill in all the required state information and give it to your client. Each time a client requests an object, your application should check whether it can reuse an existing object (with required states filled) or not; thus reducing unnecessary object creations and save memory consumption.

Microsoft says that the Intern method uses the intern pool to search for a string equal to the value of a string. If such a string exists, its reference in the intern pool is returned; otherwise, a reference to the string is added to the intern pool, then that reference is returned. In .NET Core 3.1, when I execute the following segment of code, firstString and thirdString both refer to the same string. As a result, the final line of this code segment returns True, which is not the case when you compare firstString with secondString because they refer to different objects.

```
#region test for in-built flyweight pattern
string firstString = "A simple string";
```

```
string secondString = new StringBuilder().Append("A").Append(" simple").
Append(" string").ToString();
string thirdString = String.Intern(secondString);
// Different references.
Console.WriteLine((Object)secondString == (Object)firstString);
// Same reference.
Console.WriteLine((Object)thirdString == (Object)firstString);
#endregion
```

So, you can say that the Intern method in .NET Core 3.1 follows the Flyweight pattern.

CHAPTER 11

Composite Pattern

This chapter covers the Composite pattern.

GoF Definition

Compose objects into tree structures to represent part-whole hierarchies. Composite lets clients treat individual objects and compositions of objects uniformly.

Concept

Consider a shop that sells different kinds of dry fruit, such as cashews, dates, and walnuts. Each of these items has a certain price. Let's assume that you can purchase any of these individual items, or you can purchase "gift packs" (or boxed items), which are composed of different dry fruit items. In this case, the cost of a packet is the sum of its component parts. The Composite pattern is useful in a similar situation, in which you treat both the individual parts and the combination of the parts in the same way so that you can process them uniformly.

This pattern is useful to represent part-whole hierarchies of objects. In object-oriented programming, a composite is an object with a composition of one or more similar objects, where each of these objects has similar functionality. (This is also known as a "has-a" relationship among objects.) The usage of this pattern is common in tree-structured data, and when you implement this pattern in such a data structure, you do not need to discriminate between a branch and the leaf nodes of the tree. As a result, you can achieve these two key goals using this pattern.

© Vaskaran Sarcar 2020
V. Sarcar, *Design Patterns in C#*, https://doi.org/10.1007/978-1-4842-6062-3_11

- You can compose objects into a tree structure to represent a part-whole hierarchy.

- You can access both the composite objects (branches) and the individual objects (leaf nodes) uniformly. As a result, you can reduce the complexity of the code and make the application less prone to errors.

Real-World Example

Apart from our previous example, you can also think of an organization that consists of many departments. In general, an organization has many employees. Some of these employees are grouped to form a department, and those departments can be further grouped to build the high-level structure of the organization.

Computer-World Example

I mentioned that a tree data structure could follow this concept where the clients can treat the leaves of the tree and the nonleaves (or branches of the tree) in the same way. So, when you see a hierarchical data, you can get a clue that the Composite pattern can be useful. XML files are very common examples with such tree structures.

Note   When you traverse the tree, you often use the concept of an Iterator design pattern, which is covered in Chapter 18.

Implementation

In this example, I represent a college organization. Let's assume there is a principal and two heads of departments (HODs), one for Computer Science and Engineering (CSE), and one for Mathematics (Math). Suppose that in the Mathematics department, there are currently two lecturers (or teachers), and in the Computer Science and Engineering department, there are three lecturers (teachers). The tree structure for this organization looks like Figure 11-1.

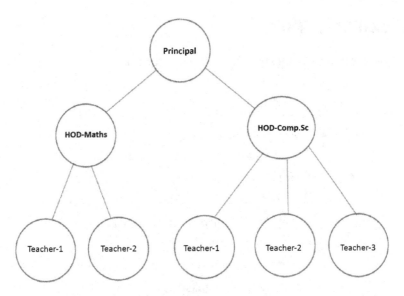

Figure 11-1. *A college organization with a principal, 2 HODs and 5 lecturers/ teachers*

Let's also assume that at the end of the year, one lecturer from the CSE department submits his resignation. The following example considers all the scenarios mentioned.

Class Diagram

Figure 11-2 shows the class diagram.

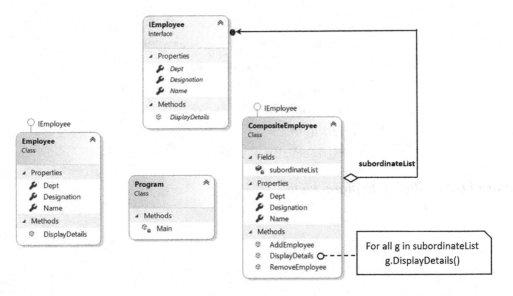

Figure 11-2. *Class diagram*

Solution Explorer View

Figure 11-3 shows the high-level structure of the program.

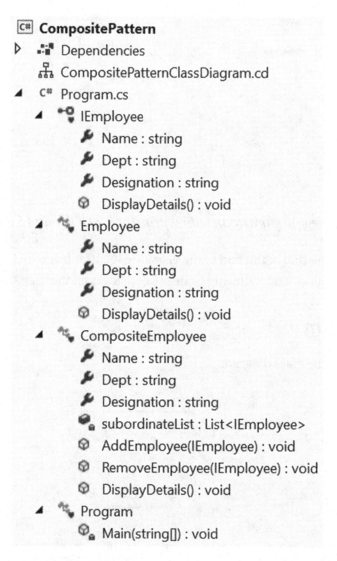

Figure 11-3. *Solution Explorer view*

Demonstration

This demonstration features a tree structure. IEmployee is an interface with three read-write properties and one method called DisplayDetails(). It looks like the following.

```
interface IEmployee
    {
        // To set an employee name
        string Name { get; set; }
        // To set an employee department
        string Dept { get; set; }
        // To set an employee designation
        string Designation { get; set; }
        // To display an employee details
        void DisplayDetails();
    }
```

From the associated comments, it's easy to understand that these three properties set an employee's name, their corresponding department, and the designation. The Employee and CompositeEmployee concrete classes implement this interface. Employee class (lecturers) acts as a leaf node, and the other one is a nonleaf node. One or more employees can report to a HOD. So, it is treated as a nonleaf (or branch) node. Similarly, all HODs report to the principal. So, Principal is another nonleaf node.

The mathematics lecturers are named M. Joy and M. Roony. The CSE teachers are named C. Sam, C. Jones, and C. Marium. These lecturers do not supervise anyone, so they are treated as leaf nodes.

The CompositeEmployee class maintains a list and two additional methods called AddEmployee(...) and RemoveEmployee(...). These methods add an employee to the list or remove an employee from the list.

Now go through the complete implementation, and refer to the supportive comments.

```
using System;
/* For List<Employee> using
 * the following namespace.
 */
using System.Collections.Generic;
```

```csharp
namespace CompositePattern
{
    interface IEmployee
    {
        // To set an employee name
        string Name { get; set; }
        // To set an employee department
        string Dept { get; set; }
        // To set an employee designation
        string Designation { get; set; }
        // To display an employee details
        void DisplayDetails();
    }
    // Leaf node
    class Employee : IEmployee
    {
        public string Name { get; set; }
        public string Dept { get; set; }
        public string Designation { get; set; }
        // Details of a leaf node
        public void DisplayDetails()
        {
            Console.WriteLine($"\t{Name} works in { Dept} department.
            Designation:{Designation}");
        }
    }
    // Non-leaf node
    class CompositeEmployee : IEmployee
    {
        public string Name { get; set; }
        public string Dept { get; set; }
        public string Designation { get; set; }

        // The container for child objects
        private List<IEmployee> subordinateList = new List<IEmployee>();
```

```csharp
    // To add an employee
    public void AddEmployee(IEmployee e)
    {
        subordinateList.Add(e);
    }

    // To remove an employee
    public void RemoveEmployee(IEmployee e)
    {
        subordinateList.Remove(e);
    }

    // Details of a composite node
    public void DisplayDetails()
    {
        Console.WriteLine($"\n{Name} works in {Dept} department.
        Designation:{Designation}");
        foreach (IEmployee e in subordinateList)
        {
            e.DisplayDetails();
        }
    }
}

class Program
{
    static void Main(string[] args)
    {
        Console.WriteLine("***Composite Pattern Demo. ***");

        #region Mathematics department
        // 2 lecturers work in Mathematics department
        Employee mathTeacher1 = new Employee { Name = "M.Joy", Dept =
        "Mathematic", Designation = "Lecturer" };
        Employee mathTeacher2 = new Employee { Name = "M.Roony", Dept =
        "Mathematics", Designation = "Lecturer" };

        // The college has a Head of Department in Mathematics
```

```
CompositeEmployee hodMaths = new CompositeEmployee { Name =
"Mrs.S.Das", Dept = "Maths", Designation = "HOD-Maths" };

// Lecturers of Mathematics directly reports to HOD-Maths
hodMaths.AddEmployee(mathTeacher1);
hodMaths.AddEmployee(mathTeacher2);
#endregion

#region Computer Science department
// 3 lecturers work in Computer Sc. department
Employee cseTeacher1 = new Employee { Name = "C.Sam", Dept =
"Computer Science", Designation = "Lecturer" };
Employee cseTeacher2 = new Employee { Name = "C.Jones", Dept =
"Computer Science.", Designation = "Lecturer" };
Employee cseTeacher3 = new Employee { Name = "C.Marium", Dept =
"Computer Science", Designation = "Lecturer" };

// The college has a Head of Department in Computer science
CompositeEmployee hodCompSc = new CompositeEmployee { Name = "Mr.
V.Sarcar", Dept = "Computer Sc.", Designation = "HOD-Computer Sc." };

/* Lecturers of Computer Sc. directly reports to HOD-CSE */
hodCompSc.AddEmployee(cseTeacher1);
hodCompSc.AddEmployee(cseTeacher2);
hodCompSc.AddEmployee(cseTeacher3);
#endregion

#region Top level management
// The college also has a Principal
CompositeEmployee principal = new CompositeEmployee { Name =
"Dr.S.Som", Dept = "Planning-Supervising-Managing", Designation =
"Principal" };

/* Head of Departments's of Maths and Computer Science directly
reports to Principal.*/
principal.AddEmployee(hodMaths);
principal.AddEmployee(hodCompSc);
#endregion
```

```csharp
/*
 * Printing the leaf-nodes and branches in the same way. i.e.
   in each case, we are calling DisplayDetails() method.
 */
Console.WriteLine("\nDetails of a Principal object is as follows:");
// Prints the complete structure
principal.DisplayDetails();

Console.WriteLine("\nDetails of a HOD object is as follows:");
/* Prints the details of Computer Science department */
hodCompSc.DisplayDetails();

// Leaf node
Console.WriteLine("\nDetails of an individual employee(leaf
node) is as follows:");
mathTeacher1.DisplayDetails();

/*
 * Suppose, one Computer Science lecturer(C.Jones)
 * is leaving now from the organization.
 */
hodCompSc.RemoveEmployee(cseTeacher2);
Console.WriteLine("\nAfter the resignation of C.Jones, the
organization has the following members:");
principal.DisplayDetails();
// Wait for user
Console.ReadKey();
    }
  }
}
```

***Composite Pattern Demo. ***

Details of a Principal object is as follows:

Dr. S.Som works in Planning-Supervising-Managing department.
Designation:Principal

Mrs. S.Das works in Maths department.Designation:HOD-Maths
        M.Joy works in Mathematic department.Designation:Lecturer
        M.Roony works in Mathematics department.Designation:Lecturer

Mr. V.Sarcar works in Computer Sc. department.Designation:HOD-Computer Sc.
        C.Sam works in Computer Science department.Designation:Lecturer
        C.Jones works in Computer Science. department.Designation:Lecturer
        C.Marium works in Computer Science department.Designation:Lecturer

Details of a HOD object is as follows:

Mr. V.Sarcar works in Computer Sc. department.Designation:HOD-Computer Sc.
        C.Sam works in Computer Science department.Designation:Lecturer
        C.Jones works in Computer Science. department.Designation:Lecturer
        C.Marium works in Computer Science department.Designation:Lecturer

Details of an individual employee(leaf node) is as follows:
        M.Joy works in Mathematic department.Designation:Lecturer

After the resignation of C.Jones, the organization has the following members:

Dr. S.Som works in Planning-Supervising-Managing department.
Designation:Principal

Mrs. S.Das works in Maths department.Designation:HOD-Maths
        M.Joy works in Mathematic department.Designation:Lecturer
        M.Roony works in Mathematics department.Designation:Lecturer

Mr. V.Sarcar works in Computer Sc. department.Designation:HOD-Computer Sc.
        C.Sam works in Computer Science department.Designation:Lecturer
        C.Marium works in Computer Science department.Designation:Lecturer

Q&A Session

11.1 What are the advantages of using the Composite design pattern?

Here are some of the advantages.

- In a tree-like structure, you can treat both the composite objects (branch nodes) and the individual objects (leaf nodes) uniformly. In this example, I used a common method called `DisplayDetails` to print both the composite object structure (the principal or department heads) and the single objects (the lecturers).

- It is common to implement a part-whole hierarchy using this design pattern.

- You can easily add a new component to the architecture or delete an existing component from the architecture.

11.2 What are the challenges associated with using the Composite design pattern?

Here are some of the disadvantages.

- If you want to maintain the ordering of child nodes (for example, if the parse trees are represented as components), you may need to take special care.

- If you are dealing with immutable objects, you cannot delete them.

- You can easily add a new component, but maintenance can be difficult over a period of time. Sometimes you may want to deal with a composite that has special components. This kind of constraint may cause additional costs to the development because you may need to implement a dynamic checking mechanism to support the concept.

11.3 In this example, you used a list data structure. Are other data structures OK to use?

Absolutely. There is no universal rule. You are free to use your preferred data structure. The GoF also confirmed that it is not necessary to use a general-purpose data structure.

11.4 How do you connect the Iterator design pattern to a Composite design pattern?

In the example, if you want to examine a composite object architecture, you may need to iterate over the objects. Also, if you want to do some special activities with some branches, you may need to iterate over its leaf nodes and non-leaf nodes.

11.5 In your implementation, in the interface, you defined only one method, DisplayDetails. But you are using additional methods for the addition and removal of objects in the composite class (CompositeEmployee). Why are you not putting these methods in the interface?

Nice observation. Even the GoF discussed this. Let's see what happens if you put the AddEmployee(...) and RemoveEmployee(...) methods in the interface. In that case, the leaf nodes need to implement these addition and removal operations. But will it be meaningful in this case? The answer is no. In this case, it may appear that you lose transparency, but I believe that you have more safety because I blocked the meaningless operations in the leaf nodes. This is why the GoF mentioned that this kind of decision involves a trade-off between safety and transparency.

11.6 I want to use an abstract class instead of an interface. Is this allowed?

In most cases, the simple answer is yes, but you need to understand the difference between an abstract class and an interface. In a typical scenario, you may find that one of them is more useful than the other. Throughout the book, I present only simple and easy-to-understand examples, so you may not see much difference between them.

Note   In the "Q&A Session" section in Chapter 3, which covered the Builder pattern, I discussed how to decide between an abstract class and an interface.

CHAPTER 12

Bridge Pattern

This chapter covers the Bridge pattern.

GoF Definition

Decouple an abstraction from its implementation so that the two can vary independently.

Concept

This pattern is also known as the Handle/Body pattern. Using it, you decouple an implementation class from an abstract class by providing a bridge between them.

This bridge interface makes the functionality of concrete classes independent from the interface implementer classes. You can alter different kinds of classes structurally without affecting each other. This pattern initially may seem to be complicated, which is why, in this chapter, there are two different implementations with a lot of explanation. The concept will be clearer to you when you go through the examples.

Real-World Example

In a software product development company, the development team and the marketing team both play crucial roles. The marketing team does a market survey and gathers customer requirements. The development team implements those requirements in the product to fulfill customer needs. Any change (e.g., in operational strategy) in one team should not have a direct impact on the other team. In this case, the marketing team is playing the role of a bridge between the clients of the product and the development team of the software company.

© Vaskaran Sarcar 2020
V. Sarcar, *Design Patterns in C#*, https://doi.org/10.1007/978-1-4842-6062-3_12

Computer-World Example

GUI frameworks can use the Bridge pattern to separate abstractions from the platform-specific implementation. For example, using this pattern, you can separate a window abstraction from a window implementation for Linux or macOS.

Implementation

Suppose that you need to design a piece of software for a seller who can sell different electronic items. For simplicity, let's assume, the seller is currently selling televisions and DVD players, and he sells them both online and offline (at different showrooms) mode.

In this case, you may start with the designs shown in Figure 12-1 or Figure 12-2.

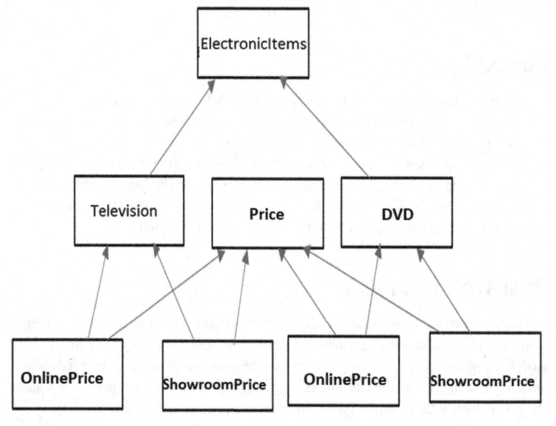

Figure 12-1. *Approach 1*

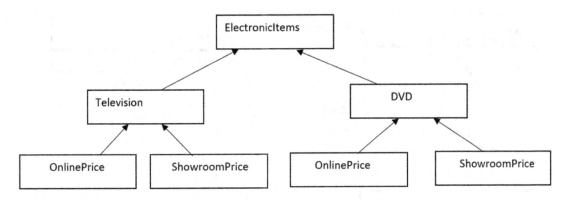

Figure 12-2. *Approach 2*

On further analysis, you discover that approach 1 is messy and will be difficult to maintain.

At first, approach 2 looks cleaner, but if you want to include new prices (e.g., ThirdPartyPrice, FestiveTimePrice, etc.), or if you want to include new electronic items (e.g., air conditioners (AC), refrigerators, etc.), you face new challenges because the elements are tightly coupled in this design. But in a real-world scenario, this kind of enhancement is often required.

So, you need to start with a loosely coupled system for future enhancements, so that either of these two hierarchies (electronics items and their prices) can grow independently. The Bridge pattern is perfect for such a scenario. So, when you use the Bridge pattern, the structure may look like Figure 12-3.

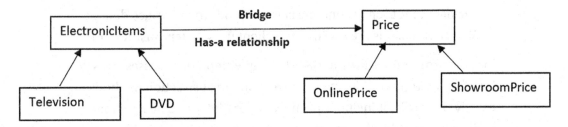

Figure 12-3. *Maintaining two separate hierarchies using the Bridge pattern*

Now let's start from the most common class diagram of a Bridge pattern (see Figure 12-4).

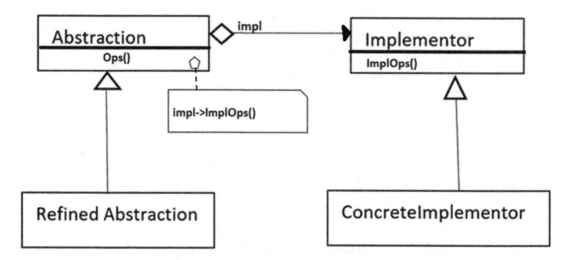

Figure 12-4. *A classical Bridge pattern*

In this class diagram,

- Abstraction defines the abstract interface and maintains the Implementor reference. In my examples, it is an abstract class, but it is very important to note that you should not assume that you need an abstract class or interface to define an abstraction. It's important to know what the word *abstraction* here says about the methods that remove the complexity. These methods simply hide the inner details of their work from the client code.

- RefinedAbstraction (a concrete class) extends the interface defined by Abstraction. It is the one that the client uses in demonstration 1.

- Implementor defines the interface for implementation classes. This interface methods don't have to correspond to abstraction methods exactly. Typically, it includes primitive operations, and abstraction defines the high-level operation based on these primitives. Also note that there does not need to be a one-to-one mapping between an abstraction class method and an implementor method. You can use a combination of the implementor method inside an abstraction class method. Demonstration 2 shows this, or you can refer to Q&A 12.5.

- ConcreteImplementor (a concrete class) implements the Implementor interface.

I follow a similar design in the upcoming demonstrations. For your reference, I point out all the participants in the implementation with comments.

Class Diagram

Figure 12-5 shows the class diagram.

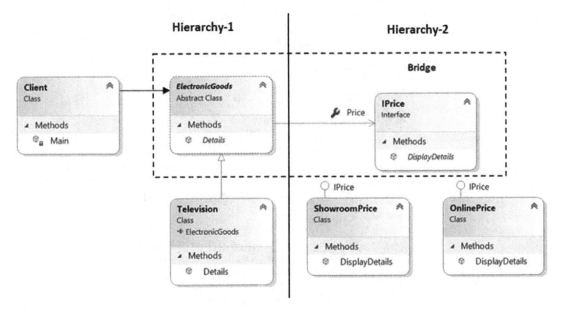

Figure 12-5. *Class diagram*

Solution Explorer View

Figure 12-6 shows the high-level structure of the program.

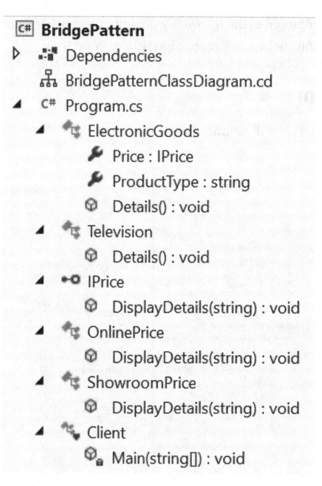

Figure 12-6. *Solution Explorer view*

Demonstration 1

In this example, ElectronicGoods is our abstraction class. It is placed in hierarchy 1. This class is defined as follows.

```
// Abstraction
    public abstract class ElectronicGoods
    {
        public IPrice Price { get; set; }
        public string ProductType { get; set; }
        public abstract void Details();
    }
```

The IPrice interface is our implementor interface. It maintains the second hierarchy and is defined as follows.

```
// Implementor
   public interface IPrice
   {
       void DisplayDetails(string product);
   }
```

Television is the concrete abstraction class that overrides the Details() method as follows.

```
// Refined Abstraction
   public class Television : ElectronicGoods
   {
       /*
        * Implementation specific:
        * Delegating the task
        * to the Implementor object.
        */

       public override void Details()
       {
           Price.DisplayDetails(ProductType);
       }
   }
```

With the supporting comments, you can see that inside the Details() method, I invoke the DisplayDetails() method from the other hierarchy and pass the information about the product type.

The concrete implementors (OnlinePrice, ShowroomPrice) catch this information and use it in DisplayDetails(...). Both concrete implementors are similar. For your reference, one of them is shown next.

```
// This is ConcreteImplementor-1
// OnlinePrice class
public class OnlinePrice : IPrice
```

```
    {
        public void DisplayDetails(string productType)
        {
            Console.Write($"\n{productType} price at online is : 2000$");
        }
    }
}
```

For simplicity, I did not vary the price in demonstration 1, but in demonstration 2, you notice the flexibility of using this pattern, and there I also vary the price. Now go through the complete demonstration, which is as follows.

```
using System;

namespace BridgePattern
{
    // Abstraction
    public abstract class ElectronicGoods
    {
        public IPrice Price { get; set; }
        public string ProductType { get; set; }
        public abstract void Details();

    }
    // Refined Abstraction
    public class Television : ElectronicGoods
    {
        /*
         * Implementation specific:
         * Delegating the task
         * to the Implementor object.
         */

        public override void Details()
        {
            Price.DisplayDetails(ProductType);
        }
    }
```

```csharp
// Implementor
public interface IPrice
{
    void DisplayDetails(string product);
}
// This is ConcreteImplementor-1
// OnlinePrice class
public class OnlinePrice : IPrice
{
    public void DisplayDetails(string productType)
    {
        Console.Write($"\n{productType} price at online is : 2000$");
    }
}
// This is ConcreteImplementor-2
// ShowroomPrice class
public class ShowroomPrice : IPrice
{
    public void DisplayDetails(string productType)
    {
        Console.Write($"\n{productType} price at showroom is : 3000$");
    }
}
// Client code
class Client
{
    static void Main(string[] args)
    {
        Console.WriteLine("***Bridge Pattern Demo.***");
        Console.WriteLine("Verifying the market price of a television.");
        ElectronicGoods eItem = new Television();
        eItem.ProductType = "Sony Television";
        // Verifying online  price
        IPrice price = new OnlinePrice();
        eItem.Price = price;
```

```
            eItem.Details();
            // Verifying showroom price
            price = new ShowroomPrice();
            eItem.Price = price;
            eItem.Details();
        }
    }
}
```

Output

Here's the output.

```
***Bridge Pattern Demo.***
Verifying the market price of a television.

Sony Television price at online is : 2000$
Sony Television price at showroom is : 3000$
```

Additional Implementation

I include an additional implementation in this chapter to help you note the flexibility of using this pattern. In this example, I used constructors, not properties. But before I show you the flexibility, let's assume that the seller provides a discount on the products for sale.

To accommodate this, in this implementation, let's add the following method in the abstraction class (ElectronicGoods).

```
// Additional method
public void Discount(int percentage)
{
    price.GetDiscount(percentage);
}
```

And the following method in the implementation interface (IPrice).

```
void GetDiscount(int percentage);
```

Since the `Discount` method is *not* abstract, the `Television` class or any derived class of `ElectronicGoods` inherits this method. But since the `GetDiscount(int percentage)` method is added in the `IPrice` interface, the concrete implementors need to implement this method. The following is such an implementation from the `OnlinePrice` class implementor.

```
public void GetDiscount(int percentage)
{
    Console.Write($"\nAt online, you can get upto {percentage}% discount.");
}
```

Note   Again, these modifications are made to provide support for the discount method only. You should not feel that the original Bridge pattern is affected by the change. To keep demonstration 1 short and simple, I did not include this method.

Now comes the flexibility part. Let's assume that the seller wants to sell electronic items called DVDs. The seller sometimes provides discounts on all products, but during the holiday seasons, additional discounts are offered for DVDs only.

So, the DVD class now need to include another method to provide the double discounts (normal discount + additional discount). You cannot add this method in the `ElectronicGoods` abstraction class because in that case, Television class will also have this method which you do not want. Most importantly, although you include the DVD class, your old code structure cannot change.

The Bridge pattern addresses this problem. The class diagram gives you a clue. In addition to this, notice how I implement the following method inside the DVD class.

```
// Specific method in DVD
public void DoubleDiscount()
{
    // Normal discount(10%)
    Discount(10);
    // Festive season additional discount(5%)
    Discount(5);
}
```

Note   You can see that inside DoubleDiscount() method, the Discount(...) method of ElectronicGoods is used, so I am coding in terms of *superclass abstraction*, which allows abstraction and implementation to vary independently.

Since I used constructors instead of properties, let's look at the changes first. The following is for abstraction with the Details(...) and Discount(...) methods.

```
// Abstraction
public abstract class ElectronicGoods
{
    //public IPrice Price { get; set; }
    private IPrice price;
    public string type;
    public double cost;
    public ElectronicGoods(IPrice price)
    {
        this.price = price;
    }
    public void Details()
    {
        price.DisplayDetails(type, cost);
    }
    // Additional method
    public void Discount(int percentage)
    {
        price.GetDiscount(percentage);
    }
}
```

Now, this is the first refined abstraction (Television class). In this class, no new method is defined, which simply means that the Television class is ready to use its parent class methods and doesn't wish to provide any new behavior.

```
// Refined Abstraction-1
// Television class uses the default discount method.
public class Television : ElectronicGoods
```

```
{
    public Television(IPrice price):base(price)
    {
        this.type = "Television";
        this.cost = 2000;
    }
    // No additional method exists for Television

}
```

The following is our second refined abstraction (DVD class), which is newly added. In this class, one new method called DoubleDiscount(...) is defined, which simply means that the client can use this DVD class-specific method if he wants. This method is coded in the superclass abstraction, and the other hierarchy is unaffected due to the addition of this DVD class. (I mean that due to the addition of the DVD class (or any other similar class) in hierarchy 1, you do not need to change ShowroomPrice, OnlinePrice, and so forth, which are placed in hierarchy 2. Even if you add some additional method(s) to the abstraction class, you do not need to make changes to hierarchy 2. Similarly, if you add a method in the implementor, you do not need to make changes in hierarchy 1.)

Note   In short, here you separate "the methods that clients use" from "how these methods are implemented."

```
// Refined Abstraction-2
// DVD class can give additional discount.
public class DVD : ElectronicGoods
{
    public DVD(IPrice price) : base(price)
    {
        this.type = "DVD";
        this.cost = 3000;
    }

    // Specic method in DVD
    public void DoubleDiscount()
    {
```

```
            // Normal discount(10%)
            Discount(10);
            // Festive season additional discount(5%)
            Discount(5);
        }
}
```

Do a crosscheck with the class diagram shown in Figure 12-7. Then directly follow the complete demonstration and output. I don't show the Solution Explorer view for this modified implementation, because it is easy to understand with the preceding discussions and the following class diagram.

Class Diagram

Figure 12-7 shows the modified class diagram.

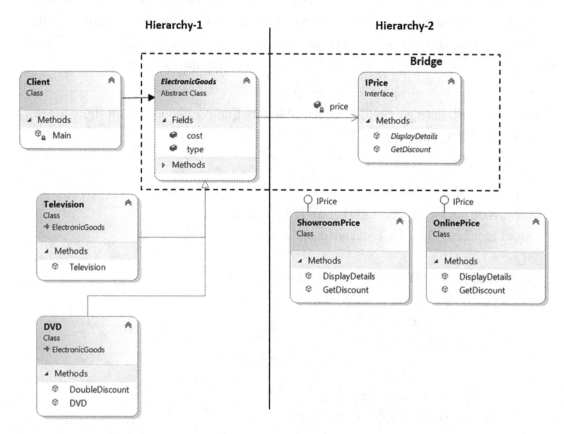

Figure 12-7. *Class diagram for demonstration 2*

Demonstration 2

Here is the complete implementation.

```
using System;

namespace BridgePatternDemo2
{
    // Abstraction
    public abstract class ElectronicGoods
    {
        //public IPrice Price { get; set; }
         private IPrice price;
         public string type;
         public double cost;
         public ElectronicGoods(IPrice price)
         {
             this.price = price;
         }
         public void Details()
         {
             price.DisplayDetails(type,cost);
         }
         // additional method
         public void Discount(int percentage)
         {
             price.GetDiscount(percentage);
         }

    }
    // Refined Abstraction-1
    // Television class uses the default discount method.
    public class Television : ElectronicGoods
```

```
{
    public Television(IPrice price):base(price)
    {
        this.type = "Television";
        this.cost = 2000;
    }
    // No additional method exists for Television

}
// Refined Abstraction-2
// DVD class can give additional discount.
public class DVD : ElectronicGoods
{
    public DVD(IPrice price) : base(price)
    {
        this.type = "DVD";
        this.cost = 3000;
    }

    // Specic method in DVD
    public void DoubleDiscount()
    {
        // Normal discount(10%)
        Discount(10);
        // Festive season additional discount
        Discount(5);
    }
}

// Implementor
public interface IPrice
{
    void DisplayDetails(string product, double price);
    // additional method
    void GetDiscount(int percentage);
}
// This is ConcreteImplementor-1
```

```csharp
// OnlinePrice class
public class OnlinePrice : IPrice
{
    public void DisplayDetails(string productType, double price)
    {
        Console.Write($"\n{productType} price at online is : {price}$");
    }
    public void GetDiscount(int percentage)
    {
        Console.Write($"\nAt online, you can get upto {percentage}%
        discount.");
    }
}
// This is ConcreteImplementor-2
// ShowroomPrice class
public class ShowroomPrice : IPrice
{
    public virtual void DisplayDetails(string productType, double price)
    {
        // Showroom price is 300$ more
        Console.Write($"\n{productType} price at showroom is : {price +
        300}$");
    }
    public void GetDiscount(int percentage)
    {
        Console.Write($"\nAt showroom, additional {percentage}%
        discount can be approved.");
    }
}
// Client code
class Client
{
    static void Main(string[] args)
    {
        Console.WriteLine("***Alternative Implementation of Bridge
        Pattern.***");
```

```csharp
#region Television details
Console.WriteLine("Verifying the market price of a television.");
 ElectronicGoods eItem = new Television(new OnlinePrice());
// Verifying online price details
eItem.Details();
// Giving 10% discount
eItem.Discount(10);
// Verifying showroom price
eItem = new Television(new ShowroomPrice());
eItem.Details();
// Giving 10% discount
eItem.Discount(10);
#endregion

#region DVD details
Console.WriteLine("\n\nNow checking the DVD details.");
// Verifying online  price
eItem = new DVD(new OnlinePrice());
eItem.Details();
// Giving 10% discount
eItem.Discount(10);
// Verifying showroom price
eItem = new DVD(new ShowroomPrice());
eItem.Details();
Console.WriteLine("\nIn showroom, you want to give double
discounts at festive season.");
Console.WriteLine("For DVD, you can get double discounts using
the DoubleDiscount() method.");
//eItem.Discount();
Console.WriteLine("For example, in festive season:");
((DVD)eItem).DoubleDiscount();
#endregion
        }
    }
}
```

Output

```
***Alternative Implementation of Bridge Pattern.***
Verifying the market price of a television.

Television price at online is : 2000$
At online, you can get upto 10% discount.
Television price at showroom is : 2300$
At showroom, additional 10% discount can be approved.

Now checking the DVD details.

DVD price at online is : 3000$
At online, you can get upto 10% discount.
DVD price at showroom is : 3300$
In showroom, you want to give double discounts at festive season.
For DVD , you can get double discounts using the DoubleDiscount() method.
For example, in festive season:

At showroom, additional 10% discount can be approved.
At showroom, additional 5% discount can be approved.
```

Q&A Session

12.1 How does this pattern make my programming life easier?
This chapter featured two examples with the following key intents.

- Avoid tight coupling between the items and their corresponding prices

- Maintain two different hierarchies in which both can be extended without impacting each other

- Deal with multiple objects in which implementations are shared among themselves

12.2 You could use simple subclassing instead of using this kind of design. Is this correct?

No. With simple subclassing, your implementations cannot vary dynamically. Your implementations may seem to behave differently, but they are bound to the abstraction at compile time.

12.3 Can I use constructors instead of properties inside the Abstraction class?

Yes. Some developers prefer constructors over properties (or getter-setter methods). Therefore, I showed you both usages in two demonstrations.

12.4 What are the key advantages of using a Bridge design pattern?

Here are some of the advantages.

- Implementations are not bound to the abstractions.

- Both the abstractions and implementations can grow independently.

- Concrete classes are independent of the interface implementer classes. In other words, changes in one of them do not affect the other. So, you can also vary the abstraction and the implementation hierarchies in different ways.

12.5 What are the challenges associated with this pattern?

The overall structure may become complex. Here you do not directly invoke a method. Instead, the abstraction layer delegates the work to the implementation layer. So, you may notice a slight performance impact when you execute an operation.

Sometimes the Bridge pattern is confused with the Adapter pattern. (Remember that the key purpose of an Adapter pattern is to deal with incompatible interfaces only.)

12.6 "You can use a combination of the implementor method when you use an abstraction class method. In demonstration 2, you see this." Can you please elaborate?

It is shown in the `DoubleDiscount()` method in demonstration 2, where you invoke the `Discount()` method twice. As another example, let's say the implementor has the following `GiveThanks()` method.

```
public interface IPrice
    {
        void DisplayDetails(string product, double price);
        // Additional method
```

```
        void GetDiscount(int percentage);
        // Added for Q&A session
        void GiveThanks();
    }
```

And the concrete implementors implemented the method. Let's say OnlinePrice implemented this method as follows.

```
public void GiveThanks()
{
  Console.Write("Thank you, please visit the site again.");
}
```

And another concrete implementor, ShowroomPrice, implements this method as follows.

```
public void GiveThanks()
{
Console.Write("Thank you for coming. please visit the shop again.");
}
```

Now, inside the abstraction, you can add this method (if you want). For example, your updated Discount may look like the following.

```
// Additional method
public void Discount(int percentage)
{
 price.GetDiscount(percentage);
 // Added for Q&A session
 price.GiveThanks();
}
```

And when you run the program (demonstration 2) with these changes, you see the following modified output.

```
***Alternative Implementation of Bridge Pattern.***
Verifying the market price of a television.

Television price at online is : 2000$
At online, you can get upto 10% discount.Thank you, please visit the site again.
```

231

Television price at showroom is : 2300$
At showroom, additional 10% discount can be approved. **Thank you for coming. Please visit the shop again.**

Now checking the DVD details.

DVD price at online is : 3000$
At online, you can get upto 10% discount. **Thank you, please visit the site again.**
DVD price at showroom is : 3300$
In showroom, you want to give double discounts at festive season.
For DVD , you can get double discounts using the DoubleDiscount() method.
For example, in festive season:

At showroom, additional 10% discount can be approved. **Thank you for coming. Please visit the shop again.**
At showroom, additional 5% discount can be approved. **Thank you for coming. Please visit the shop again.**

Note   A high-level abstraction method can include multiple implementor methods, but clients may not be aware of this.

PART I.C

Behavioral Patterns

CHAPTER 13

Visitor Pattern

This chapter covers the Visitor pattern.

GoF Definition

Represent an operation to be performed on the elements of an object structure. Visitor lets you define a new operation without changing the classes of the elements on which it operates.

Concept

In this pattern, you separate an algorithm from an object structure. So, you can add new operations on objects without modifying their existing architecture. This pattern supports the open/close principle (which says the extension is allowed, but modification is disallowed for entities such as class, function, and so on).

Note You can experience the true power of this design pattern when you combine it with the Composite pattern, as shown in an implementation later in this chapter.

To understand this pattern, let's consider a scenario in which you have an abstract class called Number as follows.

```
/// <summary>
/// Abstract class- Number
/// </summary>
abstract class Number
{
```

© Vaskaran Sarcar 2020
V. Sarcar, *Design Patterns in C#*, https://doi.org/10.1007/978-1-4842-6062-3_13

```csharp
        private int numberValue;
        private string type;
        public Number(string type, int number)
        {
            this.type = type;
            this.numberValue = number;
        }
        // I want to restrict the change in original data
        // So, no setter is present here.
        public int NumberValue
        {
            get
            {
                return numberValue;
            }
        }
        public string TypeInfo
        {
            get
            {
                return type;
            }
        }
        public abstract void SomeMethod();
    }
```

There are two concrete classes called `SmallNumber` and `BigNumber` that derive from `Number`, which is defined as follows.

```csharp
    /// <summary>
    /// Concrete class-SmallNumber
    /// </summary>

    class SmallNumber : Number
    {
        public SmallNumber(string type, int number) : base(type, number)
        { }
```

```csharp
    public override void SomeMethod()
    {
        // Some code
    }
}
/// <summary>
/// Concrete class-BigNumber
/// </summary>
class BigNumber : Number
{
    public BigNumber(string type, int number) : base(type, number)
    { }

    public override void SomeMethod
    {
        // Some code
    }
}
```

This inheritance hierarchy is easy to understand. Now let's look at an imaginary conversation between you and your customer.

Customer: I want you to create a design in which each concrete class has a method to increment the number value.

You: That's easy. I'll introduce a common method in the Number class, and as a result, each of the concrete classes can get the method.

Customer: Wait. I want you to use a method that increments the number, but in each invocation of the method in the SmallNumber class, it should increment the number by 1, and for the BigNumber class, it should increment the number by 10.

You: That won't be a problem. I can define an abstract method in the Number class, and in each of the derived classes, you can implement it differently.

Customer: That's fine with me.

You can accept this customer request as a one-off, but if your client often asks for similar requests, will it be possible for you to introduce methods like this in each class, particularly when the overall code structure is very complex? Also, in a tree structure, if it is just a branch node, can you imagine the impact of these changes across other nodes?

This time you may understand the problem and may think of some way to handle your fickle-minded customers. The Visitor pattern can help you in a situation like this. You see such an implementation in demonstration 1.

Real-World Example

Think of a taxi-booking scenario. When the taxi arrives at your door, and you enter the vehicle, the taxi driver takes control of transportation. He can take you to your destination through a route that you are not familiar with, and in the worst case, it can alter the destination (which is generated due to improper use of the Visitor pattern).

Computer-World Example

This pattern is useful when public APIs need to support *plug-in* operations. Clients can then perform their intended operations on a class (with the visiting class) without modifying the source.

Implementation

Let's continue our discussion on the Visitor pattern. You can see the class diagram in Figure 13-1. It gives you a hint on how I've implemented it in the upcoming demonstration. I introduced a new hierarchy, in which, at the top level, there is an interface called IVisitor with two methods called VisitBigNumbers(..) and VisitSmallNumbers(..). It looks like the following.

```
interface IVisitor
{
    // A visit operation for SmallNumber class
    void VisitSmallNumbers(SmallNumber number);

    // A visit operation for BigNumber class
    void VisitBigNumbers(BigNumber number);
}
```

Note   Instead of using different names (VisitSmallNumbers(..),
VisitBigNumbers(...)) for these methods, you could use the same method (for
example, VisitNumbers(...)) by using method overloading. In the Q&A session, I
discuss the reason for using different names in this example.

IncrementNumberVisitor implements this interface method, which looks like the
following.

```csharp
class IncrementNumberVisitor : IVisitor
{
    public void VisitSmallNumbers(SmallNumber number)
    {
        Number currentNumber = number as Number;
        /*
         I do not want (infact I can't change because it's readonly
         now) to modify the original data. So, I'm making a copy of it
         before I use it.
        */
        int temp = currentNumber.NumberValue;
        // For SmallNumber's incrementing by 1
        Console.WriteLine($"{currentNumber.TypeInfo} is {currentNumber.
        NumberValue}; I use it as:{++temp} for rest of my code.");
        // Remaining code, if any
    }

    public void VisitBigNumbers(BigNumber number)
    {
        Number currentNumber = number as Number;
        /*
         * I do not want (infact I can't change because it's readonly now)
         * to modify the original data.
         * So, I'm making a copy of it before I use it.
        */
        int temp = currentNumber.NumberValue;
        // For BigNumber's incrementing by 10
```

```
        Console.WriteLine($"{currentNumber.TypeInfo} is {currentNumber.
        NumberValue}; I convert it as:{temp+10} for rest of my code.");
        // Remaining code, if any
    }
}
```

One interesting point to note is that I do not want to modify the original data. So, in the Number class, you see the getter methods only. It is because I assume that once you get the data from the concrete Number classes, you can use it differently, but you are not allowed to change the original data. (It's a better practice, but it's optional).

In this example, I maintain a List data structure, called numberList, which initializes an object structure with different types of numbers. So, in demonstration 1, you get the following code segment.

```
class NumberCollection
{
    List<Number> numberList = new List<Number>();
    // List contains both SmallNumber's and BigNumber's
    public NumberCollection()
    {
        numberList.Add(new SmallNumber("small-1", 10));
        numberList.Add(new SmallNumber("small-2", 20));
        numberList.Add(new SmallNumber("small-3", 30));
        numberList.Add(new BigNumber("big-1", 200));
        numberList.Add(new BigNumber("big-2", 150));
        numberList.Add(new BigNumber("big-3", 70));
    }
        // remaining code
```

Again, you can initialize the list in this way, or once you initialize an empty list, you can supply the elements of the lists inside the client code using the AddNumberToList(...) method. Similarly, you can remove an element from your list using the RemoveNumberFromList(...) method. In demonstration 1, I did not use these methods, but I kept them for your reference. So, note the following methods.

```
public void AddNumberToList(Number number)
{
    numberList.Add(number);
}
public void RemoveNumberFromList(Number number)
{
    numberList.Remove(number);
}
```

Now we come to the most important segment. Inside the Number class, you see the following line.

```
public abstract void Accept(IVisitor visitor);
```

The concrete derived classes from Number override it as needed. For example, SmallNumber overrides it as follows.

```
public override void Accept(IVisitor visitor)
{
  visitor.VisitSmallNumbers(this);
}
```

And BigNumber implements it as follows.

```
public override void Accept(IVisitor visitor)
{
  visitor.VisitBigNumbers(this);
}
```

You can see that inside the Accept method, you can pass a "particular visitor object," which in turn can call the appropriate method across the classes. Both the SmallNumber and BigNumber classes expose themselves through this method (and here encapsulation is compromised). Now the client interacts with the visitor, and you can add new methods in the Visitor hierarchy. So, inside the client code, you notice code segments like the following.

```
NumberCollection numberCollection = new NumberCollection();
// some other code
// ....
IncrementNumberVisitor incrVisitor = new IncrementNumberVisitor();
// Visitor is visiting the list
Console.WriteLine("IncrementNumberVisitor is about to visit the list:");
numberCollection.Accept(incrVisitor);
```

Class Diagram

Figure 13-1 shows the class diagram. This time I wanted you to show the full method signature in the class diagram, so, to accommodate everything in a common place, the participants size become smaller than usual.

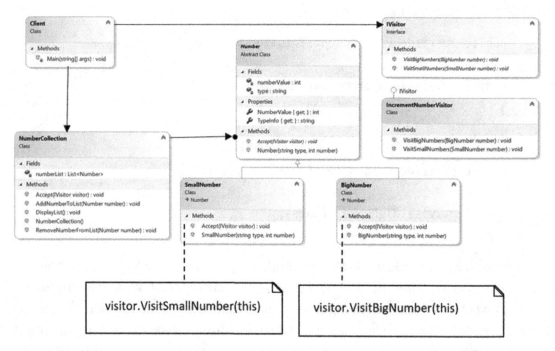

Figure 13-1. *Class diagram*

242

Solution Explorer View

Figure 13-2 shows the high-level structure of the program.

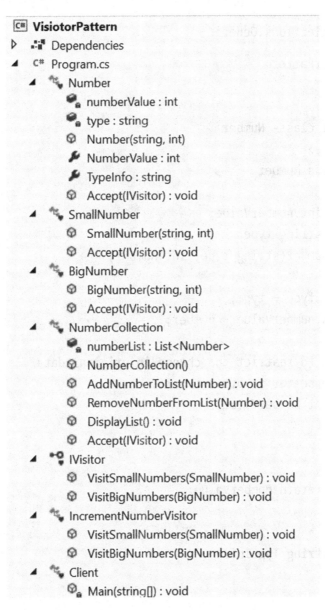

Figure 13-2. *Solution Explorer view*

Demonstration 1

Here's the complete code.

```
using System;
using System.Collections.Generic;

namespace VisitorPattern
{
    /// <summary>
    /// Abstract class- Number
    /// </summary>
    abstract class Number
    {
        private int numberValue;
        private string type;
        public Number(string type, int number)
        {
            this.type = type;
            this.numberValue = number;
        }
        //I want to restrict the change in original data
        //So, no setter is present here.
        public int NumberValue
        {
            get
            {
                return numberValue;
            }
        }
        public string TypeInfo
        {
            get
            {
                return type;
            }
        }
```

```csharp
    public abstract void Accept(IVisitor visitor);
}
/// <summary>
/// Concrete class-SmallNumber
/// </summary>

class SmallNumber : Number
{
    public SmallNumber(string type, int number) : base(type, number)
    { }

    public override void Accept(IVisitor visitor)
    {
        visitor.VisitSmallNumbers(this);
    }
}
/// <summary>
/// Concrete class-BigNumber
/// </summary>
class BigNumber : Number
{
    public BigNumber(string type, int number) : base(type, number)
    { }

    public override void Accept(IVisitor visitor)
    {
        visitor.VisitBigNumbers(this);
    }
}
class NumberCollection
{
    List<Number> numberList = new List<Number>();
    //List contains both SmallNumber's and BigNumber's
    public NumberCollection()
    {
        numberList.Add(new SmallNumber("small-1", 10));
        numberList.Add(new SmallNumber("small-2", 20));
```

```
        numberList.Add(new SmallNumber("small-3", 30));
        numberList.Add(new BigNumber("big-1", 200));
        numberList.Add(new BigNumber("big-2", 150));
        numberList.Add(new BigNumber("big-3", 70));
    }
    public void AddNumberToList(Number number)
    {
        numberList.Add(number);
    }
    public void RemoveNumberFromList(Number number)
    {
        numberList.Remove(number);
    }
    public void DisplayList()
    {
        Console.WriteLine("Current list is as follows:");
        foreach (Number number in numberList)
        {
            Console.Write(number.NumberValue+"\t");
        }
        Console.WriteLine();
    }
    public void Accept(IVisitor visitor)
    {
        foreach (Number n in numberList)
        {
            n.Accept(visitor);
        }
    }
}
/// <summary>
/// The Visitor interface.
/// GoF suggests to make visit opearation for each concrete class of
/// ConcreteElement (in our example,SmallNumber and BigNumber) in the
/// object structure
/// </summary>
```

```
interface IVisitor
{
    //A visit operation for SmallNumber class
    void VisitSmallNumbers(SmallNumber number);

    //A visit operation for BigNumber class
    void VisitBigNumbers(BigNumber number);
}
/// <summary>
/// A concrete visitor-IncrementNumberVisitor
/// </summary>
class IncrementNumberVisitor : IVisitor
{
     public void VisitSmallNumbers(SmallNumber number)
    {
        Number currentNumber = number as Number;
        /*
         I do not want( infact I can't change because it's readonly
         now) to modify the original data. So, I'm making a copy of it
         before I use it.
        */
        int temp = currentNumber.NumberValue;
        //For SmallNumber's incrementing by 1
        Console.WriteLine($"{currentNumber.TypeInfo} is {currentNumber.
        NumberValue}; I use it as:{++temp} for rest of my code.");
        //Remaining code, if any
    }

    public void VisitBigNumbers(BigNumber number)
    {
        Number currentNumber = number as Number;
        /*
         I do not want( infact I can't change because it's readonly
         now) to modify the original data. So, I'm making a copy of it
         before I use it.
        */
```

```
            int temp = currentNumber.NumberValue;
            //For BigNumber's incrementing by 10
            Console.WriteLine($"{currentNumber.TypeInfo} is {currentNumber.
            NumberValue}; I convert it as:{temp+10} for rest of my code.");
            //Remaining code, if any
        }
    }
    class Client
    {
        static void Main(string[] args)
        {
            Console.WriteLine("***Visitor Pattern Demo***\n");
            NumberCollection numberCollection = new NumberCollection();
            //Showing the current list
            numberCollection.DisplayList();
            IncrementNumberVisitor incrVisitor = new
            IncrementNumberVisitor();
            //Visitor is visiting the list
            Console.WriteLine("IncrementNumberVisitor is about to visit the
            list:");
            numberCollection.Accept(incrVisitor);
            //Showing the current list
            numberCollection.DisplayList();

            Console.ReadLine();
        }
    }
}
```

```
***Visitor Pattern Demo***

Current list is as follows:
10      20      30      200     150     70
IncrementNumberVisitor is about to visit the list:
small-1 is 10; I use it as:11 for rest of my code.
small-2 is 20; I use it as:21 for rest of my code.
small-3 is 30; I use it as:31 for rest of my code.
big-1 is 200; I convert it as:210 for rest of my code.
big-2 is 150; I convert it as:160 for rest of my code.
big-3 is 70; I convert it as:80 for rest of my code.
Current list is as follows:
10      20      30      200     150     70
```

Q&A Session

13.1 When should you consider implementing a Visitor design pattern?
Here are some use cases to consider.

- You need to add new operations to a set of objects without changing their corresponding classes. It is the primary aim to implement a Visitor pattern. When the operations change very often, this approach can be your savior.

- If you need to change the logic of various operations, you can simply do it through a visitor implementation.

13.2 Are there any drawbacks associated with this pattern?
Here are some drawbacks associated with this pattern.

- I mentioned earlier that encapsulation is not its key concern. So, you can break the power of encapsulation using visitors.

- If you need to frequently add new concrete classes to existing architecture, the visitor hierarchy becomes difficult to maintain. For example, suppose that you want to add another concrete class in the original hierarchy. In this case, you need to modify the visitor class hierarchy accordingly.

13.3 Why are you saying that a visitor class can violate the encapsulation?

Notice that inside the Accept method, you can pass a "particular visitor object," which in turn can call the appropriate method across the classes. Both SmallNumber and BigNumber class expose themselves through this method, and here encapsulation is compromised.

Also, in many cases, you may see that the visitor needs to move around a composite structure to gather information from them, and then it can modify with that information. (Though in demonstration 1, I do not allow this modification). So, when you provide this kind of support, you violate the core aim of encapsulation.

13.4 Why this pattern compromises with the encapsulation?

Here you perform some operations on a set of objects that can be heterogeneous also. But your constraint is that you cannot change their corresponding classes. So, your visitor needs a way to access the members of these objects. To fulfill this requirement, you are exposing the information to the visitor.

13.5 In demonstration 1, I see that in the visitor interfaces, you are *not* using the concept of method overloading. For example, you have written interface methods as follows.

```
// A visit operation for SmallNumber class
void VisitSmallNumbers(SmallNumber number);

// A visit operation for BigNumber class
void VisitBigNumbers(BigNumber number);
```

It appears to me that you could use something like the following.

```
// A visit operation for SmallNumber class
void VisitNumbers(SmallNumber number);

// A visit operation for BigNumber class
void VisitNumbers(BigNumber number);
```

Is this correct?

Nice catch. Yes, you can do that, but I wanted to draw your attention to the fact that these methods are doing different jobs (one is incrementing the int by 1 and the other is incrementing it by 10). By using different names, I tried to distinguish them inside the Number class hierarchy when you go through the code.

In the book *Java Design Patterns* (Apress, 2018), I used the approach that you mentioned. You can simply remember that these interface methods should target specific classes like SmallNumber or BigNumber only.

In demonstration 2, in which I combine the Visitor pattern with the Composite pattern, the overloaded methods are used.

13.6 Suppose that in demonstration 1, I added another concrete subclass of Number called UndefinedNumber. How should I proceed? Should I use another specific method in the visitor interface?

Exactly. You need to define a new method that is specific to this new class. So, your interface may look like the following (method overloading is used here).

```
interface IVisitor
{
    // A visit operation for SmallNumber class
    void VisitNumbers(SmallNumber number);
    // A visit operation for BigNumber class
    void VisitNumbers(BigNumber number);
    // A visit operation for UndefinedNumber class
    void VisitNumbers(UndefinedNumber number);
}
```

And later, you need to implement this new method in the concrete visitor class.

13.7 Suppose, I need to support new operations in the existing architecture. How should I proceed with a Visitor pattern?

For each new operation, create a new subclass of Visitor and implement the operation in it. Then, visit your existing structure the way that I showed you in the preceding examples. For example, if you want methods that investigate whether the int values of SmallNumber class instances are greater than 10, and for the BigNumber class, whether they are greater than 100. For this requirement, you can add a new concrete class, InvestigateNumberVisitor, which inherits from IVisitor and is defined as follows.

```
/// <summary>
/// Another concrete visitor-InvestigateNumberVisitor
/// </summary>
class InvestigateNumberVisitor : IVisitor
{
    public void VisitSmallNumbers(SmallNumber number)
    {
        Number currentNumber = number as Number;
        int temp = currentNumber.NumberValue;
        // Checking whether the number is greater than 10 or not
        string isTrue = temp > 10 ? "Yes" : "No";
        Console.WriteLine($"Is {currentNumber.TypeInfo} greater than 10
        ? {isTrue}");
    }
    public void VisitBigNumbers(BigNumber number)
    {
        Number currentNumber = number as Number;
        int temp = currentNumber.NumberValue;
        // Checking whether the number is greater than 100 or not
        string isTrue = temp > 100 ? "Yes" : "No";
        Console.WriteLine($"Is {currentNumber.TypeInfo} greater than
        100 ? {isTrue}");
    }
}
```

Now inside the client code, you can add the following segment to check whether it is working properly or not.

```
// Visitor-2
InvestigateNumberVisitor investigateVisitor = new
InvestigateNumberVisitor();
// Visitor is visiting the list
Console.WriteLine("InvestigateNumberVisitor is about to visit the list:");
numberCollection.Accept(investigateVisitor);
```

Once you add these segments in demonstration 1, use the client code as follows.

```
class Client
    {
        static void Main(string[] args)
        {
            Console.WriteLine("***Visitor Pattern Demo2.***\n");
            NumberCollection numberCollection = new NumberCollection();
            // Showing the current list
            numberCollection.DisplayList();
            // Visitor-1
            IncrementNumberVisitor incrVisitor = new IncrementNumberVisitor();
            // Visitor is visiting the list
            Console.WriteLine("IncrementNumberVisitor is about to visit the
            list:");
            numberCollection.Accept(incrVisitor);
            // Visitor-2
            InvestigateNumberVisitor investigateVisitor = new
            InvestigateNumberVisitor();
            // Visitor is visiting the list
            Console.WriteLine("InvestigateNumberVisitor is about to visit
            the list:");
            numberCollection.Accept(investigateVisitor);

            Console.ReadLine();

        }
    }
```

You can get the following output when you run the program.

```
***Visitor Pattern Demo2.***

Current list is as follows:
10      20      30      200     150     70
IncrementNumberVisitor is about to visit the list:
Original data:10; I use it as:11
Original data:20; I use it as:21
Original data:30; I use it as:31
```

```
Original data:200; I use it as:210
Original data:150; I use it as:160
Original data:70; I use it as:80
```

InvestigateNumberVisitor is about to visit the list:
Is small-1 greater than 10 ? No
Is small-2 greater than 10 ? Yes
Is small-3 greater than 10 ? Yes
Is big-1 greater than 100 ? Yes
Is big-2 greater than 100 ? Yes
Is big-3 greater than 100 ? No

You can download the full code for this modified example from the Apress website. I merged this in the namespace called VisitorPatternDemo2.

13.8 I see that you are initializing numberList with objects for SmallNumber and BigNumber. Is it mandatory to create such a structure?

No. I make a container that helps the client to visit smoothly in one shot. In a different variation, you could see that you initialize an empty list first and add (or remove) elements to this inside client code before you traverse the list.

To understand the previous line, you can refer to demonstration 2, where I made the container class inside the client code only.

Using Visitor Pattern and Composite Pattern Together

In demonstration 1, you saw an example of the Visitor design pattern, and in the Q&A session, you went through an extended version of it. Now I'll show you another implementation, but this time, I combine it with the Composite pattern.

Let's consider the example of the Composite design pattern from Chapter 11. In that example, there is a college with two different departments. Each of these departments has one head of department (HOD) and multiple professors/lecturers. All HODs report to the principal of the college.

Figure 13-3 shows the tree structure for this example. The college structure is the same as described in Chapter 11. The mathematics lecturers/teachers are M. Joy and M. Roony, and the CSE teachers are C. Sam, C. Jones, and C. Marium. These lecturers do not supervise anyone, so they are treated as leaf nodes in the tree diagram. Dr. S. Som is the principal and holds the highest position. Two HODs (Mrs. S. Das (HOD-Math) and Mr. V. Sarcar (HOD-Comp.Sc) reports to the principal. The HODs and principal are non-leaf nodes.

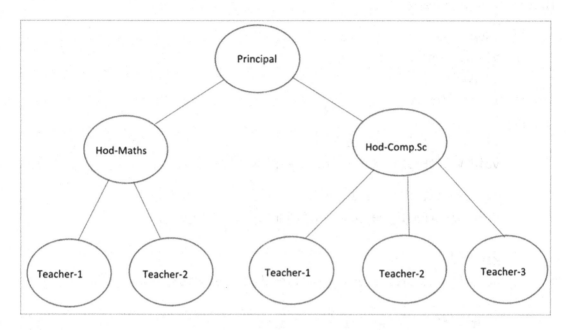

Figure 13-3. *Tree structure of the Composite design example*

Now suppose that the principal of the college wants to promote some of the employees. Let's say that teaching experience is the only criteria for promotion, but the criteria varies between senior teachers (branch nodes) and junior teachers (leaf nodes) as follows: for a junior teacher, the minimum criteria for promotion is 12 years, and for senior teachers, it is 15 years.

If you understand demonstration 1, you realize that the promotion criteria may change in the future, and there may be additional requirements from higher authorities. So, the Visitor pattern is a perfect fit to fulfill the current requirements. This is why in the upcoming example, you see that a new property and a new method are added to the Employee interface; it should be easy to understand with the supportive comments.

```
// Newly added for this example
// To set years of Experience
double Experience { get; set; }
// Newly added for this example
void Accept(IVisitor visitor);
```

Following the design in the demonstration 1, let's make a visitor interface called
IVisitor with method called VisitEmployee(...), which has two overloaded versions.
Here is the visitor hierarchy.

```
/// <summary>
/// Visitor interface
/// </summary>
interface IVisitor
{
    // To visit leaf nodes
    void VisitEmployees(Employee employee);

    // To visit composite nodes
    void VisitEmployees(CompositeEmployee employee);
}
/// <summary>
/// Concrete visitor class-PromotionCheckerVisitor
/// </summary>
class PromotionCheckerVisitor : IVisitor
{
    string eligibleForPromotion = String.Empty;
    public void VisitEmployees(CompositeEmployee employee)
    {
        //We'll promote them if experience is greater than 15 years
        eligibleForPromotion = employee.Experience > 15 ? "Yes" : "No";
        Console.WriteLine($"\t{ employee.Name } from {employee.Dept} is
        eligible for promotion? :{eligibleForPromotion}");
    }

    public void VisitEmployees(Employee employee)
    {
        //We'll promote them if experience is greater than 12 years
        eligibleForPromotion = employee.Experience > 12 ? "Yes" : "No";
        Console.WriteLine($"\t{ employee.Name } from {employee.Dept} is
        eligible for promotion? :{eligibleForPromotion}");
    }
}
```

This time, I make the container (a List data structure, called participants) in client code. When a visitor gathers the necessary details from this college structure, it can show the eligible candidates for promotion, which is the reason to include the following code segment.

```
Console.WriteLine("\n***Visitor starts visiting our composite
structure***\n");
IVisitor visitor = new PromotionCheckerVisitor();
//Visitor is traversing the participant list
foreach ( IEmployee  emp in participants)
   {
      emp.Accept(visitor);
   }
```

The visitor is collecting the data one piece at a time from the original college structure without making any modifications to it. Once the collection process is over, the visitor analyzes the data to display the intended results. To understand this visually, you can follow the arrows in Figures 13-4 through 13-8. *The principal is at the top of the organization, so you can assume that he receives no promotion.*

Step 1

Figure 13-4 shows step 1.

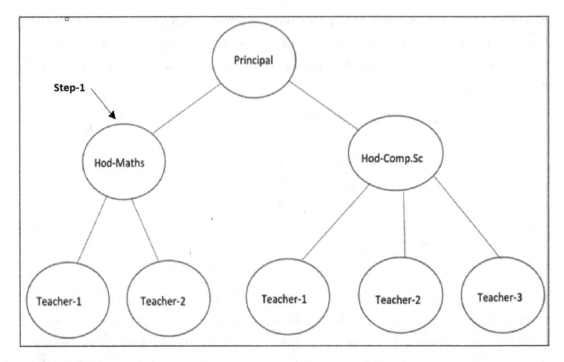

Figure 13-4. *Step 1*

Step 2

Figure 13-5 shows step 2.

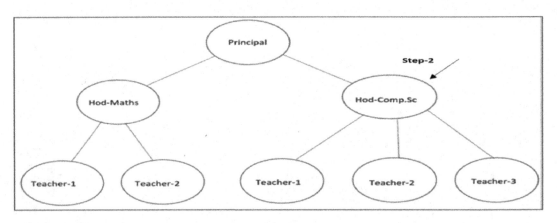

Figure 13-5. *Step 2*

Step 3

Figure 13-6 shows step 3.

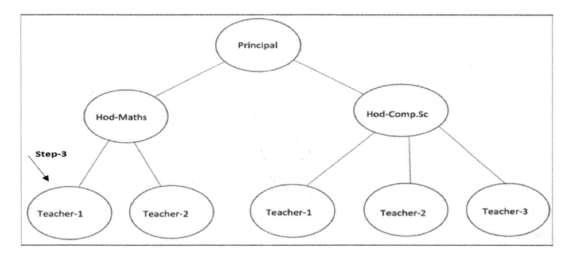

Figure 13-6. *Step 3*

Step 4

Figure 13-7 shows step 4.

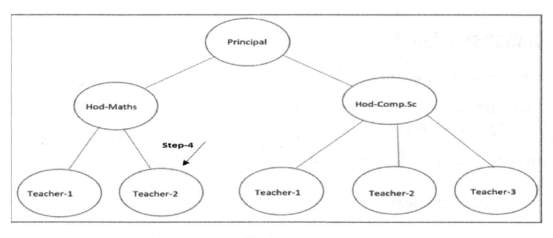

Figure 13-7. *Step 4*

Step 5

Figure 13-8 shows step 5.

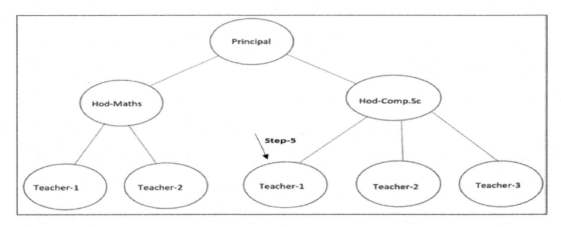

Figure 13-8. *Step 5*

And so on...

I followed a similar design in demonstration 1, and the code example is built on top of the only demonstration in Chapter 11. For brevity, I do not include the class diagram and Solution Explorer view for this example. So, go directly through the following implementation.

Demonstration 2

Here's the implementation.

```
using System;
using System.Collections.Generic;

namespace VisitorWithCompositePattern
{
    interface IEmployee
    {
        //To set an employee name
        string Name { get; set; }
        //To set an employee department
        string Dept { get; set; }
```

```csharp
    //To set an employee designation
    string Designation { get; set; }

    //To display an employee details
    void DisplayDetails();

    //Newly added for this example
    //To set years of Experience
    double Experience { get; set; }
    //Newly added for this example
    void Accept(IVisitor visitor);
}
//Leaf node
class Employee : IEmployee
{
    public string Name { get; set; }
    public string Dept { get; set; }
    public string Designation { get; set; }
    public double Experience { get; set; }
    //Details of a leaf node
    public void DisplayDetails()
    {
        Console.WriteLine($"{Name} works in { Dept} department.
        Designation:{Designation}.Experience : {Experience} years.");
    }
    public void Accept(IVisitor visitor)
    {
        visitor.VisitEmployees(this);
    }

}
//Non-leaf node
class CompositeEmployee : IEmployee
{
    public string Name { get; set; }
    public string Dept { get; set; }
    public string Designation { get; set; }
```

```csharp
    public double Experience { get; set; }

    //The container for child objects
    //private List<IEmployee> subordinateList = new List<IEmployee>();
    //Making it public now
    public List<IEmployee> subordinateList = new List<IEmployee>();

    //To add an employee
    public void AddEmployee(IEmployee e)
    {
        subordinateList.Add(e);
    }

    //To remove an employee
    public void RemoveEmployee(IEmployee e)
    {
        subordinateList.Remove(e);
    }

    //Details of a composite node
    public void DisplayDetails()
    {
        Console.WriteLine($"\n{Name} works in {Dept} department.
        Designation:{Designation}.Experience : {Experience} years.");
        foreach (IEmployee e in subordinateList)
        {
            e.DisplayDetails();
        }
    }

    public void Accept(IVisitor visitor)
    {
        visitor.VisitEmployees(this);
    }
}
/// <summary>
/// Visitor interface
/// </summary>
```

```
interface IVisitor
{
    //To visit leaf nodes
    void VisitEmployees(Employee employee);

    //To visit composite nodes
    void VisitEmployees(CompositeEmployee employee);
}
/// <summary>
/// Concrete visitor class-PromotionCheckerVisitor
/// </summary>
class PromotionCheckerVisitor : IVisitor
{
    string eligibleForPromotion = String.Empty;
    public void VisitEmployees(CompositeEmployee employee)
    {
        /*
        We'll promote them if experience is greater than 15 years.
        */
        eligibleForPromotion = employee.Experience > 15 ? "Yes" : "No";
        Console.WriteLine($"{ employee.Name } from {employee.Dept} is
        eligible for promotion? :{eligibleForPromotion}");

    }


    public void VisitEmployees(Employee employee)
    {
        /*
        We'll promote them if experience is greater
        than 12 years.
        */
        eligibleForPromotion = employee.Experience > 12 ? "Yes" : "No";
        Console.WriteLine($"{ employee.Name } from {employee.Dept} is
        eligible for promotion? :{eligibleForPromotion}");
    }
}
```

```
class Program
{
    static void Main(string[] args)
    {
        Console.WriteLine("***Visitor Pattern with Composite Pattern
        Demo. ***");

        #region Mathematics department
        //2 lecturers work in Mathematics department
        Employee mathTeacher1 = new Employee { Name = "M.Joy", Dept =
        "Mathematic", Designation = "Lecturer" ,Experience=13.7};
        Employee mathTeacher2 = new Employee { Name = "M.Roony", Dept =
        "Mathematics", Designation = "Lecturer", Experience = 6.5 };

        //The college has a Head of Department in Mathematics
        CompositeEmployee hodMaths = new CompositeEmployee { Name
        = "Mrs.S.Das", Dept = "Maths", Designation = "HOD-Maths",
        Experience = 14 };

        //Lecturers of Mathematics directly reports to HOD-Maths
        hodMaths.AddEmployee(mathTeacher1);
        hodMaths.AddEmployee(mathTeacher2);
        #endregion

        #region Computer Science department
        //3 lecturers work in Computer Sc. department
        Employee cseTeacher1 = new Employee { Name = "C.Sam", Dept =
        "Computer Science", Designation = "Lecturer", Experience = 10.2 };
        Employee cseTeacher2 = new Employee { Name = "C.Jones", Dept
        = "Computer Science.", Designation = "Lecturer", Experience =
        13.5 };
        Employee cseTeacher3 = new Employee { Name = "C.Marium", Dept =
        "Computer Science", Designation = "Lecturer", Experience = 7.3 };

        //The college has a Head of Department in Computer science
        CompositeEmployee hodCompSc = new CompositeEmployee { Name =
        "Mr. V.Sarcar", Dept = "Computer Sc.", Designation = "HOD-
        Computer Sc.", Experience = 16.5 };
```

```
//Lecturers of Computer Sc. directly reports to HOD-CSE
        hodCompSc.AddEmployee(cseTeacher1);
        hodCompSc.AddEmployee(cseTeacher2);
        hodCompSc.AddEmployee(cseTeacher3);
        #endregion

        #region Top level management
        //The college also has a Principal
        CompositeEmployee principal = new CompositeEmployee { Name =
        "Dr.S.Som", Dept = "Planning-Supervising-Managing",
        Designation = "Principal", Experience = 21 };

        /*
        Head of Departments's of Maths and Computer Science directly
        reports to Principal.
        */
        principal.AddEmployee(hodMaths);
        principal.AddEmployee(hodCompSc);
        #endregion

        /*
        Printing the leaf-nodes and branches in the same way i.e. in
        each case, we are calling DisplayDetails() method.
        */
        Console.WriteLine("\nDetails of a college structure is as follows:");
        //Prints the complete structure
        principal.DisplayDetails();

        List<IEmployee> participants = new List<IEmployee>();

        //For employees who directly reports to Principal
        foreach (IEmployee e in principal.subordinateList)
        {
            participants.Add(e);
        }
```

```
            //For employees who directly reports to HOD-Maths
            foreach (IEmployee e in hodMaths.subordinateList)
            {
                participants.Add(e);
            }
            //For employees who directly reports to HOD-Comp.Sc
            foreach (IEmployee e in hodCompSc.subordinateList)
            {
                participants.Add(e);
            }
            Console.WriteLine("\n***Visitor starts visiting our composite
            structure***\n");
            IVisitor visitor = new PromotionCheckerVisitor();
            /*
Principal is already holding the highest position.
We are not checking whether he is eligible
for promotion or not.
*/
            //principal.Accept(visitor);
            //Visitor is traversing the participant list
            foreach ( IEmployee  emp in participants)
            {
                emp.Accept(visitor);
            }

            //Wait for user
            Console.ReadKey();
        }
    }
}
```

Output

Here's the output. Some portions are in bold to show you that the visitor was able to complete its job successfully.

***Visitor Pattern with Composite Pattern Demo. ***

Details of a college structure is as follows:

Dr.S.Som works in Planning-Supervising-Managing department.
Designation:Principal.Experience : 21 years.

Mrs.S.Das works in Maths department.Designation:HOD-Maths.Experience : 14
years.
M.Joy works in Mathematic department.Designation:Lecturer.Experience : 13.7
years.
M.Roony works in Mathematics department.Designation:Lecturer.Experience :
6.5 years.

Mr. V.Sarcar works in Computer Sc. department.Designation:HOD-Computer Sc..
Experience : 16.5 years.
C.Sam works in Computer Science department.Designation:Lecturer.Experience
: 10.2 years.
C.Jones works in Computer Science. department.Designation:Lecturer.
Experience : 13.5 years.
C.Marium works in Computer Science department.Designation:Lecturer.
Experience : 7.3 years.

Visitor starts visiting our composite structure

Mrs.S.Das from Maths is eligible for promotion? :No
Mr. V.Sarcar from Computer Sc. is eligible for promotion? :Yes
M.Joy from Mathematic is eligible for promotion? :Yes
M.Roony from Mathematics is eligible for promotion? :No
C.Sam from Computer Science is eligible for promotion? :No
C.Jones from Computer Science. is eligible for promotion? :Yes
C.Marium from Computer Science is eligible for promotion? :No

CHAPTER 14

Observer Pattern

This chapter covers the Observer pattern.

GoF Definition

Define a one-to-many dependency between objects so that when one object changes state, all its dependents are notified and updated automatically.

Concept

In this pattern, there are many observers (objects) that are observing a particular subject (also an object). Observers want to be notified when there is a change made inside the subject. So, they register for that subject. When they lose interest in the subject, they simply unregister from the subject. Sometimes this model is called a Publisher-Subscriber (Pub-Sub) model. The whole idea can be summarized as follows: using this pattern, an object (subject) can send notifications to multiple observers (a set of objects) at the same time. Observers can decide how to respond to the notification, and they can perform specific actions based upon the notification.

You can visualize the scenarios with the following diagrams.

In step 1, three observers are requesting to get notifications from a subject (see Figure 14-1).

© Vaskaran Sarcar 2020
V. Sarcar, *Design Patterns in C#*, https://doi.org/10.1007/978-1-4842-6062-3_14

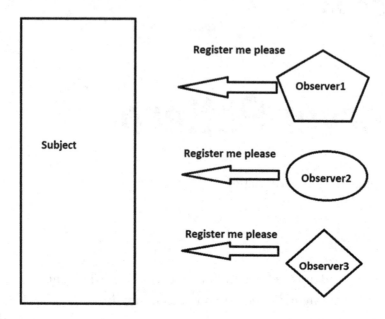

Figure 14-1. *Step 1*

In step 2, the subject can grant the requests; in other words, a connection is established (see Figure 14-2).

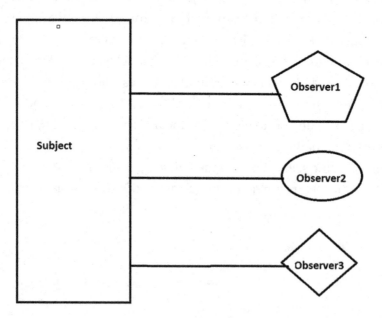

Figure 14-2. *Step 2*

In step 3, the subject is sending notifications to registered users (see Figure 14-3).

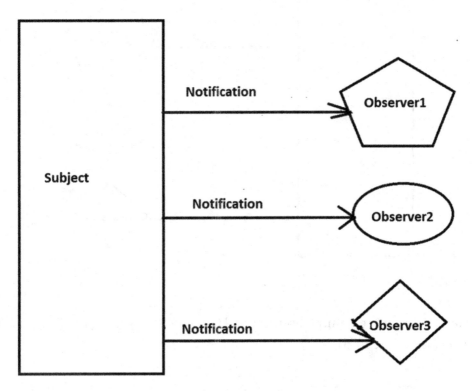

Figure 14-3. *Step 3*

In step 4 (optional), observer2 does not want to get further notifications and requests to unregister himself (or the subject doesn't want to keep observer2 in its notification list due to some specific reason, and he unregisters observer2). So, the connection between the subject and observer2 has been broken (see Figure 14-4).

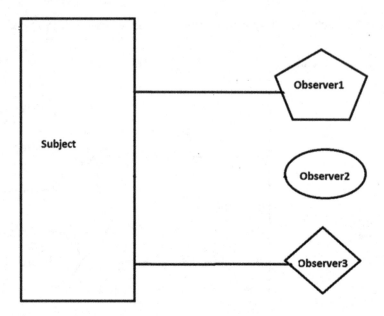

Figure 14-4. *Step 4*

In step 5, from now on, only Observer1 and Observer3 are getting notifications from the subject (see Figure 14-5).

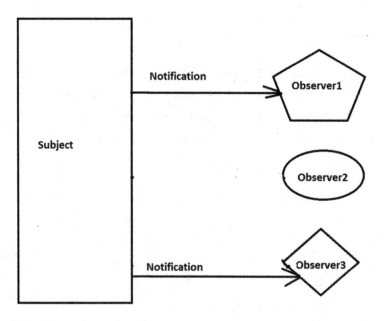

Figure 14-5. *Step 5*

Real-World Example

Think about a celebrity who has many followers on social media. Each of these followers wants to get all the latest updates from their favorite celebrity. So, they follow the celebrity until their interest wanes. When they lose interest, they simply do not follow that celebrity. Think of each of these fans or followers as an observer and the celebrity as the subject.

Computer-World Example

Let's consider a simple UI-based example in computer science. This UI is connected to some database. A user can execute a query through the UI, and after searching the database, the results are returned. With this pattern, you segregate the UI from the database. If a change occurs in the database, the UI should be notified so that it can update its display accordingly.

To simplify this scenario, assume that you are the person responsible for maintaining a database in your organization. Whenever there is a change made to the database, you want to get a notification so that you can take action if necessary. In this context, you can note the following points.

- You can see the presence of this pattern in any eventdriven software. Modern languages like C# have built-in support for handling these events following this pattern. These constructs make your life easier.

- If you are familiar with the .NET Framework, you see that in C#, you have generic `System.IObservable<T>` and `System.IObserver<T>` interfaces, in which the generic type parameter provides notifications.

Implementation

For this example, I created four observers (`Roy, Kevin, Bose`, and `Jacklin`) and two subjects (`Celebrity-1 and Celebrity-2`). A subject (in our example, `Celebrity`) maintains a list of all of its registered users. The observers receive a notification when the flag value changes in a subject.

Initially, three observers (Roy, Kevin, and Bose) registered themselves to get notifications from Celebrity-1. So, in the initial phase, all of them received notifications. But then, Kevin lost his interest in Celebrity-1. When Celebrity-1 became aware of this, he removes Kevin from his observer list. At this time, only Roy and Bose were receiving notifications (when the flag value is 50). But Kevin changed his mind later and wanted to get notifications again, so Celebrity-1 registers him again. This is why when Celebrity-1 sets the flag value to 100, all three observers have received notifications from him.

Later, you saw a celebrity named Celebrity-2. Roy and Jacklin are registered in his observer list. So, when Celebrity-2 sets the flag value to 500, both Roy and Jacklin have received the notification.

Let's look at the code. The following is the `IObserver` interface, which has an `Update(...)` method.

```
interface IObserver
{
    void Update(ICelebrity subject);
}
```

Two concrete classes—`ObserverType1` and `ObserverType2`—show you that you can have different types of observers. These classes implement the `IObserver` interface as follows.

```
// ObserverType1
class ObserverType1 : IObserver
{
    string nameOfObserver;
    public ObserverType1(String name)
    {
        this.nameOfObserver = name;
    }
    public void Update(ICelebrity celeb)
    {
        Console.WriteLine($"{nameOfObserver} has received an alert from
        {celeb.Name}.Updated value is: {celeb.Flag}");
    }
}
```

```
// ObserverType2
class ObserverType2 : IObserver
{
    string nameOfObserver;
    public ObserverType2(String name)
    {
        this.nameOfObserver = name;
    }
    public void Update(ICelebrity celeb)
    {
        Console.WriteLine($"{nameOfObserver} notified.Inside
        {celeb.Name}, the updated value is: {celeb.Flag}");
    }
}
```

The subject interface (ICelebrity) contains three methods called Register(...), Unregister(...), and NotifyRegisteredUsers(), which are easy to understand. These methods register an observer, unregister an observer, and notify all registered observers, respectively. The following is the ICelebrity interface.

```
interface ICelebrity
{
    // Name of Subject
    string Name { get; }
    int Flag { get; set; }
    // To register
    void Register(IObserver o);
    // To Unregister
    void Unregister(IObserver o);
    // To notify registered users
    void NotifyRegisteredUsers();
}
```

The Celebrity concrete class implements the ICelebrity interface. One important point is that this concrete class maintains a list of registered users. You see the following line of code inside this class.

```
List<IObserver> observerList = new List<IObserver>();
```

Note   In some examples of this pattern, you may see a slight variation where an abstract class is used instead of an interface (`ICelebrity`), and the list (`observerList`) is maintained in the abstract class. Both variations are fine. You can implement your preferred approach.

I used a constructor inside the `Celebrity` class. The constructor is as follows.

```
public Celebrity(string name)
{
    this.name = name;
}
```

I use this constructor for different celebrities. So, inside the client code, you see the following lines with comments.

```
Console.WriteLine("Working with first celebrity now.");
ICelebrity celebrity = new Celebrity("Celebrity-1");
// some other code
// Creating another celebrity
ICelebrity celebrity2 = new Celebrity("Celebrity-2");
```

Lastly, I used an expression-bodied property inside the `Celebrity` class. You can see it in this code segment.

```
//public string Name
//{
//    get
//    {
//        return name;
//    }
//}
// Or, simply use expression bodied
// properties(C# v6.0 onwards)
public string Name => name;
```

Note   If you have a version of C# prior to 6.0, then you can use the commented code block instead. The same comment applies to similar code in this book.

The remaining code is easy to understand. Follow the supportive comments if you want.

Class Diagram

Figure 14-6 shows the class diagram.

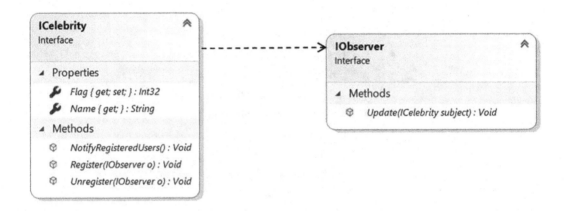

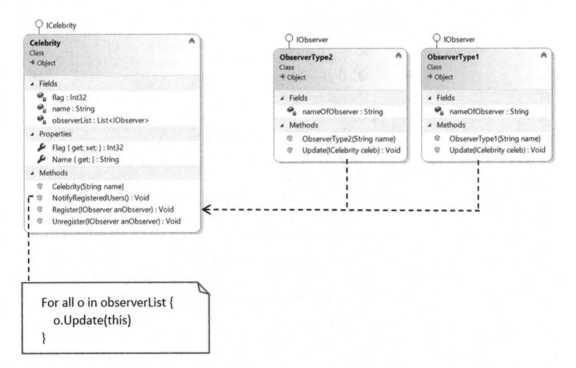

Figure 14-6. *The class diagram*

Solution Explorer View

Figure 14-7 shows the high-level structure of the program.

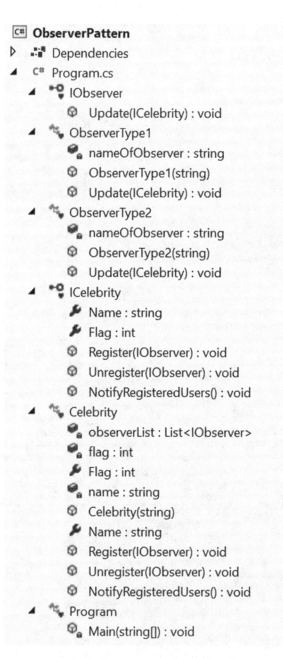

Figure 14-7. *Solution Explorer view*

Demonstration

Here's the complete demonstration.

```
using System;
// We have used List<Observer> here
using System.Collections.Generic;
namespace ObserverPattern
{
    interface IObserver
    {
        void Update(ICelebrity subject);
    }
    class ObserverType1 : IObserver
    {
        string nameOfObserver;
        public ObserverType1(String name)
        {
            this.nameOfObserver = name;
        }
        public void Update(ICelebrity celeb)
        {
            Console.WriteLine($"{nameOfObserver} has received an alert from
            {celeb.Name}. Updated value is: {celeb.Flag}");
        }
    }
    class ObserverType2 : IObserver
    {
        string nameOfObserver;
        public ObserverType2(String name)
        {
            this.nameOfObserver = name;
        }
        public void Update(ICelebrity celeb)
        {
```

```csharp
        Console.WriteLine($"{nameOfObserver} notified.Inside {celeb.
        Name}, the updated value is: {celeb.Flag}");
    }
}

interface ICelebrity
{
    // Name of Subject
    string Name { get; }
    int Flag { get; set; }
    // To register
    void Register(IObserver o);
    // To Unregister
    void Unregister(IObserver o);
    // To notify registered users
    void NotifyRegisteredUsers();

}
class Celebrity : ICelebrity
{
    List<IObserver> observerList = new List<IObserver>();
    private int flag;
    public int Flag
    {
        get
        {
            return flag;
        }
        set
        {
            flag = value;
            // Flag value changed. So notify observer(s).
            NotifyRegisteredUsers();
        }
    }
```

```csharp
    private string name;
    public Celebrity(string name)
    {
        this.name = name;
    }
    //public string Name
    //{
    //    get
    //    {
    //        return name;
    //    }
    //}
    // Or, simply use expression bodied
    // properties(C#6.0 onwards)
    public string Name => name;

    // To register an observer.
    public void Register(IObserver anObserver)
    {
        observerList.Add(anObserver);
    }
    // To unregister an observer.
    public void Unregister(IObserver anObserver)
    {
        observerList.Remove(anObserver);
    }
    // Notify all registered observers.
    public void NotifyRegisteredUsers()
    {
        foreach (IObserver observer in observerList)
        {
            observer.Update(this);
        }
    }
}
```

```csharp
class Program
{
    static void Main(string[] args)
    {
        Console.WriteLine("***Observer Pattern Demonstration.***\n");
        // We have 4 observers - 2 of them are ObserverType1, 1 is of
        // ObserverType2
        IObserver myObserver1 = new ObserverType1("Roy");
        IObserver myObserver2 = new ObserverType1("Kevin");
        IObserver myObserver3 = new ObserverType2("Bose");
        IObserver myObserver4 = new ObserverType2("Jacklin");
        Console.WriteLine("Working with first celebrity now.");
        ICelebrity celebrity = new Celebrity("Celebrity-1");
        // Registering the observers - Roy, Kevin, Bose
        celebrity.Register(myObserver1);
        celebrity.Register(myObserver2);
        celebrity.Register(myObserver3);
        Console.WriteLine(" Celebrity-1 is setting Flag = 5.");
        celebrity.Flag = 5;
        /*
        Kevin doesn't want to get further notification.
        So, unregistering the observer(Kevin)).
        */
        Console.WriteLine("\nCelebrity-1 is removing Kevin from the
        observer list now.");
        celebrity.Unregister(myObserver2);
        // No notification is sent to Kevin this time. He has
        // unregistered.
        Console.WriteLine("\n Celebrity-1 is setting Flag = 50.");
        celebrity.Flag = 50;
        // Kevin is registering himself again
        celebrity.Register(myObserver2);
        Console.WriteLine("\n Celebrity-1 is setting Flag = 100.");
        celebrity.Flag = 100;
```

```
            Console.WriteLine("\n Working with another celebrity now.");
            // Creating another celebrity
            ICelebrity celebrity2 = new Celebrity("Celebrity-2");
            // Registering the observers-Roy and Jacklin
            celebrity2.Register(myObserver1);
            celebrity2.Register(myObserver4);
            Console.WriteLine("\n --Celebrity-2 is setting Flag value as
            500.--");
            celebrity2.Flag = 500;

            Console.ReadKey();
        }
    }
}
```

Output

Here's the output.

Observer Pattern Demonstration.

Working with first celebrity now.
 Celebrity-1 is setting Flag = 5.
Roy has received an alert from Celebrity-1. Updated value is: 5
Kevin has received an alert from Celebrity-1. Updated value is: 5
Bose notified.Inside Celebrity-1, the updated value is: 5

Celebrity-1 is removing Kevin from the observer list now.

 Celebrity-1 is setting Flag = 50.
Roy has received an alert from Celebrity-1. Updated value is: 50
Bose notified.Inside Celebrity-1, the updated value is: 50

 Celebrity-1 is setting Flag = 100.
Roy has received an alert from Celebrity-1. Updated value is: 100
Bose notified.Inside Celebrity-1, the updated value is: 100
Kevin has received an alert from Celebrity-1. Updated value is: 100

Working with another celebrity now.

```
--Celebrity-2 is setting Flag value as 500.--
Roy has received an alert from Celebrity-2. Updated value is: 500
Jacklin notified.Inside Celebrity-2, the updated value is: 500
```

Q&A Session

14.1 If there is only one observer, then I do not need to set up the interface. Is this correct?

Yes. But if you want to follow the pure object-oriented programming guidelines, you may always prefer interfaces (or abstract classes) over a concrete class. Aside from this point, there are usually multiple observers, and you implement them following the contracts. That's where you benefit from this kind of design.

14.2 Can you have different type of observers?

Yes. Think about this in a real-world scenario. When anyone is making a crucial change in the organization's database, multiple groups of people from different departments may want to know about the change (such as your boss and the owner of the database, who work at different levels) and act accordingly. So, you may need to provide support for different type of observers in your application. This is why in this chapter, I showed you an example involving multiple observers with multiple celebrities.

14.3 Can you add or remove observers at runtime?

Yes. Notice that at the beginning of the program, to get notifications, Kevin registers himself. Later, he unregisters and then reregisters.

14.4 It appears to me that there are similarities between the Observer pattern and the Chain of Responsibility pattern (see Chapter 22). Is this correct?

In an Observer pattern, all registered users receive notifications at the same time; but in the Chain of Responsibility pattern, objects in the chain are notified one by one, which happens until an object handles the notification fully (or, you reach at the end of the chain). Figure 14-8 and Figure 14-9 summarize the differences.

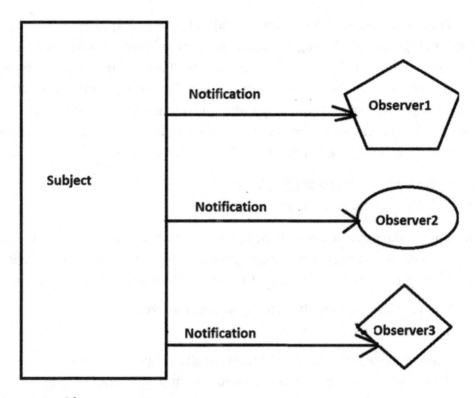

Figure 14-8. *Observer pattern*

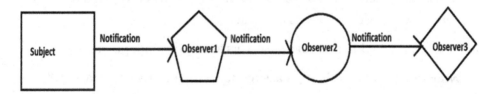

Figure 14-9. *Chain of Responsibility pattern*

In Figure 14-9, I assume that Observer3 was able to process the notification completely. So, it is the end node of the chain. In this case, you also need to remember that you may need to take special action if the notification reaches at the end of the chain, but no one handles it properly.

14.5 Does this model support one-to-many relationships?

Yes, the GoF definition confirms this. Since a subject can send notifications to multiple observers, this kind of dependency is depicting a one-to-many relationship.

14.6 There are ready-made constructs available (for example, System. IObservable<T>). Instead of using them, why are you writing your own code?

You cannot change ready-made functionalities, but I believe that when you try to implement the concept yourself, you better understand the ready-made constructs.

Another important point to note is that when you use the System.IObservable<T> and System.IObserver<T> interfaces, you need to be familiar with generic programming. Not only that, if you look closely at these interfaces, you see the following.

```
public interface IObservable<out T>
public interface IObserver<in T>
```

This simply means that you need to be familiar with covariance and contravariance in C# too. At first, these concepts may seem difficult. In my book *Getting Started with Advanced C#* (Apress, 2020), I discuss these concepts in detail with code examples.

14.7 What are the key benefits of the Observer pattern?

Here are some key advantages.

- Subjects (celebrities in our example) and their registered users (observers) make up a loosely coupled system. They do not need to know each other explicitly.

- You do not need to make changes to the subject when you add or remove an observer from its notification lists.

- Also, you can add or remove observers at runtime independently.

14.8 What are the key challenges associated with an Observer pattern?

Here are some key challenges when you implement (or use) this pattern.

- Undoubtedly, a memory leak is the greatest concern when you deal with events in C# (also known as a *lapsed listener problem*). An automatic garbage collector may not always help you in this context.

- The order of notification is not dependable.

CHAPTER 15

Strategy Pattern

This chapter covers the Strategy pattern. It is also known as the Policy pattern.

GoF Definition

Define a family of algorithms, encapsulates each one, and makes them interchangeable. Strategy lets the algorithm vary independently from clients that use it.

Concept

A client can select an algorithm from a set of algorithms dynamically at runtime. This pattern also provides a simple way to use the selected algorithm.

You know that an object can have states and behaviors. And some of these behaviors may vary among the objects of a class. This pattern focuses on the changing behaviors that can be associated with an object at a specific time.

In our example, you see a Vehicle class. You can create a vehicle object using this class. Once a Vehicle object is created, you can add and set behaviors to this object. Inside the client code, you can replace the current behavior with a new behavior too. Most interestingly, you see that since the behaviors can be changed, the vehicle class is *not* defining the behavior; it is simply delegating the task to an object referenced by a vehicle. The overall implementation can make the concept clearer to you.

Real-World Example

In a soccer match, if Team A is leading 1–0 over Team B toward the end of the game, instead of attacking, Team A becomes defensive to maintain the lead. At the same time, Team B goes for an all-out attack to score the equalizer.

© Vaskaran Sarcar 2020
V. Sarcar, *Design Patterns in C#*, https://doi.org/10.1007/978-1-4842-6062-3_15

Computer-World Example

Suppose that you have a backup memory slot. If your primary memory is full, but you need to store more data, you can use a backup memory slot. If you do not have this backup memory slot and you try to store the additional data into your primary memory, the data is discarded (when the primary memory is full). In these cases, you may get exceptions, or you may encounter some peculiar behavior (based on the architecture of the program). So, a runtime check is necessary before you store the data. Then you can proceed further.

Implementation

In this implementation, I focus on the changing behaviors of a vehicle only. In the implementation, you see that once a vehicle object is created, it is associated with an InitialBehavior, which simply states that in this state, the vehicle cannot do anything special. But once you set a FlyBehavior, the vehicle can fly. When you set the FloatBehavior, it can float. All *changing* behaviors are maintained in a separate hierarchy.

```
/// <summary>
/// Abstract Behavior
/// </summary>
public abstract class VehicleBehavior
{
    public abstract void AboutMe(string vehicle);
}
/// <summary>
/// Floating capability
/// </summary>
class FloatBehavior : VehicleBehavior
{
    public override void AboutMe(string vehicle)
    {
        Console.WriteLine($"My {vehicle} can float now.");
    }
}
```

```csharp
/// <summary>
/// Flying capability
/// </summary>
class FlyBehavior : VehicleBehavior
{
    public override void AboutMe(string vehicle)
    {
        Console.WriteLine($"My {vehicle} can fly now.");
    }
}
/// <summary>
/// Initial behavior. Cannot do anything special.
/// </summary>
class InitialBehavior : VehicleBehavior
{
    public override void AboutMe(string vehicle)
    {
Console.WriteLine($"My {vehicle} is just born. It cannot do anything special.");
    }
}
```

In many examples, you see a term called a *context class*. Vehicle is the context class in this demonstration. This class is defined as follows.

```csharp
/// <summary>
/// Context class-Vehicle
/// </summary>
public class Vehicle
{
    VehicleBehavior behavior;
    string vehicleType;
    public Vehicle(string vehicleType)
    {
        this.vehicleType = vehicleType;
        // Setting the initial behavior
        this.behavior = new InitialBehavior();
```

```
        }
        /*
         * It's your choice. You may prefer to use a setter
         * method instead of using a constructor.
         * You can call this method whenever we want
         * to change the "vehicle behavior" on the fly.
         */
        public void SetVehicleBehavior(VehicleBehavior behavior)
        {
            this.behavior = behavior;
        }
        /*
        This method will help us to delegate the behavior to
        the object referenced by vehicle.You do not know about the object
        type, but you simply know that this object can tell something about
        it, i.e. "AboutMe()" method
        */
        public void DisplayAboutMe()
        {
            behavior.AboutMe(vehicleType);
        }
    }
```

You can see, inside the constructor, I set the initial behavior, which can be altered later using the SetVehicleBehavior(...) method. DisplayAboutMe() delegates the task to a particular object.

Class Diagram

Figure 15-1 shows the important parts of the class diagram.

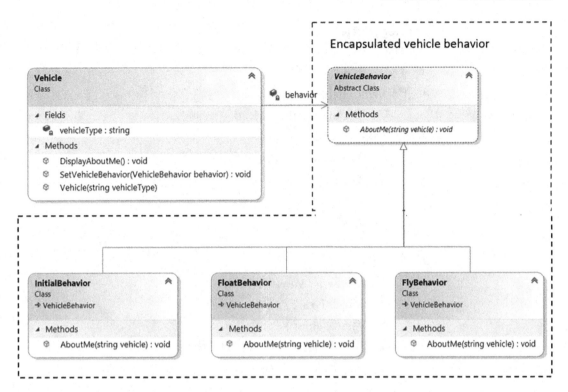

Figure 15-1. *Class diagram*

Solution Explorer View

Figure 15-2 shows the high-level structure of the program.

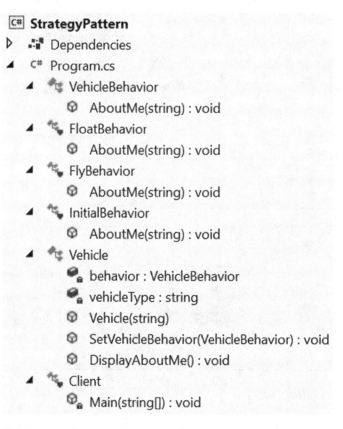

Figure 15-2. *Solution Explorer view*

Demonstration

Here's the implementation.

```
using System;

namespace StrategyPattern
{
    /// <summary>
    /// Abstract Behavior
    /// </summary>
    public abstract class VehicleBehavior
    {
        public abstract void AboutMe(string vehicle);
    }
```

```csharp
/// <summary>
/// Floating capability
/// </summary>
class FloatBehavior : VehicleBehavior
{
    public override void AboutMe(string vehicle)
    {
        Console.WriteLine($"My {vehicle} can float now.");
    }
}
/// <summary>
/// Flying capability
/// </summary>
class FlyBehavior : VehicleBehavior
{
    public override void AboutMe(string vehicle)
    {
        Console.WriteLine($"My {vehicle} can fly now.");
    }
}
/// <summary>
/// Initial behavior.Cannot do anything special.
/// </summary>
class InitialBehavior : VehicleBehavior
{
    public override void AboutMe(string vehicle)
    {
Console.WriteLine($"My{vehicle}is just born.It cannot do anything special.");
    }
}
/// <summary>
/// Context class-Vehicle
/// </summary>
public class Vehicle
{
```

```csharp
        VehicleBehavior behavior;
        string vehicleType;
        public Vehicle(string vehicleType)
        {
            this.vehicleType = vehicleType;
            //Setting the initial behavior
            this.behavior = new InitialBehavior();
        }
        /*
         * It's your choice. You may prefer to use a setter
         * method instead of using a constructor.
         * You can call this method whenever we want
         * to change the "vehicle behavior" on the fly.
         */
        public void SetVehicleBehavior(VehicleBehavior behavior)
        {
            this.behavior = behavior;
        }
        /*
        This method will help us to delegate the behavior to
        the object referenced by vehicle.You do not know about the object
        type, but you simply know that this object can tell something about
        it, i.e. "AboutMe()" method
        */
        public void DisplayAboutMe()
        {
            behavior.AboutMe(vehicleType);
        }
    }
    /// <summary>
    /// Client code
    /// </summary>
```

```
class Client
{
    static void Main(string[] args)
    {
        Console.WriteLine("***Strategy Pattern Demo.***\n");
        Vehicle context = new Vehicle("Aeroplane");
        context.DisplayAboutMe();
        Console.WriteLine("Setting flying capability to vehicle.");
        context.SetVehicleBehavior(new FlyBehavior());
        context.DisplayAboutMe();

        Console.WriteLine("Changing the vehicle behavior again.");
        context.SetVehicleBehavior(new FloatBehavior());
        context.DisplayAboutMe();

        Console.ReadKey();
    }
}
}
```

Output

Here's the output.

```
***Strategy Pattern Demo.***

My Aeroplane is just born.It cannot do anything special.
Setting flying capability to vehicle.
My Aeroplane can fly now.
Changing the vehicle behavior again.
My Aeroplane can float now.
```

Q&A Session

15.1 It appears to me that you are complicating everything by focusing on changing behaviors. Also, I do not understand why I need the Context class at all. You could simply use the inheritance mechanism and proceed. Can you please address these concerns?

If a behavior is common for all subtypes, it's okay to use inheritance, for example, you can make an abstract class and put the common behavior into it so that all child classes get the common behavior. But the real power of strategy comes into picture when the behaviors can vary across the objects, and maintaining them using inheritance is difficult.

For example, let's say that you start with different behaviors, and you place them in an abstract class as follows.

```
public abstract class Vehicle
{
    public abstract void AboutMe();
    public abstract void FloatBehavior();
    public abstract void FlyBehavior();

    public virtual void DefaultJob()
    {
        Console.WriteLine("By default, I float.");
    }
}
```

Now let's say that `Boat` and `Aeroplane` are two concrete classes that inherit from it. You know that a `Boat` object should not fly, so inside the `Boat` class, you can simply override `FlyBehavior` as follows.

```
public override void FlyBehavior()
{
    throw new NotImplementedException();
}
```

Similarly, an `Aeroplane` object should not float in water (in a normal situation). So, inside the `Aeroplane` class, you may override `FloatBehavior` as follows.

```
public override void FloatBehavior()
```

```
{
  throw new NotImplementedException();
}
```

Now consider when you have lots of changing behaviors across objects like these. This kind of maintenance can be overhead.

Apart from this, let's consider a special vehicle that has specialized features. If you simply put those special features in the abstract class, all other vehicle object inherits those and need to implement those. But it is not over yet. Further, assume that there is a constraint on the Boat class, which simply says that it cannot have any such special behavior. Now you encounter a deadlock situation. If you implement this special method, you are violating the constraint. If you do not implement it, the system architecture breaks because the language construct requires you to implement the behavior. (Or, you need to mark the class with the abstract keyword, but at the same time, remember that you cannot create an instance from an abstract class.)

To overcome this, I can create a separate inheritance hierarchy with an interface to hold all the specialized features, and my classes can implement the interface if needed. But again, it may solve the problem partially because the interface may contain multiple methods, and your class may need to implement only one of them. In the end, in any of these cases, the overall maintenance becomes tough. Apart from this, the special behaviors may change, and in that case, you need to track down all the classes that implement these behaviors.

In a situation like this, the context class acts as a savior. For example, for the Boat class object, the client does *not* set the fly behavior, or for Aeroplane class objects, the client does *not* set the float behavior; he simply knows which behavior is expected from the particular vehicle. So, if you want, you can guard against a situation in which a client mistakenly sets an incorrect behavior to a vehicle.

To simplify this, the context class holds a reference variable for the changing behavior and delegates the task to the appropriate behavior class. This is why you see the following segment in our Vehicle context class.

```
public class Vehicle
{
    VehicleBehavior behavior;
    //Some other code
```

```
/*
 * It's your choice. You may prefer to use a setter
 * method instead of using a constructor.
 * You can call this method whenever we want
 * to change the "vehicle behavior" on the fly.
 */
public void SetVehicleBehavior(VehicleBehavior behavior)
{
    this.behavior = behavior;
}
//Some other code
}
```

A "has-a" relationship fits better than an "is-a" relationship for this example, and it is one of the primary reasons that most of the design patterns encourage composition over inheritance.

15.2 What are the key advantages of using a Strategy design pattern?
Here are some of the key advantages.

- This design pattern makes your classes independent from algorithms. Here a class delegates the algorithms to the strategy object (that encapsulates the algorithm) dynamically at runtime. So, the choice of algorithms is not bound at compile time.

- It's easier to maintain your codebase.

- It's easily extendable.

You can refer to the answer in Q&A 15.1 in this context.

15.3 What are the key challenges associated with a Strategy design pattern?
The disadvantages can be summarized as follows.

- The addition of context classes causes more objects to exits in your application.

- Users of the application must be aware of different strategies; otherwise, the output may surprise them.

CHAPTER 16

Template Method Pattern

This chapter covers the Template Method pattern.

GoF Definition

Define the skeleton of an algorithm in an operation, deferring some steps to subclasses. Template method lets subclasses redefine certain steps of an algorithm without changing the algorithm's structure.

Concept

Using this pattern, you begin with the minimum or essential structure of an algorithm. Then you defer some responsibilities to the subclasses. As a result, the derived class can redefine some steps of an algorithm without changing the flow of the algorithm.

Simply, this design pattern is useful when you implement a multistep algorithm but allow customization through subclasses.

Real-World Example

When you order a pizza, the chef of the restaurant can use a basic mechanism to prepare the pizza, but he may allow you to select the final materials. For example, a customer can opt for different toppings such as bacon, onions, extra cheese, mushrooms, and so on. So, just before the delivery of the pizza, the chef can include these choices.

© Vaskaran Sarcar 2020
V. Sarcar, *Design Patterns in C#*, https://doi.org/10.1007/978-1-4842-6062-3_16

Computer-World Example

Suppose that you have been hired to design an online engineering degree course. You know that, in general, the first semester of the course is the same for all courses. For subsequent semesters, you need to add new papers or subjects to the application based on the course opted by a student.

The Template Method pattern makes sense when you want to avoid duplicate code in your application but allow subclasses to change some specific details of the base class workflow to bring varying behavior to the application. (However, you may not want to override the base methods entirely to make radical changes in the subclasses. In this way, the pattern differs from simple polymorphism.)

Implementation

Assume that each engineering student needs to pass mathematics and demonstrate soft skills (such as communication skills, people management skills, and so on) in their initial semesters to obtain their degrees. Later, you add special papers to their courses based on their chosen paths (computer science or electronics).

To serve the purpose, a template method `DisplayCourseStructure()` is defined in an abstract class `BasicEngineering,` which is as follows.

```
/// <summary>
/// Basic skeleton of actions/steps
/// </summary>
public abstract class BasicEngineering
{
    //The following method(step) will NOT vary
    private void Math()
    {
        Console.WriteLine("1.Mathematics");
    }
    //The following method(step) will NOT vary
    private  void SoftSkills()
```

```
    {
        Console.WriteLine("2.SoftSkills");
    }
    /*
    The following method will vary.It will be
    overridden by derived classes.
    */

    public abstract void SpecialPaper();

    //The "Template Method"
    public void DisplayCourseStructure()
    {
        //Common Papers:
        Math();
        SoftSkills();
        //Specialized Paper:
        SpecialPaper();
    }
}
```

Note that subclasses of `BasicEngineering` cannot alter the flow of
`DisplayCourseStructure()` method, but they can override the `SpecialPaper()` method
to include course-specific details and make the final course list different from each other.

The concrete classes called `ComputerScience` and `Electronics` are the subclasses of
`BasicEngineering,` and they take the opportunity to override the `SpecialPaper()` method.
The following code segment shows such a sample from the `ComputerScience` class.

```
//The concrete derived class-ComputerScience
public class ComputerScience : BasicEngineering
{
  public override void SpecialPaper()
  {
        Console.WriteLine("3.Object-Oriented Programming");
  }
}
```

Class Diagram

Figure 16-1 shows the important parts of the class diagram.

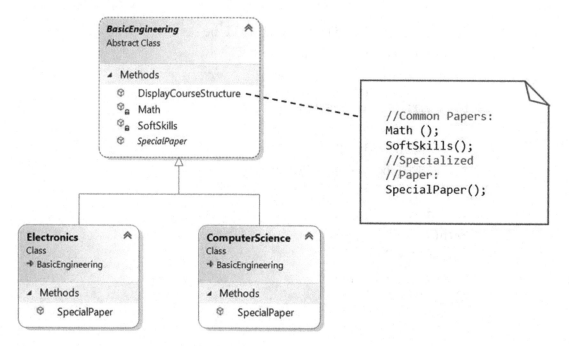

Figure 16-1. *Class diagram*

Solution Explorer View

Figure 16-2 shows the high-level structure of the program.

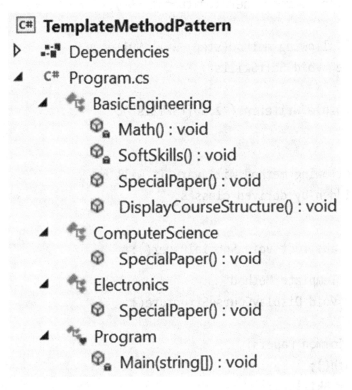

Figure 16-2. *Solution Explorer view*

Demonstration 1

Here's the implementation.

```
using System;

namespace TemplateMethodPattern
{
    /// <summary>
    /// Basic skeleton of actions/steps
    /// </summary>
    public abstract class BasicEngineering
    {
```

```csharp
//The following method(step) will NOT vary
private void Math()
{
    Console.WriteLine("1.Mathematics");
}
//The following method(step) will NOT vary
private  void SoftSkills()
{
    Console.WriteLine("2.SoftSkills");
}
/*
The following method will vary.It will be
overridden by derived classes.
*/

public abstract void SpecialPaper();

//The "Template Method"
public void DisplayCourseStructure()
{
    //Common Papers:
    Math();
    SoftSkills();
    //Specialized Paper:
    SpecialPaper();
}
}

//The concrete derived class-ComputerScience
public class ComputerScience : BasicEngineering
{
    public override void SpecialPaper()
    {
        Console.WriteLine("3.Object-Oriented Programming");
    }
}
```

```csharp
//The concrete derived class-Electronics
public class Electronics : BasicEngineering
{
    public override void SpecialPaper()
    {
        Console.WriteLine("3.Digital Logic and Circuit Theory");
    }
}

//Client code
class Program
{
    static void Main(string[] args)
    {
        Console.WriteLine("***Template Method Pattern Demonstration--
        1.***\n");
        BasicEngineering bs = new ComputerScience();
        Console.WriteLine("Computer Science course includes the
        following subjects:");
        bs.DisplayCourseStructure();
        Console.WriteLine();
        bs = new Electronics();
        Console.WriteLine("Electronics course includes the following
        subjects:");
        bs.DisplayCourseStructure();
        Console.ReadLine();
    }
}
}
```

```
***Template Method Pattern Demonstration-1.***

Computer Science course includes the following subjects:
1.Mathematics
2.SoftSkills
3.Object-Oriented Programming

Electronics course includes the following subjects:
1.Mathematics
2.SoftSkills
3.Digital Logic and Circuit Theory
```

Q&A Session

16.1 In this pattern, subclasses can simply redefine the methods based on their needs. Is this correct?

Yes.

16.2 In the abstract class BasicEngineering, **only one method is abstract, and the other two methods are concrete methods. What is the reason behind this?**

This is a simple example with only three methods, and you want the subclasses to override only the SpecialPaper() method here. Other methods are common to both courses, and they do not need to be overridden by the subclasses.

16.3 Suppose that you want to add some more methods in the BasicEngineering **class, but you want to work on those methods if and only if your child classes need them; otherwise, you ignore them. This type of situation is common in some PhD programs where some courses are mandatory, but if a student has certain qualifications, the student may not need to attend the lectures for those subjects. Can you design this kind of situation with the Template Method pattern?**

Yes, you can. Basically, you want to use a hook, which is a method that can help you to control the flow in an algorithm.

To show an example of this kind of design, now I add one more method in BasicEngineering called IncludeAdditionalPaper(). Let's assume that by default, this subject is included in the course list, but electronics students can opt-out of this course.

The modified BasicEngineering class now looks like the following (note the bold lines that indicate the important changes).

```csharp
/// <summary>
/// Basic skeleton of actions/steps
/// </summary>
public abstract class BasicEngineering
{
    //The following method(step) will NOT vary
    private void Math()
    {
        Console.WriteLine("1.Mathematics");
    }
    //The following method(step) will NOT vary
    private void SoftSkills()
    {
        Console.WriteLine("2.SoftSkills");
    }
    /*
    The following method will vary.It will be
    overridden by derived classes.
    */

    public abstract void SpecialPaper();

    //The "Template Method"
    public void DisplayCourseStructure()
    {
        //Common Papers:
        Math();
        SoftSkills();
        //Specialized Paper:
        SpecialPaper();
```

```
        //Include an additional subject if required.
        if (IsAdditionalPaperNeeded())
        {
            IncludeAdditionalPaper();
        }
    }

    private void IncludeAdditionalPaper()
    {
        Console.WriteLine("4.Compiler Design.");
    }
    //A hook method.
    //By default,an additional subject is needed
    public virtual bool IsAdditionalPaperNeeded()
    {
        return true;
    }
}
```

Since Electronics class doesn't need to include the additional method, it is defined as follows:

```
//The concrete derived class-Electronics
public class Electronics : BasicEngineering
{
    public override void SpecialPaper()
    {
        Console.WriteLine("3.Digital Logic and Circuit Theory");
    }
    //Using the hook method now.
    //Additional paper is not needed for Electronics.
    public override bool IsAdditionalPaperNeeded()
    {
        return false;
    }

}
```

Let's go through the program and output now.

Demonstration 2

Here's the modified implementation. The key changes are shown in bold.

```
using System;

namespace TemplateMethodPattern
{
    /// <summary>
    /// Basic skeleton of actions/steps
    /// </summary>
    public abstract class BasicEngineering
    {
        //The following method(step) will NOT vary
        private void Math()
        {
            Console.WriteLine("1.Mathematics");
        }
        //The following method(step) will NOT vary
        private void SoftSkills()
        {
            Console.WriteLine("2.SoftSkills");
        }
        /*
        The following method will vary.It will be
        overridden by derived classes.
        */

        public abstract void SpecialPaper();

        //The "Template Method"
        public void DisplayCourseStructure()
        {
            //Common Papers:
            Math();
```

```
            SoftSkills();
            //Specialized Paper:
            SpecialPaper();
    ·       //Include an additional subject if required.
            if (IsAdditionalPaperNeeded())
            {
                IncludeAdditionalPaper();
            }
        }

        private void IncludeAdditionalPaper()
        {
            Console.WriteLine("4.Compiler Design.");
        }
        //A hook method.
        //By default,an additional subject is needed.
        public virtual bool IsAdditionalPaperNeeded()
        {
            return true;
        }
    }

    //The concrete derived class-ComputerScience
    public class ComputerScience : BasicEngineering
    {
        public override void SpecialPaper()
        {
            Console.WriteLine("3.Object-Oriented Programming");
        }
        //Not tested the hook method.
        //An additional subject is needed
    }

    //The concrete derived class-Electronics
    public class Electronics : BasicEngineering
    {
```

```csharp
    public override void SpecialPaper()
    {
        Console.WriteLine("3.Digital Logic and Circuit Theory");
    }
    //Using the hook method now.
    //Additional paper is not needed for Electronics.
    public override bool IsAdditionalPaperNeeded()
    {
        return false;
    }

}

//Client code
class Program
{
    static void Main(string[] args)
    {
        Console.WriteLine("***Template Method Pattern Demonstration--
        2.***\n");
        BasicEngineering bs = new ComputerScience();
        Console.WriteLine("Computer Science course includes the
        following subjects:");
        bs.DisplayCourseStructure();
        Console.WriteLine();
        bs = new Electronics();
        Console.WriteLine("Electronics course includes the following
        subjects:");
        bs.DisplayCourseStructure();
        Console.ReadLine();
    }
}
}
```

Output

Here's the modified output.

```
***Template Method Pattern Demonstration-2.***

Computer Science course includes the following subjects:
1.Mathematics
2.SoftSkills
3.Object-Oriented Programming
```
4.Compiler Design.

```
Electronics course includes the following subjects:
1.Mathematics
2.SoftSkills
3.Digital Logic and Circuit Theory
```

Note   You may prefer an alternative approach. For example, you could directly include the default method called IncludeAdditionalPaper() in BasicEngineering. After that, you could override the method in the Electronics class and make the method body empty. But this approach does not look better when you compare it to the previous approach.

16.4 It looks like this pattern is similar to the Builder pattern. Is this correct?

No. Don't forget the core intent; the Template Method pattern is a behavioral design pattern, and Builder is a creational design pattern. In the Builder pattern, the clients/customers are the bosses. They can control the order of the algorithm. In the Template Method pattern, you (or the developers) are the boss. You put your code in a central location (for example, the abstract class BasicEngineering.cs in this example), and you have absolute control over the flow of the execution, which cannot be altered by the client. For example, you can see that Mathematics and SoftSkills always appear at the top, following the execution order in the template method DisplayCourseStructure(). The clients need to obey this flow.

If you alter the flow in your template method, other participants will also follow the new flow.

16.5 What are the key advantages of using a Template Method design pattern?

Here are some of the key advantages.

- You can control the flow of the algorithms. Clients cannot change them.

- Common operations are in a centralized location. For example, in an abstract class, the subclasses can redefine only the varying parts so that you can avoid redundant code.

16.6 What are the key challenges associated with a Template Method design pattern?

The disadvantages can be summarized as follows.

- The client code cannot direct the sequence of steps. If you want that type of functionality, use the Builder pattern.

- A subclass can override a method defined in the parent class (in other words, hiding the original definition in the parent class), which can go against the Liskov substitution principle that basically says that if S is a subtype of T, then objects of type T can be replaced with objects of type S.

- Having more subclasses means more scattered code and difficult maintenance.

16.7 What happens if a subclass tries to override the other parent methods in BasicEngineering?

This pattern suggests not to do that. When you use this pattern, you should not override all the parent methods entirely to bring a radical change in the subclasses. In this way, it differs from simple polymorphism.

16.8 How does this pattern differ from the Strategy pattern?

You have identified a good point. Yes, the Strategy and the Template Method patterns have similarities. In Strategy, you can vary the entire algorithm using delegation; however, the Template Method pattern suggests that you vary certain steps in an algorithm using inheritance, but the overall flow of the algorithm is unchanged.

CHAPTER 17

Command Pattern

This chapter covers the Command pattern.

GoF Definition

Encapsulate a request as an object, thereby letting you parameterize clients with different requests, queue, or log requests, and support undoable operations.

Concept

Using this pattern, you encapsulate a method invocation process. Here an object can invoke an operation through some crystalized method and doesn't worry about how to perform the operation. This pattern is among those patterns that are normally tough to understand by merely reading the description. The concept becomes clearer when you see the implementations. So, stay with me and keep reading until you see demonstration 1.

In general, four terms are important here: *invoker, client, command,* and *receiver,* which are as follows.

- The command object consists of the actions that a receiver performs.

- A *command* object can invoke a method of the receiver in a way that is specific to that receiver's class. The *receiver* then starts processing the job (or the action).

- A command object is separately passed to the *invoker* object to invoke the command. The invoker object contains the crystallized methods through which a client can perform a job without worrying about how the target receiver performs the actual job.

- The *client* object holds the invoker object and the command objects. The client only makes the decision (i.e., which commands to execute) and then passes the command to the invoker object for execution.

© Vaskaran Sarcar 2020
V. Sarcar, *Design Patterns in C#*, https://doi.org/10.1007/978-1-4842-6062-3_17

Real-World Example

When you are drawing a picture, you may need to redraw (undo) some parts of it to make it better.

Computer-World Example

In general, you can observe this pattern in the menu system of an editor or integrated development environment (IDE). For example, you can use the Command pattern to support undo, multiple undos, or similar operations in a software application.

Microsoft uses this pattern in Windows Presentation Foundation (WPF). A 2012 article that appeared in *Visual Studio Magazine* (`https://visualstudiomagazine.com/articles/2012/04/10/command-pattern-in-net.aspx`) describes it in detail.

> *The command pattern is well suited for handling GUI interactions. It works so well that Microsoft has integrated it tightly into the Windows Presentation Foundation (WPF) stack. The most important piece is the ICommand inter- face from the System.Windows.Input namespace. Any class that imple- ments the ICommand interface can be used to handle a keyboard or mouse event through the common WPF controls. This linking can be done either in XAML or in a code-behind.*

In addition, if you are familiar with Java or Swing, you see that Action is also a command object.

Implementation

In this example, RemoteControl is the Invoker class. GameStartCommand and GameStartCommand are concrete classes to represent commands. These two classes implement the common interface ICommand, which is as follows (the associated comments state the purpose of each method).

```
public interface ICommand
{
    // To execute a command
    void Execute();
    // To undo last command execution
    void Undo();
}
```

The Game is the receiver class, which has the following definition.

```
public class Game
{
  string gameName;
  public Game(string name)
    {
      this.gameName = name;
    }
  public void Start()
    {
      Console.WriteLine($"{gameName} is on.");
    }
  public void DisplayScore()
    {
      Console.WriteLine("The score is changing time to time.");
    }
  public void Finish()
    {
      Console.WriteLine($"---The game of {gameName} is over.----");
    }
}
```

When the client uses a GameStopCommand command and calls the ExecuteCommand method on an Invoker object as follows.

```
invoker.ExecuteCommand();
```

The target receiver (Game class object in this example) performs the following action only.

```
game.Finish();
```

But when the client uses a GameStartCommand command and calls the ExecuteCommand method on an Invoker object using the same code as follows.

```
invoker.ExecuteCommand();
```

The target receiver (Game class object in this example) performs the following set of actions.

```
game.Start();
game.DisplayScore();
```

So, you can see that a command doesn't need to perform only a single action; instead, based on your needs, you can perform a series of actions on a target receiver and encapsulate them in a command object.

POINTS TO NOTE

The examples in this chapter show simple demonstrations of undo operations. The implementation of an undo depends on the specification and can be complex in some scenarios. For demonstration 1, I simply assume that an undo call simply undoes the last command that was performed successfully. The Execute() and Undo() methods of the GameStartCommand and GameStopCommand classes are doing the opposite. That is, when a client invokes an undo operation using GameStopCommand, the game restarts and displays the score (which is a simple console message in this example). But if the client invokes the undo operation using GameStartCommand, the game stops immediately. It's similar to switching on a light and switching off the same light; or adding a number to a target number and as a reverse case, substrating the same number from the resultant number again.

Lastly, look at the following code segments, which is how I create a command object.

```
Game gameName = new Game("Golf");
// Command to start the game
GameStartCommand gameStartCommand = new GameStartCommand(gameName);
```

I set the command to an invoker and use its ExecuteCommand() method to execute the command. Later, I undo this again. I kept the console messages to help you understand.

```
Console.WriteLine("**Starting the game and performing undo
immediately.**");
invoker.SetCommand(gameStartCommand);
invoker.ExecuteCommand();
```

```
// Performing undo operation
Console.WriteLine("\nUndoing the previous command now.");
invoker.UndoCommand();
```

Class Diagram

Figure 17-1 shows the class diagram.

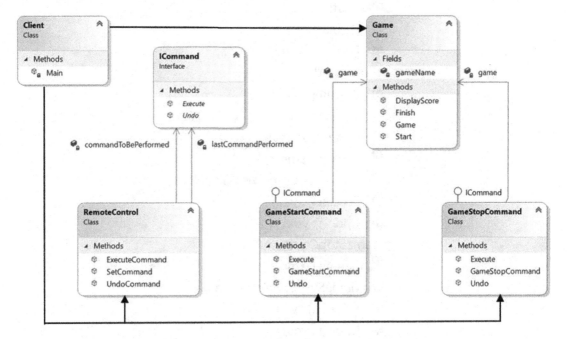

Figure 17-1. *Class diagram*

Solution Explorer View

Figure 17-2 shows the high-level structure of the program.

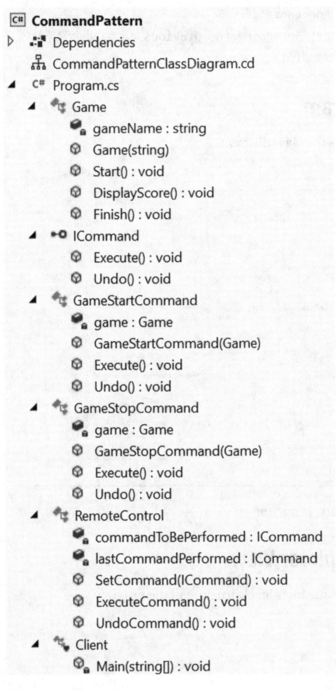

Figure 17-2. *Solution Explorer view*

Demonstration 1

Here's the complete program.

```csharp
using System;

namespace CommandPattern
{
    /// <summary>
    ///  Receiver Class
    /// </summary>
    public class Game
    {
        string gameName;
        public Game(string name)
        {
            this.gameName = name;
        }
        public void Start()
        {
            Console.WriteLine($"{gameName} is on.");
        }
        public void DisplayScore()
        {
            Console.WriteLine("The score is changing time to time.");
        }
        public void Finish()
        {
            Console.WriteLine($"---The game of {gameName} is over.---");
        }

    }
    /// <summary>
    /// The command interface
    /// </summary>
```

```csharp
public interface ICommand
{
    // To execute a command
    void Execute();
    // To undo last command execution
    void Undo();

}
/// <summary>
/// GameStartCommand
/// </summary>
public class GameStartCommand : ICommand
{
    private Game game;
    public GameStartCommand(Game game)
    {
        this.game = game;
    }
    public void Execute()
    {
        game.Start();
        game.DisplayScore();
    }

    public void Undo()
    {
        Console.WriteLine("Undoing start command.");
        game.Finish();
    }
}
/// <summary>
/// GameStopCommand
/// </summary>
```

```
public class GameStopCommand : ICommand
{
    private Game game;
    public GameStopCommand(Game game)
    {
        this.game = game;
    }
    public void Execute()
    {
        Console.WriteLine("Finishing the game.");
        game.Finish();
    }

    public void Undo()
    {
        Console.WriteLine("Undoing stop command.");
        game.Start();
        game.DisplayScore();
    }
}

/// <summary>
/// Invoker class
/// </summary>
public class RemoteControl
{
    ICommand commandToBePerformed, lastCommandPerformed;
    public void SetCommand(ICommand command)
    {
        this.commandToBePerformed = command;
    }
    public void ExecuteCommand()
    {
        commandToBePerformed.Execute();
        lastCommandPerformed = commandToBePerformed;
    }
```

```csharp
        public void UndoCommand()
        {
            // Undo the last command executed
            lastCommandPerformed.Undo();
        }
    }
    /// <summary>
    /// Client code
    /// </summary>
    class Client
    {
        static void Main(string[] args)
        {
            Console.WriteLine("***Command Pattern Demonstration***\n");

            /* Client holds both the Invoker and Command Objects */
            RemoteControl invoker = new RemoteControl();

            Game gameName = new Game("Golf");
            // Command to start the game
            GameStartCommand gameStartCommand = new
            GameStartCommand(gameName);
            // Command to stop the game
            GameStopCommand gameStopCommand = new
            GameStopCommand(gameName);

            Console.WriteLine("**Starting the game and performing undo
            immediately.**");
            invoker.SetCommand(gameStartCommand);
            invoker.ExecuteCommand();
            // Performing undo operation
            Console.WriteLine("\nUndoing the previous command now.");
            invoker.UndoCommand();

            Console.WriteLine("\n**Starting the game again.Then stopping it
            and undoing the stop operation.**");
            invoker.SetCommand(gameStartCommand);
```

```
            invoker.ExecuteCommand();
            // Stop command to finish the game
            invoker.SetCommand(gameStopCommand);
            invoker.ExecuteCommand();
            // Performing undo operation
            Console.WriteLine("\nUndoing the previous command now.");
            invoker.UndoCommand();

            Console.ReadKey();
        }
    }
}
```

Output

Here's the output.

```
***Command Pattern Demonstration***

**Starting the game and performing undo immediately.**
Golf is on.
The score is changing time to time.

Undoing the previous command now.
Undoing start command.
---The game of Golf is over.---

**Starting the game again.Then stopping it and undoing the stop
operation.**
Golf is on.
The score is changing time to time.
Finishing the game.
---The game of Golf is over.---

Undoing the previous command now.
Undoing stop command.
Golf is on.
The score is changing time to time.
```

Q&A Session

17.1 The GoF definition starts with "Encapsulate a request." How are you implementing the encapsulation in demonstration 1?

The command object contains the set of actions that target a specific receiver. When you set the command and invoke ExecuteCommand() on the invoker object, the intended actions are performed at the receiver's end. From the outside, no other objects know how this happens; they simply know that if they call ExecuteCommand(), their requests are processed.

17.2 Following the GoF definition, how did you parameterize other objects with different requests?

Note that I first set GameStartCommand in invoker, and later, I replaced it with GameStopCommand. Invoker object simply invoked ExecuteCommand() in both cases.

17.3 In this example, you are dealing with a single receiver only. How do you deal with multiple receivers?

In this example, Game is the receiver class, but no one restricts you from creating a new class and following the implementation that is shown in demonstration 1. Also, note that you created a Game class object using the following line.

```
Game gameName = new Game("Golf");
```

Since the Game class constructor accepts a string parameter, you could also pass a different value and create a different object. The following code segment is a sample.

```
Console.WriteLine("\nPlaying another game now.(Optional for you)");

gameName = new Game("Soccer");
// Command to start the game
gameStartCommand = new GameStartCommand(gameName);
// Command to stop the game
gameStopCommand = new GameStopCommand(gameName);

// Starting the game
invoker.SetCommand(gameStartCommand);
invoker.ExecuteCommand();
```

```
// Stopping the game
invoker.SetCommand(gameStopCommand);
invoker.ExecuteCommand();
```

The previous code segment can generate the following output as expected:
Playing another game now.(Optional for you)
Soccer is on.
The score is changing time to time.
Finishing the game.
---The game of Soccer is over.---

17.4 Can I ignore the invoker object?

Most of the time, programmers try to encapsulate data and the corresponding methods in object-oriented programming (OOP). But you find that in the Command pattern, you are trying to encapsulate command objects. In other words, you are implementing encapsulation from a different perspective.

I told you earlier that when ExecuteCommand() of the invoker object is called, the intended actions are performed at the receiver's end. From the outside, no other object knows how it happens; they simply know that if they call ExecuteCommand(), their requests are processed. So, simply an invoker contains some crystalized method through which a client can perform a job without worrying about how the actual job is performed at the receiver's end.

This approach makes sense when you need to deal with a complex set of commands.

Let's review the terms again. You create command objects that you pass to some receivers to access them, and you execute those commands through an invoker that calls the methods of the command objects (for example, ExecuteCommand in this example). For a simple use case, this invoker class is not mandatory. For example, consider a case in which a command object has only one method to execute, and you are trying to dispense with the invoker to invoke the method. But invokers may play an important role when you want to keep track of a series of commands in a log file (or in a queue).

17.5 Why would you want to keep track of these logs?

You may want to create undo or redo operations.

17.6 What are the key advantages associated with the Command pattern?
Here are some advantages.

- Requests for the creation and the ultimate execution are decoupled. Clients may not know how an invoker is performing the operations.

- You can create macro commands (these are sequences of multiple commands and can be invoked together. For example, for macro command, you can create a class that has a constructor to accept a list of commands. And in its Execute() method, you can invoke Execute() of these commands sequentially using a for loop/foreach loop).

- New commands can be added without affecting the existing system.

- Most importantly, you can support the much-needed undo (and redo) operations.

- It should be noted that once you simply create a command object, it does not mean that the computation starts immediately. You could schedule it for later or place them in a job queue and execute them later. Also, by using a thread pool, you can execute them asynchronously in a multithreaded environment. (Asynchronous programming is discussed in Chapter 27 of this book.)

17.7 What are the challenges associated with the Command pattern?
Here are some of the disadvantages.

- To support more commands, you need to create more classes. So, maintenance can be difficult as time goes on.

- How to handle errors or make a decision about what to do with return values when an erroneous situation occurs becomes tricky. A client may want to know about those. But here you decouple the command with client code, so these situations are difficult to handle. The challenge becomes significant in a multithreaded environment where the invoker can run in a different thread.

17.8 In demonstration 1, you are undoing only the last command? Is there any way to implement "undo all"? Also, how do you log requests?

Good question. You can simply maintain a stack that can store the commands, and then you can simply pop the items from your stack and invoke its undo() method. In Chapter 19 (on the Memento pattern, which is similar to this pattern), I further discuss the undos and various implementations. For now, let me show you a simple example, in which you can undo all the previous commands. Demonstration 2 is made for that. It's a simple modification of demonstration 1, so class diagram and solution explorer view are omitted; you can directly jump into the implementation.

You have asked another question on how to log the requests. In demonstration 2, when I maintain the list to store the commands that execute, I use this list to support "undo all commands" using a single method invocation. The same list can serve as a history of commands which you can print in the console. Or, you can make a separate file to maintain the details each time a command executes. Later you can retrieve the file for a detailed look if necessary.

Modified Implementation

This example shows you a way to invoke multiple undo operations. There are some small changes made to the invoker class. I maintain a list to store all the commands that execute. Whenever a command is executed, it is added in the list, and later when I call UndoAll(), I can simply iterate over this list and call the corresponding undo operations. The invoker is shown with key changes in bold as follows.

```
/// <summary>
/// Invoker class
/// </summary>
public class RemoteControl
{
  ICommand commandToBePerformed, lastCommandPerformed;
  List<ICommand> savedCommands = new List<ICommand>();
  public void SetCommand(ICommand command)
  {
    this.commandToBePerformed = command;
  }
}
```

```
public void ExecuteCommand()
{
   commandToBePerformed.Execute();
   lastCommandPerformed = commandToBePerformed;
   savedCommands.Add(commandToBePerformed);
}
public void UndoCommand()
{
   // Undo the last command executed
   lastCommandPerformed.Undo();
}
public void UndoAll()
{
   for (int i = savedCommands.Count; i > 0; i--)
   {
      // Get a restore point and call Undo()
      savedCommands[i - 1].Undo();
   }
}
}
```

The Game class does not have the Start() method now; instead, it has two new methods called UpLevel() and DownLevel(), as follows.

```
public void UpLevel()
{
 ++level;
 Console.WriteLine("Level upgraded.");
}
public void DownLevel()
{
 --level;
 Console.WriteLine("Level downgraded.");
}
```

The UpLevel() method upgrades the level of the game. The DownLevel() method does the reverse, so it is used in the Undo operation of the GameStartCommand class. To serve my key purpose (showing you "undo all"), I do not need the GameStopCommand class in this example, so to make the example short and simple, I omitted that class too. Lastly, I made a simple assumption that when the game level is set to 0 (i.e., in the born state), if you execute Undo(), the game stops. The remaining code is easy to understand, and you can go through demonstration 2 now.

Demonstration 2

Here's complete program.

```
using System;
using System.Collections.Generic;

namespace CommandPatternDemonstration2
{
    // Receiver Class
    public class Game
    {
        string gameName;
        public int level;
        public Game(string name)
        {
            this.gameName = name;
            level = -1;
            Console.WriteLine($"Game started.");
        }
        public void DisplayLevel()
        {
            Console.WriteLine($"Current level is set to {level}.");
        }
        public void UpLevel()
        {
            ++level;
            Console.WriteLine("Level upgraded.");
        }
```

```
    public void DownLevel()
    {
        --level;
        Console.WriteLine("Level downgraded.");
    }
    public void Finish()
    {
        Console.WriteLine($"---The game of {gameName} is over.---");
    }

}
public interface ICommand
{
    void Execute();
    void Undo();

}
/// <summary>
/// GameStartCommand
/// </summary>
public class GameStartCommand : ICommand
{
    private Game game;
    public GameStartCommand(Game game)
    {
        this.game = game;
    }
    public void Execute()
    {
        game.UpLevel();
        game.DisplayLevel();
    }

    public void Undo()
    {
        if (game.level > 0)
        {
```

```
            game.DownLevel();
            game.DisplayLevel();
        }
        else
        {
            game.Finish();
        }
    }
}

/// <summary>
/// Invoker class
/// </summary>
public class RemoteControl
{
    ICommand commandToBePerformed, lastCommandPerformed;
    List<ICommand> savedCommands = new List<ICommand>();
    public void SetCommand(ICommand command)
    {
        this.commandToBePerformed = command;
    }
    public void ExecuteCommand()
    {
        commandToBePerformed.Execute();
        lastCommandPerformed = commandToBePerformed;
        savedCommands.Add(commandToBePerformed);
    }

    public void UndoCommand()
    {
        // Undo the last command executed
        lastCommandPerformed.Undo();
    }
    public void UndoAll()
    {
        for (int i = savedCommands.Count; i > 0; i--)
```

```csharp
        {
            // Get a restore point and call Undo()
            savedCommands[i - 1].Undo();
        }
    }
}
/// <summary>
/// Client code
/// </summary>
class Client
{
    static void Main(string[] args)
    {
        Console.WriteLine("***Command Pattern Demonstration2***\n");

        // Client holds both the Invoker and Command Objects
        RemoteControl invoker = new RemoteControl();

        Game gameName = new Game("Golf");
        // Command to start the game
        GameStartCommand gameStartCommand = new GameStartCommand(gameName);

        Console.WriteLine("**Starting the game and upgrading the level
        3 times.**");
        invoker.SetCommand(gameStartCommand);
        invoker.ExecuteCommand();
        invoker.ExecuteCommand();
        invoker.ExecuteCommand();

        // Performing undo operation(s) one at a time
        //invoker.UndoCommand();
        //invoker.UndoCommand();
        //invoker.UndoCommand();
```

```
        Console.WriteLine("\nUndoing all the previous commands at one shot.");
        invoker.UndoAll();
        Console.ReadKey();
      }
    }
}
```

Output

Here's the new output.

```
***Command Pattern Demonstration2***

Game started.
**Starting the game and upgrading level 3 times.**
Level upgraded.
Current level is set to 0.
Level upgraded.
Current level is set to 1.
Level upgraded.
Current level is set to 2.

Undoing all the previous commands at one shot.
Level downgraded.
Current level is set to 1.
Level downgraded.
Current level is set to 0.
---The game of Golf is over.---
```

CHAPTER 18

Iterator Pattern

This chapter covers the Iterator pattern.

GoF Definition

Provide a way to access the elements of an aggregate object sequentially without exposing its underlying representation.

Concept

Iterators are generally used to traverse a container (or a collection of objects) to access its elements without knowing how the data are stored internally. It is very useful when you need to traverse different kinds of collection objects in a standard and uniform way. Figure 18-1 shows a sample and most common diagram for an Iterator pattern.

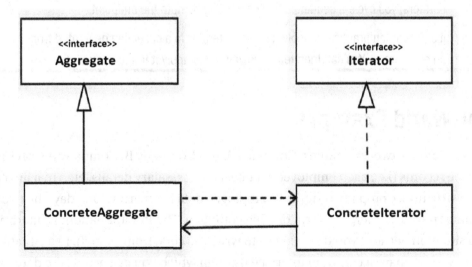

Figure 18-1. *A sample diagram for an Iterator pattern*

© Vaskaran Sarcar 2020
V. Sarcar, *Design Patterns in C#*, https://doi.org/10.1007/978-1-4842-6062-3_18

The participants are described as follows.

- **Iterator** is an interface that accesses or traverses elements.

- **ConcreteIterator** implements the `Iterator` interface methods. It can also keep track of the current position in the traversal of the aggregate.

- **Aggregate** defines an interface that can create an `Iterator` object.

- **ConcreteAggregate** implements the `Aggregate` interface. It returns an instance of the `ConcreteIterator`.

POINTS TO NOTE

- It is frequently used to traverse the nodes of a tree-like structure. In many examples, you may notice the Iterator pattern with the Composite pattern.

- The role of an iterator is not limited to traversing. This role can vary to support various requirements. For example, you can filter the elements in various ways.

- Clients cannot see the actual traversal mechanism. A client program only uses public iterator methods.

- The concept of iterators and enumerators has existed for a long time. Enumerators produce the next element based on a criterion, whereas using iterators, you cycle a sequence from a starting point to the endpoint.

- It's a common practice to apply a foreach iterator to a collection generated from an enumerator. You can then fetch the value and apply it in the body of the loop.

Real-World Example

Suppose there are two companies: Company A and Company B. Company A stores its employee records (i.e., each employee's name, address, salary details, etc.) in a linked list data structure. Company B stores its employee data in an array. One day, the two companies decide to merge to form one big company. The Iterator pattern is handy in such a situation because you do need not to write the code from scratch. In a situation like this, you can have a common interface through which you can access the data for both companies. So, you can simply call those methods without rewriting the code.

Consider another example. Suppose your company has decided to promote some employees based on their performances. So, all the managers get together and set a common criterion for promotion. Then they iterate over the records of the employees one by one to mark the potential candidates for promotion.

You can consider the example from a different domain too. For example, when you store songs in your preferred audio devices (for example, into an MP3 player) or your mobile devices, you can iterate over them through various button press or swipe movements. The basic idea is to provide you a mechanism so that you can iterate over your list smoothly.

Computer-World Example

Go through the following two bullet points. These are common examples of Iterator pattern.

- C# has iterators that were introduced in Visual Studio 2005. The `foreach` statement is frequently used in this context. To learn more about these built-in functionalities, refer to `https://docs. microsoft.com/en-us/dotnet/csharp/iterators`.

- If you are familiar with Java, you may have used Java's built-in `Iterator` interface, `java.util.Iterator`. This pattern is used in interfaces like `java.util.Iterator` or `java.util.Enumeration`.

Implementation

Similar to our real-world example, let's assume that there is a college with two departments: the sciences and the arts. The arts department uses an array data structure to maintain its course details, but the science department is using a linked list data structure to keep the same. The administrative department does not interfere with how a department maintains these details. It is simply interested in getting the data from each department and wants to access the data uniformly. Now assume you are a member of the administrative department, and at the beginning of a new session, you want to advertise the curriculum using the iterators. Let's see how we can implement it in the upcoming demonstration.

Let's assume that you have an iterator called IIterator, which acts as the common interface in the upcoming example, and it currently supports four basic methods: First(), Next(), CurrentItem(), and IsCollectionEnds(), which are as follows.

- The First() method reset the pointer to the first element before you start traversing a data structure.

- The Next() method returns the next element in the container.

- The CurrentItem() method returns the current element of the container that the iterator is pointing at a particular time.

- The IsCollectionEnds() validates whether any next element is available for further processing or not. So, this method helps you to decide whether you have reached the end of your container.

These methods are implemented in each of the ScienceIterator and ArtsIterator classes. You'll see that the CurrentItem() method is defined differently in the ScienceIterator and ArtIterator classes. Also, to print the curriculum, I used only two of these methods: IsCollectionEnds() and Next(). If you want, you can experiment with the two remaining methods, First() and currentItem(). I mentioned the four methods and provided some sample implementations for them because they are very common in Iterator pattern implementations. These sample implementations can help you understand those examples too.

POINT TO NOTE

The code size of the program can be halved if you consider either the sciences or the arts subjects only. But I kept them both to show you that the Iterator pattern can help you to traverse without knowing how the data are stored internally. For sciences, the subjects are stored in a linked list, but for arts, subjects are stored in an array. Still, by using this pattern, you can traverse and print the subjects in a uniform way.

Class Diagram

Figure 18-2 shows the class diagram.

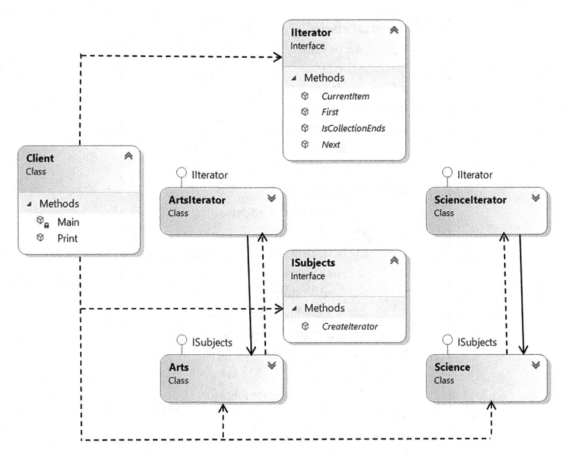

Figure 18-2. *Class diagram*

Solution Explorer View

Figure 18-3 shows the high-level structure of the program. It's a big program and tough to accommodate everything properly in a single screenshot, so I expanded only the details for the Science department.

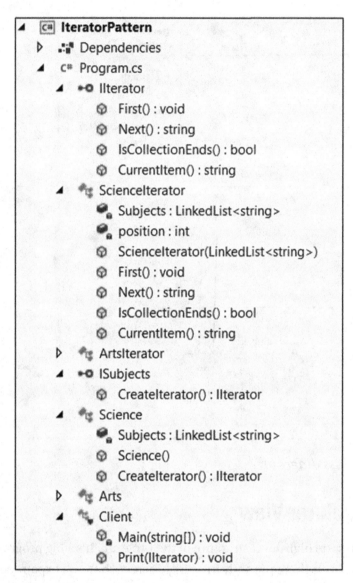

Figure 18-3. Solution Explorer view

Demonstration 1

Here's the implementation.

```
using System;
using System.Collections.Generic;
using System.Linq;
```

```csharp
namespace IteratorPattern
{
    #region Iterator
    public interface IIterator
    {
        // Reset to first element
        void First();
        // Get next element
        string Next();
        // End of collection check
        bool IsCollectionEnds();
        // Retrieve Current Item
        string CurrentItem();
    }

    /// <summary>
    ///   ScienceIterator
    /// </summary>
    public class ScienceIterator : IIterator
    {
        private LinkedList<string> Subjects;
        private int position;

        public ScienceIterator(LinkedList<string> subjects)
        {
            this.Subjects = subjects;
            position = 0;
        }

        public void First()
        {
            position = 0;
        }

        public string Next()
        {
            return Subjects.ElementAt(position++);
        }
```

```csharp
        public bool IsCollectionEnds()
        {
            if (position < Subjects.Count)
            {
                return false;
            }
            else
            {
                return true;
            }
        }

        public string CurrentItem()
        {
            return Subjects.ElementAt(position);
        }
    }
    /// <summary>
    ///  ArtsIterator
    /// </summary>
    public class ArtsIterator : IIterator
    {
        private string[] Subjects;
        private int position;
        public ArtsIterator(string[] subjects)
        {
            this.Subjects = subjects;
            position = 0;
        }
        public void First()
        {
            position = 0;
        }
```

```csharp
    public string Next()
    {
        //Console.WriteLine("Currently pointing to the subject: "+
        this.CurrentItem());
        return Subjects[position++];
    }

    public bool IsCollectionEnds()
    {
        if (position >= Subjects.Length)
        {
            return true;
        }
        else
        {
            return false;
        }
    }

    public string CurrentItem()
    {
        return Subjects[position];
    }
}
#endregion

#region Aggregate

public interface ISubjects
{
    IIterator CreateIterator();
}
public class Science : ISubjects
{
    private LinkedList<string> Subjects;
```

```csharp
        public Science()
        {
            Subjects = new LinkedList<string>();
            Subjects.AddFirst("Mathematics");
            Subjects.AddFirst("Computer Science");
            Subjects.AddFirst("Physics");
            Subjects.AddFirst("Electronics");
        }

        public IIterator CreateIterator()
        {
            return new ScienceIterator(Subjects);
        }
    }
    public class Arts : ISubjects
    {
        private string[] Subjects;

        public Arts()
        {
            Subjects = new[] { "English", "History", "Geography",
            "Psychology" };
        }

        public IIterator CreateIterator()
        {
            return new ArtsIterator(Subjects);
        }
    }
    #endregion

    /// <summary>
    /// Client code
    /// </summary>
    class Client
    {
        static void Main(string[] args)
        {
```

```
        Console.WriteLine("***Iterator Pattern Demonstration.***");
        // For Science
        ISubjects subjects= new Science();
        IIterator iterator = subjects.CreateIterator();
        Console.WriteLine("\nScience subjects :");
        Print(iterator);

        // For Arts
        subjects = new Arts();
        iterator = subjects.CreateIterator();
        Console.WriteLine("\nArts subjects :");
        Print(iterator);

        Console.ReadLine();
    }
    public static void Print(IIterator iterator)
    {
        while (!iterator.IsCollectionEnds())
        {
            Console.WriteLine(iterator.Next());
        }
    }
    }
    }

}
```

Output

Here's the output.

```
***Iterator Pattern Demonstration.***

Science subjects :
Electronics
Physics
Computer Science
Mathematics
```

```
Arts subjects :
English
History
Geography
Psychology
```

Note   You may use two or more different data structures in an implementation to demonstrate the power of this pattern. You have seen that in the previous demonstration, I used the `First ()`, `Next()`, `IsCollectionEnds()`, and `CurrentItem()` methods with different implementations that vary due to their internal data structures.

One use of `CurrentItem()` is also shown in the commented code. If you want to test it, you can uncomment the line.

Demonstration 2

Now let's look at another implementation using C#'s built-in support for iterator pattern. I used the IEnumerable interface, so you do not need to define a custom iterator. But to use this interface, you need to include the following line at the beginning of the program.

```
using System.Collections;
```

If you see the definition in Visual Studio, it describes the following.

```
//
// Summary:
//      Exposes an enumerator, which supports a simple iteration over a
//      non-generic collection.
[NullableContextAttribute(1)]
public interface IEnumerable
{
 //
 // Summary:
 //      Returns an enumerator that iterates through a collection.
 //
```

```
// Returns:
//  An System.Collections.IEnumerator object that can be used to iterate
//  through the collection.
IEnumerator GetEnumerator();
}
```

So, you can easily predict that each concrete iterator needs to implement the GetEnumerator() method. In the following implementation (demonstration 2), both concrete iterators define it as follows.

```
public IEnumerator GetEnumerator()
{
 foreach( string subject in Subjects)
  {
    yield return subject;
  }
}
```

You may wonder about the yield return. Microsoft discusses it at https://docs. microsoft.com/en-us/dotnet/csharp/language-reference/keywords/yield.

> *When you use the yield contextual keyword in a statement, you indicate that the method, operator, or get accessor in which it appears is an iterator. Using yield to define an iterator removes the need for an explicit extra class (the class that holds the state for an enumeration, see IEnumerator<T> for an example) when you implement the IEnumerable and IEnumerator pattern for a custom collection type.*

> *You use a yield return statement to return each element one at a time. The sequence returned from an iterator method can be consumed by using a foreach statement or LINQ query. Each iteration of the foreach loop calls the iterator method. When a yield return statement is reached in the iterator method, expression is returned, and the current location in code is retained. Execution is restarted from that location the next time that the iterator function is called.*

These comments are self-explanatory. In short, the foreach of GetEnumerator can remember where it was after last yield return and can give you the next value.

In the upcoming demonstration, the remaining code is easy to understand. Since the overall concept and intent are similar to demonstration 1, now you can directly jump to demonstration 2. Here's the complete implementation.

```csharp
using System;
using System.Collections;
using System.Collections.Generic;

namespace SimpleIterator
{
    public class Arts : IEnumerable
    {
        private string[] Subjects;

        public Arts()
        {
            Subjects = new[] { "English", "History", "Geography",
            "Psychology" };
        }

        public IEnumerator GetEnumerator()
        {
            foreach (string subject in Subjects)
            {
                yield return subject;
            }
        }
    }

    public class Science : IEnumerable
    {
        private LinkedList<string> Subjects;

        public Science()
        {
            Subjects = new LinkedList<string>();
            Subjects.AddFirst("Mathematics");
            Subjects.AddFirst("Computer Science");
            Subjects.AddFirst("Physics");
```

```
        Subjects.AddFirst("Electronics");
    }

    public IEnumerator GetEnumerator()
    {
        foreach (string subject in Subjects)
        {
            yield return subject;
        }
    }
}
class Program
{
    static void Main(string[] args)
    {
        Console.WriteLine("***Iterator Pattern.A simple demonstration
        using built-in constructs.***");
        Arts artsPapers = new Arts();
        Console.WriteLine("\nArts subjects are as follows:");
        /*
          Consume values from the
          collection's GetEnumerator()
         */
        foreach (string subject in artsPapers)
        {
            Console.WriteLine(subject);
        }

        Science sciencePapers = new Science();
        Console.WriteLine("\nScience subjects are as follows:");
        /*
          Consume values from the
          collection's GetEnumerator()
         */
        foreach (string subject in sciencePapers)
        {
```

```
            Console.WriteLine(subject);
        }

    }

    }

}
```

Output

Here's the output.

```
***Iterator Pattern.A simple demonstration using built-in constructs.***

Arts subjects are as follows:
English
History
Geography
Psychology

Science subjects are as follows:
Electronics
Physics
Computer Science
Mathematics
```

Q&A Session

18.1 What is the Iterator pattern used for?
The following discusses some of its usage.

- You can traverse an object structure without knowing its internal details. As a result, if you have a collection of different subcollections (for example, your container is mixed with arrays, lists, linked lists, and so on), you can still traverse the overall collection and deal with the elements in a universal way without knowing the internal details or differences among them.

- You can traverse a collection in different ways. If they are designed properly, multiple traversals are also possible in parallel.

18.2 What are the key challenges associated with this pattern?

You must make sure that no accidental modification has taken place during the traversal procedure.

18.3 But to deal with the challenge mentioned earlier, you can simply take a backup and then proceed. Am I right?

Taking a backup and re-examining it later is a costly operation.

18.4 In the code, I see a region named `Aggregate`. Is there any reason behind that naming?

An aggregate defines an interface to create an `Iterator` object. I adopted the name from the GoF book.

18.5 Throughout the discussion, you have talked about collections. What is a collection?

When you manage (or create) a related group of objects, in C#, you have the following choices.

- You can consider arrays.

- You can consider collections.

Collections are preferred in many cases because they can grow or shrink dynamically. In some collections, you can even assign keys to objects so that you can retrieve them at a later stage more efficiently with those keys. (For example, a dictionary is such a collection that is often used for fast lookups.) Lastly, a collection is a class, so before you add elements to it, you need to create instances. Here's an example.

```
LinkedList<string> Subjects = new LinkedList<string>();
Subjects.AddLast("Maths");
Subjects.AddLast("Comp. Sc.");
Subjects.AddLast("Physics");
```

In this example, instead of `AddFirst()` method, I used the `AddLast()` method for a variation. Both methods are available and in-built in C#. The `AddLast()` method adds the node at the end of the `LinkedList<T>`, whereas the `AddFirst()` method adds the node at the beginning of `LinkedList<T>`.

18.6 In this implementation, you could simply consider using either of the science or arts subjects to demonstrate an implementation of an Iterator pattern and reduce the code size. Is this correct?

Yes, and I mentioned it before. But when you use two different data structures, you may visualize the real power of the Iterator design pattern. So, I kept them both here.

CHAPTER 19

Memento Pattern

This chapter covers the Memento pattern.

GoF Definition

Without violating encapsulation, capture and externalize an object's internal state so that the object can be restored to this state later.

Concept

The word *memento* is a reminder of past events. By following an object-oriented approach, you can also track (or save) the states of an object. So, whenever you want to restore an object to its previous state, you can consider using this pattern.

In this pattern, you commonly see three participants: memento, originator, and caretaker (often used as a client). The working flow can be summarized as follows: The originator object has an internal state, and a client can set a state in it. To save the current internal state of the originator, a client (or caretaker) requests a memento from it. A client can also pass a memento (which it holds) back to the originator to restore a previous state. By following the proper approach, these saving and restoring operations do not violate encapsulation.

Real-World Example

You can see a classic example of the Memento pattern in the states of a finite state machine. It is a mathematical model, but one of its simplest applications is a turnstile. A turnstile has some rotating arms, which initially are locked. When you go through it (for example, putting some coins in), the locks are open, and the arms can rotate. Once you pass through, the arms return to a locked state.

© Vaskaran Sarcar 2020
V. Sarcar, *Design Patterns in C#*, https://doi.org/10.1007/978-1-4842-6062-3_19

Computer-World Example

In a drawing application, you may need to revert to an older state. Also, in database transactions, you may need to roll back some specific transactions. Memento patterns can be used in those scenarios.

Implementation

The following are some important suggestions from the GoF.

- A memento saves an originator's internal state.

- Only the originator should create the mementos. Later it can use a memento to restore a previous internal state.

- A caretaker class is the container of mementos. This class is used for memento's safekeeping, but it never operates or examines the content of a memento. A caretaker can get the memento from the originator.

Note   In this pattern, the originator sees a wide interface, whereas a caretaker sees a narrow interface. The caretaker is not allowed to make any changes to mementos. So, the memento object should be used as an opaque object.

A memento design pattern can have varying implementation using different techniques. In this chapter, you see two demonstrations. Demonstration 1 is relatively simple and easy to understand. But it is improved in demonstration 2. In both implementations, I did *not* use a separate caretaker class; instead, I used the client code to play the role of the caretaker.

In demonstration 1, the caretaker holds an Originator object and asks for memento objects from it. It holds the mementos in a list. So, you see the following lines of code inside the client.

```
Originator originatorObject = new Originator();
Memento currentMemento;
IList<Memento> savedStates = new List<Memento>();
/*
```

Adding a memento the list. This memento stores
the current state of the Originator.
*/
savedStates.Add(originatorObject.CurrentMemento());

The memento class is very simple, and it has a simple getter-setter to get or set the state of an originator. The class is as follows.

```
class Memento
    {
        private string state;
        public string State
        {
            get
            {
                return state;
            }
            set
            {
                state = value;
            }
        }
    }
```

Note From C# 3.0 onward, you can make the code size shorter by using automatic properties such as public string State { get; set; }.

Apart from the state, the Originator class has a constructor and two methods called CurrentMemento()and RestoreMemento(...). The first one supplies a memento in response to a caretaker request and is defined as follows.

```
        public Memento CurrentMemento()
        {
            myMemento = new Memento();
            myMemento.State = state;
            return myMemento;
        }
```

The second one restores the originator to a previous state. This state is contained in a memento (that comes as a method argument) from the caretaker. The caretaker can send the mementos that it saved earlier. This method is defined as follows.

```
public void RestoreMemento(Memento restoreMemento)
{
    this.state = restoreMemento.State;
    Console.WriteLine($"Restored to state : {state}");
}
```

The remaining code is easy but refer to the comments to get a better understanding.

Class Diagram

Figure 19-1 shows the class diagram.

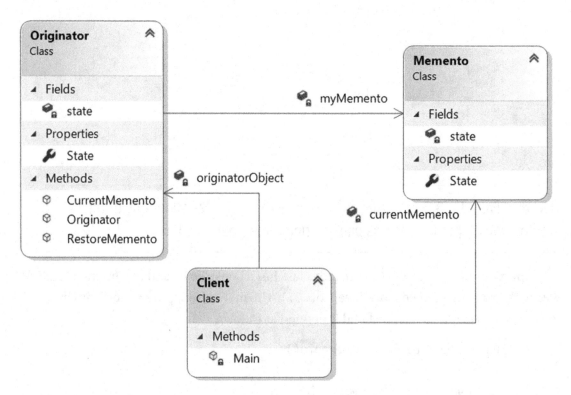

Figure 19-1. *Class diagram*

Solution Explorer View

Figure 19-2 shows the high-level structure of the program.

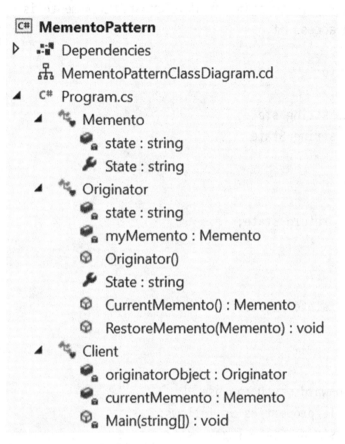

Figure 19-2. Solution Explorer view

Demonstration 1

Here's the implementation.

```
using System;
using System.Collections.Generic;

namespace MementoPattern
{
/// <summary>
/// Memento class
```

```csharp
/// As per GoF:
/// 1.A Memento object stores the snapshot of Originator's
/// internal state.
/// 2.Ideally,only the originator that created a memento is
/// allowed to access it.
/// </summary>
    class Memento
    {
        private string state;
        public string State
        {
            get
            {
                return state;
            }
            set
            {
                state = value;
            }
        }
        /*
        C#3.0 onwards, you can use
        automatic properties as follows:
        public string State { get; set; }
        */

    }

/// <summary>
/// Originator class
/// As per GoF:
/// 1.It creates a memento that contains a snapshot of
/// its current internal state.
/// 2.It uses a memento to restore its internal state.
/// </summary>
```

```csharp
class Originator
{
    private string state;
    Memento myMemento;
    public Originator()
    {
        //Creating a memento with born state.
        state = "Snapshot #0.(Born state)";
        Console.WriteLine($"Originator's current state is: {state}");

    }
    public string State
    {
        get { return state; }
        set
        {
            state = value;
            Console.WriteLine($"Originator's current state is:
            {state}");
        }
    }

    /*
    Originator will supply the memento
    (which contains it's current state)
    in respond to caretaker's request.
    */
    public Memento CurrentMemento()
    {
        myMemento = new Memento();
        myMemento.State = state;
        return myMemento;
    }
```

```csharp
        // Back to an old state (Restore)
        public void RestoreMemento(Memento restoreMemento)
        {
            this.state = restoreMemento.State;
            Console.WriteLine($"Restored to state : {state}");
        }
    }

/// <summary>
/// The 'Caretaker' class.
/// As per GoF:
/// 1.This class is responsible for memento's safe-keeping.
/// 2.Never operates or Examines the content of a Memento.

/// Additional notes( for your reference):
/// The originator object has an internal state, and a client can set a
/// state in it.A client(or, caretaker) requests a memento from the
/// originator to save the current internal state of the originator).
/// It can also pass a memento back to the originator to restore it
/// to a previous state that the memento holds in it.This enables to save
/// and restore the internal state of an originator without violating its
/// encapsulation.
/// </summary>

    class Client
    {
        static Originator originatorObject;
        static Memento currentMemento;
        static void Main(string[] args)
        {
            Console.WriteLine("***Memento Pattern Demonstration-1.***\n");
            //Originator is initialized.The constructor will create a
            born state.
            originatorObject = new Originator();
            //Memento currentMemento;
            IList<Memento> savedStates = new List<Memento>();
```

```csharp
/*
 Adding a memento the list.This memento stores
 the current state of the Origintor.
*/
savedStates.Add(originatorObject.CurrentMemento());

//Snapshot #1.
originatorObject.State = "Snapshot #1";
//Adding this memento as a  restore point
 savedStates.Add(originatorObject.CurrentMemento());

//Snapshot #2.
originatorObject.State = "Snapshot #2";
//Adding this memento as a  restore point
savedStates.Add(originatorObject.CurrentMemento());

//Snapshot #3.
originatorObject.State = "Snapshot #3";
//Adding this memento as a  restore point
savedStates.Add(originatorObject.CurrentMemento());

//Snapshot #4. It is not added as a restore point.
originatorObject.State = "Snapshot #4";

//Available restore points
Console.WriteLine("\nCurrently available restore points are :");
foreach (Memento m in savedStates)
{
    Console.WriteLine(m.State);
}

//Undo's
//Roll back starts...
Console.WriteLine("\nPerforming undo's now.");
for (int i = savedStates.Count; i > 0; i--)
{
    //Get a restore point
    currentMemento = savedStates[i - 1];
    originatorObject.RestoreMemento(currentMemento);
}
```

```
        //Redo's
        Console.WriteLine("\nPerforming redo's now.");
        for (int i = 1; i < savedStates.Count; i++)
        {
            currentMemento = savedStates[i];
            originatorObject.RestoreMemento(currentMemento);
        }
        // Wait for user
        Console.ReadKey();
    }
  }
}
```

Output

Here's the output.

```
***Memento Pattern Demonstration-1.***

Originator's current state is: Snapshot #0.(Born state)
Originator's current state is: Snapshot #1
Originator's current state is: Snapshot #2
Originator's current state is: Snapshot #3
Originator's current state is: Snapshot #4

Currently available restore points are :
Snapshot #0.(Born state)
Snapshot #1
Snapshot #2
Snapshot #3

Performing undo's now.
Restored to state : Snapshot #3
Restored to state : Snapshot #2
Restored to state : Snapshot #1
Restored to state : Snapshot #0.(Born state)
```

```
Performing redo's now.
Restored to state : Snapshot #1
Restored to state : Snapshot #2
Restored to state : Snapshot #3
```

Analysis

Using the concept of this program, you can use three different variations of undo operations, as follows.

- You can go back to the previous restore point.

- You can go back to your specified restore point (directly using the index property). For example, to go back directly to Snapshot #2, you can use the following lines of code:

  ```
  //Directly going back to Snapshot #2
   currentMemento = savedStates[2];
   originatorObject.RestoreMemento(currentMemento);
  ```

- You can revert all the restore points (which is shown using a for loop and an index property)

Note   If an application is using the Memento pattern and there is a state which is a mutable reference type, you may see the implementation of a deep copy technique to store the state inside the Memento object. You learned about deep copy in Chapter 2.

Q&A Session

19.1 Can you use a nongeneric version, such as ArrayList, in the previous example?
I like to follow the advice of the experts, who generally prefer generic versions over nongeneric versions. This is why I like data structures such as List, Dictionary, and so on, over their counterparts, like ArrayList and HashTable. I discuss generics in detail in two of my earlier books: *Interactive C#* (Apress, 2017) and *Getting Started with Advanced C#* (Apress, 2020).

19.2 What are the key advantages of using the Memento design pattern?
Here are some of the advantages.

- The biggest advantage is that you can always discard the unwanted changes and restore them to an intended or stable state.

- You do not compromise with the encapsulation associated with the key objects that are participating in this model.

- You can maintain high cohesion.

- It provides an easy recovery technique.

19.3 What are the key challenges associated with the Memento design pattern?
Here are some of the disadvantages.

- Having more mementos requires more storage. In addition, they put an additional burden on a caretaker.

- The previous point increases maintenance costs.

- You cannot ignore the time it takes to save these states, which can decrease the overall performance of the application.

Note that in a language such as C# or Java, developers may prefer to use serialization/deserialization techniques instead of directly implementing the Memento design pattern. Each of these techniques has its pros and cons, but you can combine both techniques in your application.

19.4 I'm confused. To support undo operations, which pattern should I use— Memento or Command?
The GoF said that these are related patterns. It primarily depends on how you want to handle the situation. Suppose you are adding 25 to an integer. After this addition operation, you can undo it by doing a reverse operation. Simply put, $50 + 25 = 75$, so $75 - 25 = 50$. In this type of operation, you do not need to store the previous state.

But consider a situation where you need to store the state of your objects prior to the operation. In this case, you use Memento. For example, in a paint application, you can avoid the cost of undoing some painting operations by storing the list of objects before executing the commands. This stored list can be treated as mementos, and you can keep this list with the associated commands. A similar concept applies to a long-running game application that has multiple levels and in which you save your last performance level. So, an application can use both patterns to support undo operations.

In the end, you must remember that storing a memento object is mandatory in the Memento pattern so that you can revert to a previous state. In the Command pattern, it is not necessary to store the commands. Once you execute a command, its job is done. If you do not support "undo" operations, you may not be interested in storing these commands at all.

19.5 I understand that a caretaker should not operate on mementos. So, demonstration 1 is fine. But I see that inside the client code, I can create a Memento object and set a state using the following lines of code, and no one is blocking me. Is this correct?

```
//For Q&A session only(Shouldn't be used)
currentMemento = new Memento();
currentMemento.State = "Arbitrary state set by caretaker";
```

Good catch. It is the potential drawback of demonstration 1. For a caretaker class, try to remember the following points from the GoF.

- This class is responsible for the memento's safekeeping.

- It never operates or examines the content of a memento.

In demonstration 2, I took care of these points. So, go through it; it is a relatively complicated example.

Modified Implementation

In this example, I tried to block direct access to a memento from the client code. The following are some of the important changes.

- The Memento class has a private constructor. As a result, this class cannot be initialized using a new operator outside.

- The Memento class is nested inside the Originator class and placed in a separate file (Originator.cs). I also made the Memento class internal.

- To accommodate these changes, the CurrentMemento() method is modified as follows:

  ```
  public Memento CurrentMemento()
  ```

```
    {
            //Code segment used in Demonstration-1
            //myMemento = new Memento();//error now
            //myMemento.State = state;
            //return myMemento;

            //Modified code for Demonstration-2
            return new Memento(this.State);
    }
```

The caretaker (client) is very similar to demonstration 1, except this time, you need to use **Originator.Memento** instead of Memento. Let's go through demonstration 2 now.

Class Diagram

Figure 19-3 shows the modified class diagram. (Note that the association lines can go to the outermost shapes but not to the nested types in Visual Studio class diagrams.)

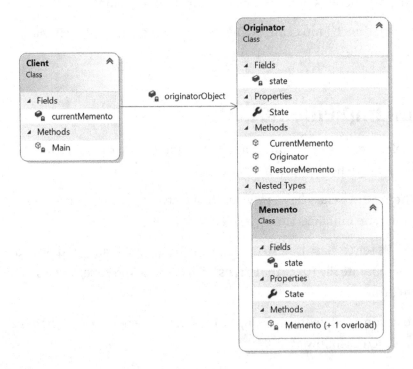

Figure 19-3. *Class diagram for demonstration 2*

Solution Explorer View

Figure 19-4 shows the modified high-level structure of the program.

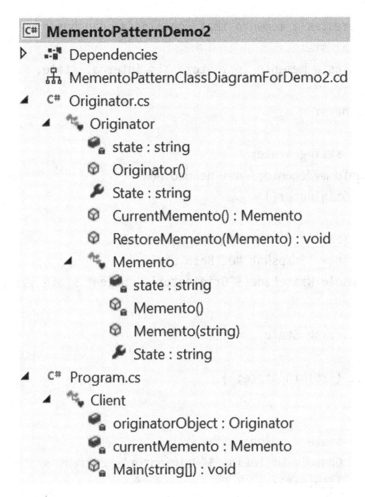

Figure 19-4. *Solution Explorer view of demonstration 2*

Demonstration 2

Here's the modified implementation.

```
//Originator.cs
using System;

namespace MementoPatternDemo2
```

```csharp
{
    /// <summary>
    ///   Originator class
    ///   As per GoF:
    ///   1.It creates a memento that contains a snapshot of its current
    ///   internal state.
    ///   2.It uses a memento to restore its internal state.
    /// </summary>
    class Originator
    {
        private string state;
        //Memento myMemento;//not needed now
        public Originator()
        {
            //Creating a memento with born state.
            state = "Snapshot #0.(Born state)";
            Console.WriteLine($"Originator's current state is: {state}");

        }
        public string State
        {
            get { return state; }
            set
            {
                state = value;
                Console.WriteLine($"Originator's current state is:
                {state}");
            }
        }

        /*
        Originator will supply the memento
        (which contains it's current state)
        in respond to caretaker's request.
        */
        public Memento CurrentMemento()
```

```csharp
{
    //Code segment used in Demonstration-1
    //myMemento = new Memento();
    //error now, because of private constructor
    //myMemento.State = state;
    //return myMemento;

    //Modified code for Demonstration-2
    return new Memento(this.State);
}

// Back to an old state (Restore)
public void RestoreMemento(Memento restoreMemento)
{
    this.state = restoreMemento.State;
    Console.WriteLine($"Restored to state : {state}");
}
/// <summary>
/// Memento class
/// As per GoF:
/// 1.A Memento object stores the snapshot of Originator's internal
/// state.
/// 2.Ideally,only the originator that created a memento is allowed
/// to access it.
/// </summary>
internal class Memento
{
    private string state;
    //Now Memento class cannot be initialized outside
    private Memento() { }
    public Memento(string state)
    {
        this.state = state;
    }
    public string State
    {
```

```
                get
                {
                    return state;
                }
                set
                {
                    state = value;
                }
            }
        }

    }
}
//Client.cs
using System;
using System.Collections.Generic;

namespace MementoPatternDemo2
{
    class Client
    {
        static Originator originatorObject;
        static Originator.Memento currentMemento;
        static void Main(string[] args)
        {
            Console.WriteLine("***Memento Pattern Demonstration-2.***");
            Console.WriteLine("Originator (with nested internal class
            'Memento') is maintained in a separate file.\n");
            //Originator is initialized.The constructor will create a
            //born state.
            originatorObject = new Originator();
            //Cannot create memento inside client code now
            //currentMemento = new Originator.Memento();
            //error:inaccessible
            //currentMemento.State = "test";
            //Also error, because previous line cannot be used
```

```
IList<Originator.Memento> savedStates = new List<Originator.
Memento>();
/*
 Adding a memento the list.This memento stores
 the current state of the Origintor.
*/
savedStates.Add(originatorObject.CurrentMemento());

//Snapshot #1.
originatorObject.State = "Snapshot #1";
//Adding this memento as a  restore point
savedStates.Add(originatorObject.CurrentMemento());

//Snapshot #2.
originatorObject.State = "Snapshot #2";
//Adding this memento as a  restore point
savedStates.Add(originatorObject.CurrentMemento());

//Snapshot #3.
originatorObject.State = "Snapshot #3";
//Adding this memento as a  restore point
savedStates.Add(originatorObject.CurrentMemento());

//Snapshot #4. It is not added as a restore point.
originatorObject.State = "Snapshot #4";

//Available restore points
Console.WriteLine("\nCurrently available restore points are :");
foreach (Originator.Memento m in savedStates)
{
    Console.WriteLine(m.State);
}

//Undo's
//Roll back starts...
Console.WriteLine("\nPerforming undo's now.");
for (int i = savedStates.Count; i > 0; i--)
```

```
        {
            //Get a restore point
            currentMemento = savedStates[i - 1];
            originatorObject.RestoreMemento(currentMemento);
        }
        //Redo's
        Console.WriteLine("\nPerforming redo's now.");
        for (int i = 1; i < savedStates.Count; i++)
        {
            currentMemento = savedStates[i];
            originatorObject.RestoreMemento(currentMemento);
        }
        // Wait for user
        Console.ReadKey();
        }
    }
}
```

Output

Here is the output. You can see that apart from the initial console messages, the output of demonstration 1 and demonstration 2 are the same, but programmatically, I put more constraints in this example.

```
***Memento Pattern Demonstration-2.***
Originator (with nested internal class 'Memento') is maintained in a
separate file.

Originator's current state is: Snapshot #0.(Born state)
Originator's current state is: Snapshot #1
Originator's current state is: Snapshot #2
Originator's current state is: Snapshot #3
Originator's current state is: Snapshot #4

Currently available restore points are :
Snapshot #0.(Born state)
Snapshot #1
```

Snapshot #2
Snapshot #3

Performing undo's now.
Restored to state : Snapshot #3
Restored to state : Snapshot #2
Restored to state : Snapshot #1
Restored to state : Snapshot #0.(Born state)

Performing redo's now.
Restored to state : Snapshot #1
Restored to state : Snapshot #2
Restored to state : Snapshot #3

CHAPTER 20

State Pattern

This chapter covers the State pattern.

GoF Definition

Allow an object to alter its behavior when its internal state changes. The object will appear to change its class.

Concept

The GoF definition is easy to understand. It simply states that an object can change what it does based on its current state.

Suppose that you are dealing with a large-scale application where the codebase is rapidly growing. As a result, the situation becomes complex, and you may need to introduce lots of if-else blocks/switch statements to guard the various conditions. The State pattern fits in such a context. It allows your objects to behave differently based on their current state, and you can define state-specific behaviors with different classes.

In this pattern, you think in terms of your application's possible states, and you segregate the code accordingly. Ideally, each of the states is independent of other states. You keep track of these states, and your code responds according to the behavior of the current state. For example, suppose that you are watching a program on your television (TV). Now, if you press the Mute button on the TV's remote control, there is a state change on your TV. But there is no change if the TV is already in a switched-off mode.

So, the basic idea is that if your code can track the current state of the application, you can centralize the task, segregate your code, and respond accordingly.

© Vaskaran Sarcar 2020
V. Sarcar, *Design Patterns in C#*, https://doi.org/10.1007/978-1-4842-6062-3_20

Real-World Example

Consider a scenario for a network connection, such as a TCP connection. An object can be in various states; for example, a connection might be just established, a connection might be closed, or the object is listening through the connection. When this connection receives a request from other objects, it responds according to its present state.

The functionalities of a traffic signal or television are other examples of the State pattern. For example, you can change the channel if the TV is already in switched-on mode. It does not respond to the channel change requests if it is in switched-off mode.

Computer-World Example

The TCP connection example can fit into this category. Consider another example. Suppose that you have a job-processing system that can process a certain number of jobs at a time. When a new job appears, either the system processes the job, or it signals that it is busy with the maximum number of jobs that it can process at that time. This busy signal simply indicates that its total number of job-processing capabilities has been reached, and the new job request cannot be fulfilled immediately.

Implementation

This example models the functionalities related to a TV, which has a control panel to support on, off, and mute operations. For simplicity, assume that at any given time, the TV is in any of these three states: On, Off, or Mute. The following shows an interface called IPossibleStates.

```
interface IPossibleStates
{
    //Users can press any of these buttons-On, Off or Mute
    void PressOnButton(TV context);
    void PressOffButton(TV context);
    void PressMuteButton(TV context);
}
```

Three concrete classes—On, Off, and Mute—implement this interface. The basic functionality can be described as follows. Initially, the TV is in the Off state. So, when you press the On button on the control panel, the TV moves to the On state, and then if you press the Mute button, it goes into the Mute state.

Assume that if you press the Off button when the TV is in the Off state; if you press the On button when the TV is in the On state; or if you press the Mute button when the TV is in Mute mode, there is no state change to the TV. The TV can go into the Off state from the On state or the Mute state (when you press the Off button). Figure 20-1 is a state diagram that reflects all possible scenarios.

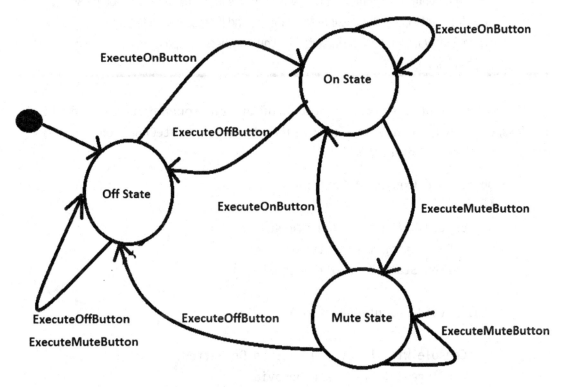

Figure 20-1. *Different states of a TV*

POINTS TO REMEMBER

- In this diagram, I did not mark any state as the final state, although in Figure 20-1, I switch to turn off the TV.

- To make the design simpler, assume that if you press the Off (or Mute) button when the TV is in the Off state; or if you press the On button when the TV is in the On state; or if you press the Mute button when the TV is in Mute mode, there is no state change to the TV. But in the real world, a remote control may work differently. For example, if the TV is currently in the On state and you press the Mute button, the TV goes into Mute mode; and if press the Mute button again, the TV may return to On state. So, you may need to update your program logic accordingly.

The TV has a control panel to support on, off, and mute operations. So, inside the TV class, there are three methods: ExecuteOffButton(), ExecuteOnButton(), and ExecuteMuteButton() as follows.

```
public void ExecuteOffButton()
{
    Console.WriteLine("You pressed Off button.");
    //Delegating the state behavior
    currentState.PressOffButton(this);
}
public void ExecuteOnButton()
{
    Console.WriteLine("You pressed On button.");
    //Delegating the state behavior
    currentState.PressOnButton(this);
}
public void ExecuteMuteButton()
{
    Console.WriteLine("You pressed Mute button.");
    //Delegating the state behavior
    currentState.PressMuteButton(this);
}
```

I delegated the state behavior. For example, when you press ExecuteMuteButton(), the control invokes PressMuteButton(...) based on the current state of the television.

Let's follow the class diagram now.

Class Diagram

Figure 20-2 shows the important parts of the class diagram.

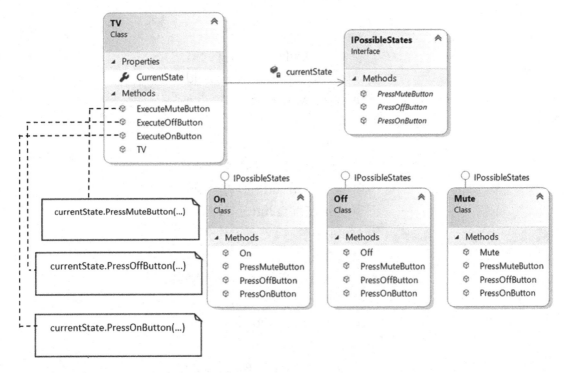

Figure 20-2. *Class diagram*

Solution Explorer View

Figure 20-3 shows the high-level structure of the program.

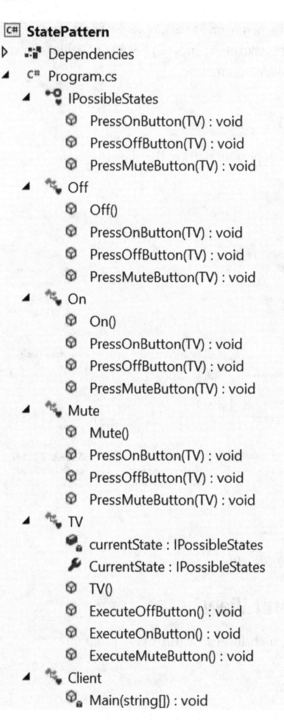

Figure 20-3. *Solution Explorer view*

Demonstration

Here's the complete implementation.

```
using System;
namespace StatePattern
{
    interface IPossibleStates
    {
        //Users can press any of these buttons-On, Off or Mute
        void PressOnButton(TV context);
        void PressOffButton(TV context);
        void PressMuteButton(TV context);
    }
    //Subclasses does not contain any local state.
    //Only one unique instance of IPossibleStates is required.
    /// <summary>
    /// Off state behavior
    /// </summary>
    class Off : IPossibleStates
    {
        public Off()
        {
            Console.WriteLine("---TV is Off now.---\n");
        }

        //TV is Off now, user is pressing On button
        public void PressOnButton(TV context)
        {
            Console.WriteLine("TV was Off.Going from Off to On state.");
            context.CurrentState = new On();
        }
```

```csharp
        //TV is Off already, user is pressing Off button again
        public void PressOffButton(TV context)
        {
            Console.WriteLine("TV was already in Off state.So, ignoring
            this opeation.");
        }
        //TV is Off now, user is pressing Mute button
        public void PressMuteButton(TV context)
        {
            Console.WriteLine("TV was already off.So, ignoring this
            operation.");
        }
    }
    /// <summary>
    /// On state behavior
    /// </summary>
    class On : IPossibleStates
    {
        public On()
        {
            Console.WriteLine("---TV is On now.---\n");
        }
        //TV is On already, user is pressing On button again
        public void PressOnButton(TV context)
        {
            Console.WriteLine("TV is already in On state.Ignoring repeated
            on button press operation.");
        }
        //TV is On now, user is pressing Off button
        public void PressOffButton(TV context)
        {
            Console.WriteLine("TV was on.So,switching off the TV.");
            context.CurrentState = new Off();
        }
```

```csharp
        //TV is On now, user is pressing Mute button
        public void PressMuteButton(TV context)
        {
            Console.WriteLine("TV was on.So,moving to silent mode.");
            context.CurrentState = new Mute();
        }
}
/// <summary>
/// Mute state behavior
/// </summary>
class Mute : IPossibleStates
{

        public Mute()
        {
            Console.WriteLine("---TV is in Mute mode now.---\n");
        }
        /*
        Users can press any of these buttons at this state-On, Off or Mute.
        TV is in mute, user is pressing On button.
        */
        public void PressOnButton(TV context)
        {
            Console.WriteLine("TV was in mute mode.So, moving to normal
            state.");
            context.CurrentState = new On();
        }
        //TV is in mute, user is pressing Off button
        public void PressOffButton(TV context)
        {
            Console.WriteLine("TV was in mute mode. So, switching off the
            TV.");
            context.CurrentState = new Off();
        }
```

```csharp
        //TV is in mute already, user is pressing mute button again
        public void PressMuteButton(TV context)
        {
            Console.WriteLine(" TV is already in Mute mode, so, ignoring
            this operation.");
        }
    }
    /// <summary>
    /// TV is the context class
    /// </summary>
    class TV
    {
        private IPossibleStates currentState;
        public IPossibleStates CurrentState
        {
            get
            {
                return currentState;
            }
            /*
            Usually this value will be set by the class that implements the
            interface "IPossibleStates"
            */
            set
            {
                currentState = value;
            }
        }
        public TV()
        {
            //Starting with Off state
            this.currentState = new Off();
        }
```

```csharp
        public void ExecuteOffButton()
        {
            Console.WriteLine("You pressed Off button.");
            //Delegating the state behavior
            currentState.PressOffButton(this);
        }
        public void ExecuteOnButton()
        {
            Console.WriteLine("You pressed On button.");
            //Delegating the state behavior
            currentState.PressOnButton(this);
        }
        public void ExecuteMuteButton()
        {
            Console.WriteLine("You pressed Mute button.");
            //Delegating the state behavior
            currentState.PressMuteButton(this);
        }
    }
    /// <summary>
    /// Client code
    /// </summary>
    class Client
    {
        static void Main(string[] args)
        {
            Console.WriteLine("***State Pattern Demo***\n");
            //TV is initialized with Off state.
            TV tv = new TV();
            Console.WriteLine("User is pressing buttons in the following
            sequence:");
            Console.WriteLine("Off->Mute->On->On->Mute->Mute->Off\n");
            //TV is already in Off state
            tv.ExecuteOffButton();
```

```
            //TV is already in Off state, still pressing the Mute button
            tv.ExecuteMuteButton();
            //Making the TV on
            tv.ExecuteOnButton();
        //TV is already in On state, pressing On button again
            tv.ExecuteOnButton();
            //Putting the TV in Mute mode
            tv.ExecuteMuteButton();
        //TV is already in Mute, pressing Mute button again
            tv.ExecuteMuteButton();
            //Making the TV off
            tv.ExecuteOffButton();
            // Wait for user
            Console.Read();
        }
    }
}
```

Output

Here's the output.

```
***State Pattern Demo***

---TV is Off now.---

User is pressing buttons in the following sequence:
Off->Mute->On->On->Mute->Mute->Off

You pressed Off button.
TV was already in Off state.So, ignoring this opeation.
You pressed Mute button.
TV was already off.So, ignoring this operation.
You pressed On button.
TV was Off.Going from Off to On state.
---TV is On now.---
```

```
You pressed On button.
TV is already in On state.Ignoring repeated on button press operation.
You pressed Mute button.
TV was on.So,moving to silent mode.
```
---TV is in Mute mode now.---

```
You pressed Mute button.
 TV is already in Mute mode, so, ignoring this operation.
You pressed Off button.
TV was in mute mode. So, switching off the TV.
```
---TV is Off now.---

Q&A Session

20.1 Can you elaborate on how this pattern works in a real-world scenario?

Psychologists have repeatedly documented the fact that human beings can perform their best when they are in a relaxed mood. In the reverse scenario, however, when their minds are filled with tension, they cannot produce great results. That is why they always suggest you working in a relaxed mood. So, the same work can be enjoyable or boring, depending on your current mood.

You can think about our demonstration example again. Suppose that you want to watch the live telecast of the winning moments of your favorite team. To watch and enjoy the moment, you need to power on the TV first. If the TV is not functioning properly at that moment and cannot be in the On state, you cannot enjoy the moment. So, if you want to enjoy the moment through your TV, the first criterion is that the TV should change its state from Off to On. The State pattern is helpful if you want to design a similar kind of behavior change in an object when its internal state changes.

20.2 In this example, you have considered only three states of a TV: On, Off, and Mute. There can be many other states; for example, there may be a state that deals with connection issues or different display conditions. Why have you ignored those issues?

The straightforward answer is I ignored those states to keep things simple. If the number of states increases significantly in the system, then it becomes difficult to maintain the system (and this is one of the key challenges associated with this design pattern). But if you understand this implementation, you can easily add any states that you want.

20.3 I noticed that the GoF represented a similar structure for both the State pattern and the Strategy pattern in their famous book. I'm confused by that.

Yes, the structures are similar, but you need to remember that their intents are different. When you use the Strategy pattern, you are getting a better alternative to subclassing. In a State design pattern, different types of behaviors can be encapsulated in a state object, and the context is delegated to any of these states. When a context's internal state changes, its behavior also changes. So, the State pattern can be thought of as a dynamic version of the Strategy pattern.

State patterns can also help you avoid a lot of if conditions in some contexts. For example, if a TV is in the Off state, it cannot go into the Mute state. From this state, it can move to the On state only. So, if you do not like the State design pattern, you may need to write the code like this.

```
class TV
{
//Some code before
public void ExecuteOnButton()
{
if(currentState==Off )
{
Console.WriteLine("You pressed On button. Going from Off to OnState");
//Some code after
}
if(currentState==On )
{
Console.WriteLine("You pressed On button. TV is already in on state.
So, ignoring this opeation.");
//Some code after
}
else
{
Console.WriteLine("TV was on. Moving into mute mode now.");
}
//Some code after
}
```

You need to repeat these checks for different kinds of button presses (For example, for the ExecuteOffButton() and ExecuteMuteButton() method, you need to repeat these checks and program accordingly). So, if you do not think in terms of states, over time, handling different conditions with a lot of if-else is very challenging, and it can be difficult when the codebase continually grows.

20.4 How are you implementing the open/close principle in your example?

Each of these TV states is closed for modification, but you can add a new state to the TV class.

20.5 What are the common characteristics between the Strategy pattern and the State pattern?

The State pattern can be considered as a dynamic Strategy pattern. Both patterns promote composition and delegation.

20.6 It appears to me that these state objects are acting like singletons. Is this correct?

Yes, it's a nice observation. The concrete subclasses of IPossibleStates do not contain any local state in this example, and as a result, in this application, only one state instance is working. Most of the time, this pattern acts similarly.

20.7 Why are you using context as a method parameter? Can you avoid them in statements like this?

```
void PressOnButton(TV context);
```

Using the context, I'm saving states. Also, the concrete subclasses of IPossibleStates do not contain any local state. So, in this application, only one state instance is working. So, this construct helps you evaluate whether you are changing between states or you are already in the same state. Note the output. These contexts help you get output like the following.

```
"You pressed Mute button.
TV was already off.So, ignoring this operation."
```

20.8 What are the pros and cons of the State design pattern?

The advantages are as follows.

- You have seen that by following the open/close principle, you can add new states and extend a state's behavior easily. Also, a state behavior can be extended without hassle. For example, in this implementation, you can add a new state and new behavior for a TV class without changing the TV class itself.

- It reduces if-else statements. In other words, conditional complexity is reduced. (Refer to the answer to question 20.3.)

There is a downside to using this pattern.

- The State pattern is also known as Objects for States, so you can assume that more states need more code, and the obvious side effect is more difficult maintenance.

20.9 In these implementations, TV is a concrete class. Why are you not programming to interface in this case?

I assume that the TV class is not going to change and so ignored that part to reduce some code size of the program. But yes, you can always start from an interface, for example, ITv, in which you can define the contracts.

20.10 In the TV class constructor, you are initializing the TV with an Off state. So, both states and the context class can trigger the state transitions?

Yes.

CHAPTER 21

Mediator Pattern

This chapter covers the Mediator pattern.

GoF Definition

Define an object that encapsulates how a set of objects interact. Mediator promotes loose coupling by keeping objects from referring to each other explicitly, and it lets you vary their interaction independently.

Concept

A mediator is an intermediary through whom a group of objects communicates, but they cannot refer to each other directly. The mediator takes responsibility for controlling and coordinating the interactions among them. As a result, you can reduce the direct number of interconnections among different objects. So, using this pattern, you can reduce the coupling in an application.

Real-World Example

When an airplane needs to take off, a series of verifications take place. These kinds of verifications confirm that all components and individual parts (which can be dependent on each other) are in perfect condition.

Another example is when the pilots of different airplanes (who are approaching or departing the terminal area) communicate with the airport towers. They do not explicitly communicate with other pilots in different airlines. They simply send their status to the controlling tower only. These towers send signals to confirm who can take off (or land). You must note that these towers do not control the whole flight. They enforce constraints only in the terminal areas.

© Vaskaran Sarcar 2020
V. Sarcar, *Design Patterns in C#*, https://doi.org/10.1007/978-1-4842-6062-3_21

Computer-World Example

When a client processes a business application, you may need to implement some constraints. For example, suppose you have a form where clients need to supply their user IDs and passwords to access their accounts. In the same form, you may need to supply other mandatory fields such as email ID, communication address, age, and so on. Let's assume you are applying the constraints as follows.

Initially, you check whether the user ID supplied by a user is a valid one. If it is a valid ID, then only the password field is enabled. After supplying these two fields, you may need to check whether the user provides an email ID. Let's further assume that after providing all this information (a valid user ID, a password, a correctly formatted email ID, and so on), your Submit button is enabled. In other words, the Submit button is enabled if the user supplies a valid user ID, password, a valid email ID, and other mandatory details. You can also ensure that the user ID is an integer, so if a user by mistake provides any character in that field, the Submit button stays in disabled mode. The Mediator pattern becomes handy in such a scenario.

In short, when a program consists of many classes, and the logic is distributed among them, the code becomes harder to read and maintain. In those scenarios, if you want to bring new changes to the system's behavior, it can be difficult unless you use the Mediator pattern.

Implementation

Wikipedia describes the Mediator pattern, as shown in Figure 21-1 (which is adopted from the GoF).

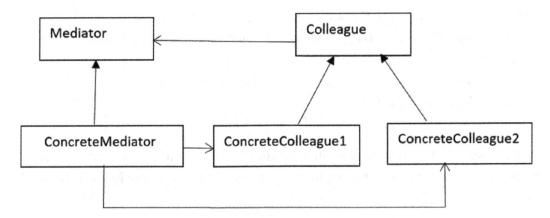

Figure 21-1. *Mediator pattern example*

The participants are described as follows.

- `Mediator`: This defines the interface that provides communication among `Colleague` objects.

- `ConcreteMediator`: This knows and maintains the list of `Colleague` objects. It implements the `Mediator` interface and coordinates the communication among the `Colleague` objects.

- `Colleague`: This defines the interface for communication with other colleagues.

- `ConcreteColleague(s)`: A concrete colleague must implement the `Colleague` interface. These objects communicate with each other through the mediator.

In demonstration 1, I replaced `Colleague` and `ConcreteColleague(s)` *with* `AbstractFriend` and `Friend`. (Yes, you can assume that it is a friendly environment.) In this example, there are three participants named Amit, Sohel, and Joseph, who communicate with each other through a chat server. The chat server plays the role of a mediator in this scenario.

In the following example, `IMediator` is the interface and defined with comments that are easy to understand.

```
interface IMediator
{
    // To register a friend
    void Register(AbstractFriend friend);
```

```
// To send a message from one friend to another friend
void Send(AbstractFriend fromFriend, AbstractFriend toFriend,string
msg);
// To display currently registered objects/friends.
void DisplayDetails();
}
```

The ConcreteMediator class implements this interface, and this class maintains the list of registered participants. So, inside this class, you also see the following lines of code.

```
// List of friends
List<AbstractFriend> participants = new List<AbstractFriend>();
```

Apart from this, the mediator allows only registered users to communicate with each other and post messages successfully. So, the Send() method in the ConcreteMediator class checks whether both the sender and receiver are registered users. The method is defined as follows.

```
public void Send(AbstractFriend fromFriend, AbstractFriend toFriend,string
msg)
{
    // Verifying whether the sender is a registered user or not.
    if (participants.Contains(fromFriend))
    {
            // Verifying whether the receiver is a registered user or not.
            if (participants.Contains(toFriend))
            {
                Console.WriteLine($"\n[{fromFriend.Name}] posts: {msg}
                Last message posted {DateTime.Now}");
                System.Threading.Thread.Sleep(1000);
                // Target receiver will receive this message.
                toFriend.ReceiveMessage(fromFriend, msg);
            }
```

```
    // Target receiver is NOT a registered user
    else
    {
        Console.WriteLine($"\n{fromFriend.Name}, you cannot
        send message to {toFriend.Name} because he is NOT a
        registered user.");
    }
}
// Message sender is NOT a registered user
else
{
    Console.WriteLine($"\nAn outsider named {fromFriend.Name}
    of [{fromFriend.GetType()}] is trying to send a message to
    {toFriend.Name}.");
}
}
```

In this example, there is another inheritance hierarchy, in which I use AbstractFriend as an abstract class so that you cannot directly instantiate it. Instead, you can instantiate objects from the concrete classes Friend or Stranger, which inherit from AbstractFriend. This inheritance hierarchy is as follows.

```
/// <summary>
/// AbstractFriend class
/// Making it an abstract class, so that you cannot instantiate it directly.
/// </summary>
    abstract class AbstractFriend
    {
        IMediator mediator;

        // Using auto property
        public string Name { get; set; }
```

```csharp
    // Constructor
    public AbstractFriend(IMediator mediator)
    {
        this.mediator = mediator;
    }
    public void SendMessage(AbstractFriend toFriend,string msg)
    {
        mediator.Send(this,toFriend, msg);
    }
    public void ReceiveMessage(AbstractFriend fromFriend, string msg)
    {
        Console.WriteLine($"{this.Name} has received a message from
        {fromFriend.Name} saying: {msg} ");
    }
}
/// <summary>
/// Friend class
/// </summary>

class Friend : AbstractFriend
{
    // Constructor
    public Friend(IMediator mediator)
        : base(mediator)
    {

    }
}
/// <summary>
/// Another class called Stranger
/// </summary>
class Stranger : AbstractFriend
{
    // Constructor
```

```
    public Stranger(IMediator mediator)
        : base(mediator)
    {

    }
}
```

Note Following the core architecture of a basic Mediator pattern, I used two different concrete classes to demonstrate the fact that you should *not* assume that the communicating objects should be from the same class only.

In the client code, you see the following participants: two from the Friend class and one from the Stranger class.

```
// 3 persons-Amit,Sohel,Joseph
// Amit and Sohel from Friend class
Friend friend1 = new Friend(mediator);
friend1.Name = "Amit";
Friend friend2 = new Friend(mediator);
friend2.Name = "Sohel";
// Joseph is from Stranger class
Stranger stranger1 = new Stranger(mediator);
stranger1.Name = "Joseph";
```

These people can communicate among them through a chat server. So, before passing the messages, they first register themselves to the chat server as follows.

```
// Registering the participants
mediator.Register(friend1);
mediator.Register(friend2);
mediator.Register(stranger1);
```

At the end of the program, I introduced two people: Todd and Jack. Todd is a Friend class object, and Jack is a Stranger class object. But neither of them registered with the mediator object; so the mediator is not allowing them to post messages to the desired object.

Jack can send the message properly if he registers with the mediator before sending a message, as follows.

```
mediator.Register(stranger1); // Disabled in Demonstration1
stranger1.SendMessage(friend3,"Hello friend...");
```

And the same comment applies for Todd too.

Class Diagram

Figure 21-2 shows the important parts of the class diagram.

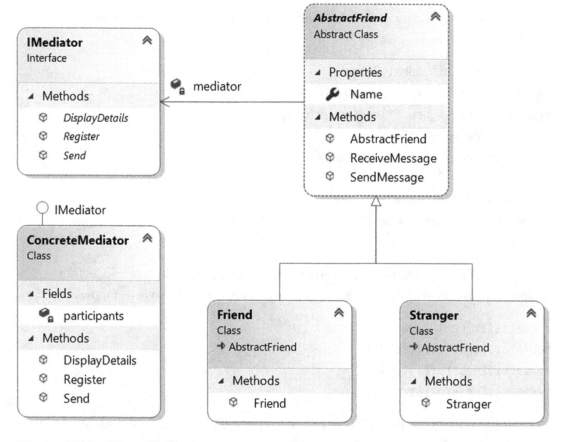

Figure 21-2. *Class diagram*

Solution Explorer View

Figure 21-3 shows the high-level structure of the program.

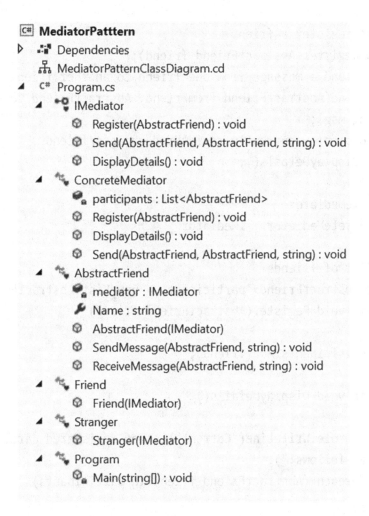

Figure 21-3. *Solution Explorer view*

Demonstration 1

Here's the complete demonstration.

```
using System;
using System.Collections.Generic;
```

```csharp
namespace MediatorPattern
{
    interface IMediator
    {
        // To register a friend
        void Register(AbstractFriend friend);
        // To send a message from one friend to another friend
        void Send(AbstractFriend fromFriend, AbstractFriend toFriend,
        string msg);
        // To display currently registered objects/friends.
        void DisplayDetails();
    }
    // ConcreteMediator
    class ConcreteMediator : IMediator
    {
        // List of friends
        List<AbstractFriend> participants = new List<AbstractFriend>();
        public void Register(AbstractFriend friend)
        {
            participants.Add(friend);
        }
        public void DisplayDetails()
        {
            Console.WriteLine("Current list of registered participants is
            as follows:");
            foreach (AbstractFriend friend in participants)
            {
                Console.WriteLine($"{friend.Name}");
            }
        }
        /*
         The mediator allows only registered users
         to communicate each other and post messages
         successfully. So, the following method
```

checks whether both the sender and receiver
are registered users or not.
*/

```
public void Send(AbstractFriend fromFriend, AbstractFriend
toFriend, string msg)
{
    // Verifying whether the sender is a registered user or not
    if (participants.Contains(fromFriend))

    {
        /* Verifying whether the receiver is a registered user or
        not */
        if (participants.Contains(toFriend))
        {
            Console.WriteLine($"\n[{fromFriend.Name}] posts: {msg}
            Last message posted {DateTime.Now}");
            System.Threading.Thread.Sleep(1000);
            /* Target receiver will receive this message.*/
            toFriend.ReceiveMessage(fromFriend, msg);
        }
        else
        {
            Console.WriteLine($"\n{fromFriend.Name}, you cannot
            send message to {toFriend.Name} because he is NOT a
            registered user.");
        }
    }
    // Message sender is NOT a registered user.
    else
    {
        Console.WriteLine($"\nAn outsider named {fromFriend.Name}
        of [{fromFriend.GetType()}] is trying to send a message to
        {toFriend.Name}.");
    }
}
}
```

```csharp
/// <summary>
/// AbstractFriend class
/// Making it an abstract class, so that you cannot instantiate it directly.
/// </summary>
abstract class AbstractFriend
{
    IMediator mediator;

    // Using auto property
    public string Name { get; set; }

    // Constructor
    public AbstractFriend(IMediator mediator)
    {
        this.mediator = mediator;
    }
    public void SendMessage(AbstractFriend toFriend, string msg)
    {
        mediator.Send(this, toFriend, msg);
    }
    public void ReceiveMessage(AbstractFriend fromFriend, string msg)
    {
        Console.WriteLine($"{this.Name} has received a message from
        {fromFriend.Name} saying: {msg} ");
    }
}
/// <summary>
/// Friend class
/// </summary>

class Friend : AbstractFriend
{
    // Constructor
```

```csharp
        public Friend(IMediator mediator)
            : base(mediator)
        {

        }
}
/// <summary>
/// Another class called Stranger
/// </summary>
class Stranger : AbstractFriend
{
    // Constructor
    public Stranger(IMediator mediator)
        : base(mediator)
    {

    }
}

class Program
{
    static void Main(string[] args)
    {
        Console.WriteLine("***Mediator Pattern Demonstration.***\n");

        IMediator mediator = new ConcreteMediator();
        //AbstractFriend afriend = new AbstractFriend(mediator);//error

        // 3 persons-Amit, Sohel, Joseph
        // Amit and Sohel from Friend class
        Friend friend1 = new Friend(mediator);
        friend1.Name = "Amit";
        Friend friend2 = new Friend(mediator);
        friend2.Name = "Sohel";
        // Joseph is from Stranger class
        Stranger stranger1 = new Stranger(mediator);
        stranger1.Name = "Joseph";
```

```
// Registering the participants
mediator.Register(friend1);
mediator.Register(friend2);
mediator.Register(stranger1);

// Displaying the participant's list
mediator.DisplayDetails();

Console.WriteLine("Communication starts among
participants...");
friend1.SendMessage(friend2, "Hi Sohel, can we discuss the
mediator pattern?");
friend2.SendMessage(friend1, "Hi Amit, Yup, we can discuss
now.");
stranger1.SendMessage(friend1, " How are you?");

// Another friend who does not register to the mediator
Friend friend4 = new Friend(mediator);
friend4.Name = "Todd";
/*
Todd is NOT a registered user.
So,he cannot send this message to Joseph.
*/
friend4.SendMessage(stranger1, "Hello Joseph...");
/*
Todd is NOT a registered user.
So,he cannot receive this message from Amit.
*/
friend1.SendMessage(friend4, "Hello Todd...");

// An outsider person tries to participate
Stranger stranger2 = new Stranger(mediator);
stranger2.Name = "Jack";
//mediator.Register(stranger1);
// This message cannot reach Joseph, because Jack
// is not the registered user.
stranger2.SendMessage(stranger1, "Hello friend...");
```

```
        // Wait for user
        Console.Read();
    }
}
}
```

Output

Here's the output.

```
***Mediator Pattern Demonstration.***

Current list of registered participants is as follows:
Amit
Sohel
Joseph
Communication starts among participants...

[Amit] posts: Hi Sohel, can we discuss the mediator pattern?Last message
posted 15-05-2020 11:13:08
Sohel has received a message from Amit saying: Hi Sohel, can we discuss the
mediator pattern?

[Sohel] posts: Hi Amit, Yup, we can discuss now. Last message posted 15-05-
2020 11:13:09
Amit has received a message from Sohel saying: Hi Amit, Yup, we can discuss
now.

[Joseph] posts:  How are you? Last message posted 15-05-2020 11:13:10
Amit has received a message from Joseph saying:  How are you?

An outsider named Todd of [MediatorPattern.Friend] is trying to send a
message to Joseph.

Amit, you cannot send message to Todd because he is NOT a registered user.

An outsider named Jack of [MediatorPattern.Stranger] is trying to send a
message to Joseph.
```

Analysis

Note that only registered users can communicate with each other and post messages successfully. The mediator is not allowing any outsider in the system. (Notice the last few lines of the output).

POINT TO REMEMBER

You should not assume that there should always be one-to-one communication. It is because the GoF states that a mediator replaces many-to-many interactions with one-to-many interactions. But in this chapter, I assume that all the messages are private and should not be broadcasted to everyone; so, I gave an example where the mediator is sending the messages to intended receivers only. The mediator is broadcasting the messages to warn others only when an outsider is trying to post messages in the chat server.

Q&A Session

21.1 Why are you complicating things? In the previous example, each of the participants could talk to each other directly, and you could bypass the mediator. Is this correct?

In this example, you have only three *registered* participants, and the mediator allows them only to communicate with each other. So, it may appear that since there are only three participants, they could communicate with each other directly. But think about a more complicated scenario, and let's add another constraint to this application, which states that a participant can send a message to a target participant if and only if the target participant stays in online mode only (which is the common scenario for a chat server). If you do not use the mediator pattern, it is not sufficient to check whether the participant is a valid user; in addition to this, you need to check the target recipient's online status before you post a message. And if the number of participants keeps growing, can you imagine the complexity of the system? So, a mediator can rescue you from such a scenario because you can put all the validation criteria inside the mediator. Figures 21-4 and 21-5 depict the scenario better.

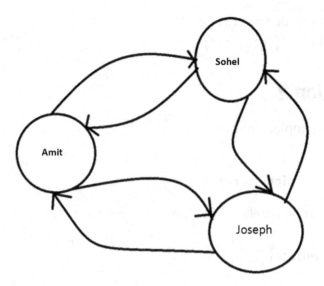

Figure 21-4. *Case 1: Without using a mediator*

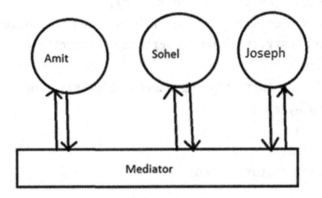

Figure 21-5. *Case 2: With a mediator*

Modified Implementation

In the modified example, a participant can send messages to another participant if both are registered users, and the receiver is online only. The mediator takes care of sending the messages to the correct destination, but before it sends a message, the participant's online status is known to him.

Figure 21-5 hints that in similar scenarios, the mediator can check the status of all the objects and maintain the logic of sending the messages. So, let's modify the program. Notice that I added a state for each participant. So, you see this new code segment inside the AbstractFriend class.

409

```
// New property for Demonstration 2
public string Status { get; set; }
```

Demonstration 2

Here's the modified implementation.

```
using System;
using System.Collections.Generic;

namespace MediatorPatternModifiedDemo
{
    interface IMediator
    {
        // To register a friend
        void Register(AbstractFriend friend);
        // To send a message from one friend to another friend
        void Send(AbstractFriend fromFriend, AbstractFriend toFriend,
        string msg);
        // To display currently registered objects/friends.
        void DisplayDetails();
    }
    // ConcreteMediator
    class ConcreteMediator : IMediator
    {
        // List of friends
        List<AbstractFriend> participants = new List<AbstractFriend>();
        public void Register(AbstractFriend friend)
        {
            participants.Add(friend);
        }
        public void DisplayDetails()
        {
            Console.WriteLine("Current list of registered participants is
            as follows:");
            foreach (AbstractFriend friend in participants)
            {
```

```
        Console.WriteLine($"{friend.Name}");
    }
}
/*
The mediator allows only registered users
to communicate with each other and post messages
successfully. So, the following method
checks whether both the sender and receiver
are registered users or not.
*/
public void Send(AbstractFriend fromFriend, AbstractFriend
toFriend, string msg)
{
    // Verifying whether the sender is a registered user or not.
    if (participants.Contains(fromFriend))

    {
        /* Verifying whether the receiver is a registered user and
        he is online.*/
        if (participants.Contains(toFriend) && toFriend.
        Status=="On")
        {
            Console.WriteLine($"\n[{fromFriend.Name}] posts: {msg}
            Last message posted {DateTime.Now}");
            System.Threading.Thread.Sleep(1000);
            //Target receiver will receive this message.
            toFriend.ReceiveMessage(fromFriend, msg);
        }
        else
        {
            Console.WriteLine($"\n{fromFriend.Name},at this moment,
            you cannot send message to {toFriend.Name} because he
            is either not a registered user or he is currently
            offline.");
        }
    }
```

```csharp
            //Message sender is NOT a registered user.
            else
            {
                Console.WriteLine($"\nAn outsider named {fromFriend.Name}
                of [{fromFriend.GetType()}] is trying to send a message to
                {toFriend.Name}.");
            }
        }
    }
    /// <summary>
    /// AbstractFriend class
    /// Making it an abstract class, so that you cannot instantiate it
    /// directly.
    /// </summary>
    abstract class AbstractFriend
    {
        IMediator mediator;

        // Using auto property
        public string Name { get; set; }
        // New property for Demonstration 2
        public string Status { get; set; }

        // Constructor
        public AbstractFriend(IMediator mediator)
        {
            this.mediator = mediator;
        }
        public void SendMessage(AbstractFriend toFriend, string msg)
        {
            mediator.Send(this, toFriend, msg);
        }
        public void ReceiveMessage(AbstractFriend fromFriend, string msg)
        {
            Console.WriteLine($"{this.Name} has received a message from
            {fromFriend.Name} saying: {msg} ");
```

```csharp
        }
    }
    /// <summary>
    /// Friend class
    /// </summary>
    class Friend : AbstractFriend
    {
// Constructor
        public Friend(IMediator mediator)
            : base(mediator)
        {

        }
    }
    /// <summary>
    /// Another class called Stranger
    /// </summary>
    class Stranger : AbstractFriend
    {
        // Constructor
        public Stranger(IMediator mediator)
            : base(mediator)
        {

        }
    }

    class Program
    {
        static void Main(string[] args)
        {
            Console.WriteLine("***Mediator Pattern Modified
            Demonstration.***\n");

            IMediator mediator = new ConcreteMediator();
            //AbstractFriend afriend = new AbstractFriend(mediator);//error
```

```
// 3 persons-Amit, Sohel, Joseph
// Amit and Sohel from Friend class
Friend friend1 = new Friend(mediator);
friend1.Name = "Amit";
friend1.Status = "On";
Friend friend2 = new Friend(mediator);
friend2.Name = "Sohel";
friend2.Status = "On";
// Joseph is from Stranger class
Stranger stranger1 = new Stranger(mediator);
stranger1.Name = "Joseph";
stranger1.Status = "On";

// Registering the participants
mediator.Register(friend1);
mediator.Register(friend2);
mediator.Register(stranger1);

// Displaying the participant's list
mediator.DisplayDetails();

Console.WriteLine("Communication starts among
participants...");
friend1.SendMessage(friend2, "Hi Sohel,can we discuss the
mediator pattern?");
friend2.SendMessage(friend1, "Hi Amit,Yup, we can discuss
now.");
stranger1.SendMessage(friend1, " How are you?");

// Another friend who does not register to the mediator
Friend friend4 = new Friend(mediator);
friend4.Name = "Todd";
// This message cannot reach Joseph, because Todd
// is not the registered user.
friend4.SendMessage(stranger1, "Hello Joseph...");
```

```
            // This message will NOT reach Todd because he
            // is not a registered user.
            friend1.SendMessage(friend4, "Hello Todd...");

            // An outsider tries to participate
            Stranger stranger2 = new Stranger(mediator);
            stranger2.Name = "Jack";
            //mediator.Register(stranger1);
            // This message cannot reach Joseph, because Jack
            // is not the registered user.
            stranger2.SendMessage(stranger1, "Hello friend...");

            Console.WriteLine("Sohel is going to offline now.");
            friend2.Status = "Off";
            /*
             Since Sohel is offline, he will NOT receive
             this message.
             */
            friend1.SendMessage(friend2, "Hi Sohel, I have a gift for
            you.");
            Console.WriteLine("Sohel is online again.");
            friend2.Status = "On";
            stranger1.SendMessage(friend2, "Hi Sohel, Amit was looking for
            you.");

            // Wait for user
            Console.Read();
        }
    }
}
```

Output

Here's the modified output.

Mediator Pattern Modified Demonstration.

Current list of registered participants is as follows:
Amit
Sohel
Joseph
Communication starts among participants...

[Amit] posts: Hi Sohel,can we discuss the mediator pattern?Last message posted 15-05-2020 11:30:50
Sohel has received a message from Amit saying: Hi Sohel,can we discuss the mediator pattern?

[Sohel] posts: Hi Amit,Yup, we can discuss now.Last message posted 15-05-2020 11:30:51
Amit has received a message from Sohel saying: Hi Amit,Yup, we can discuss now.

[Joseph] posts: How are you?Last message posted 15-05-2020 11:30:52
Amit has received a message from Joseph saying: How are you?

An outsider named Todd of [MediatorPatternModifiedDemo.Friend] is trying to send a message to Joseph.

Amit,at this moment, you cannot send message to Todd because **he is either not a registered user or he is currently offline.**

An outsider named Jack of [MediatorPatternModifiedDemo.Stranger] is trying to send a message to Joseph.
Sohel is going to offline now.

Amit,at this moment, you cannot send message to Sohel because he is either not a registered user or he is currently offline.
Sohel is online again.

[Joseph] posts: Hi Sohel, Amit was looking for you.Last message posted 15-05-2020 11:30:53
Sohel has received a message from Joseph saying: Hi Sohel, Amit was looking for you.

> **Note**   Some of the lines from the previous output are bold to demonstrate the impact of the modified program (demonstration 2).

Now you can see that a participant can send messages to another participant if and only if he is online. The mediator takes care of sending the messages to the correct destination, and before it sends a message, it ensures that both participants are registered users.

21.2 What are the advantages of using the Mediator pattern?

The following are some of the advantages.

- You can reduce the complexity of objects communicating in a system.

- The pattern promotes loose coupling. So, objects can be reused.

- The pattern reduces the number of subclasses in the system.

- You replace a many-to-many relationship with a one-to-many relationship, so the code is much easier to read and understand. And as an obvious effect of this, maintenance becomes easier.

- You can provide a centralized control with this pattern.

- In short, it is always a good aim to remove tight coupling from your code, and the Mediator pattern scores high in that context.

21.3 What are the disadvantages of using the Mediator pattern?

The following points address the challenges.

- In some cases, implementing the proper encapsulation becomes tricky, and the mediator object's architecture becomes complex.

- Sometimes maintaining a complex mediator becomes a big concern.

21.4 If you need to add a new rule or logic, you can directly add it to the mediator. Is this correct?

Yes.

21.5 I'm finding some similarities between the Facade pattern and the Mediator pattern. Is this correct?

Yes. In his book *Design Pattern for Dummies* (For Dummies, 2006), Steve Holzner mentions the similarity by describing the Mediator pattern as a multiplexed Facade pattern. In the Mediator pattern, instead of working with an interface of a single object, you are making a multiplexed interface among multiple objects to do smooth transitions.

21.6 In this pattern, you are reducing the number of interconnections among various objects. What are the key benefits you have achieved because of this reduction?

More interconnections among objects can create a monolithic system that becomes difficult to change (because the behaviors are distributed among many objects). As a side effect, you may need to create many subclasses to bring those changes into the system.

21.7 In both implementations, you are using `Thread.Sleep(1000)`. What is the reason for this?

You can ignore that. I used this to mimic a real-life scenario. I assume that participants are posting the messages after reading them properly, and this activity takes a minimum of 1 second.

CHAPTER 22

Chain of Responsibility Pattern

This chapter covers the Chain of Responsibility pattern.

GoF Definition

Avoid coupling the sender of a request to its receiver by giving more than one object a chance to handle the request. Chain the receiving objects and pass the request along the chain until an object handles it.

Concept

In this pattern, you form a chain of objects in which you pass the responsibility of a task from one object to another until an object accepts the responsibility of completing the task. Each object in the chain can handle a particular kind of request. If an object cannot handle the request fully, it passes the request to the next object in the chain. This process may continue until the end of the chain. This kind of request-handling mechanism gives you the flexibility to add a new processing object (handler) in the chain. Figure 22-1 shows such a chain with N number of handlers.

© Vaskaran Sarcar 2020
V. Sarcar, *Design Patterns in C#*, https://doi.org/10.1007/978-1-4842-6062-3_22

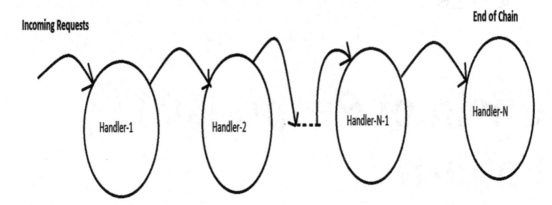

Figure 22-1. *Chain of Responsibility pattern*

Real-World Example

Most software organizations have some customer care representatives who take feedback from customers and forward any issues to the appropriate departments in the organization. However, the departments do not fix the issue simultaneously. The department that seems responsible looks at the issue first, and if those employees believe that the issue should be forwarded to another department, they forward it.

You may see a similar scenario when a patient visits a hospital. Doctors from one department can refer the patient to a different department (for further diagnosis) if they think it's needed.

You can consider a mobile company organization too. For example, in India, the Vodafone mobile company runs a customer care department. If you have a complaint, you first raise the issue to the customer care department. If they fail to solve your problem, you can escalate it to a nodal officer. If you are not satisfied with the solution given by the nodal officer, you can further escalate the issue to an appellate officer.

Computer-World Example

Consider a software application (e.g., a printer) that can send emails and faxes. As a result, any customer can report either fax issues or email issues, so you need to have two different types of error handlers: EmailErrorHandler and FaxErrorHandler.You can safely assume that EmailErrorHandler handles email errors only, and it is not responsible for fax errors. In the same manner, FaxErrorHandler handles fax errors and does not care about email errors.

You can form a chain like this: whenever your application finds an error, it just raises a ticket and forwards the error with the hope that one of those handlers will handle it. Let's assume that the request first comes to `FaxErrorhandler`. If this handler agrees that it is a fax issue, it handles it; otherwise, it forwards the issue to `EmailErrorHandler`.

Note that here the chain is ending with `EmailErrorHandler`. But if you need to handle another type of issue, such as an authentication issue, because of security vulnerabilities, you can make an `AuthenticationErrorHandler` and put it after `EmailErrorHandler`. Now, if an `EmailErrorHandler` also cannot fix the issue completely, it forwards the issue to `AuthenticationErrorHandler`, and the chain ends there.

POINTS TO REMEMBER

This is just an example; you are free to place these handlers in any order that you like. The bottom line is that the processing chain may end in either of these two scenarios:

- A handler can process the request completely.

- You have reached the end of the chain.

You see a similar mechanism when you are implementing an exception handling mechanism with multiple catch blocks in your C# application. If an exception occurs in a try block, the first catch block tries to handle it. If it cannot handle that type of exception, the next catch block tries to handle it, and the same mechanism is followed until the exception is handled properly by some handlers (catch blocks). If the last catch block in your application is also unable to handle it, the exception is thrown outside of this chain.

Implementation

Let's assume that in the following example, you write the program for the computer world example I've just discussed. In this example, I assume that we need to process different kinds of messages that may come from either email or fax. Customers can also tag either a normal priority or a high priority to these messages. So, at the beginning of the program, you see the following segments of code.

```
/// <summary>
/// Message priorities
/// </summary>
```

```
public enum MessagePriority
{
  Normal,
  High
}
/// <summary>
/// Message class
/// </summary>
public class Message
{
 public string Text { get; set; }
 public MessagePriority Priority;
 public Message(string msg, MessagePriority priority)
  {
    this.Text = msg;
    this.Priority = priority;
  }
}
```

I chose an abstract Receiver class this time because I wanted to share some common functionality across its derived classes.

POINTS TO NOTE

Alternatively, you can choose an interface and use the concept of default interface methods, which are supported in C# 8. Since the legacy versions do not support this, I chose the abstract class for this example.

The Receiver class looks like the following.

```
abstract class Receiver
{
  protected Receiver nextReceiver;
  //To set the next handler in the chain.  public void
  NextReceiver(Receiver nextReceiver)
```

```
  {
    this.nextReceiver = nextReceiver;
  }
 public abstract void HandleMessage(Message message);
}
```

The FaxErrorHandler and EmailErrorHandler classes inherit from Receiver, and they act as the concrete handlers in this program. To demonstrate a very simple use case, I could use the following code segment in FaxErrorHandler.

```
if (message.Text.Contains("fax"))
{
    Console.WriteLine($"FaxErrorHandler processed { message.Priority }
    priority issue: { message.Text }");
}
else if (nextReceiver != null)
{
    nextReceiver.HandleMessage(message);
}
```

POINTS TO REMEMBER

In the previous code segment, you can see that if a message contains the word *fax*, then the FaxErrorHandler handles it; otherwise, it passes the issue to the next handler. Similarly, in the upcoming example, if a message contains the word *email*, then EmailErrorHandler handles the message and so forth. So, you may question what happens if both *email* and *fax* are included in a message? I took care of this in the upcoming example, but for simplicity, you can ignore the case using this segment of code. In a real-world problem, one error can cause another error; so when an error occurs in the Fax code base, the same error can propagate to the Email code base (if they share a common code base). A common fix can solve both issues. In the upcoming example, I show you when you should pass the issue and how to pass the issue to the next handler. So, at first, you may ignore the individual pillar complexities.

In actuality, an organization may prefer to implement an AI-based mechanism to analyze an issue first, and then based on the symptoms, they can forward the issue to a particular department, but at the core, you may see this pattern.

To demonstrate a situation in which a message contains both the word *email* and the word fax, I used a relatively complex structure for FaxErrorHandler, which is as follows (the associated comments can be your guide).

```
class FaxErrorHandler : Receiver
{
    bool messagePassedToNextHandler = false;
    public override void HandleMessage(Message message)
    {
        // Start processing if the error message contains "fax"
        if (message.Text.Contains("fax"))
        {
            Console.WriteLine("FaxErrorHandler processed {0} priority
            issue: {1}", message.Priority, message.Text);
                /*
                Do not leave now, if the error message contains 'email' too.
                */
                if (nextReceiver != null && message.Text.Contains("email"))
                {
                    Console.WriteLine("I've fixed fax side defect.Now email
                    team needs to work on top of this fix.");
                    nextReceiver.HandleMessage(message);
                    // We'll not pass the message repeatedly to next
                    handler
                    messagePassedToNextHandler = true;
                }
        }
        if (nextReceiver != null && messagePassedToNextHandler != true)
        {
            nextReceiver.HandleMessage(message);
        }
    }
}
```

The EmailErrorHandler is similar to this. Now if you have a message that contains both *email* and *fax*, like "Neither the fax nor email is working," this relatively complex structure can help you to get the following output, where you can see that both teams worked on the defect:

```
FaxErrorHandler processed High priority issue: Neither fax nor email are
working.
I've fixed fax side defect. Now email team needs to work on top of this fix.
EmailErrorHandler processed High priority issue: Neither fax nor email are
working.
Email side defect is fixed. Now fax team needs to cross verify this fix.
```

At the end of my chain, there is an UnknownErrorHandler that states that the issue is neither from Email nor from Fax; so you need to consult the expert developers to tackle the issue.

```
class UnknownErrorHandler : Receiver
    {
        public override void HandleMessage(Message message)
        {
            if (!(message.Text.Contains("fax")|| message.Text.
            Contains("email")))
            {
                Console.WriteLine("Unknown error occurs.Consult experts
                immediately.");
            }
            else if (nextReceiver != null)
            {
                nextReceiver.HandleMessage(message);
            }
        }
}
}
```

Lastly, the forming of the error handler objects is quite easy and straightforward which are as follows.

```
// Different handlers
Receiver emailHandler = new EmailErrorHandler();
Receiver faxHandler = new FaxErrorHandler();
Receiver unknownHandler = new UnknownErrorHandler();
```

From the following code segment, you can easily understand how to form a chain of handlers.

```
/*
Making the chain :
FaxErrorhandler->EmailErrorHandler->UnknownErrorHandler.
*/
faxHandler.NextReceiver(emailHandler);
emailHandler.NextReceiver(unknownHandler);
```

Class Diagram

Figure 22-2 shows the class diagram.

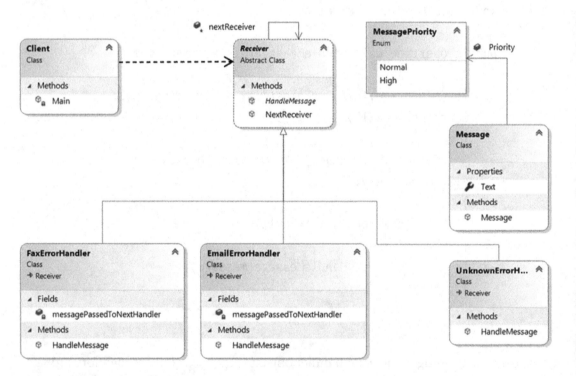

Figure 22-2. *Class diagram*

Solution Explorer View

Figure 22-3 shows the high-level structure of the program.

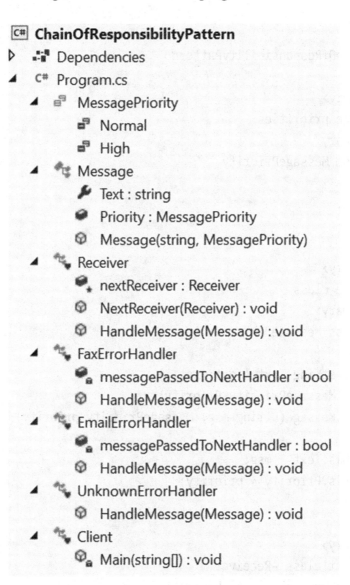

Figure 22-3. *Solution Explorer View*

Demonstration

Here's the complete program.

```csharp
using System;

namespace ChainOfResponsibilityPattern
{
    /// <summary>
    /// Message priorities
    /// </summary>
    public enum MessagePriority
    {
        Normal,
        High
    }
    /// <summary>
    /// Message class
    /// </summary>
    public class Message
    {
        public string Text { get; set; }
        public MessagePriority Priority;
        public Message(string msg, MessagePriority priority)
        {
            this.Text = msg;
            this.Priority = priority;
        }
    }
    /// <summary>
    /// Abstract class -Receiver
    /// The abstract class is chosen to share
    /// the common codes across derived classes.
    /// </summary>
```

```csharp
abstract class Receiver
{
    protected Receiver nextReceiver;
    //To set the next handler in the chain.
    public void NextReceiver(Receiver nextReceiver)
    {
        this.nextReceiver = nextReceiver;
    }
    public abstract void HandleMessage(Message message);
}
/// <summary>
/// FaxErrorHandler class
/// </summary>
class FaxErrorHandler : Receiver
{
    bool messagePassedToNextHandler = false;
    public override void HandleMessage(Message message)
    {
        //Start processing if the error message contains "fax"
        if (message.Text.Contains("fax"))
        {
            Console.WriteLine($"FaxErrorHandler processed {message.
            Priority} priority issue: {message.Text}");
            //Do not leave now, if the error message contains email too.
            if (nextReceiver != null && message.Text.Contains("email"))
            {
                Console.WriteLine("I've fixed fax side defect.Now email
                team needs to work on top of this fix.");
                nextReceiver.HandleMessage(message);
                //We'll not pass the message repeatedly to next handler.
                messagePassedToNextHandler = true;
            }
        }
```

```
            if (nextReceiver != null && messagePassedToNextHandler != true)
            {
                nextReceiver.HandleMessage(message);
            }
        }
    }
    /// <summary>
    /// EmailErrorHandler class
    /// </summary>
    class EmailErrorHandler : Receiver
    {
        bool messagePassedToNextHandler = false;
        public override void HandleMessage(Message message)
        {
            //Start processing if the error message contains "email"
            if (message.Text.Contains("email"))
            {
                Console.WriteLine($"EmailErrorHandler processed {message.
                Priority} priority issue: {message.Text}");
                //Do not leave now, if the error message contains "fax" too.
                if (nextReceiver != null && message.Text.Contains("fax"))
                {
                    Console.WriteLine("Email side defect is fixed.Now fax
                  team needs to cross verify this fix.");
                    //Keeping the following code here.
                    //It can be useful if you place this handler before fax
                    //error handler
                     nextReceiver.HandleMessage(message);
                    //We'll not pass the message repeatedly to the next
                    //handler.
                    messagePassedToNextHandler = true;
                }
            }
```

```
        if (nextReceiver != null && messagePassedToNextHandler != true)
        {
            nextReceiver.HandleMessage(message);
        }
    }
}
/// <summary>
/// UnknownErrorHandler class
/// </summary>
class UnknownErrorHandler : Receiver
{
    public override void HandleMessage(Message message)
    {
        if (!(message.Text.Contains("fax") || message.Text.
        Contains("email")))
        {
            Console.WriteLine("Unknown error occurs.Consult experts
            immediately.");
        }
        else if (nextReceiver != null)
        {
            nextReceiver.HandleMessage(message);
        }
    }
}
/// <summary>
/// Client code
/// </summary>
class Client
{
    static void Main(string[] args)
    {
        Console.WriteLine("***Chain of Responsibility Pattern
        Demo***\n");
```

```
            //Different handlers
            Receiver emailHandler = new EmailErrorHandler();
            Receiver faxHandler = new FaxErrorHandler();
            Receiver unknownHandler = new UnknownErrorHandler();
            /*
            Making the chain :
            FaxErrorhandler->EmailErrorHandler->UnknownErrorHandler.
            */
            faxHandler.NextReceiver(emailHandler);
            emailHandler.NextReceiver(unknownHandler);

            Message msg = new Message("The fax is reaching late to the
            destination.", MessagePriority.Normal);
            faxHandler.HandleMessage(msg);
            msg = new Message("The emails are not reaching to the
            destinations.", MessagePriority.High);
            faxHandler.HandleMessage(msg);
            msg = new Message("In email, CC field is disabled always.",
            MessagePriority.Normal);
            faxHandler.HandleMessage(msg);
            msg = new Message("The fax is not reaching to the
            destination.", MessagePriority.High);
            faxHandler.HandleMessage(msg);
            msg = new Message("Cannot login  into the system.",
            MessagePriority.High);
            faxHandler.HandleMessage(msg);
            msg = new Message("Neither fax nor email are working.",
            MessagePriority.High);
            faxHandler.HandleMessage(msg);
            Console.ReadKey();
        }
    }
}
```

```
***Chain of Responsibility Pattern Demo***

FaxErrorHandler processed Normal priority issue: The fax is reaching late
to the destination.
EmailErrorHandler processed High priority issue: The emails are not
reaching to the destinations.
EmailErrorHandler processed Normal priority issue: In email, CC field is
disabled always.
FaxErrorHandler processed High priority issue: The fax is not reaching to
the destination.
Unknown error occurs.Consult experts immediately.
FaxErrorHandler processed High priority issue: Neither fax nor email are
working.
I've fixed fax side defect.Now email team needs to work on top of this fix.
EmailErrorHandler processed High priority issue: Neither fax nor email are
working.
Email side defect is fixed.Now fax team needs to cross verify this fix.
```

Q&A Session

22.1 In the previous example, why do you need the message priorities?

Good catch. Actually, you can ignore the message priorities because, for simplicity, you are just searching for the text *Email* or *Fax* in the handlers. I added these priorities to beautify the code. Instead of using separate handlers for *Email* and *Fax*, you could make a different kind of chain that can handle the messages based on the priorities. But I did not form the priority-based chain in our demonstration because I assume that the developers who are working in the Fax pillar do not know much about the Email pillar and vice versa.

22.2 What are the advantages of using the Chain of Responsibility design pattern?

Some notable advantages are as follows.

- You have more than one object to handle a request. (If a handler cannot handle the whole request, it can forward the responsibility to the next handler in the chain.)

- The nodes of the chain can be added or removed dynamically. Also, you can shuffle their order. For example, in the previous application, if you see that most defects come from email, then you may place `EmailErrorHandler` as the first handler to save the average processing time of the application.

- A handler does not need to know how the next handler in the chain handles the request. It can focus on its handling mechanism.

- In this pattern, you are decoupling the senders (of requests) from the receivers.

22.3 What are the challenges associated with using the Chain of Responsibility design pattern?

The following points describe some of the challenges.

- There is no guarantee that the request is handled because you may reach the end of the chain but have not found any explicit receiver to handle the request.

- Debugging becomes tricky with this kind of design.

22.4 How do you handle the scenario where you have reached the end of the chain, but no handler handled the request?

One simple solution is through try/catch (or try/finally or try/catch/finally) blocks. You can put all the handlers in the `try` block, and if none handles the request, you can raise an exception with the appropriate messages and catch the exception in the `catch` block to draw your attention to it (or handle it in some different way).

The GoF talked about Smalltalk's automatic forwarding mechanism (doesNotUnderstand) in a similar context. If a message cannot find a proper handler, it is caught in doesNotUnderstand implementations, which can be overridden to forward the message in the object's successor, log it in a file, and store it in a queue for later processing, or you can simply perform any other operations. But you must make a note that by default, this method raises an exception that needs to be handled properly.

22.5 I can say that a handler either handles the request fully or passes it to the next handler. Is this correct?

Yes.

22.6 It appears to me that there are similarities between the Observer pattern and the Chain of Responsibility pattern. Is this correct?

In an Observer pattern, all registered users get notifications in parallel, but in the Chain of Responsibility pattern, objects in the chain are sequentially notified one by one, and this process continues until an object handles the notification fully (or you reach at the end of the chain). The comparisons are shown with diagrams in the "Q&A Session" section of the Observer pattern (see Q&A 14.4 in Chapter 14).

CHAPTER 23

Interpreter Pattern

This chapter covers the Interpreter pattern.

GoF Definition

Given a language, define a representation for its grammar along with an interpreter that uses the representation to interpret sentences in the language.

Concept

This pattern plays the role of a translator, and it is often used to *evaluate sentences in a language*. So, you first need to define a grammar to represent the language. Then the interpreter deals with that grammar. This pattern is best when the grammar is simple.

POINTS TO NOTE

To better understand this pattern, it is helpful to be familiar with words (or sentences), grammar, languages, and so forth in Automata, which is a big topic. The detailed discussion of it is beyond the scope of the book. For now, you know that in a formal language, the alphabet may contain an infinite number of elements, a word can be a finite sequence of letters (simply strings), and a set of all strings generated by grammar is called the language generated the grammar (G). Normally, grammar is represented by a tuple (V,T,S,P) where V is a set of nonterminal symbols, T is a set of terminal symbols (S) is the start symbol, and P is the production rules. For example, if you have a grammar G = (V,T,S,P) where

```
V={S},
T={a,b},
P={S->aSbS,S->bSaS,S->ε },
S={S};
```

© Vaskaran Sarcar 2020
V. Sarcar, *Design Patterns in C#*, https://doi.org/10.1007/978-1-4842-6062-3_23

The ε denotes an empty string. The grammar can generate an equal number of a's and b's, like ab, ba, abab, baab, and so forth. For example, the following steps show a derivation process of getting **abba.**

```
S
aSbS [since S->aSbS]
abS [since S->ε]
abbSaS [since S->bSaS]
abbaS [since S->ε]
abba [sinceS->ε]
```

In the same way, you can generate **baab**. Here are the derivation steps as a quick reference.

```
S
bSaS [since S->bSaS]
baS [sinceS->ε]
baaSbS [since S->aSbS]
baabS [sinceS->ε]
baab [sinceS->ε]
```

Each class in this pattern may represent a rule in the language, and it should have a method to interpret an expression. So, to handle a greater number of rules, you need to create a greater number of classes, and this is why an Interpreter pattern is seldom used to handle very complex grammar.

Let's consider different arithmetic expressions in a calculator program. Though these expressions are different, they all constructed using some basic rules, and these rules are defined in the grammar of the language (of these arithmetic expressions). So, it is a better idea if you can interpret a generic combination of these rules rather than treating each different combination of rules as separate cases. An Interpreter pattern can be used in such a scenario, which will be clear to you when you see demonstration 2 in detail. But before that, let's look at a relatively simple example in demonstration 1.

A typical structure of this pattern is often described with a diagram similar to Figure 23-1.

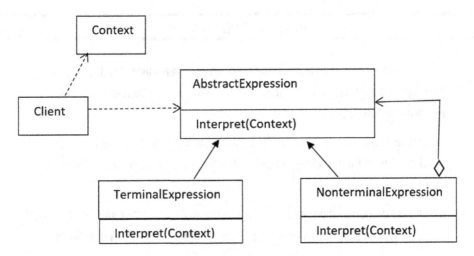

Figure 23-1. *Structure of a typical Interpreter pattern*

The terms are described as follows.

- **AbstractExpression** is typically an interface with an interpret method. You need to pass a context object to this method.

- **TerminalExpression** is used for terminal expressions. A terminal expression is the one that does not need other expressions to interpret. They are leaf nodes (i.e., they do not have child nodes) in the data structure.

- **NonterminalExpression** is used for nonterminal expressions. It is also known as AlternationExpression, RepetitionExpression, and SequenceExpression. These are like composites that can contain both the terminal and nonterminal expressions. When you call the Interpret() method on this, you call Interpret() on all of its children. In demonstration 2, you see them in action.

- **Context** holds the global information that the interpreter needs.

- **Client** calls the Interpret() method. Optionally, it can build the syntax tree based on the rules of the language.

POINTS TO REMEMBER

- An interpreter processes a language with simple grammar rules. Ideally, developers do not want to create their own languages, which is why they seldom use this pattern.

- There are two demonstrations in this chapter, which are *not* related to one another. The first is relatively simple, but the second is complex and involves more code.

- In the first demonstration, you transform a three-digit number into its equivalent word form. This program is fine-tuned from the previous edition of this book.

- The second program uses the Interpreter pattern as a rule validator and explains the details. My book *Java Design Patterns* (Apress, 2018) discusses the same concept with multiple examples.

Real-World Example

Real-world examples include a translator who translates a foreign language. Musicians play the role of interpreters of music notes, which is the "grammar."

Computer-World Example

The Java compiler interprets the Java source code into bytecode that a Java virtual machine understands. In C#, the source code is converted to MSIL intermediate code, which is interpreted by the Common Language Runtime (CLR). Upon execution, this MSIL is converted to native code (binary executable code) by the Just-In-Time (JIT) compiler.

Implementation

In general, you represent each of these grammar rules with a class. Let's define a simple rule, as shown here.

$E ::= E_1 \, E_2 \, E_3$

$E_1: = Zero \, Hundred(s) \mid One \, Hundred(s) \mid Two \, Hundred(s) \mid ... \mid$ $Nine \, Hundred(s)$

$E_2: = Zero \, Ten(s) \mid One \, Ten(s) \mid$ "$Two \, Ten(s) \mid ... \mid Ninety$

$E_3: = and \, Zero \mid and \, One \mid and \, Two \mid and \, Three \mid ... \mid and \, Nine$

For simplicity and better readability, I am representing this grammar with four classes: InputExpression for E (an abstract class), HundredExpression for E_1, TensExpression for E_2, and UnitExpression for E_3. So, in the upcoming program (demonstration 1), 789 is interpreted as Seven hundred(s) Eight ten(s) and Nine.

In demonstration 1, the Context class is very easy to understand. It has a public constructor that accepts a string parameter called input, which is later interpreted in word forms. The class also contains a read-only property Input and a read-write property called Output, and it is defined as follows.

```
public class Context
{
    private string input;
    public string Input {
        get
        {
            return input;
        }
    }
    public string Output { get; set; }

    // The constructor
    public Context(string input)
    {
        this.input = input;
    }

}
```

The abstract class InputExpression holds the abstract method Interpret(...),
which is overridden by its concrete subclasses called HundredExpression,
TensExpression, and UnitExpression. This class also contains a concrete method
GetWord(string str), which is used in all the concrete subclasses. I placed this method
in this abstract class so that I can simply avoid repeating this code in concrete subclasses.
This class is as follows.

```
// The abstract class-will hold the common code.
abstract class InputExpression
{
    public abstract void Interpret(Context context);
    public string GetWord(string str)
    {
        switch (str)
        {
            case "1":
                return "One";
            case "2":
                return "Two";
            case "3":
                return "Three";
            case "4":
                return "Four";
            case "5":
                return "Five";
            case "6":
                return "Six";
            case "7":
                return "Seven";
            case "8":
                return "Eight";
            case "9":
                return "Nine";
            case "0":
                return "Zero";
```

```
        default:
            return "*";
    }
  }
}
```

Inside the concrete subclass, you see the built-in Substring method to pick the intended digit from the input. The following line shows this.

```
string hundreds = context.Input.Substring(0, 1);
```

Finally, in the client code, I used a separate method called EvaluateInputWithContext to build the parse tree before I interpret the input in the given context. So, you see the following lines.

```
// Building the parse tree
List<InputExpression> expTree = new List<InputExpression>();
expTree.Add(new HundredExpression());
expTree.Add(new TensExpression());
expTree.Add(new UnitExpression());
// Interpret the input
foreach (InputExpression inputExp in expTree)
{
    inputExp.Interpret(context);
}
// some other code..
```

The remaining code is easy to understand, so let's move ahead.

Class Diagram

Figure 23-2 shows the class diagram.

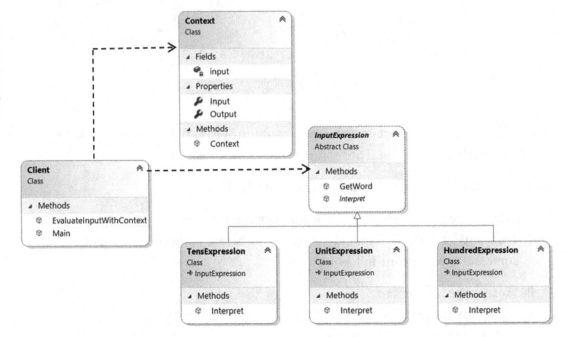

Figure 23-2.   Class diagram

Solution Explorer View

Figure 23-3 shows the high-level structure of the parts of the program.

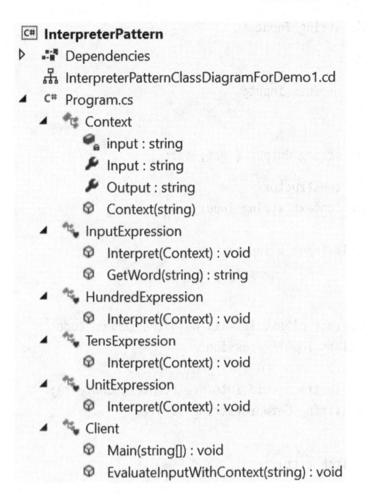

this figure will be printed in b/w

Figure 23-3. *Solution Explorer view*

Demonstration 1

Here's the complete demonstration.

```
using System;
using System.Collections.Generic;

namespace InterpreterPattern
{
    public class Context
    {
        private string input;
```

```csharp
    public string Input {
        get
        {
            return input;
        }
    }
    public string Output { get; set; }

    // The constructor
    public Context(string input)
    {
        this.input = input;
    }

}
// The abstract class. It will hold the common code
abstract class InputExpression
{
    public abstract void Interpret(Context context);
    public string GetWord(string str)
    {

        switch (str)
        {
            case "1":
                return "One";
            case "2":
                return "Two";
            case "3":
                return "Three";
            case "4":
                return "Four";
            case "5":
                return "Five";
            case "6":
                return "Six";
```

```
            case "7":
                return "Seven";
            case "8":
                return "Eight";
            case "9":
                return "Nine";
            case "0":
                return "Zero";
            default:
                return "*";
        }
    }
}

class HundredExpression : InputExpression
{
    public override void Interpret(Context context)
    {
     string hundreds = context.Input.Substring(0,1);
     context.Output += GetWord(hundreds) + " hundred(s) ";
    }
}
class TensExpression : InputExpression
{
    public override void Interpret(Context context)
    {
        string tens = context.Input.Substring(1,1);
        context.Output += GetWord(tens) + " ten(s) ";
    }
}
class UnitExpression : InputExpression
{
    public override void Interpret(Context context)
    {
        string units = context.Input.Substring(2, 1);
```

```
            context.Output += "and "+GetWord(units);
        }
    }

    // Client Class
    class Client
    {
        public static void Main(String[] args)
        {
            Console.WriteLine("***Interpreter Pattern Demonstation-
            1.***\n");
            Console.WriteLine(" It will validate first three digit of a
            valid number.");
            string inputString="789";
            EvaluateInputWithContext(inputString);
            inputString = "456";
            EvaluateInputWithContext(inputString);
            inputString = "123";
            EvaluateInputWithContext(inputString);
            inputString = "075";
            EvaluateInputWithContext(inputString);
            inputString = "Ku79";//invalid input
            EvaluateInputWithContext(inputString);

            Console.ReadLine();
        }
        public static void EvaluateInputWithContext(string inputString)
        {
            Context context = new Context(inputString);
            //Building the parse tree
            List<InputExpression> expTree = new List<InputExpression>();
            expTree.Add(new HundredExpression());
            expTree.Add(new TensExpression());
            expTree.Add(new UnitExpression());
            // Interpret the input
```

```
        foreach (InputExpression inputExp in expTree)
        {
            inputExp.Interpret(context);
        }
        if (!context.Output.Contains("*"))
            Console.WriteLine($" {context.Input} is interpreted as
            {context.Output}");
        else
        {
            Console.WriteLine($" {context.Input} is not a valid
            input.");
        }
        }
    }
}
```

Output

Here's the output.

```
***Interpreter Pattern Demonstation-1.***

It will validate first three digit of a valid number.
789 is interpreted as Seven hundred(s) Eight ten(s) and Nine
456 is interpreted as Four hundred(s) Five ten(s) and Six
123 is interpreted as One hundred(s) Two ten(s) and Three
075 is interpreted as Zero hundred(s) Seven ten(s) and Five
Ku79 is not a valid input.
```

Another Implementation

Let's look at another usage of this pattern. There are some important steps (which are followed in this example) when you consider implementing the pattern. These are as follows.

- **Step 1** Define the rules of the language for which you want to build an interpreter.

- **Step 2** Define an abstract class or an interface to represent an expression. It should contain a method to interpret an expression.

  - **Step 2A** Identify terminal and nonterminal expressions. For example, in the upcoming example, the `IndividualEmployee` class is a terminal expression class.

  - **Step 2B** Create nonterminal expression classes. Each of them calls the Interpret method on their children. For example, in the upcoming example, `OrExpression` and `AndExpression` classes are non- terminal expression classes.

- **Step 3** Build the abstract syntax tree using these classes. *You can do this inside the client code, or you can create a separate class to accomplish the task.*

- **Step 4** A client now uses this tree to interpret a sentence.

- **Step 5** Pass the context to the interpreter. It typically has sentences to be interpreted. An interpreter can also perform some additional tasks using this context.

POINTS TO NOTE

In the upcoming program, I use the Interpreter pattern as a rule validator.

Here I instantiate different employees with their "years of experience" and the current grades. For simplicity, there are four employees in four different grades: G1, G2, G3, and G4. So, you see the following lines.

```
Employee emp1 = new IndividualEmployee(5, "G1");
Employee emp2 = new IndividualEmployee(10, "G2");
Employee emp3 = new IndividualEmployee(15, "G3");
Employee emp4 = new IndividualEmployee(20, "G4");
```

I want to validate a rule against the context, which tells you that *to be promoted, an employee should have minimum 10 years of experience, and he should be from G2 grade or G3 grade. Once these expressions are interpreted, you see the output in terms of a boolean value.* You see the following lines of code inside the Main() method.

```
// Minimum Criteria for promoton is:
// The year of experience is minimum 10 yrs. and
// Employee grade should be either G2 or G3
List<string> allowedGrades = new List<string> { "G2", "G3" };
Context context = new Context(10, allowedGrades);
```

You can see that the allowed grades are stored in a list and passed to the Context class constructor. So, the following segment of code in Context class can make sense to you.

```
private int experienceReqdForPromotion;
private List<string> allowedGrades;
public Context(int experience, List<string> allowedGrades)
{
    this.experienceReqdForPromotion = experience;
    this.allowedGrades = new List<string>();
    foreach (string grade in allowedGrades)
    {
        this.allowedGrades.Add(grade);
    }
}
```

Employee is an interface with the Interpret(...) method as follows.

```
interface Employee
{
    bool Interpret(Context context);
}
```

As I told you before, the IndividualEmployee class acts as the leaf node in this example. This class implements Employee interface method as follows.

```
public bool Interpret(Context context)
{
    if (this.yearOfExperience >= context.GetYearofExperience()
    && context.GetPermissibleGrades().Contains(this.currentGrade))
    {
        return true;
    }
    return false;
}
```

Now let's handle some complex rules or expressions in this example. In the client code, you see the first complex rule in the following forms.

```
Console.WriteLine("Is emp1 and any of emp2, emp3, emp4 is eligible for
promotion?" + builder.BuildTreeBasedOnRule1(emp1, emp2, emp3, emp4).
Interpret(context));
Console.WriteLine("Is emp2 and any of emp1, emp3, emp4 is eligible for
promotion?"+ builder.BuildTreeBasedOnRule1(emp2, emp1, emp3, emp4).
Interpret(context));
// and so on..
```

And the second complex rule is in the following form.

```
Console.WriteLine("Is emp1 or (emp2 but not emp3) is eligible for
promotion?"+ builder.BuildTreeBasedOnRule2(emp1, emp2, emp3).
Interpret(context));
Console.WriteLine("Is emp2 or (emp3 but not emp4) is eligible for
promotion?"+ builder.BuildTreeBasedOnRule2(emp2, emp3, emp4).
Interpret(context));
```

So, the question may come into your mind how these rules are working? Here is the answer: another class, EmployeeBuilder, has methods to evaluate these rules. You'll see the detailed implementation shortly, but for now, let's look at the step by step process to form the first rule, which is as follows with supporting comments.

```
// Building the tree
//Complex Rule-1: emp1 and (emp2 or (emp3 or emp4))
public Employee BuildTreeBasedOnRule1(Employee emp1, Employee emp2,
Employee emp3, Employee emp4)
{
    // emp3 or emp4
    Employee firstPhase = new OrExpression(emp3, emp4);
    // emp2 or (emp3 or emp4)
    Employee secondPhase = new OrExpression(emp2, firstPhase);
    // emp1 and (emp2 or (emp3 or emp4))
    Employee finalPhase = new AndExpression(emp1, secondPhase);
    return finalPhase;
}
```

AndExpression, OrExpression, and NotExpression are three concrete classes implementing the interface Employee, and hence each of them has its own Interpret(...) method. For example, AndExpression implements Interpret(...) method as follows.

```
public bool Interpret(Context context)
{
    return emp1.Interpret(context) && emp2.Interpret(context);
}
```

Similarly, OrExpression implements Interpret(...) method as follows.

```
public bool Interpret(Context context)
{
    return emp1.Interpret(context) || emp2.Interpret(context);
}
```

And NotExpression implements the same method as follows.

```
public bool Interpret(Context context)
{
    return !emp.Interpret(context);
}
```

You can see that each of the composite expressions is invoking the Interpret()
method on all its children. The remaining code is easy to understand, so let's move on.

Note   This design pattern does not instruct you on how to build a syntax tree or
how to parse sentences. It gives you freedom in how you want to proceed.

Class Diagram

Figure 23-4 shows the class diagram.

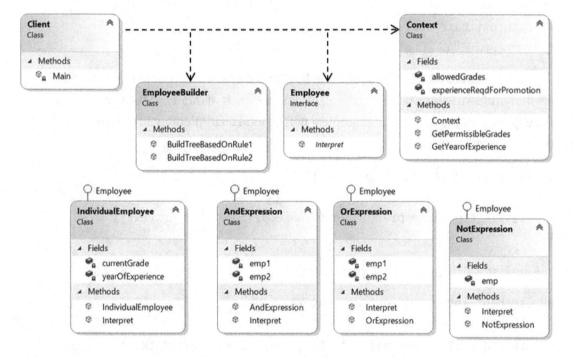

Figure 23-4.   *Class diagram*

Solution Explorer View

Figure 23-5 shows the high-level structure of the parts of the program.

C# **InterpreterPatternDemo2**

▷ ⋅⋅⋅ Dependencies

🔠 InterpreterPatternClassDiagramForDemo2.cd

◢ C# Program.cs

    ◢ ⚬ Employee

        ⚙ Interpret(Context) : bool

    ◢ ⚙ IndividualEmployee

        🔒 yearOfExperience : int

        🔒 currentGrade : string

        ⚙ IndividualEmployee(int, string)

        ⚙ Interpret(Context) : bool

    ◢ ⚙ OrExpression

        🔒 emp1 : Employee

        🔒 emp2 : Employee

        ⚙ OrExpression(Employee, Employee)

        ⚙ Interpret(Context) : bool

    ▷ ⚙ AndExpression

    ◢ ⚙ NotExpression

        🔒 emp : Employee

        ⚙ NotExpression(Employee)

        ⚙ Interpret(Context) : bool

    ◢ ⚙ Context

        🔒 experienceReqdForPromotion : int

        🔒 allowedGrades : List<string>

        ⚙ Context(int, List<string>)

        ⚙ GetYearofExperience() : int

        ⚙ GetPermissibleGrades() : List<string>

    ◢ ⚙ EmployeeBuilder

        ⚙ BuildTreeBasedOnRule1(Employee, Employee, Employee, Employee) : Employee

        ⚙ BuildTreeBasedOnRule2(Employee, Employee, Employee) : Employee

    ◢ ⚙ Client

        ⚙ Main(string[]) : void

Figure 23-5. *Solution Explorer view*

Demonstration 2

Here's the complete implementation.

```
using System;
using System.Collections.Generic;
```

```csharp
namespace InterpreterPatternDemo2
{
    interface Employee
    {
        bool Interpret(Context context);
    }
    /// <summary>
    /// IndividualEmployee class
    /// </summary>
    class IndividualEmployee : Employee
    {
        private int yearOfExperience;
        private string currentGrade;
        public IndividualEmployee(int experience, string grade)
        {
            this.yearOfExperience = experience;
            this.currentGrade = grade;
        }
        public bool Interpret(Context context)
        {
            if (this.yearOfExperience >= context.GetYearofExperience()
                && context.GetPermissibleGrades().Contains(this.
                currentGrade))
            {
                return true;
            }
            return false;
        }
    }
    /// <summary>
    /// OrExpression class
    /// </summary>
    class OrExpression : Employee
    {
        private Employee emp1;
        private Employee emp2;
```

```csharp
    public OrExpression(Employee emp1, Employee emp2)
    {
        this.emp1 = emp1;
        this.emp2 = emp2;
    }
    public bool Interpret(Context context)
    {
        return emp1.Interpret(context) || emp2.Interpret(context);
    }
}
/// <summary>
/// AndExpression class
/// </summary>
class AndExpression : Employee
{
    private Employee emp1;
    private Employee emp2;
    public AndExpression(Employee emp1, Employee emp2)
    {
        this.emp1 = emp1;
        this.emp2 = emp2;
    }
    public bool Interpret(Context context)
    {
        return emp1.Interpret(context) && emp2.Interpret(context);
    }
}
/// <summary>
/// NotExpression class
/// </summary>
class NotExpression : Employee
{
    private Employee emp;
```

```csharp
        public NotExpression(Employee expr)
        {
            this.emp = expr;
        }
        public bool Interpret(Context context)
        {
            return !emp.Interpret(context);
        }
    }
    /// <summary>
    /// Context class
    /// </summary>
    class Context
    {
        private int experienceReqdForPromotion;
        private List<string> allowedGrades;
        public Context(int experience, List<string> allowedGrades)
        {
            this.experienceReqdForPromotion = experience;
            this.allowedGrades = new List<string>();
            foreach (string grade in allowedGrades)
            {
                this.allowedGrades.Add(grade);
            }
        }
        public int GetYearofExperience()
        {
            return experienceReqdForPromotion;
        }
        public List<string> GetPermissibleGrades()
        {
            return allowedGrades;
        }
    }
```

```csharp
/// <summary>
/// EmployeeBuilder class
/// </summary>
class EmployeeBuilder
{
    // Building the tree
    // Complex Rule-1: emp1 and (emp2 or (emp3 or emp4))
    public Employee BuildTreeBasedOnRule1(Employee emp1, Employee emp2,
    Employee emp3, Employee emp4)
    {
        // emp3 or emp4
        Employee firstPhase = new OrExpression(emp3, emp4);
        // emp2 or (emp3 or emp4)
        Employee secondPhase = new OrExpression(emp2, firstPhase);
        // emp1 and (emp2 or (emp3 or emp4))
        Employee finalPhase = new AndExpression(emp1, secondPhase);
        return finalPhase;
    }
    // Complex Rule-2: emp1 or (emp2 and (not emp3 ))
    public Employee BuildTreeBasedOnRule2(Employee emp1, Employee emp2,
    Employee emp3)
    {
        // Not emp3
        Employee firstPhase = new NotExpression(emp3);
        // emp2 or (not emp3)
        Employee secondPhase = new AndExpression(emp2, firstPhase);
        // emp1 and (emp2 or (not emp3 ))
        Employee finalPhase = new OrExpression(emp1, secondPhase);
        return finalPhase;
    }
}
public class Client
{
```

```
static void Main(string[] args)
{
    Console.WriteLine("***Interpreter Pattern Demonstration-
    2***\n");

    // Minimum Criteria for promoton is:
    // The year of experience is minimum 10 yrs. and
    // Employee grade should be either G2 or G3
    List<string> allowedGrades = new List<string> { "G2", "G3" };
    Context context = new Context(10, allowedGrades);
    Employee emp1 = new IndividualEmployee(5, "G1");
    Employee emp2 = new IndividualEmployee(10, "G2");
    Employee emp3 = new IndividualEmployee(15, "G3");
    Employee emp4 = new IndividualEmployee(20, "G4");

    EmployeeBuilder builder = new EmployeeBuilder();

    // Validating the 1st complex rule
    Console.WriteLine("----- Validating the first complex
    rule.-----");
    Console.WriteLine("Is emp1 and any of emp2, emp3, emp4 is
    eligible for promotion?"
        + builder.BuildTreeBasedOnRule1(emp1, emp2, emp3, emp4).
        Interpret(context));
    Console.WriteLine("Is emp2 and any of emp1, emp3, emp4 is
    eligible for promotion?"
        + builder.BuildTreeBasedOnRule1(emp2, emp1, emp3, emp4).
        Interpret(context));
    Console.WriteLine("Is emp3 and any of emp1, emp2, emp3 is
    eligible for promotion?"
        + builder.BuildTreeBasedOnRule1(emp3, emp1, emp2, emp4).
        Interpret(context));
    Console.WriteLine("Is emp4 and any of emp1, emp2, emp3 is
    eligible for promotion?"
        + builder.BuildTreeBasedOnRule1(emp4, emp1, emp2, emp3).
        Interpret(context));
```

```
        Console.WriteLine("-----Validating the second complex rule
        now.-----");
        //Validating the 2nd complex rule
        Console.WriteLine("Is emp1 or (emp2 but not emp3) is eligible
        for promotion?"
            + builder.BuildTreeBasedOnRule2(emp1, emp2, emp3).
            Interpret(context));
        Console.WriteLine("Is emp2 or (emp3 but not emp4) is eligible
        for promotion?"
            + builder.BuildTreeBasedOnRule2(emp2, emp3, emp4).
            Interpret(context));
        Console.ReadKey();
        }
    }
}
```

Output

Here's the output.

```
***Interpreter Pattern Demonstration-2***

----- Validating the first complex rule.-----
Is emp1 and any of emp2, emp3, emp4 is eligible for promotion?False
Is emp2 and any of emp1, emp3, emp4 is eligible for promotion?True
Is emp3 and any of emp1, emp2, emp3 is eligible for promotion?True
Is emp4 and any of emp1, emp2, emp3 is eligible for promotion?False
-----Validating the second complex rule now.-----
Is emp1 or (emp2 but not emp3) is eligible for promotion?False
Is emp2 or (emp3 but not emp4) is eligible for promotion?True
```

Q&A Session

23.1 When should you use this pattern?

To be honest, it is not needed much in daily programming. However, in some rare situations, you may need to work with your own programming language, where it could come in handy. But before you proceed, you must ask yourself, what is the return on investment (ROI)?

23.2 What are the advantages of using the Interpreter design pattern?

The following are some of the advantages.

- You are involved in the process of defining grammar for a language and how to represent and interpret sentences. You can change and extend the grammar also.

- You have full freedom over how to interpret these expressions.

23.3 What are the challenges associated with using the Interpreter design pattern?

I believe that the amount of work is the biggest concern. Also, maintaining a complex grammar becomes tricky because you may need to create (and maintain) separate classes to deal with different rules.

That's the end of part 1 of the book. I hope you enjoyed all the detailed implementations of all the GoF patterns. Now you can move to the next part of the book, which covers some other interesting patterns.

PART II

Additional Design Patterns

CHAPTER 24

Simple Factory Pattern

This chapter covers the Simple Factory pattern.

Definition

The Simple Factory pattern creates an object without exposing the instantiation logic to the client.

Concept

In object-oriented programming (OOP), a factory is such an object that can create other objects. A factory can be invoked in many ways, but most often, it uses a method that can return objects with varying prototypes. Any subroutine that helps create these new objects is considered a factory. Most importantly, it helps you abstract the process of object creation from the consumers of the application.

Real-World Example

In a South Indian restaurant, when you place an order for your favorite biryani dish, the waiter may ask whether you like to have your Biryani with more spice or whether it should be prepared with less spice. Based on your choice, the chef adds spices to the core material and makes the appropriate dish for you.

© Vaskaran Sarcar 2020
V. Sarcar, *Design Patterns in C#*, https://doi.org/10.1007/978-1-4842-6062-3_24

Computer-World Example

The Simple Factory pattern is common to software applications, but before proceeding, note the following.

- The Simple Factory pattern is not treated as a standard design pattern in the GoF's famous book, but the approach is common to any application you write where you want to separate the code that varies a lot from the part of code that does not vary. It is assumed that you follow this approach in all the applications you write.

- The Simple Factory pattern is considered the simplest form of the Factory Method pattern (and Abstract Factory pattern). So, you can assume that any application that follows either the Factory Method pattern or the Abstract Factory pattern also follows the concept of the Simple Factory pattern's design goals.

In the following implementation, I discuss this pattern with a common use case. Let's go through the implementation.

Implementation

These are the important characteristics of the following implementation.

- In this example, you are dealing with two different types of animals: dogs and tigers. There are two concrete classes: Dog.cs and Tiger. cs. Each class has a common parent, IAnimal.cs. You see the following code:

```
// IAnimal.cs
namespace SimpleFactory
{
    public interface IAnimal
    {
        void AboutMe();
    }
}
```

```
// Dog.cs

using System;
namespace SimpleFactory
{
    public class Dog : IAnimal
    {
        public void AboutMe()
        {
            Console.WriteLine("The dogs says: Bow-Wow.I prefer
            barking.");
        }
    }
}
//Tiger.cs
using System;

namespace SimpleFactory
{
    public class Tiger : IAnimal
    {
        public void AboutMe()
        {
            Console.WriteLine("The tiger says: Halum.I prefer
            hunting.");
        }
    }
}
```

- I put the code for creating objects in a different place (specifically, in a factory class). Using this approach, when you create either a dog or a tiger, you are not directly using the new operator in client code. So, in the client code, you see the following line:

```
preferredType = simpleFactory.CreateAnimal();
```

- In the upcoming example, the process of creating an object depends on the user input. I separated the code that can vary from the code that is least likely to vary. This mechanism can help you to remove tight coupling in the system. So, inside Main(), you see the following code with supportive comments:

```
IAnimal preferredType = null;
SimpleFactory simpleFactory = new SimpleFactory();
#region The code region that can vary based on users preference
/*
 * Since this part may vary, we're moving the
 * part to CreateAnimal() of SimpleFactory class.
 */
preferredType = simpleFactory.CreateAnimal();
#endregion
#region The codes that do not change frequently.
preferredType.AboutMe();
#endregion
```

Note   In some places, you may see a variation of this pattern where objects are created through a parameterized constructor such as `preferredType=simpleFactory.CreateAnimal("Tiger")`.

In the upcoming example, I select the animal based on users' input, and a parameterized constructor is not needed. In the earlier edition of this book, I used two methods: `Speak()` and `Action()`. But to make this example short and simple, I chose a single method called `AboutMe()`. I merged the previous two methods into a single method.

Class Diagram

Figure 24-1 shows the class diagram.

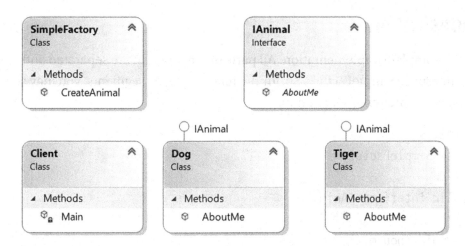

Figure 24-1. *Class diagram*

Solution Explorer View

Figure 24-2 shows the high-level structure of the program.

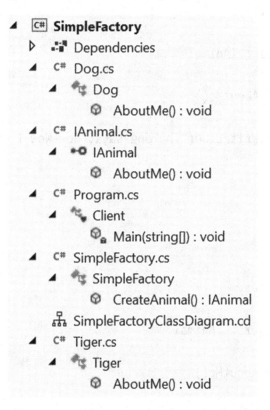

Figure 24-2. *Solution Explorer view*

Demonstration

Here's the complete implementation. All parts of the program are separated and placed in the namespace SimpleFactory. So, for the following code segments, you may see the namespace declaration multiple times.

```
//IAnimal.cs
namespace SimpleFactory
{
    public interface IAnimal
    {
        void AboutMe();
    }
}
//Dog.cs

using System;
namespace SimpleFactory
{
    public class Dog : IAnimal
    {
        public void AboutMe()
        {
            Console.WriteLine("The dog says: Bow-Wow.I prefer barking.");
        }
    }
}

//Tiger.cs
using System;

namespace SimpleFactory
{
    public class Tiger : IAnimal
    {
        public void AboutMe()
        {
            Console.WriteLine("The tiger says: Halum.I prefer hunting.");
```

```
            }
        }
}

//SimpleFactory.cs
using System;
namespace SimpleFactory
{
    public class SimpleFactory
    {
        public IAnimal CreateAnimal()
        {
            IAnimal intendedAnimal = null;
            Console.WriteLine("Enter your choice(0 for Dog, 1 for Tiger)");
            string b1 = Console.ReadLine();
            int input;
            if (int.TryParse(b1, out input))
            {
                Console.WriteLine("You have entered {0}", input);
                switch (input)
                {
                    case 0:
                        intendedAnimal = new Dog();
                        break;
                    case 1:
                        intendedAnimal = new Tiger();
                        break;
                    default:
                        Console.WriteLine("You must enter either 0 or 1");
                        //We'll throw a runtime exception for any other
                        //choices.
                        throw new ApplicationException(String.Format
                        (" Unknown Animal cannot be instantiated."));
                }
            }
```

```
            return intendedAnimal;
        }
    }
}

//Program.cs(Client)
 using System;
namespace SimpleFactory
{
    /*
     * A client is interested to get an animal
     * who can tell something about it.
     */
    class Client
    {
        static void Main(string[] args)
        {
            Console.WriteLine("*** Simple Factory Pattern Demo.***\n");
            IAnimal preferredType = null;
            SimpleFactory simpleFactory = new SimpleFactory();
            #region The code region that can vary based on users preference
            /*
             * Since this part may vary,we're moving the
             * part to CreateAnimal() in SimpleFactory class.
             */
            preferredType = simpleFactory.CreateAnimal();
            #endregion

            #region The codes that do not change frequently.
            preferredType.AboutMe();
            #endregion

            Console.ReadKey();
        }
    }
}
```

Output

The following is case 1, with user input 0.

```
*** Simple Factory Pattern Demo.***

Enter your choice(0 for Dog, 1 for Tiger)
0
You have entered 0
The dog says: Bow-Wow.I prefer barking.
```

The following is case 2, with user input 1.

```
*** Simple Factory Pattern Demo.***

Enter your choice(0 for Dog, 1 for Tiger)
1
You have entered 1
The tiger says: Halum.I prefer hunting.
```

The following is case 3, with user input 3.

```
*** Simple Factory Pattern Demo.***

Enter your choice(0 for Dog, 1 for Tiger)
3
You have entered 3
You must enter either 0 or 1
```

In this case, you get the following exception: "Unknown Animal cannot be instantiated" (see Figure 24-3).

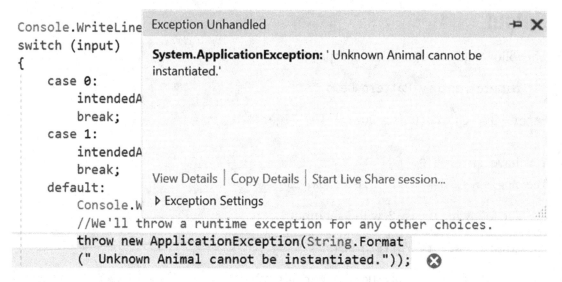

```
Console.WriteLine   Exception Unhandled                              ⊨ ✕
switch (input)
{                   System.ApplicationException: ' Unknown Animal cannot be
                    instantiated.'
    case 0:
        intendedA
        break;
    case 1:
        intendedA
        break;          View Details │ Copy Details │ Start Live Share session...
    default:
        Console.W    ▷ Exception Settings
        //We'll throw a runtime exception for any other choices.
        throw new ApplicationException(String.Format
        (" Unknown Animal cannot be instantiated."));   ✕
```

Figure 24-3. *Exception encountered due to an invalid input*

Q&A Session

24.1 In this example, I see that the clients are delegating the object's creation through the Simple Factory pattern. But instead of this, they could directly create objects with the new operator. Is this correct?

No. These are the key reasons behind the previous design.

- One of the key object-oriented design principles is to separate the parts of your code that are most likely to change from the rest.

- In this case, only the creation process for objects changes. You can assume that there is code fragment to describe something about an animal, and that part of the code does not need to vary inside the client code. So, in the future, if there is any change required in the creation process, you need to change only the CreateAnimal() method of the SimpleFactory class. The client code is unaffected because of those changes.

- You do not want to put lots of if-else blocks (or switch statements) inside the client body. That makes your code clumsy.

- How you are creating the objects is hidden from the client code. This kind of abstraction promotes security.

24.2 What are the challenges associated with this pattern?

If you want to add a new animal or delete an existing animal, you need to modify the CreateAnimal() method. This process violates the open/closed principle (which says that a code module should be open for extension but closed for modification) of the SOLID principles.

Note   The SOLID principles were promoted by Robert C. Martin. There are many online sources available. If you are interested in a quick introduction, go to https://en.wikipedia.org/wiki/SOLID.

24.3 Can you make the factory class static?

You can, but you have to remember the restrictions associated with a static class. For example, you cannot inherit them, and so on. It can make sense when you deal with some value objects which do not have an implementation class or a separate interface. It is also useful when you work with immutable classes, and your factory class doesn't need to return a brand-new object each time you use it.

In short, a value object is an object whose equality is based on the values rather than the identity. The most important characteristic of a value object is that it is immutable without an identity.

A simple real-life example can be given using five-rupee currency notes and five-rupee coins in India. Their money values are the same, but they are different instances.

In general, a static factory class can promote global states, which are not ideal for object-oriented programming.

CHAPTER 25

Null Object Pattern

This chapter covers the Null Object pattern.

Definition

The Null Object pattern is not a GoF design pattern. I am taking the definition from Wikipedia, which says the following.

In object-oriented computer programming, a null object is an object with no referenced value or with defined neutral ('null') behavior. The null object design pattern describes the uses of such objects and their behavior (or lack thereof). It was first published in the Pattern Languages of Program Design book series.

Concept

The pattern can implement a "do-nothing" relationship, or it can provide a default behavior when an application encounters a null object instead of a real object. With this pattern, our core aim is to make a better solution by avoiding a "null objects check" or "null collaborations check" through `if` blocks and you encapsulate the absence of an object by providing a default behavior that does nothing. The basic structure of this pattern is shown in Figure 25-1.

© Vaskaran Sarcar 2020
V. Sarcar, *Design Patterns in C#*, https://doi.org/10.1007/978-1-4842-6062-3_25

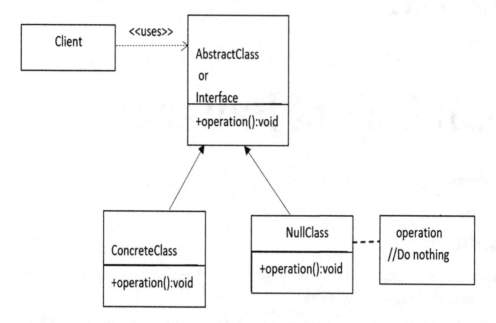

Figure 25-1. *The basic structure of a Null Object pattern*

This chapter begins with a program that seems to be OK, but it has a serious potential bug. When you analyze the bug with a potential solution, you understand the need for the Null Object pattern. So, let's jump to the next section.

A Faulty Program

Let's assume that you have two different types of vehicles: Bus and Train, and a client can pass different input (e.g., a and b) to create a Bus object or a Train object. The following program demonstrates this. This program runs smoothly when the input is valid, but a potential bug is revealed when you supply an invalid input. Here's the faulty program.

```
using System;

namespace ProgramWithOnePotentialBug
{
    interface IVehicle
    {
        void Travel();
    }
```

```csharp
class Bus : IVehicle
{
    public static int busCount = 0;
    public Bus()
    {
        busCount++;
    }
    public void Travel()
    {
        Console.WriteLine("Let us travel with Bus");
    }
}
class Train : IVehicle
{
    public static int trainCount = 0;
    public Train()
    {
        trainCount++;
    }
    public void Travel()
    {
        Console.WriteLine("Let us travel with Train");
    }
}

class Program
{
    static void Main(string[] args)
    {
        Console.WriteLine("***This program demonstrates the need of
        null object pattern.***\n");
        string input = String.Empty;
        int totalObjects = 0;
```

```csharp
while (input != "exit")
{
    Console.WriteLine("Enter your choice(Type 'a' for Bus, 'b'
    for Train.Type 'exit' to quit application.");
    input = Console.ReadLine();
    IVehicle vehicle = null;
    switch (input)
    {
        case "a":
            vehicle = new Bus();
            break;
        case "b":
            vehicle = new Train();
            break;
        case "exit":
            Console.WriteLine("Creating one more bus and
            closing the application");
            vehicle = new Bus();
            break;
    }
    totalObjects = Bus.busCount + Train.trainCount;
    vehicle.Travel();
    Console.WriteLine($"Total objects created in the system
    ={totalObjects}");
}
}
}
}
```

Output with Valid Input

You may have an immediate concern; when you type exit, you create an unnecessary object. It's true. We'll handle it later. For now, let's focus on the other bug, which is more dangerous for us. Here is some output with valid input.

```
***This program demonstrates the need of null object pattern.***

Enter your choice(Type 'a' for Bus, 'b' for Train.Type 'exit' to quit
application.
a
Let us travel with Bus
Total objects created in the system =1
Enter your choice(Type 'a' for Bus, 'b' for Train.Type 'exit' to quit
application.
b
Let us travel with Train
Total objects created in the system =2
Enter your choice(Type 'a' for Bus, 'b' for Train.Type 'exit' to quit
application.
a
Let us travel with Bus
Total objects created in the system =3
Enter your choice(Type 'a' for Bus, 'b' for Train.Type 'exit' to quit
application.
```

Analysis with an Unwanted Input

Let's assume that the user has mistakenly supplied a different character, such as *e*, as shown here.

```
Enter your choice(Type 'a' for Bus, 'b' for Train.Type 'exit' to quit
application.
e
```

This time, you get a runtime exception called System.NullReferenceException, as shown in Figure 25-2.

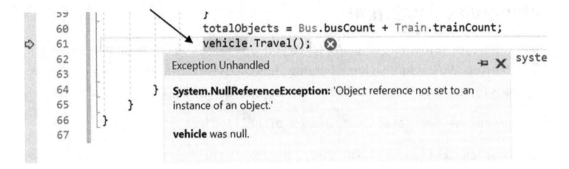

Figure 25-2. *A runtime exception occurs when the user supplies an invalid input*

A Potential Fix

The immediate remedy that may come into your mind is to do a null check before invoking the operation, as shown here.

```
if (vehicle != null)
{
  vehicle.Travel();
}
```

Analysis

The prior solution works in this case. But think of an enterprise application. When you do null checks for each scenario, if you place if conditions like this in each case, you make your code dirty. At the same time, you may notice the side effect of difficult maintenance. The concept of Null Object pattern is useful in similar cases.

POINT TO REMEMBER

In the prior example, I can avoid creating unnecessary objects when the user types *exit* and avoid the null check if I use a **null conditional operator** like the following:

```
vehicle?.Travel();
```

This operator is available in C# 6 and later versions only. Still it can be beneficial for you to look into the implementation details of the Null Object pattern. For example, when you use Null Object pattern, instead of doing nothing, you can supply a default behavior (that suits your application best) for those null objects.

Real-World Example

A washing machine works properly when there is a water supply without any internal leakage. But suppose that on one occasion, you forget to supply the water before you start washing the clothes, but you pressed the button that initiates washing the clothes. The washing machine should not damage itself in such a situation; so, it can beep some alarm to draw your attention and indicate that there is no water supply at the moment.

Computer-World Example

Assume that in a client-server architecture, the server does calculations based on the client input. The server needs to be intelligent enough not to initiate any calculation unnecessarily. Before processing the input, it may want to do a cross-verification to ensure whether it needs to start the calculation at all, or it should ignore an invalid input. You may notice the Command pattern with a Null Object pattern in such a case.

Basically, in an enterprise application, you can avoid big number of **null checks and if/else blocks** using this design pattern. The following implementation gives an overview of this pattern.

Implementation

Let's modify the faulty program that we discussed before. You handle the invalid input through a NullVehicle object this time. So, if by mistake the user supplies any invalid data (in other words, any input other than *a* or *b* in this case), the application does nothing; that is, it can ignore those invalid input through a NullVehicle object, which does nothing. The class is defined as follows.

```
/// <summary>
/// NullVehicle class
/// </summary>
class NullVehicle : IVehicle
{
 private static readonly NullVehicle instance = new NullVehicle();
 private NullVehicle()
 {
  nullVehicleCount++;
 }
 public static int nullVehicleCount;
 public static NullVehicle Instance
 {
  get
  {
    return instance;
  }
 }
 public void Travel()
{
   // Do Nothing
}
}
```

You can see that I applied the concept of Singleton design pattern when I create a NullVehicle object. It is because there can be an infinite number of invalid input, so in the following example, I do not want to create the NullVehicle object repeatedly. Once there is a NullVehicle object, I'd like to reuse that object.

Note   For a null object method, you need to return whatever seems sensible as a default. In our example, you cannot travel with a vehicle that does not exist. So, it makes sense that for the NullVehicle class, the Travel() method does nothing.

Class Diagram

Figure 25-3 shows the class diagram.

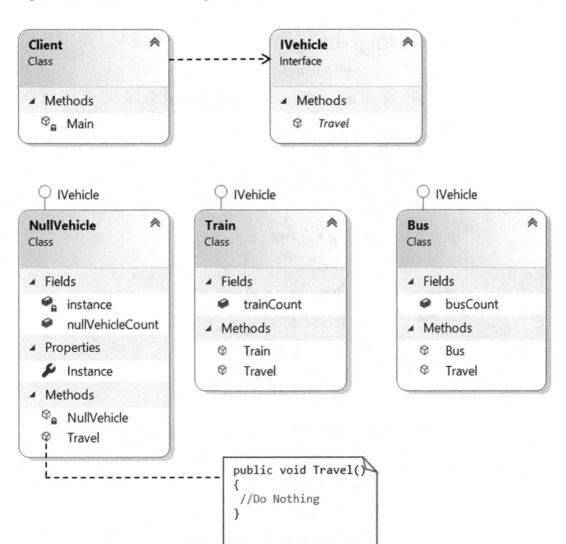

Figure 25-3. *Class diagram*

Solution Explorer View

Figure 25-4 shows the high-level structure of the program.

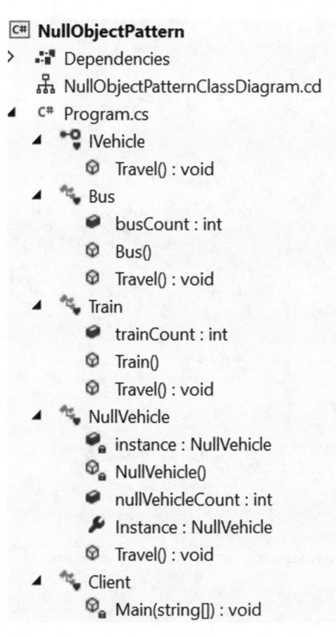

Figure 25-4. *Solution Explorer view*

Demonstration

Here's the complete implementation.

```
using System;
namespace NullObjectPattern
{
    interface IVehicle
    {
        void Travel();
    }
    /// <summary>
    /// Bus class
    /// </summary>
    class Bus : IVehicle
    {
        public static int busCount = 0;
        public Bus()
        {
            busCount++;
        }
        public void Travel()
        {
            Console.WriteLine("Let us travel with Bus.");
        }
    }
    /// <summary>
    /// Train class
    /// </summary>
    class Train : IVehicle
    {
        public static int trainCount = 0;
        public Train()
        {
            trainCount++;
        }
```

```csharp
        public void Travel()
        {
            Console.WriteLine("Let us travel with Train.");
        }
    }
    /// <summary>
    /// NullVehicle class
    /// </summary>
    class NullVehicle : IVehicle
    {
        private static readonly NullVehicle instance = new NullVehicle();
        private NullVehicle()
        {
            nullVehicleCount++;
        }

        public static int nullVehicleCount;
        public static NullVehicle Instance
        {
            get
            {
                return instance;
            }
        }
        public void Travel()
        {
            // Do Nothing
        }
    }
    /// <summary>
    /// Client code
    /// </summary>
```

```csharp
class Client
{
    static void Main(string[] args)
    {
        Console.WriteLine("***Null Object Pattern Demonstration.***\n");
        string input = String.Empty;
        int totalObjects = 0;

        while (input != "exit")
        {
            Console.WriteLine("Enter your choice( Type 'a' for Bus,
            'b' for Train.Type 'exit' to quit) ");
            input = Console.ReadLine();
            IVehicle vehicle = null;
            switch (input)
            {
                case "a":
                    vehicle = new Bus();
                    break;
                case "b":
                    vehicle = new Train();
                    break;
                case "exit":
                    Console.WriteLine("Closing the application.");
                    vehicle = NullVehicle.Instance;
                    break;
                default:
                    Console.WriteLine("Please supply the correct
                    input(a/b/exit)");
                    vehicle = NullVehicle.Instance;
                    break;
            }
            totalObjects = Bus.busCount + Train.trainCount +
            NullVehicle.nullVehicleCount;
            // No need to do null check now.
```

```
                //if (vehicle != null)
                vehicle.Travel();
                //}
                Console.WriteLine("Total objects created in the system ={0}",
                totalObjects);

            }
            Console.ReadKey();
        }
    }
}
```

Output

Here's the output.

```
***Null Object Pattern Demonstration.***

Enter your choice( Type 'a' for Bus, 'b' for Train.Type 'exit' to quit)
a
Let us travel with Bus.
Total objects created in the system =2
Enter your choice( Type 'a' for Bus, 'b' for Train.Type 'exit' to quit)
b
Let us travel with Train.
Total objects created in the system =3
Enter your choice( Type 'a' for Bus, 'b' for Train.Type 'exit' to quit)
c
Please supply the correct input(a/b/exit)
Total objects created in the system =3
Enter your choice( Type 'a' for Bus, 'b' for Train.Type 'exit' to quit)
d
Please supply the correct input(a/b/exit)
Total objects created in the system =3
Enter your choice( Type 'a' for Bus, 'b' for Train.Type 'exit' to quit)
b
Let us travel with Train.
```

```
Total objects created in the system =4
Enter your choice( Type 'a' for Bus, 'b' for Train.Type 'exit' to quit)
exit
Closing the application.
Total objects created in the system =4
```

Analysis

I draw your attention to the following points.

- Invalid input and their effects are shown in bold.

- The objects count is not increasing because of null vehicle objects/ invalid input.

- You did not perform any null check. Still, the program execution is not interrupted because of invalid user input.

Q&A Session

25.1 At the beginning of the implementation, I see an additional object is created. Is this intentional?

To save some computer memory/storage, I followed a Singleton design pattern that supports early initialization when I constructed the NullVehicle class. You do not want to create a NullVehicle object for each invalid input because your application may receive a large number of invalid input. If you do not guard against the situation, a huge number of NullVehicle objects may reside in the system (which is useless), and they can occupy a large amount of computer memory, which in turn can cause some unwanted side effects. (For example, the system may become slow, applications response time may increase, etc.)

25.2 When should you use this pattern?

This pattern can be useful in the following cases.

- You do not want to encounter a NullReferenceException (for example, if by mistake you try to invoke a method of a null object).

- You like to ignore lots of null checks in your code.

- You want to make your code cleaner and easily maintainable.

Note   You learn another use of this pattern at the end of this chapter.

25.3 What are the challenges associated with the Null Object pattern?

You need to be aware of the following scenarios.

- Most often, you may want to find and fix the root cause of a failure. So, if you throw a `NullReferenceException`, that can work better for you. You can always handle those exceptions in a `try/catch` block or a `try/catch/finally` block and update the log information accordingly.

- The Null Object pattern helps you to implement a default behavior when you unconsciously want to deal with an object that is not present at all. But trying to supply such a default behavior may not always be appropriate.

- Incorrect implementations of the Null Object pattern can suppress the true bug that may appear as normal in your program execution.

25.4. It looks as if null objects are working like proxies. Is this correct?

No. In general, proxies act on real objects at some point in time, and they may also provide some behavior. But a null object should not do any such thing.

25.5. The Null Object pattern is always associated with `NullReferenceException`. Is this correct?

The concept is the same, but the exception name can be different or language-specific. For example, in Java, you can use this pattern to guard java.lang.NullPointerException, but in a language like C#, you use it to guard System.NullReferenceException.

Finally, I want to draw your attention to another interesting point. The Null Object pattern can be useful in another context. For example, consider the following segment of code.

```
//A case study in another context.
List<IVehicle> vehicleList = new List<IVehicle>();
vehicleList.Add(new Bus());
vehicleList.Add(new Train());
vehicleList.Add(null);
```

```
foreach (IVehicle vehicle in vehicleList)
{
    vehicle.Travel();
}
```

When you use the previous code segment, you get System.NullReferenceException again. But if you replace vehicleList.Add(null); with vehicleList.Add(NullVehicle. Instance);, there is no runtime exception. So, you can loop through easily, which is another important usage of this pattern.

CHAPTER 26

MVC Pattern

This chapter covers the MVC pattern.

Definition

MVC (model-view-controller) is an architectural pattern. This pattern is commonly used in web applications and in developing powerful user interfaces. Trygve Reenskaug first described MVC in 1979 in a paper titled "Applications programming in Smalltalk-80TM: How to use Model-View-Controller," which was written before the existence of the World Wide Web. So, at that time, there was no concept of web applications. But modern-day applications are an adaptation of that original concept. Instead of treating it a true design pattern, some developers prefer to say this an "MVC architecture."

Wikipedia defines it as follows.

> Model-view-controller (MVC) is an architectural pattern commonly used for developing user interfaces that divides an application into three interconnected parts. This is done to separate internal representations of information from the way information is presented to and accepted by the user. The MVC design pattern decouples these major components allowing for efficient code reuse and parallel development. (https://en.wikipedia.org/wiki/Model-view-controller)

My favorite description of MVC comes from Connelly Barnes, who said,

> An easy way to understand MVC: the model is the data, the view is the window on the screen, and the controller is the glue between the two. (http://wiki.c2.com/?ModelViewController)

495

© Vaskaran Sarcar 2020
V. Sarcar, *Design Patterns in C#*, https://doi.org/10.1007/978-1-4842-6062-3_26

Concept

Using this pattern, you separate the user interface logic from the business logic and decouple the major components in such a way that those can be reused efficiently. This approach promotes parallel development.

From the definition, it is apparent that the pattern consists of these major components: model, view, and controller. The controller is placed between the view and model in such a way that they can communicate with each other only through the controller. This model separates the mechanism for how the data is displayed from the mechanism for how the data is manipulated. Figure 26-1 shows the MVC pattern.

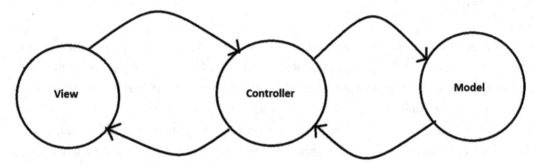

Figure 26-1. *A typical MVC architecture*

Key Points to Remember

These are brief descriptions of the key components in this pattern.

- View represents the final output. It can also accept user input. It is a presentation layer, and you can think of it as a graphical user interface (GUI). You can design it with various technologies. For example, in a .NET application, you can use HTML, CSS, WPF, and so on, and for a Java application, you can use AWT, Swing, JSF, JavaFX, and so forth.

- The model manages the data and business logic, and it acts as the actual brain of your application. It manages the data and business logic. It knows how to store, manage, or manipulate the data and handle the requests that come from the controller. But this component is separated from the view component. A typical example is a database, a file system, or a similar kind of storage. It can be designed with Oracle, SQL Server, DB2, Hadoop, MySQL, and so on.

- The controller is the intermediary. It accepts a user's input from the view component and passes the request to the model. When it gets a response from the model, it passes the data to a view. It can be designed with C# .NET, ASP.NET, VB.NET, Core Java, JSP, Servlets, PHP, Ruby, Python, and so on.

You may notice varying implementations in different applications. Here are some examples.

- You can have multiple views.

- Views can pass runtime values (for example, using JavaScript) to controllers.

- Your controller can validate the user's input.

- Your controller can receive input in various ways. For example, it can get input from a web request via a URL, or input can be passed by clicking a Submit button on a form.

- In some applications, you may notice that the model can update the view component.

In short, you need to use this pattern to support your own need. Figures 26-2, 26-3, and 26-4 show known variations of an MVC architecture.

Variation 1

Figure 26-2 shows variation 1.

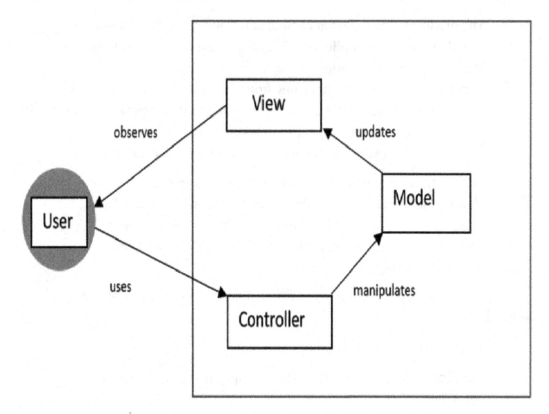

Figure 26-2. *A typical MVC framework*

Variation 2

Figure 26-3 shows variation 2.

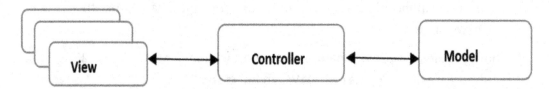

Figure 26-3. *An MVC framework with multiple views*

Variation 3

Figure 26-4 shows variation 3.

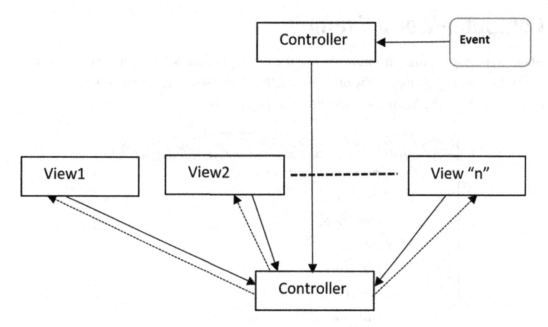

Figure 26-4. *An MVC pattern implemented with an Observer pattern/event-based mechanism*

One of the best descriptions for MVC comes from wiki.c2.com (`http://wiki.c2.com/?ModelViewController`), where it says, "We need *smart* models, *thin* controllers, and *dumb* views."

Real-World Example

Consider our Template Method pattern's real-life example. But this time, let's interpret it differently. I said that in a restaurant, based on customer input, a chef adjusts the taste and makes the final dish. But you know that the customers do not place their orders directly with the chef. The customers see the menu card (View), may consult with the waiter/waitress, and then place the order. The waiter passes the order slip to the chef who gathers the required materials from the restaurant's kitchen (similar to storehouses or, computer databases). Once prepared, the waiter carries the plate to the customer's table. So, you can consider the role of a waiter as the controller, the chefs in the kitchen as the model, and the food preparation materials as the data.

Computer-World Example

Many web programming frameworks use the concept of the MVC framework. Typical examples include Django, Ruby on Rails, ASP.NET, and so on. A typical ASP.NET MVC project can have the following view shown in Figure 26-5.

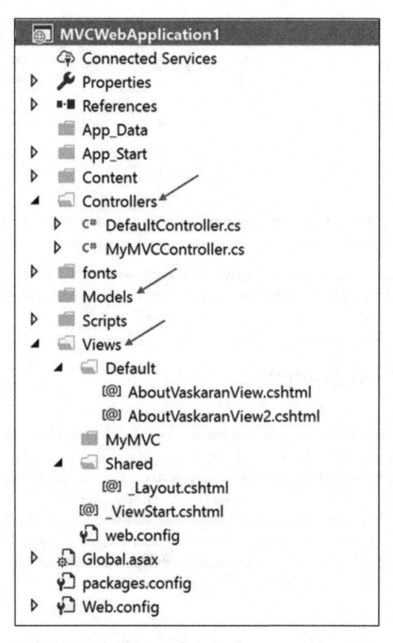

Figure 26-5. *Solution Explorer view of a typical ASP.NET MVC Project*

POINTS TO NOTE

Different technologies follow different structures, so you don't need a folder structure with the strict naming convention shown in Figure 26-5.

Implementation

For simplicity and to match our theory, I also divided the upcoming implementation into three major parts: model, view, and controller. Once you note the Solution Explorer view, you can identify the separate folders created to accomplish this task. Here are some important points.

- **IModel, IView,** and **IController** are three interfaces that are implemented by the concrete classes **EmployeeModel, ConsoleView,** and **EmployeeController,** respectively. Seeing these names, you can assume that these are representatives of the model, view, and controller layers of our MVC architecture.

- In this application, the requirement is very simple. Some employees need to register on an application. Initially, the application has three different registered employees: Amit, Jon, and Sam. These employees have ID's as E1, E2, and E3. So, you see the following constructor:

```
public EmployeeModel()
{
    // Adding 3 employees at the beginning.
    enrolledEmployees = new List<Employee>();
    enrolledEmployees.Add(new Employee("Amit", "E1"));
    enrolledEmployees.Add(new Employee("John", "E2"));
    enrolledEmployees.Add(new Employee("Sam", "E3"));
}
```

- At any point in time, you should be able to see the enrolled employees in the system. In the client code, you invoke DisplayEnrolledEmployees() on a Controller object as follows:

```
controller.DisplayEnrolledEmployees();
```

Then the controller passes the call to view layer as follows:

```
view.ShowEnrolledEmployees(enrolledEmployees);
```

And you see that a concrete implementor of View Interface (ConsoleView.cs) describes the method as follows:

```
public void ShowEnrolledEmployees (List<Employee>
enrolledEmployees)
{
        Console.WriteLine("\n ***This is a console view of
        currently enrolled employees.*** ");
        foreach (Employee emp in enrolledEmployees)
        {
                Console.WriteLine(emp);
        }
        Console.WriteLine("--------------------");
}
```

- You can add a new employee or delete an employee from the registered employees list. The AddEmployeeToModel(Employee employee) and RemoveEmployeeFromModel(string employeeIdToRemove) methods are used for this purpose. Let's look at the method signature of RemoveEmployeeFromModel(...). To delete an employee, you need to supply the employee ID (which is nothing more than a string). But if the employee ID is not found, the application ignores this delete request.

- A simple check is added in the Employee class to ensure that you are not adding an employee with the same ID repeatedly in the application.

Now go through the implementation. Yes, it's big, but when you analyze it part by part with the help of the previous bullet points and the supporting diagrams, you should not face any difficulties with understanding the code. You can also consider the comments for your immediate reference.

POINTS TO NOTE

Typically, you want to use MVC with technologies that offer built-in support and perform much of the groundwork. For example, when you use ASP.NET (or a similar technology) to implement the MVC pattern because you have a lot of built-in support. In these cases, you need to learn the new terminologies.

Throughout this book, I use console applications for design pattern implementations. Let's continue to use the same for the upcoming implementation, because our focus is only on MVC architecture.

Class Diagram

Figure 26-6 shows the class diagram.

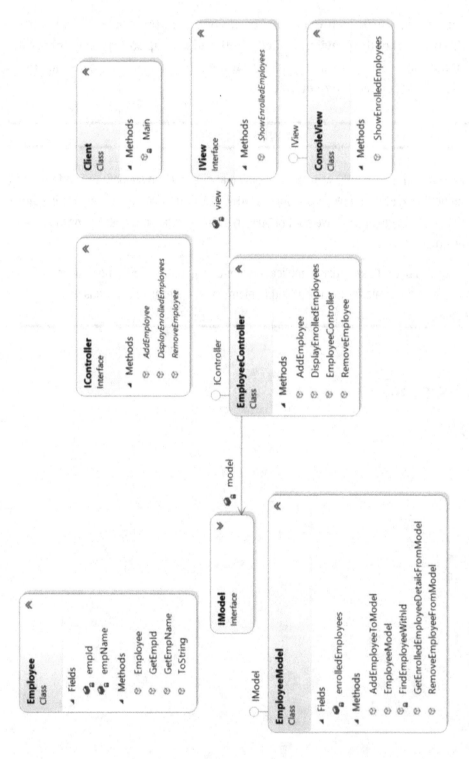

Figure 26-6. Class diagram

Solution Explorer View

Figure 26-7 shows the high-level structure of the program.

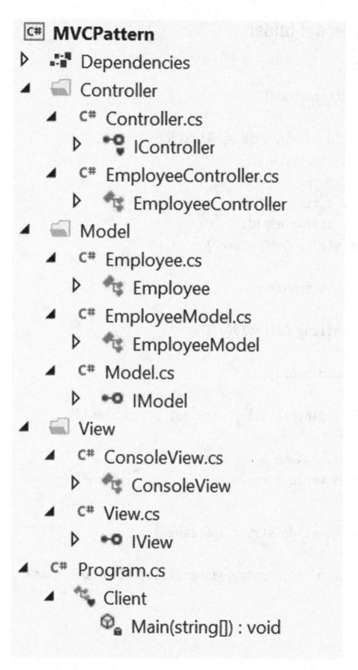

Figure 26-7. *Solution Explorer view*

Demonstration 1

Here is the complete demonstration.

Contents in Model folder

// Employee.cs

```
namespace MVCPattern.Model
{
    // The key "data" in this application
    public class Employee
    {
        private string empName;
        private string empId;
        public string GetEmpName()
        {
            return empName;
        }
        public string GetEmpId()
        {
            return empId;
        }
        public Employee(string empName, string empId)
        {
            this.empName = empName;
            this.empId = empId;
        }

        public override string ToString()
        {
            return  $"{empName} is enrolled with id : {empId}.";
        }
    }
}
```

// Model.cs

```csharp
using System.Collections.Generic;

namespace MVCPattern.Model
{
    public interface IModel
    {

        List<Employee> GetEnrolledEmployeeDetailsFromModel();
        void AddEmployeeToModel(Employee employeee);
        void RemoveEmployeeFromModel(string employeeId);
    }
}
```

// EmployeeModel.cs

```csharp
using System;
using System.Collections.Generic;

namespace MVCPattern.Model
{
    public class EmployeeModel : IModel
    {
        List<Employee> enrolledEmployees;

        public EmployeeModel()
        {
            // Adding 3 employees at the beginning.
            enrolledEmployees = new List<Employee>();
            enrolledEmployees.Add(new Employee("Amit", "E1"));
            enrolledEmployees.Add(new Employee("John", "E2"));
            enrolledEmployees.Add(new Employee("Sam", "E3"));
        }

        public List<Employee> GetEnrolledEmployeeDetailsFromModel()
        {
            return enrolledEmployees;
        }
```

```csharp
// Adding an employee to the model(registered employee list)
public void AddEmployeeToModel(Employee employee)
{
    Console.WriteLine($"\nTrying to add an employee to the
    registered list.The employee name is {employee.GetEmpName()}
    and id is {employee.GetEmpId()}.");

    if (!enrolledEmployees.Contains(employee))
    {
        enrolledEmployees.Add(employee);
        Console.WriteLine(employee + " [added recently.]");
    }
    else
    {
        Console.WriteLine("This employee is already added in the
        registered list.So, ignoring the request of addition.");
    }
}
// Removing an employee from model(registered employee list)

public void RemoveEmployeeFromModel(string employeeIdToRemove)
{
    Console.WriteLine($"\nTrying to remove an employee from the
    registered list.The employee id is {employeeIdToRemove}.");
    Employee emp = FindEmployeeWithId(employeeIdToRemove);
    if (emp != null)
    {
        Console.WriteLine("Removing this employee.");
        enrolledEmployees.Remove(emp);
    }
    else
    {
        Console.WriteLine($"At present, there is no employee with
        id {employeeIdToRemove}.Ignoring this request.");
    }
}
```

```
Employee FindEmployeeWithId(string employeeIdToRemove)
{
    Employee removeEmp = null;
    foreach (Employee emp in enrolledEmployees)
    {
        if (emp.GetEmpId().Equals(employeeIdToRemove))
        {
            Console.WriteLine($" Employee Found.{emp.GetEmpName()}
            has id: { employeeIdToRemove}.");
            removeEmp = emp;
        }
    }
    return removeEmp;
}
}
}
```

Contents in View folder

// View.cs

```
using MVCPattern.Model;
using System.Collections.Generic;

namespace MVCPattern.View
{
    public interface IView
    {
        void ShowEnrolledEmployees(List<Employee> enrolledEmployees);
    }
}
```

// ConsoleView.cs

```
using System;
using System.Collections.Generic;
using MVCPattern.Model;
```

```csharp
namespace MVCPattern.View
{
    public class ConsoleView : IView
    {
        public void ShowEnrolledEmployees(List<Employee> enrolledEmployees)
        {
            Console.WriteLine("\n ***This is a console view of currently
            enrolled employees.*** ");
            foreach (Employee emp in enrolledEmployees)
            {
                Console.WriteLine(emp);
            }
            Console.WriteLine("---------------------");
        }
    }
}
```

Contents in Controller folder

// Controller.cs

```csharp
using MVCPattern.Model;

namespace MVCPattern.Controller
{
    interface IController
    {
        void DisplayEnrolledEmployees();
        void AddEmployee(Employee employee);
        void RemoveEmployee(string employeeId);
    }

}
```

// EmployeeController.cs

```csharp
using System.Collections.Generic;
using MVCPattern.Model;
using MVCPattern.View;
```

510

```csharp
namespace MVCPattern.Controller
{
    public class EmployeeController : IController
    {
        IModel model;
        IView view;

        public EmployeeController(IModel model, IView view)
        {
            this.model = model;
            this.view = view;
        }

        public void DisplayEnrolledEmployees()
        {
            // Get data from Model
            List<Employee> enrolledEmployees = model.
            GetEnrolledEmployeeDetailsFromModel();
            // Connect to View
            view.ShowEnrolledEmployees(enrolledEmployees);
        }

        // Sending a request to model to add an employee to the list.
        public void AddEmployee(Employee employee)
        {
            model.AddEmployeeToModel(employee);
        }
        // Sending a request to model to remove an employee from the list.
        public void RemoveEmployee(string employeeId)
        {
            model.RemoveEmployeeFromModel(employeeId);

        }
    }
}
```

Client code

// Program.cs

```csharp
using MVCPattern.Controller;
using MVCPattern.Model;
using MVCPattern.View;
using System;

namespace MVCPattern
{
    class Client
    {
        static void Main(string[] args)
        {
            Console.WriteLine("***MVC architecture Demo***\n");
            // Model
            IModel model = new EmployeeModel();

            // View
            IView view = new ConsoleView();

            // Controller
            IController controller = new EmployeeController(model, view);
            controller.DisplayEnrolledEmployees();

            // Add an employee
            Employee empToAdd = new Employee("Kevin", "E4");
            controller.AddEmployee(empToAdd);
            // Printing the current details
            controller.DisplayEnrolledEmployees();

            // Remove an existing employee using the employee id.
            controller.RemoveEmployee("E2");
            // Printing the current details
            controller.DisplayEnrolledEmployees();
```

```
        /* Cannot remove an  employee who does not belong to the
        list.*/
        controller.RemoveEmployee("E5");
        // Printing the current details
        controller.DisplayEnrolledEmployees();

        // Avoiding a duplicate entry
        controller.AddEmployee(empToAdd);
        // Printing the current details
        controller.DisplayEnrolledEmployees();

        /* This segment is added to discuss a question in "Q&A Session"
        and initially commented out. */
        // view = new MobileDeviceView();
        // controller = new EmployeeController(model, view);
        // controller.DisplayEnrolledEmployees();
        Console.ReadKey();
      }
    }
}
```

Output

Here is the output.

```
***MVC architecture Demo***

 ***This is a console view of currently enrolled employees.***
Amit is enrolled with id : E1.
John is enrolled with id : E2.
Sam is enrolled with id : E3.
---------------------

Trying to add an employee to the registered list.The employee name is Kevin
and id is E4.
Kevin is enrolled with id : E4. [added recently.]
```

```
 ***This is a console view of currently enrolled employees.***
Amit is enrolled with id : E1.
John is enrolled with id : E2.
Sam is enrolled with id : E3.
Kevin is enrolled with id : E4.
---------------------

Trying to remove an employee from the registered list.The employee id is E2.
 Employee Found.John has id: E2.
Removing this employee.

 ***This is a console view of currently enrolled employees.***
Amit is enrolled with id : E1.
Sam is enrolled with id : E3.
Kevin is enrolled with id : E4.
---------------------

Trying to remove an employee from the registered list.The employee id is E5.
At present, there is no employee with id E5.Ignoring this request.

 ***This is a console view of currently enrolled employees.***
Amit is enrolled with id : E1.
Sam is enrolled with id : E3.
Kevin is enrolled with id : E4.
---------------------

Trying to add an employee to the registered list.The employee name is Kevin
and id is E4.
This employee is already added in the registered list.So, ignoring the
request of addition.

 ***This is a console view of currently enrolled employees.***
Amit is enrolled with id : E1.
Sam is enrolled with id : E3.
Kevin is enrolled with id : E4.
---------------------
```

Q&A Session

26.1 Suppose that you have a programmer, a DBA, and a graphic designer. Can you predict their roles in an MVC architecture?

The graphic designer designs the view layer, the DBA creates the model, and the programmer works to make an intelligent controller.

26.2 What are the key advantages of using the MVC design pattern?

Some important advantages are as follows.

- High cohesion and low coupling are the benefits of MVC. You have probably noticed that tight coupling between the model and the view is easily removed in this pattern. So, the application can be easily extendable and reusable.

- The pattern supports parallel development.

- You can also accommodate multiple runtime views.

26.3 What are the challenges associated with the MVC pattern?

Here are some challenges.

- It requires highly skilled personnel.

- For a tiny application, it may not be suitable.

- Developers may need to be familiar with multiple languages, platforms, and technologies.

- Multi-artifact consistency is a big concern because you are separating the overall project into three major parts.

26.4 Can you provide multiple views in this implementation?

Sure. Let's add a new shorter view called MobileDeviceView in the application. Let's add this class inside the View folder as follows.

```
using System;
using System.Collections.Generic;
using MVCPattern.Model;
namespace MVCPattern.View
{
```

```
public class MobileDeviceView:IView
{

    public void ShowEnrolledEmployees(List<Employee> enrolledEmployees)
    {
        Console.WriteLine("\n +++This is a mobile device view of
        currently enrolled employees.+++ ");
        foreach (Employee emp in enrolledEmployees)
        {
            Console.WriteLine(emp.GetEmpId() + "\t" + emp.
            GetEmpName());
        }
        Console.WriteLine("++++++++++++++++++++++");
    }
}
}
```

Once you add this class, your modified Solution Explorer view should be similar to Figure 26-8.

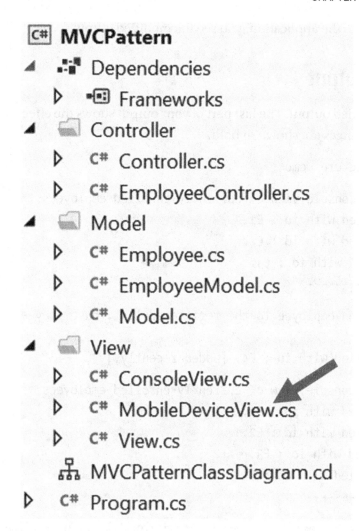

Figure 26-8. *Modified Solution Explorer view*

Now add the following segment of code at the end of your client code(Refer the comment for your reference).

```
/* This segment is added to discuss a question in "Q&A Session and was
   initially commented out.Now I'm uncommenting the following three lines
   of code."
*/
view = new MobileDeviceView();
controller = new EmployeeController(model, view);
controller.DisplayEnrolledEmployees();
```

Now if you run the application, you see the modified output.

Modified Output

Here is the modified output. The last part of your output shows the effects of the new changes. The changes are shown in bold.

```
***MVC architecture Demo***

 ***This is a console view of currently enrolled employees.***
Amit is enrolled with id : E1.
John is enrolled with id : E2.
Sam is enrolled with id : E3.
---------------------

Trying to add an employee to the registered list.The employee name is Kevin
and id is E4.
Kevin is enrolled with id : E4. [added recently.]

 ***This is a console view of currently enrolled employees.***
Amit is enrolled with id : E1.
John is enrolled with id : E2.
Sam is enrolled with id : E3.
Kevin is enrolled with id : E4.
---------------------

Trying to remove an employee from the registered list.The employee id is E2.
 Employee Found.John has id: E2.
Removing this employee.

 ***This is a console view of currently enrolled employees.***
Amit is enrolled with id : E1.
Sam is enrolled with id : E3.
Kevin is enrolled with id : E4.
---------------------

Trying to remove an employee from the registered list.The employee id is E5.
At present, there is no employee with id E5.Ignoring this request.
```

```
 ***This is a console view of currently enrolled employees.***
Amit is enrolled with id : E1.
Sam is enrolled with id : E3.
Kevin is enrolled with id : E4.
---------------------
```

Trying to add an employee to the registered list.The employee name is Kevin and id is E4.
This employee is already added in the registered list.So, ignoring the request of addition.

```
 ***This is a console view of currently enrolled employees.***
Amit is enrolled with id : E1.
Sam is enrolled with id : E3.
Kevin is enrolled with id : E4.
---------------------
 +++This is a mobile device view of currently enrolled employees.+++
E1      Amit
E3      Sam
E4      Kevin
+++++++++++++++++++++
```

CHAPTER 27

Patterns in Asynchronous Programming

You see many interesting patterns in asynchronous programming, which is tough and challenging but interesting. It is often referred to as *asynchrony*. The overall concept did not evolve in one day, it took time, and in C# 5.0, you got `async` and `await` keywords to make it easier. Before that, programmers implemented the concept with various techniques. Each technique has its pros and cons. The goal of this chapter to introduce you with different asynchronous programming patterns.

Overview

To begin, let's discuss asynchronous programming. In simple terms, you take a code segment in your application and run it on a separate thread. What is the key benefit? The simple answer is that you can free the original thread and let it continue to do its remaining tasks, while in a separate thread, you can perform a different task. This mechanism helps you develop modern-day applications; for example, when you implement a highly responsive user interface, these concepts are very useful.

POINTS TO REMEMBER

Broadly you notice three different patterns in asynchronous programming which are as follows:

- **IAsyncResult Pattern:** Alternatively, it is known as the Asynchronous Programming Model (APM). In this pattern, at the core, you see the `IAsyncResult` interface to support the asynchronous behavior. In a synchronous model, if you have a synchronous method called XXX(), in the

---

© Vaskaran Sarcar 2020
V. Sarcar, *Design Patterns in C#*, https://doi.org/10.1007/978-1-4842-6062-3_27

asynchronous version, you see the `BeginXXX()` and `EndXXX()` methods for the corresponding synchronous method. For example, in synchronous version, if you have the `Read()` method to support read operation; in asynchronous programming, you normally have `BeginRead()` and `EndRead()` methods to support the corresponding read operation asynchronously. Using this concept, from demonstration 5 to demonstration 7, you see the `BeginInvoke` and `EndInvoke` methods. But this pattern is not recommended for upcoming and new development.

- **Event-based Asynchronous Pattern (EAP):** This pattern came with the .NET Framework 2.0. It is based on the event mechanism. Here you see the method name with *the* `Async` suffix, one or multiple events, and `EventArg` derived types. This pattern is still in use, but not recommended for new development.

- **Task-based Asynchronous Pattern (TAP):** It first appeared in.NET Framework 4; it is the recommended practice for asynchronous programming. In C#, you often see the `async` and `await` keywords in this pattern.

To keep the chapter short, I could have omitted the discussions on APM and EAP, but I discuss them in this chapter so that you understand legacy code. At the same time, you discover the pathway of the continuous development of asynchronous programming.

To understand asynchronous programming better, let's start our discussion with its counterpart: synchronous programming. A synchronous approach is straightforward, and the code paths are easy to understand, but in this kind of programming, you need to wait to get the results from a particular segment of code, and until you cannot do anything fruitful. For example, when a segment of code tries to open a webpage that takes time to load, or when a segment of code is exercising a long-running algorithm, and so forth. In these cases, if you follow the synchronous approach, you need to sit idle. As a result, even if your computer is super fast and it has more computational power, you are not using its full potential, which is not a good idea. Therefore, to support modern-day demands and build highly responsive applications, the need for asynchronous programming is growing day by day. So, you benefit when you know different implementation patterns in this category.

Using Synchronous Approach

In demonstration 1, I execute a simple program, starting with a synchronous approach. Here there are two simple methods called ExecuteMethodOne() and ExecuteMethodTwo(). Inside the Main() method, I call these methods synchronously (i.e., I invoked ExecuteMethodOne() first and then ExecuteMethodTwo()). To focus on the key discussion, I made these methods very simple. I put simple sleep statements inside them to ensure that the jobs performed by these methods take a measurable amount of time to complete. Once you run the application and notice the output, you see that only after ExecuteMethodOne() finishes its execution, can ExecuteMethodTwo() begin its execution. In this case, the Main() method cannot complete until the methods complete their executions.

Note   Throughout this chapter, you see these methods with slight variations. I tried to maintain similar methods so that you can compare different techniques of asynchronous programming easily. For the simple demonstration purposes, in these examples, I assume ExecuteMethodOne() takes more time to finish because it'll perform some lengthy operation. So, I forced a relatively long sleep inside it. On the contrary, I assume that ExecuteMethodTwo() performs a small task, so I placed a relatively short sleep inside it.

Demonstration 1

Here is the complete demonstration.

```
using System;
using System.Threading;

namespace SynchronousProgrammingExample
{
    class Program
    {
        static void Main(string[] args)
        {
```

```
        Console.WriteLine("***A Synchronous Program
        Demonstration.***");
        Console.WriteLine("ExecuteMethodTwo() needs to wait for
        ExecuteMethodOne() to finish first.");
        ExecuteMethodOne();
        ExecuteMethodTwo();
        Console.WriteLine("End Main().");
        Console.ReadKey();
    }
    // First Method
    private static void ExecuteMethodOne()
    {
        Console.WriteLine("MethodOne has started.");
        // Some big task
        Thread.Sleep(1000);
        Console.WriteLine("MethodOne has finished.");
    }
    // Second Method
    private static void ExecuteMethodTwo()
    {
        Console.WriteLine("MethodTwo has started.");
        // Some small task
        Thread.Sleep(100);
        Console.WriteLine("MethodTwo has finished.");
    }
}
}
```

Output

Here is the output.

```
***A Synchronous Program Demonstration.***
ExecuteMethodTwo() needs to wait for ExecuteMethodOne() to finish first.
MethodOne has started.
MethodOne has finished.
```

```
MethodTwo has started.
MethodTwo has finished.
End Main().
```

Using Thread Class

If you look closely at the methods in demonstration 1, you find that those methods were not dependent on each other. If you can execute them in parallel, the response time of your application is improved, and you can reduce the overall execution time. So, let's find some better approaches.

You can implement the concepts of multithreading in this case. Demonstration 2 is a simple solution using threads. It shows substituting the ExecuteMethodOne() method inside a new thread.

Demonstration 2

```csharp
using System;
using System.Threading;

namespace UsingThreadClass
{
    class Program
    {
        static void Main(string[] args)
        {
            Console.WriteLine("***Asynchronous Programming using Thread
            class.***");
            //ExecuteMethodOne();
            //Old approach.Creating a separate thread for the following
            //task(i.e. ExecuteMethodOne.)
            Thread newThread = new Thread(() =>
            {
                Console.WriteLine("MethodOne has started on a separate
                thread.");
                // Some big task
```

```
            Thread.Sleep(1000);
            Console.WriteLine("MethodOne has finished.");
        }
        );
        newThread.Start();
        /*
            Taking a small sleep to increase the probability of
            executing ExecuteMethodOne() before ExecuteMethodTwo().
         */
        Thread.Sleep(20);
        ExecuteMethodTwo();
        Console.WriteLine("End Main().");
        Console.ReadKey();
    }

    // Second Method
    private static void ExecuteMethodTwo()
    {
        Console.WriteLine("MethodTwo has started.");
        // Some small task
        Thread.Sleep(100);
        Console.WriteLine("MethodTwo has finished.");
    }
  }
}
```

Output

The following is a possible output.

```
***Asynchronous Programming using Thread class.***
MethodOne has started on a separate thread.
MethodTwo has started.
MethodTwo has finished.
End Main().
MethodOne has finished.
```

Analysis

Notice that although ExecuteMethodOne() started early, ExecuteMethodTwo() did not wait for ExecuteMethodOne() to finish its execution. Also, since ExecuteMethodTwo() is doing very little (sleep time is 100 milliseconds), it was able to finish before ExecuteMethodOne() finished its execution. Not only this, since the main thread was not blocked, it was able to continue its execution.

Q&A Session

27.1 Why do you put a sleep statement before the execution of Method2() inside Main?

Good catch. It was not necessary, but in some cases, you may notice that even though you try to start ExecuteMethodOne() to execute on a separate thread before ExecuteMethodTwo() in the current thread, it doesn't happen. As a result, you may notice the following output.

```
***Asynchronous Programming using Thread class.***
MethodTwo has started.
MethodOne has started in a separate thread.
MethodTwo has finished.
End Main().
MethodOne has finished.
```

This simple sleep statement helps you increase the probability of starting ExecuteMethodOne() before ExecuteMethodTwo() in this example.

Using ThreadPool Class

Creating threads directly in a real-world application is normally discouraged. Some key reasons behind this are as follows.

- Maintaining too many threads incur tough and costly operations.

- A large amount of time is wasted due to context switching, instead of doing real work.

To avoid directly creating threads, C# gives you the facility to use the built-in ThreadPool class. With this class, you can use the existing threads, which can be reused to serve your purpose. The ThreadPool class is very effective in maintaining the optimal number of threads in your application. So, if needed, you can execute some of your tasks asynchronously using this facility.

ThreadPool is a static class that contains some static methods; some of them have an overloaded version too. For your quick reference, Figure 27-1 is a partial screenshot from Visual Studio IDE that shows the methods in the ThreadPool class.

```
namespace System.Threading
{
    ...public static class ThreadPool
    {
        ...public static bool BindHandle(SafeHandle osHandle);
        ...public static bool BindHandle(IntPtr osHandle);
        ...public static void GetAvailableThreads(out int workerThreads, out int completionPortThreads);
        ...public static void GetMaxThreads(out int workerThreads, out int completionPortThreads);
        ...public static void GetMinThreads(out int workerThreads, out int completionPortThreads);
        ...public static bool QueueUserWorkItem(WaitCallback callBack);
        ...public static bool QueueUserWorkItem(WaitCallback callBack, object state);
        ...public static RegisteredWaitHandle RegisterWaitForSingleObject(WaitHandle waitObject, WaitOrT:
        ...public static RegisteredWaitHandle RegisterWaitForSingleObject(WaitHandle waitObject, WaitOrT:
        ...public static RegisteredWaitHandle RegisterWaitForSingleObject(WaitHandle waitObject, WaitOrT:
        ...public static RegisteredWaitHandle RegisterWaitForSingleObject(WaitHandle waitObject, WaitOrT:
        ...public static bool SetMaxThreads(int workerThreads, int completionPortThreads);
        ...public static bool SetMinThreads(int workerThreads, int completionPortThreads);
        ...public static bool UnsafeQueueNativeOverlapped(NativeOverlapped* overlapped);
        ...public static bool UnsafeQueueUserWorkItem(WaitCallback callBack, object state);
        ...public static RegisteredWaitHandle UnsafeRegisterWaitForSingleObject(WaitHandle waitObject, Wa
        ...public static RegisteredWaitHandle UnsafeRegisterWaitForSingleObject(WaitHandle waitObject, Wa
        ...public static RegisteredWaitHandle UnsafeRegisterWaitForSingleObject(WaitHandle waitObject, Wa
        ...public static RegisteredWaitHandle UnsafeRegisterWaitForSingleObject(WaitHandle waitObject, Wa
    }
}
```

Figure 27-1. *A screenshot of ThreadPool class from Visual Studio 2019 IDE*

In this section, our focus is on the QueueUserWorkItem method. Figure 27-1 shows that this method has two overloaded versions. Now to know the details of this method, let's expand the method description in Visual Studio. For example, once you expand the first overloaded version of this method, you notice the following.

```
//
// Summary:
//     Queues a method for execution. The method executes when a thread
//     pool thread becomes available.
//
```

```
// Parameters:
//   callBack:
//     A System.Threading.WaitCallback that represents the method to be
//     executed.
//
// Returns:
//     true if the method is successfully queued; System.NotSupportedException
//     is thrown if the work item could not be queued.
//
// Exceptions:
//   T:System.ArgumentNullException:
//     callBack is null.
//
//   T:System.NotSupportedException:
//     The common language runtime (CLR) is hosted, and the host does not
//     support this action.
[SecuritySafeCritical]
public static bool QueueUserWorkItem(WaitCallback callBack);
```

If you further investigate the method parameter, you find that WaitCallBack is a delegate with the following description.

```
//
// Summary:
//     Represents a callback method to be executed by a thread pool thread.
//
// Parameters:
//   state:
//     An object containing information to be used by the callback method.
[ComVisible(true)]
public delegate void WaitCallback(object state);
```

The second overloaded version of QueueUserWorkItem can take an additional object parameter named state. It is as follows.

```
public static bool QueueUserWorkItem(WaitCallback callBack, object state);
```

It tells that using this overloaded version, you can pass some valuable data to your method through this parameter. In the upcoming demonstration, I use both overloaded versions, and that's why, in the upcoming example, in addition to ExecuteMethodOne() and ExecuteMethodTwo() (which you saw in the previous demonstrations), I introduce another method called ExecuteMethodThree() in which I pass an object parameter.

People often use the words- arguments and parameter interchangeably. But an expert programmer is often particular about this. The variable(s) used in a method definition is called parameters of the method. For example, if you see a method definition inside a class something like the following:

```
public void Sum(int firstNumber,int secondNumber)
```

you say that the firstNumber and secondNumber are the parameters of the method Sum. Now assume you have an object of the class, say ob. So, when you invoke the method using the following line:

```
ob.Sum(1,2)
```

you say that 1 and 2 are the arguments that you've passed to the Sum method.

In short, you can say that we pass the arguments to a method, and these values are assigned to the method parameters. Following these definitions, I should say in my comments that I have passed 10 as an argument to ExecuteMethodThree. But for the sake of simplicity, often programmers do not emphasize on these terms too much, and you may see these terms are used interchangeably.

Demonstration 3

To use the QueueUserWorkItem method effectively, you need to use a method that matches a WaitCallBack delegate signature. In the following demonstration, I queue two methods in a ThreadPool. In demonstration 1 and demonstration 2, ExecuteMethodTwo() did not accept any parameter. So, if you want to use this method as it is and pass it to QueueUserWorkItem, you get the following compilation error.

```
No overload for 'ExecuteMethodTwo' matches delegate 'WaitCallback'
```

So, let's modify the ExecuteMethodTwo() method with a dummy object parameter as follows. (I kept the comments for your reference.)

```
/*
The following method's signature should match
the delegate WaitCallback.It is as follows:
public delegate void WaitCallback(object state)
*/
private static void ExecuteMethodTwo(object state)
{
  Console.WriteLine("--MethodTwo has started.");
  // Some small task
  Thread.Sleep(100);
  Console.WriteLine("--MethodTwo has finished.");
}
```

Let's now introduce another method named ExecuteMethodThree(...), which truly uses the parameter. This method is described as follows.

```
private static void ExecuteMethodThree(object number)
{
 Console.WriteLine("---MethodThree has started.");
 int upperLimit = (int)number;
 for (int i = 0; i < upperLimit; i++)
 {
  Console.WriteLine("---MethodThree prints 3.0{0}", i);
 }
 Thread.Sleep(100);
 Console.WriteLine("---MethodThree has finished.");
}
```

Now go through the following demonstration and corresponding output.

```
using System;
using System.Threading;

namespace UsingThreadPool
{
```

```csharp
class Program
{
    static void Main(string[] args)
    {
        Console.WriteLine("***Asynchronous Programming using ThreadPool
        class.***");

        // Using Threadpool
        // Not passing any argument to ExecuteMethodTwo
        ThreadPool.QueueUserWorkItem(new WaitCallback(ExecuteMethodTwo));
        /*
         Passing 10 as the argument to
         ExecuteMethodThree.
        */
        ThreadPool.QueueUserWorkItem(new WaitCallback(ExecuteMethod
        Three), 10);
        ExecuteMethodOne();

        Console.WriteLine("End Main().");
        Console.ReadKey();
    }

    private static void ExecuteMethodOne()
    {
        Console.WriteLine("-MethodOne has started.");
        // Some big task
        Thread.Sleep(1000);
        Console.WriteLine("-MethodOne has finished.");
    }

    /*
    The following method's signature should match
    the delegate WaitCallback.It is as follows:
    public delegate void WaitCallback(object state)
    */
```

```
private static void ExecuteMethodTwo(object state)
{
    Console.WriteLine("--MethodTwo has started.");
    // Some small task
    Thread.Sleep(100);
    Console.WriteLine("--MethodTwo has finished.");
}
/*
The following method has a parameter.
This method's signature also matches the WaitCallBack
delegate signature.
*/
private static void ExecuteMethodThree(object number)
{
    Console.WriteLine("---MethodThree has started.");
    int upperLimit = (int)number;
    for (int i = 0; i < upperLimit; i++)
    {
        Console.WriteLine($"---MethodThree prints 3.0{i}");
    }
    Thread.Sleep(100);
    Console.WriteLine("---MethodThree has finished.");
}
    }
}
```

Output

The following is a possible output.

```
***Asynchronous Programming using ThreadPool class.***
-MethodOne has started.
--MethodTwo has started.
---MethodThree has started.
---MethodThree prints 3.00
---MethodThree prints 3.01
```

```
---MethodThree prints 3.02
---MethodThree prints 3.03
---MethodThree prints 3.04
---MethodThree prints 3.05
---MethodThree prints 3.06
---MethodThree prints 3.07
---MethodThree prints 3.08
---MethodThree prints 3.09
--MethodTwo has finished.
---MethodThree has finished.
-MethodOne has finished.
End Main().
```

Q&A Session

27.2 Using the simple delegate instantiation technique, if I use the following first line instead of the second line, will the application compile and run?

```
ThreadPool.QueueUserWorkItem(ExecuteMethodTwo);
ThreadPool.QueueUserWorkItem(new WaitCallback(ExecuteMethodTwo));
```

Yes, but since you are learning to use the WaitCallback delegate now, I used the detailed way of instantiation to draw your special attention to it.

Using Lambda Expression with the ThreadPool Class

If you like lambda expressions, you can use it in a similar context. For example, in the previous demonstration, you can replace ExecuteMethodThree(...) using the lambda expression as follows.

```
// Using lambda Expression
// Here the method needs a parameter(input).
// Passing 10 as an argument to ExecuteMethodThree
ThreadPool.QueueUserWorkItem((number) =>
```

```
{
  Console.WriteLine("--MethodThree has started.");
  int upperLimit = (int)number;
  for (int i = 0; i < upperLimit; i++)
  {
   Console.WriteLine("---MethodThree prints 3.0{0}", i);
  }
  Thread.Sleep(100);
  Console.WriteLine("--MethodThree has finished.");
  }, 10

);
```

So, in the previous demonstration, you can comment out the following line and replace ExecuteMethodThree(...) with the lambda expression introduced earlier.

```
ThreadPool.QueueUserWorkItem(new WaitCallback(ExecuteMethodThree), 10);
```

If you execute the program again, you get a similar output. For your reference, I present the full implementation in demonstration 4.

Demonstration 4

```
using System;
using System.Threading;

namespace UsingThreadPoolWithLambdaExpression
{
    class Program
    {
        static void Main(string[] args)
        {
            Console.WriteLine("***Asynchronous Programming
            Demonstration.***");
            Console.WriteLine("***Using ThreadPool with Lambda
            Expression.***");
```

```csharp
            // Using Threadpool
            // Not passing any parameter for ExecuteMethodTwo
            ThreadPool.QueueUserWorkItem(ExecuteMethodTwo);
            // Using lambda Expression
            // Here the method needs a parameter(input).
            // Passing 10 as an argument to ExecuteMethodThree
            ThreadPool.QueueUserWorkItem((number) =>
            {
                Console.WriteLine("--MethodThree has started.");
                int upperLimit = (int)number;
                for (int i = 0; i < upperLimit; i++)
                {
                    Console.WriteLine("---MethodThree prints 3.0{0}", i);
                }
                Thread.Sleep(100);
                Console.WriteLine("--MethodThree has finished.");
            }, 10
        );

            ExecuteMethodOne();
            Console.WriteLine("End Main().");
            Console.ReadKey();
        }
        /// <summary>
        /// ExecuteMethodOne()
        /// </summary>
        private static void ExecuteMethodOne()
        {
            Console.WriteLine("-MethodOne has started.");
            // Some big task
            Thread.Sleep(1000);
            Console.WriteLine("-MethodOne has finished.");
        }
```

```
/*
The following method's signature should match
the delegate WaitCallback.It is as follows:
public delegate void WaitCallback(object state)
*/

private static void ExecuteMethodTwo(Object state)
{
    Console.WriteLine("--MethodTwo has started.");
    // Some small task
    Thread.Sleep(100);
    Console.WriteLine("--MethodTwo has finished.");
}
    }
}
```

Output

The following is a possible output.

```
***Asynchronous Programming Demonstration.***
***Using ThreadPool with Lambda Expression.***
--MethodTwo has started.
-MethodOne has started.
--MethodThree has started.
---MethodThree prints 3.00
---MethodThree prints 3.01
---MethodThree prints 3.02
---MethodThree prints 3.03
---MethodThree prints 3.04
---MethodThree prints 3.05
---MethodThree prints 3.06
---MethodThree prints 3.07
---MethodThree prints 3.08
---MethodThree prints 3.09
```

```
--MethodTwo has finished.
--MethodThree has finished.
-MethodOne has finished.
End Main().
```

Note   This time, you saw lambda expressions with the `ThreadPool` class. In demonstration 2, you saw lambda expressions with the `Thread` class.

Using IAsyncResult Pattern

I mentioned that the `IAsyncResult` interface helps you implement asynchronous behavior. I also told you that in a synchronous model, if you have a synchronous method called XXX, in the asynchronous version, you see the `BeginXXX` and `EndXXX` methods for the corresponding synchronous method. Now you see these in detail.

Polling Using Asynchronous Delegates

In demonstration 3 and demonstration 4, you saw a built-in `WaitCallBack` delegate. In general, delegates have many different uses. In this section, you see another important usage. Let's consider *polling*, which is a mechanism that repeatedly checks a condition. In our upcoming example, let's check whether a delegate instance completes its task or not.

Demonstration 5

This time, I modify the `ExecuteMethodOne(...)` and `ExecuteMethodTwo()` methods slightly. These methods can print the thread IDs. Instead of blindly sleeping for 1000 milliseconds, this time, I allow `ExecuteMethodOne(...)` to accept an `int` parameter, which supplies sleep times.

As in previous cases, `ExecuteMethodTwo()` sleeps only for 100 milliseconds, but `ExecuteMethodOne(...)` takes more time to complete its task compared to `ExecuteMethodTwo()`. To make it happen, in this example, I pass 3000 milliseconds inside `ExecuteMethodOne(...)` as the method argument.

Let's look at the important segment of the code. Now my ExecuteMethodOne is as follows:

```
// First Method
private static void ExecuteMethodOne(int sleepTimeInMilliSec)
{
  Console.WriteLine("MethodOne has started.");
  Console.WriteLine($"Inside ExecuteMethodOne(),Thread id {Thread.
CurrentThread.ManagedThreadId}.");
  // Some big task
  Thread.Sleep(sleepTimeInMilliSec);
  Console.WriteLine("\nMethodOne has finished.");
}
```

To match the signature, I declare the delegate Method1Delegate as follows.

```
public delegate void Method1Delegate(int sleepTimeinMilliSec);
```

And later I instantiate it as follows.

```
Method1Delegate method1Del = ExecuteMethodOne;
```

Everything is straightforward so far. Now come to the most important line of the code, which is as follows.

```
IAsyncResult asyncResult = method1Del.BeginInvoke(3000, null, null);
```

Do you remember that in the context of a delegate, you can use the Invoke() method? But that time your code followed a synchronous path. Now you are exploring asynchronous programming, and so you see the BeginInvoke and EndInvoke methods. When the C# compiler sees the delegate keyword, it supplies these methods for a dynamically generated class.

BeginInvoke method's return type is IAsyncResult. If you hover your mouse on BeginInvoke or notice its structure, you see that although ExecuteMethodOne accepts only one parameter, the BeginInvoke method always takes two additional parameters: one of type AsyncCallback and one of type object. You see the discussion on them shortly. In this example, I used the first parameter only and passed 3000 milliseconds as ExecuteMethodOne's argument. But for the last two parameters of BeginInvoke, I passed null values.

The returned result of BeginInvoke is important and I hold the result in an IAsyncResult object. The IAsyncResult has the following the read-only properties.

```
public interface IAsyncResult
{
  bool IsCompleted { get; }
  WaitHandle AsyncWaitHandle { get; }
  object AsyncState { get; }
  bool CompletedSynchronously { get; }
}
```

For now, my focus is on the isCompleted property. If you expand these definitions further, you see that isCompleted is defined as follows.

```
//
// Summary:
//      Gets a value that indicates whether the asynchronous  operation has
//      completed.
//
// Returns:
//      true if the operation is complete; otherwise, false.
bool IsCompleted { get; }
```

So, it's clear that you can use this property to verify whether the delegate has completed its work.

In the following example, I check whether the delegate in other thread completes its work. If the work is not completed, I print asterisks (*) in the console window and forcing the main thread to take a short sleep, which is why you see the following segment of code in this demonstration.

```
while (!asyncResult.IsCompleted)
{
    // Keep working in main thread
    Console.Write("*");
    Thread.Sleep(5);
}
```

Lastly, the EndInvoke method accepts an argument of type IAsyncResult. So, I passed asyncResult as an argument in this method. Now go through the complete demonstration.

```
using System;
using System.Threading;

namespace PollingDemoInDotNetFramework
{
    //WILL NOT WORK ON .NET CORE.
    //RUN THIS PROGRAM ON .NET FRAMEWORK.
    class Program
    {
        public delegate void Method1Delegate(int sleepTimeinMilliSec);
        static void Main(string[] args)
        {
            Console.WriteLine("***Polling Demo.Run it in .NET
            Framework.***");
            Console.WriteLine("Inside Main(),Thread id {0} .", Thread.
            CurrentThread.ManagedThreadId);
            // Synchronous call
            //ExecuteMethodOne(3000);

            Method1Delegate method1Del = ExecuteMethodOne;
            IAsyncResult asyncResult = method1Del.BeginInvoke(3000, null,
            null);
            ExecuteMethodTwo();
            while (!asyncResult.IsCompleted)
            {
                // Keep working in main thread
                Console.Write("*");
                Thread.Sleep(5);
            }

            method1Del.EndInvoke(asyncResult);
            Console.ReadKey();
        }
```

```
    // First Method
    private static void ExecuteMethodOne(int sleepTimeInMilliSec)
    {
        Console.WriteLine("MethodOne has started.");
        Console.WriteLine($"Inside ExecuteMethodOne(),Thread id
        {Thread.CurrentThread.ManagedThreadId}.");
        // Some big task
        Thread.Sleep(sleepTimeInMilliSec);
        Console.WriteLine("\nMethodOne has finished.");
    }
    // Second Method
    private static void ExecuteMethodTwo()
    {
        Console.WriteLine("MethodTwo has started.");
        Console.WriteLine($"Inside ExecuteMethodTwo(),Thread id
        {Thread.CurrentThread.ManagedThreadId}.");
        // Some small task
        Thread.Sleep(100);
        Console.WriteLine("MethodTwo has finished.");
    }

    }
}
```

Output

The following is a possible output.

```
***Polling Demo.Run it in .NET Framework.***
Inside Main(),Thread id 1 .
MethodTwo has started.
Inside ExecuteMethodTwo(),Thread id 1.
MethodOne has started.
Inside ExecuteMethodOne(),Thread id 3.
MethodTwo has finished.
*************************************************************************
*************************************************************************
```

```
***********************************************************************
***********************************************************************
***********************************************************************
********************************************************************
```
MethodOne has finished.

Q&A Session

27.3 In a previous case, ExecuteMethodOne(...) takes only one parameter, and the BeginInvoke takes three parameters. So, can I simply say that if ExecuteMethodOne(...) accepts n number of parameters, then BeginInvoke has n+2 parameters?

Yes, the initial set of parameters is based on your methods, but for the last two parameters, one is of type AsyncCallback, and the final one is of type object.

POINTS TO REMEMBER

- This type of example was run in .NET Framework 4.7.2. If you execute the program in .NET Core 3.0, you get this exception: System. PlatformNotSupportedException: 'Operation is not supported on this platform. One of the primary reasons for this is that async delegates implementations depend on remoting features that are not present in .NET Core. The detailed discussion on this can be found at https://github.com/dotnet/runtime/issues/16312.

- If you do not want to examine and print the asterisks (*) in the console window, you can simply call the EndInvoke() method of the delegate type once your main thread completes its execution. The EndInvoke() itself waits until the delegate completes its work.

- If you don't explicitly examine whether the delegate finishes its execution or not, or you simply forget to call EndInvoke(), the thread of the delegate stops after the main thread dies. For instance, if you comment out the following segment of code from the prior example.

```
//while (!asyncResult.IsCompleted)
//{
//    Keep working in main thread
```

```
//      Console.Write("*");
//      Thread.Sleep(5);
//}
//method1Del.EndInvoke(asyncResult);
//Console.ReadKey();
```

And run the application again, you may NOT see the statement "MethodOne has finished."

- BeginInvoke helps the calling thread get the result of the asynchronous method invocation at a later time by using `EndInvoke`.

Using AsyncWaitHandle of IAsyncResult

Did you notice `WaitHandle AsyncWaitHandle { get; }` inside `IAsyncResult`? It is important, and this time, I show you an alternative approach using this property. If you see it closely, you find that `AsyncWaitHandle` returns a `WaitHandle`, and it has the following description.

```
//
// Summary:
//      Gets a System.Threading.WaitHandle that is used to wait for an
//      asynchronous operation to complete.
//
// Returns:
//      A System.Threading.WaitHandle that is used to wait for an
//      asynchronous operation to complete.
WaitHandle AsyncWaitHandle { get; }
```

The Visual Studio IDE confirms that `WaitHandle` is an abstract class that waits for exclusive access to shared resources. Inside `WaitHandle`, you see `WaitOne()` method with five different overloaded versions, which are as follows.

```
public virtual bool WaitOne(int millisecondsTimeout);
public virtual bool WaitOne(int millisecondsTimeout, bool exitContext);
public virtual bool WaitOne(TimeSpan timeout);
public virtual bool WaitOne(TimeSpan timeout, bool exitContext);
```

```
public virtual bool WaitOne();
```

In the upcoming demonstration, I used the first overloaded version and provided an optional timeout value in milliseconds. If you expand the method, you see the following summary associated with it.

```
// Summary:
// Blocks the current thread until the current System.Threading.WaitHandle
// receives a signal, using a 32-bit signed integer to specify the time
// interval in milliseconds.
//(Some other details omitted)
public virtual bool WaitOne(int millisecondsTimeout);
```

So, it's clear that by using WaitHandle, you can wait for a delegate thread to finish its work. In the following program, if the wait is successful, the control exits from the while loop. But if a timeout occurs, WaitOne() returns false, and the while loop continues and prints asterisks (*) in the console.

Demonstration 6

```
using System;
using System.Threading;
//RUN THIS PROGRAM ON .NET FRAMEWORK.

namespace UsingWaitHandleInDotNetFramework
{
    class Program
    {
        public delegate void Method1Delegate(int sleepTimeinMilliSec);
        static void Main(string[] args)
        {
            Console.WriteLine("***Polling and WaitHandle Demo.***");
            Console.WriteLine("Inside Main(),Thread id {0} .", Thread.
            CurrentThread.ManagedThreadId);
            // Synchronous call
            //ExecuteMethodOne(3000);
```

```
// Asynchrous call using a delegate
Method1Delegate method1Del = ExecuteMethodOne;
IAsyncResult asyncResult = method1Del.BeginInvoke(3000, null,
null);
ExecuteMethodTwo();
while (true)
{
    // Keep working in main thread
    Console.Write("*");
    /*
     There are 5 different overload method for WaitOne().
     Following method blocks the current thread until the
     current System.Threading.WaitHandle receives a
     signal,using a 32-bit signed integer to specify the time
      interval in milliseconds.
    */
    if (asyncResult.AsyncWaitHandle.WaitOne(10))
    {
        Console.Write("\nResult is available now.");
        break;
    }
}
method1Del.EndInvoke(asyncResult);
Console.WriteLine("\nExiting Main().");
Console.ReadKey();
}

// First Method
private static void ExecuteMethodOne(int sleepTimeInMilliSec)
{
    Console.WriteLine("MethodOne has started.");
    // It will have a different thread id
    Console.WriteLine($"Inside ExecuteMethodOne(),Thread id
    {Thread.CurrentThread.ManagedThreadId}.");
    // Some big task
```

```csharp
        Thread.Sleep(sleepTimeInMilliSec);
        Console.WriteLine("\nMethodOne has finished.");
    }

    // Second Method
    private static void ExecuteMethodTwo()
    {
        Console.WriteLine("MethodTwo has started.");
        Console.WriteLine($"Inside ExecuteMethodTwo(),Thread id
        {Thread.CurrentThread.ManagedThreadId}.");
        // Some small task
        Thread.Sleep(100);
        Console.WriteLine("MethodTwo has finished.");
    }
  }
}
```

Output

Here is one possible output.

```
***Polling and WaitHandle Demo.***
Inside Main(),Thread id 1 .
MethodTwo has started.
Inside ExecuteMethodTwo(),Thread id 1.
MethodOne has started.
Inside ExecuteMethodOne(),Thread id 3.
MethodTwo has finished.
************************************************************************
************************************************************************
************************************************************************
*********************************
MethodOne has finished.
***
Result is available now.
Exiting Main().
```

Analysis

If you compare this demonstration with the previous one, here you wait for the asynchronous operation to complete differently. Instead of using IsCompleted property, this time, you used the AsyncWaitHandle property of IAsyncResult. I showed you both variations, which can be seen in different applications.

Using Asynchronous Callback

Revisit the BeginInvoke method, which was used in the previous two demonstrations. Let's review how I used it.

```
// Asynchrous call using a delegate
Method1Delegate method1Del = ExecuteMethodOne;
IAsyncResult asyncResult = method1Del.BeginInvoke(3000, null, null);
```

This code segment shows that inside the BeginInvoke method, I passed two null arguments for the last two method parameters. If you hover your mouse over the line of these prior demonstrations, you notice that BeginInvoke is expecting an IAsyncCallback delegate as the second parameter and an object for the third parameter in this case.

Let's investigate the IAsyncCallback delegate. Visual Studio IDE tells that this delegate is defined in System namespace, and it has the following description.

```
//
// Summary:
//     References a method to be called when a corresponding asynchronous
//     operation completes.
//
// Parameters:
//   ar:
//     The result of the asynchronous operation.
  [ComVisible(true)]
  public delegate void AsyncCallback(IAsyncResult ar);
```

You can use a callback method to execute something useful (for example, some housekeeping works). The AsyncCallback delegate has a void return type, and it accepts an IAsyncResult parameter. So, let's define a method that can match this delegate signature and call this method once the Method1Del instance finishes its execution. Here is a sample method (let's call it ExecuteCallbackMethod) that is used in an upcoming demonstration.

```
/*
It's a callback method.This method will be invoked
when Method1Delegate completes its work.
*/
private static void ExecuteCallbackMethod(IAsyncResult asyncResult)
{
 //if null you can throw some exception

    if (asyncResult != null)
    {
     Console.WriteLine("\nCallbackMethod has started.");
     Console.WriteLine($"Inside ExecuteCallbackMethod(...), Thread id
     {Thread.CurrentThread.ManagedThreadId} .");
     // Do some housekeeping work/ clean-up operation
     Thread.Sleep(100);
     Console.WriteLine("CallbackMethod has finished.");
    }
 }
```

Demonstration 7

Now go through the complete implementation.

```
using System;
using System.Threading;

namespace UsingAsynchronousCallback
{
    class Program
    {
        public delegate void Method1Delegate(int sleepTimeinMilliSec);
        static void Main(string[] args)
        {
            Console.WriteLine("***Using Asynchronous Callback.***");
```

```
        Console.WriteLine("Inside Main(),Thread id {0} .", Thread.
        CurrentThread.ManagedThreadId);

        // Asynchrous call using a delegate
        Method1Delegate method1Del = ExecuteMethodOne;
        IAsyncResult asyncResult = method1Del.BeginInvoke(3000,
        ExecuteCallbackMethod, null);

        ExecuteMethodTwo();
        while (!asyncResult.IsCompleted)
        {
            // Keep working in main thread
            Console.Write("*");
            Thread.Sleep(5);
        }

        method1Del.EndInvoke(asyncResult);
        Console.WriteLine("Exit Main().");
        Console.ReadKey();
    }
    // First Method
    private static void ExecuteMethodOne(int sleepTimeInMilliSec)
    {
        Console.WriteLine("MethodOne has started.");
        Console.WriteLine($"Inside ExecuteMethodOne(),Thread id
        {Thread.CurrentThread.ManagedThreadId}.");
        // Some big task
        Thread.Sleep(sleepTimeInMilliSec);
        Console.WriteLine("\nMethodOne has finished.");
    }

    // Second Method
    private static void ExecuteMethodTwo()
    {
        Console.WriteLine("MethodTwo has started.");
        Console.WriteLine($"Inside ExecuteMethodTwo(),Thread id
        {Thread.CurrentThread.ManagedThreadId}.");
```

```
        // Some small task
        Thread.Sleep(100);
        Console.WriteLine("MethodTwo has finished.");
    }

    /*
     It's a callback method.This method will be invoked
     when Method1Delegate instance completes its work.
     */
    private static void ExecuteCallbackMethod(IAsyncResult asyncResult)
    {
        if (asyncResult != null)//if null you can throw some exception
        {
            Console.WriteLine("\nCallbackMethod has started.");
            Console.WriteLine($"Inside ExecuteCallbackMethod(...),
            Thread id {Thread.CurrentThread.ManagedThreadId} .");
            // Do some housekeeping work/ clean-up operation
            Thread.Sleep(100);
            Console.WriteLine("CallbackMethod has finished.");
        }
    }
  }
}
```

Output

The following is a possible output.

```
***Using Asynchronous Callback.***
Inside Main(),Thread id 1 .
MethodTwo has started.
Inside ExecuteMethodTwo(),Thread id 1.
MethodOne has started.
Inside ExecuteMethodOne(),Thread id 3.
```

```
MethodTwo has finished.
************************************************************************
************************************************************************
************************************************************************
************************************************************************
************************************************************************
************************************************************************
**********
MethodOne has finished.

CallbackMethod has started.
Inside ExecuteCallbackMethod(...),Thread id 3 .
Exit Main().
CallbackMethod has finished.
```

Analysis

The callback method started its work only after ExecuteMethodOne finished its execution. Also, note that the ExecuteMethodOne and ExecuteCallbackMethod thread IDs are the same. It is because the callback method was invoked from the thread in which ExecuteMethodOne was running.

Q&A Session

27.4 What is a callback method?

Normally, it is a method that is invoked after a specific operation is completed. You often see this kind of method in asynchronous programming when you do not know the exact finishing time of an operation, but you want to start a new task once a certain task is done. For example, in the previous example, ExecuteCallbackMethod can perform some clean-up work if ExecuteMethodOne allocates some resources during its execution.

27.5 I see that the callback method was not invoked from the main thread. Is it expected?

Yes. In this example, ExecuteCallbackMethod is the callback method that can start its execution only after ExecuteMethodOne completes its work. So, it makes sense that you call ExecuteCallbackMethod from the same thread in which ExecuteMethodOne was running.

27.6 Can I use a lambda expression in this example?

Good catch. To get a similar output, in the previous demonstration, instead of creating a new ExecuteCallbackMethod method and using the following line,

```
IAsyncResult asyncResult = method1Del.BeginInvoke(3000,
ExecuteCallbackMethod, null);
```

you could replace it using a lambda expression as follows.

```
IAsyncResult asyncResult = method1Del.BeginInvoke(3000,
 (result) =>
{
    if (result != null)//if null you can throw some exception
    {
        Console.WriteLine("\nCallbackMethod has started.");
        Console.WriteLine($"Inside ExecuteCallbackMethod(),Thread id {
        Thread.CurrentThread.ManagedThreadId }.");
        // Do some housekeeping work/ clean-up operation
        Thread.Sleep(100);
        Console.WriteLine("CallbackMethod has finished.");
    }
 },
null);
```

27.7 I see that when you used the callback method inside the **BeginInvoke** method, instead of passing an object as the final parameter, you passed a null value. Is there any specific reason for this?

No, I did not use that parameter in these demonstrations. Since it is an object parameter, you can pass anything meaningful to you. When you use a callback method, you can pass the delegate instance itself. It can help your callback method to analyze the result of the asynchronous method.

But for simplicity, let's modify the previous demonstration and pass a string message as the last argument inside BeginInvoke. Let's assume now you are modifying the existing line of code

```
IAsyncResult asyncResult = method1Del.BeginInvoke(3000,ExecuteCallback
Method, null);
```

with the following one.

```
IAsyncResult asyncResult = method1Del.BeginInvoke(3000,
ExecuteCallbackMethod, "Method1Delegate, Thank you for using me." );
```

To accommodate this change, lets modify the ExecuteCallbackMethod() method too. The newly added lines are shown in bold.

```
private static void ExecuteCallbackMethod(IAsyncResult asyncResult)
{
    if (asyncResult != null)//if null you can throw some exception
     {
       Console.WriteLine("\nCallbackMethod has started.");
       Console.WriteLine($"Inside ExecuteCallbackMethod(...),Thread id {
       Thread.CurrentThread.ManagedThreadId} .");
       // Do some housekeeping work/ clean-up operation
       Thread.Sleep(100);
       // For Q&A 27.7
       string msg = (string)asyncResult.AsyncState;
       Console.WriteLine($"Callback method says : '{msg}'");
       Console.WriteLine("CallbackMethod has finished.");
       }
   }
```

If you run the program again, this time you can see the following output which conforms the new string message:

```
***Using Asynchronous Callback.***
Inside Main(),Thread id 1 .
MethodTwo has started.
Inside ExecuteMethodTwo(),Thread id 1.
MethodOne has started.
Inside ExecuteMethodOne(),Thread id 3.
```

```
MethodTwo has finished.
********************************************************************
********************************************************************
********************************************************************
********************************************************************
********************************************************************
*************************************************************
MethodOne has finished.

CallbackMethod has started.
Exit Main().
Inside ExecuteCallbackMethod(...),Thread id 3 .
Callback method says : `Method1Delegate, Thank you for using me.'
CallbackMethod has finished.
```

POINTS TO REMEMBER

You have seen the implementation of polling, wait handles, and asynchronous callbacks using delegates. This programming model can be seen in other places in .NET Framework also, for example BeginGetResponse, BeginGetRequestStream of HttpWebRequest class or BeginExecuteNonQuery(), BeginExecuteReader(), BeginExecuteXmlReader() of SqlCommand class. These methods have overloaded versions too.

Using Event-based Asynchronous Pattern

In this section, you see the usage of event-based asynchronous patterns, which are initially tough to understand. Based on the complexity of your application, this pattern can take various forms. Here are some key characteristics of this pattern.

- In general, an asynchronous method can be a replica of its synchronous version, but when you call it, it starts on a separate thread and then return immediately. This mechanism allows you to call a thread to continue while the intended operations run in the background. Examples of these operations can be a long-running process such as loading a large image, downloading a large file, connecting, establishing a connection to a database, and so forth. Event-based asynchronous patterns are helpful in these contexts. For example, once the long-running download operation is completed, an event can be raised to notify the information. The subscribers of the event can act based on this notification immediately.

- You can execute multiple methods simultaneously and receive a notification when each one completes.

- Using this pattern, you take advantage of multithreading, but at the same time, you hide the overall complexity.

- In the simplest case, your method name has an `Async` suffix to tell others that you are using an asynchronous version of the method. At the same time, you have a corresponding event with a `Completed` suffix. In an ideal case, you should have a corresponding cancel method, and it should support displaying the progress bar/report. The method that supports the cancel operation can also be named `MethodNameAsyncCancel` (or simply `CancelAsync`).

- Components like SoundPlayer, PictureBox, WebClient, and BackgroundWorker are commonly known representatives of this pattern.

I made a simple application using WebClient. Let's look at it.

Demonstration 8

At the beginning of the program, you see that I needed to include some specific namespaces. I used the comments to tell you about their importance in this demonstration.

In this example, I want to download a file into my local system. But instead of using a true URL from the Internet, I stored the source file in my local system. This gives two major benefits.

- You do not need an Internet connection to run this application.

- Since you're not using the Internet connection, the download operation is relatively faster.

Now look at the following block of code before you see the complete example.

```
WebClient webClient = new WebClient();
// File location
Uri myLocation = new Uri(@"C:\TestData\testfile_original.txt");
// Target location for download
string targetLocation = @"C:\TestData\downloaded_file.txt";
webClient.DownloadFileAsync(myLocation, targetLocation);
webClient.DownloadFileCompleted += new AsyncCompletedEventHandler(Download
Completed);
```

So far, things are straightforward and simple. But I draw your attention to the following lines of code.

```
webClient.DownloadFileAsync(myLocation, targetLocation);
webClient.DownloadFileCompleted += new AsyncCompletedEventHandler(Download
Completed);
```

You can see that in the first line, I use a method defined in WebClient called DownloadFileAsync. In Visual Studio, the method description tells us the following.

```
// Summary:
//     Downloads, to a local file, the resource with the specified
//     URI. This method does not block the calling thread.
//
// Parameters:
//   address:
//     The URI of the resource to download.
//
//   fileName:
//     The name of the file to be placed on the local computer.
//
// Exceptions:
//   T:System.ArgumentNullException:
//     The address parameter is null. -or- The fileName parameter is null.
//
//   T:System.Net.WebException:
```

```
//      The URI formed by combining System.Net.WebClient.BaseAddress and
        address is invalid.
//      -or- An error occurred while downloading the resource.
//
//   T:System.InvalidOperationException:
//      The local file specified by fileName is in use by another thread.
public void DownloadFileAsync(Uri address, string fileName);
```

When you use this method, the calling thread is not blocked. (Actually, DownloadFileAsync is the asynchronous version of the DownloadFile method, which is also defined in WebClient.)

Now we come to the next line of code.

```
webClient.DownloadFileCompleted += new
AsyncCompletedEventHandler(DownloadCompleted);
```

Visual Studio describes DownloadFileCompleted event as follows.

```
/ Summary:
//      Occurs when an asynchronous file download operation completes.
public event AsyncCompletedEventHandler DownloadFileCompleted;
```

It further describes AsyncCompletedEventHandler as follows.

```
// Summary:
//      Represents the method that will handle the MethodNameCompleted event  ·
//      of an asynchronous operation.
//
// Parameters:
//   sender:
//      The source of the event.
//
//   e:
//      An System.ComponentModel.AsyncCompletedEventArgs that contains the
//      event data.
public delegate void AsyncCompletedEventHandler(object sender,
AsyncCompletedEventArgs e);
```

You can subscribe to the DownloadFileCompleted event to show a notification that the download operation is finished. To do that, I used the following method.

```
private static void DownloadCompleted(object sender,
AsyncCompletedEventArgs e)
{
    Console.WriteLine("Successfully downloaded the file now.");
}
```

Note The DownloadCompleted method matches the signature of AsyncCompletedEventHandler delegate.

I assume that you have mastered the concept of delegates and events before you run this application. So, you know that I could replace the line of code.

```
webClient.DownloadFileCompleted += new AsyncCompletedEventHandler(Download
Completed);
```

with the following line of code.

```
webClient.DownloadFileCompleted += DownloadCompleted;
```

But I like to keep the long version for better readability. Now go through the complete example and output.

```
using System;
// For AsyncCompletedEventHandler delegate
using System.ComponentModel;
using System.Net; // For WebClient
using System.Threading; // For Thread.Sleep() method

namespace UsingWebClient
{
    class Program
    {
        static void Main(string[] args)
        {
            Console.WriteLine("***Event Based Asynchronous Program
            Demo.***");
```

```csharp
            // Method1();
            #region The lenghty operation(download)
            Console.WriteLine("Starting a download operation.");
            WebClient webClient = new WebClient();
            // File location
            Uri myLocation = new Uri(@"C:\TestData\OriginalFile.txt");
            // Target location for download
            string targetLocation = @"C:\TestData\DownloadedFile.txt";
            webClient.DownloadFileAsync(myLocation, targetLocation);
            webClient.DownloadFileCompleted += new AsyncCompletedEvent
            Handler(DownloadCompleted);
            #endregion
            ExecuteMethodTwo();
            Console.WriteLine("End Main()...");
            Console.ReadKey();
        }
        // ExecuteMethodTwo
        private static void ExecuteMethodTwo()
        {
            Console.WriteLine("MethodTwo has started.");
            // Some very small task
            Thread.Sleep(10);
            Console.WriteLine("MethodTwo has finished.");
        }

        private static void DownloadCompleted(object sender,
        AsyncCompletedEventArgs e)
        {
            Console.WriteLine("Successfully downloaded the file now.");
        }
    }
}
```

Output

The following is a possible output.

```
***Event Based Asynchronous Program Demo.***
Starting a download operation.
MethodTwo has started.
MethodTwo has finished.
End Main()...
Successfully downloaded the file now.
```

Analysis

You can see that the download operation started before ExecuteMethodTwo() starts its execution. Still, ExecuteMethodTwo() completed its job before the download operation completed. If you are interested in the content of Original.txt, here it is.

```
Dear Reader,
This is my test file.It is originally stored at C:\TestData in my system.
```

You can test with a similar file and contents for a quick verification at your end.

Additional Note

You can make this example even better when you introduce a progress bar. In that case, you can use a Windows Form App to get built-in support for the progress bar. Let's ignore ExecuteMethodTwo() for now, and focus on the asynchronous download operation solely. You can make a basic form, as shown in Figure 27-2, which contains three simple buttons and one progress bar. (You need to drag and drop these controls on your form first and name them as shown in Figure 27-2. I assume that you know these simple activities.)

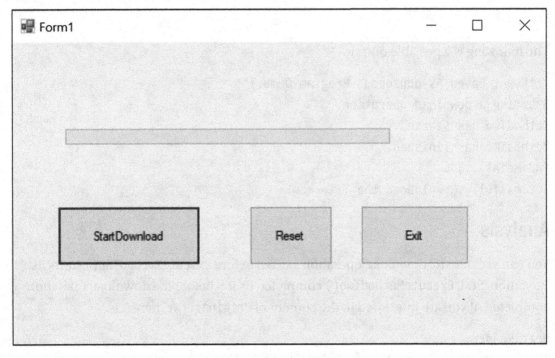

Figure 27-2. *A simple UI application to demonstrate event-based asynchrony*

The following segment of code is self-explanatory.

```
using System;
using System.ComponentModel;
using System.Net;
using System.Windows.Forms;

namespace UsingWebClentWithWinForm
{
    public partial class Form1 : Form
    {
        public Form1()
        {
            InitializeComponent();
        }

        private void StartDownload_Click(object sender, EventArgs e)
        {
         WebClient webClient = new WebClient();
```

```csharp
    Uri myLocation = new Uri(@"C:\TestData\testfile_original.txt");
    string targetLocation = @"C:\TestData\downloaded_file.txt";
    webClient.DownloadFileAsync(myLocation, targetLocation);
    webClient.DownloadFileCompleted += new          AsyncCompletedEvent
    Handler(DownloadCompleted);
    webClient.DownloadProgressChanged += new DownloadProgressChanged
    EventHandler(ProgressChanged);
    MessageBox.Show("Executed download operation.");
}
private void DownloadCompleted(object sender, AsyncCompletedEventArgs e)
{
    MessageBox.Show("Successfully downloaded the file now.");
}
private void ProgressChanged(object sender,
DownloadProgressChangedEventArgs e)
{
    progressBar.Value = e.ProgressPercentage;
}

private void ResetButton_Click(object sender, EventArgs e)
{
    progressBar.Value = 0;
}

private void ExitButton_Click(object sender, EventArgs e)
{
    this.Close();
}
}
}
```

Note   You can download the complete code for this application from the Apress website.

Output

Once you click StartDownloadButton, you get the output shown in Figure 27-3 and Figure 27-4.

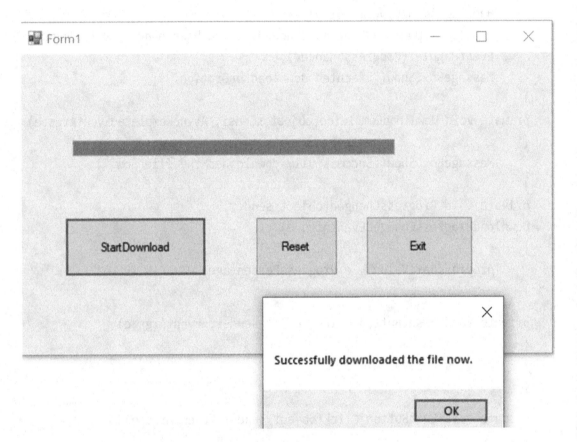

Figure 27-3. *A runtime screenshot of the UI application*

Once you click the OK button, you see the message box shown in Figure 27-4.

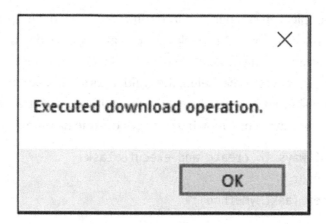

Figure 27-4. *Another message box pops up when you click the OK button*

Q&A Session

27.8 What are the pros and cons associated with an event-based asynchronous program?

Here are some common pros and cons associated with this approach.

Pros

- You can invoke a long-running method and return immediately. When the method completes, you can get a notification that you can use effectively.

Cons

- Since you have segregated code, it's often difficult to understand, debug, and maintain.

- A major problem occurs when you subscribe to an event but later forget to unsubscribe. This mistake can lead to memory leaks in your application, and the impact can be severe; for example, your system hangs or is unresponsive, and you need to reboot it often.

Understanding Tasks

To understand the task-based asynchronous pattern (TAP), first, you must know what a task is. A task is simply a unit of work that you want to perform. You can complete this work in the same thread or a different thread. Using tasks, you can have better control over the threads; for example, you can perform a continuation work once a particular task is finished. A parent task can create child tasks, so you can organize the hierarchy. This kind of hierarchy is important when you cascade your messages. Consider an example. In your application, once a parent task is canceled, the child tasks should be canceled too.

You can create tasks in different ways. In the following demonstration, I created three tasks in three different ways. The following segment of code has supporting comments.

```
#region Different ways to create and execute task
// Using constructor
Task taskOne = new Task(MyMethod);
taskOne.Start();
// Using task factory
TaskFactory taskFactory = new TaskFactory();
// StartNew Method creates and starts a task.
// It has different overloaded version.
Task taskTwo = taskFactory.StartNew(MyMethod);
// Using task factory via a task
Task taskThree = Task.Factory.StartNew(MyMethod);
#endregion
```

You can see that all three tasks (taskOne, taskTwo, taskThree) try to do a similar operation: they simply execute MyMethod(), which is described as follows.

```
private static void MyMethod()
{
    Console.WriteLine("Task.id={0} with Thread id {1} has started.", Task.
    CurrentId, Thread.CurrentThread.ManagedThreadId);
    // Some task
    Thread.Sleep(100);
    Console.WriteLine("MyMethod for Task.id={0} and Thread id {1} is
    completed.", Task.CurrentId,  Thread.CurrentThread.ManagedThreadId);
    }
```

You can see that inside MyMethod(), to distinguish the tasks and threads, I printed their corresponding IDs in the console. Apart from this, I passed the method name as an argument inside the StartNew() method. This method has 16 overloaded versions (at the time of this writing), and I used the one that is defined as follows.

```
//
// Summary:
//     Creates and starts a task.
//
// Parameters:
//   action:
//     The action delegate to execute asynchronously.
//
// Returns:
//     The started task.
//
// Exceptions:
//   T:System.ArgumentNullException:
//     The action argument is null.
public Task StartNew(Action action);
```

Since MyMethod() matches the signature of the Action delegate in this case, there was no problem for me to use this method with StartNew.

POINTS TO REMEMBER

For your reference, let's recollect the theory behind the Action delegate. The method summary of the following code:

```
public delegate void Action();
```

says that it encapsulates a method that has no parameters and does not return a value.

In the upcoming example (demonstration 9), you see that MyMethod() doesn't accept any argument, and its return type is void; this is why I could use the method name inside StartNew().

But it is important to note that in advanced programming, you frequently see the generic versions of Action delegates. I selected the following lines from my book *Getting Started with Advanced C#* (Apress, 2020):

Action delegates can take 1 to 16 input parameters but do not have a return type. The overloaded versions are as follows:

```
Action<in T>
Action<in T1,in T2>
Action<in T1,in T2, in T3>
....
Action<in T1, in T2, in T3,in T4, in T5, in T6,in T7,in T8,in T9,in T10,in
T11,in T12,in T13,in T14,in T15,in T16>
```

For example, if you have a method called CalculateSumOfThreeInts that takes three int's as input parameters and whose return type is void, as follows:

```
private static void CalculateSumOfThreeInts(int i1, int i2, int i3)
{
    int sum = i1 + i2 + i3;
    Console.WriteLine("Sum of {0},{1} and {2} is: {3}", i1, i2, i3, sum);
}
```

You can use an Action delegate to get the sum of three integers, as follows:

```
Action<int, int, int> sum = new Action<int, int, int>(
CalculateSumOfThreeInts);
sum(10, 3, 7);
```

Otherwise, you can use the short form as follows:

```
Action<int, int, int> sum = CalculateSumOfThreeInts;
sum(10, 3, 7);
```

Demonstration 9

Now go through the complete demonstration and output.

```
using System;
using System.Threading;
using System.Threading.Tasks;

namespace DifferentWaysToCreateTask
{
```

```csharp
class Program
{
    static void Main(string[] args)
    {
        Console.WriteLine("***Using different ways to create
        tasks.****");
        Console.WriteLine($"Inside Main().Thread ID:{Thread.
        CurrentThread.ManagedThreadId}");

        #region Different ways to create and execute task
        // Using constructor.
        Task taskOne = new Task(MyMethod);
        taskOne.Start();
        // Using task factory.
        TaskFactory taskFactory = new TaskFactory();
        // StartNew Method creates and starts a task.
        // It has different overloaded versions.
        Task taskTwo = taskFactory.StartNew(MyMethod);
        // Using task factory via a task.
        Task taskThree = Task.Factory.StartNew(MyMethod);
        #endregion
        Console.ReadKey();
    }

    private static void MyMethod()
    {
        Console.WriteLine($"Task.id={Task.CurrentId} with Thread id
        {Thread.CurrentThread.ManagedThreadId} has started.");
        Thread.Sleep(100);
        Console.WriteLine($"MyMethod for Task.id={Task.CurrentId}
        and Thread id {Thread.CurrentThread.ManagedThreadId} is
        completed.");
    }
}
```

Output

The following is a possible output.

```
***Using different ways to create tasks.****
Inside Main().Thread ID:1
Task.id=3 with Thread id 6 has started.
Task.id=2 with Thread id 4 has started.
Task.id=1 with Thread id 5 has started.
MyMethod for Task.id=3 and Thread id 6 is completed.
MyMethod for Task.id=1 and Thread id 5 is completed.
MyMethod for Task.id=2 and Thread id 4 is completed.
```

Note   ManagedThreadId gets a unique identifier *only* for a particular managed thread. You may notice a different value when you run the application on your machine. So, you should not feel that since you have created *n* number of threads, you should see the thread ids between 1 to *n* only. There may be other threads running in the background.

Q&A Session

27.9 **StartNew()** **can be used for the methods that match the Action delegate signature. Is this correct?**

Not at all. I used it in one of the StartNew overloads that accepts a parameter, which is the name of a method that matches an Action delegate signature. But, there are other overloaded versions of StartNew; for example, consider the following, in which you see the Func delegates.

```
public Task<TResult> StartNew<[NullableAttribute(2)]TResult>
(Func<TResult> function, TaskCreationOptions creationOptions);
```

Or,

```
public Task<TResult> StartNew<[NullableAttribute(2)]TResult>
(Func<TResult> function, CancellationToken cancellationToken);
```

27.10 In a previous Q&A, I saw TaskCreationOptions. What does it mean?

It is an enum. You can set a task's behavior using it. Here is the details of it.

```
public enum TaskCreationOptions
{
        None = 0,
        PreferFairness = 1,
        LongRunning = 2,
        AttachedToParent = 4,
        DenyChildAttach = 8,
        HideScheduler = 16,
        RunContinuationsAsynchronously = 64,
}
```

In an upcoming demonstration, you see another important enum called TaskContinuationOptions, which can also help you set a task behavior.

Using Task-based Asynchronous Pattern (TAP)

Task-based Asynchronous Pattern (TAP) came in C# 4.0. It is the foundation for async/await, which came in C# 5.0. TAP introduced the Task class and its generic variant Task<TResult>. Task is used when the return value of an asynchronous chunk of code is not a big concern. But when you do care about this return value, you should use the generic version, Task<TResult>. You have had an overview of Task. Let's use this concept to implement a task-based asynchronous pattern using ExecuteMethodOne() and ExecuteMethodTwo().

Demonstration 10

Here is a complete demonstration.

```
using System;
using System.Threading;
using System.Threading.Tasks;
```

```csharp
namespace UsingTAP
{
    class Program
    {
        static void Main(string[] args)
        {
            Console.WriteLine("***Using Task-based Asynchronous
            Pattern.****");
            Console.WriteLine($"Inside Main().The thread ID:{Thread.
            CurrentThread.ManagedThreadId}");
            Task taskForMethod1 = new Task(ExecuteMethodOne);
            taskForMethod1.Start();
            ExecuteMethodTwo();
            Console.ReadKey();
        }

        private static void ExecuteMethodOne()
        {
            Console.WriteLine("Method1 has started.");
            Console.WriteLine($"Inside ExecuteMethodOne(),Thread id
            {Thread.CurrentThread.ManagedThreadId}.");
            // Some big task
            Thread.Sleep(1000);
            Console.WriteLine("Method1 has completed its job now.");
        }

        private static void ExecuteMethodTwo()
        {
            Console.WriteLine("Method2 has started.");
            Console.WriteLine($"Inside ExecuteMethodTwo(),Thread id
            {Thread.CurrentThread.ManagedThreadId}.");
            Thread.Sleep(100);
            Console.WriteLine("Method2 is completed.");
        }
    }
}
```

Output

The following is a possible output.

```
***Using Task-based Asynchronous Pattern.****
Inside Main().The thread ID:1
Method2 has started.
Inside ExecuteMethodTwo(),Thread id 1.
Method1 has started.
Inside ExecuteMethodOne(),Thread id 4.
Method2 is completed.
Method1 has completed its job now.
```

You have just seen a sample demo of a task-based asynchronous pattern. I did not care about the return value of ExecuteMethodOne(). But let's say that you are interested in whether ExecuteMethodOne() executed successfully or not. For simplicity, I use a string message to indicate successful completion in the upcoming example. And this time, you see a generic variant of Task, which is Task<string> in this example. For lambda expression lovers, I modified ExecuteMethodOne() with a lambda expression in this example, and to fulfill the key requirement, I adjusted the return type.

In this example, I added another method called, ExecuteMethodThree(). For comparison, this method is initially commented out; the program is executed, and the output is analyzed. Later, I uncomment it and create a task hierarchy using the method. Once this is done, the program is executed again, and you notice that ExecuteMethodThree() runs when ExecuteMethodOne() completes its job. I kept the comments to help you understand.

Now go through demonstration 11.

Demonstration 11

Here is a complete demonstration.

```
using System;
using System.Threading;
using System.Threading.Tasks;
```

```csharp
namespace TAPDemonstration2
{
    class Program
    {
        static void Main(string[] args)
        {
            Console.WriteLine("***Using Task-based Asynchronous Pattern.
            Using lambda expression into it.****");
            Console.WriteLine("Inside Main().Thread ID:{0}", Thread.
            CurrentThread.ManagedThreadId);
            // Task taskForMethod1 = new Task(Method1);
            // taskForMethod1.Start();
            Task<string> taskForMethod1 = ExecuteMethodOne();
            /*
             Wait for task to complete.
             If you use Wait() method as follows, you'll not see
             the  asynchonous behavior.
             */
            // taskForMethod1.Wait();
            // Continue the task
            // The taskForMethod3 will continue once taskForMethod1 is
            // finished
            // Task taskForMethod3 = taskForMethod1.ContinueWith(Execute
            MethodThree, TaskContinuationOptions.OnlyOnRanToCompletion);
            ExecuteMethodTwo();
            Console.WriteLine($"Task for Method1 was a : {taskForMethod1.
            Result}");
            Console.ReadKey();
        }
        // Using lambda expression
        private static Task<string> ExecuteMethodOne()
        {
            return Task.Run(() =>
            {
                string result = "Failure";
```

```
        try
        {
            Console.WriteLine("Method1 has started.");
            Console.WriteLine($"Inside Method1(),Task.id={Task.
            CurrentId}");
            Console.WriteLine($"Inside Method1(),Thread id {Thread.
            CurrentThread.ManagedThreadId}.");
            //Some big task
            Thread.Sleep(1000);
            Console.WriteLine("Method1 has completed its job
            now.");
            result = "Success";
        }
        catch (Exception ex)
        {
            Console.WriteLine("Exception caught:{0}", ex.Message);
        }
        return result;
    }
    );
}

private static void ExecuteMethodTwo()
{
    Console.WriteLine("Method2 has started.");
    Console.WriteLine($"Inside ExecuteMethodTwo(),Thread id
    {Thread.CurrentThread.ManagedThreadId}.");
    Thread.Sleep(100);
    Console.WriteLine("Method2 is completed.");
}
private static void ExecuteMethodThree(Task task)
{
    Console.WriteLine("Method3 starts now.");
    Console.WriteLine($"Task.id is:{Task.CurrentId} with Thread id
    is:{Thread.CurrentThread.ManagedThreadId}");
    Thread.Sleep(20);
```

```
            Console.WriteLine($"Method3 with Task.id {Task.CurrentId}
            and Thread id {Thread.CurrentThread.ManagedThreadId} is
            completed.");
        }
    }
}
```

Output

The following is a possible output.

```
***Using Task-based Asynchronous Pattern.Using lambda expression into
it.****
Inside Main().Thread ID:1
Method2 has started.
Inside ExecuteMethodTwo(),Thread id 1.
Method1 has started.
Inside Method1(),Task.id=1
Inside Method1(),Thread id 4.
Method2 is completed.
Method1 has completed its job now.
Task for Method1 was a : Success
```

Analysis

Did you notice that this time, I did not use the Start() method for taskForMethod1? Instead, I used the Run() method from the Task class to execute Method1(). Why did I do that? Well, inside the Task class, Run is a static method. The method summary in Visual Studio states the following about this Run method: "Queues the specified work to run on the thread pool and returns a System.Threading.Tasks.Task`1 object that represents that work." At the time of writing, this method had eight overloaded versions, which are as follows.

```
public static Task Run(Action action);
public static Task Run(Action action, CancellationToken cancellationToken);
public static Task<TResult> Run<TResult>(Func<TResult> function);
public static Task<TResult> Run<TResult>(Func<TResult> function,
CancellationToken cancellationToken);
```

```
public static Task Run(Func<Task> function);
public static Task Run(Func<Task> function, CancellationToken
cancellationToken);
public static Task<TResult> Run<TResult>(Func<Task<TResult>> function);
public static Task<TResult> Run<TResult>(Func<Task<TResult>> function,
CancellationToken cancellationToken);
```

Now check another important point in this example. If you uncomment the following line,

```
// Task taskForMethod3 = taskForMethod1.ContinueWith(ExecuteMethodThree,
TaskContinuationOptions.OnlyOnRanToCompletion);
```

and run the application again, you get output similar to the following.

```
***Using Task-based Asynchronous Pattern.Using lambda expression into
it.****
Inside Main().Thread ID:1
Method2 has started.
Inside ExecuteMethodTwo(),Thread id 1.
Method1 has started.
Inside Method1(),Task.id=1
Inside Method1(),Thread id 4.
Method2 is completed.
Method1 has completed its job now.
Task for Method1 was a : Success
Method3 starts now.
Task.id is:2 with Thread id is:5
Method3 with Task.id 2 and Thread id 5 is completed.
```

You can see the `ContinueWith()` method helps continue a task. You may also notice the following.

```
TaskContinuationOptions.OnlyOnRanToCompletion
```

It simply states that the task will continue when `taskForMethod1` completes its job. Similarly, you can opt for other options using the enum `TaskContinuationOptions`, which has the following description.

```
public enum TaskContinuationOptions
{
    None = 0,
    PreferFairness = 1,
    LongRunning = 2,
    AttachedToParent = 4,
    DenyChildAttach = 8,
    HideScheduler = 16,
    LazyCancellation = 32,
    RunContinuationsAsynchronously = 64,
    NotOnRanToCompletion = 65536,
    NotOnFaulted = 131072,
    OnlyOnCanceled = 196608,
    NotOnCanceled = 262144,
    OnlyOnFaulted = 327680,
    OnlyOnRanToCompletion = 393216,
    ExecuteSynchronously = 524288
}
```

Q&A Session

27.11 Can I assign multiple tasks at a time?

Yes, you can. For example, in the previously modified example, if you have another method called ExecuteMethodFour with the following description.

```
private static void ExecuteMethodFour(Task task)
{
    Console.WriteLine("Method4 starts now.");
    Console.WriteLine($"Task.id is:{ Task.CurrentId } with Thread id is :{
    Thread.CurrentThread.ManagedThreadId } ");
          Thread.Sleep(10);
    Console.WriteLine($"Method4 with Task.id { Task.CurrentId } and Thread
    id { Thread.CurrentThread.ManagedThreadId } is completed."); ,
}
```

You can write the following lines.

```
Task<string> taskForMethod1 = Method1();
Task taskForMethod3 = taskForMethod1.ContinueWith(ExecuteMethodThree,
TaskContinuationOptions.OnlyOnRanToCompletion);
 taskForMethod3 = taskForMethod1.ContinueWith(ExecuteMethodFour,
 TaskContinuationOptions.OnlyOnRanToCompletion);
```

This means that once `taskForMethod1` completes the task, you see the continuation work with `taskForMethod3`, which executes both `ExecuteMethodThree` and `ExecuteMethodFour`.

It is also important to note that a continuation work can have another continuation work. For example, if you want something like the following.

- Once taskForMethod1 finishes, then to continue with taskForMethod3; and

- Once taskForMethod3 finishes, then only to continue with taskForMethod4

you can write something similar to the following.

```
// Method1 starts
Task<string> taskForMethod1 = Method1();
// Task taskForMethod3 starts after taskForMethod1
Task taskForMethod3 = taskForMethod1.ContinueWith(ExecuteMethodThree,
TaskContinuationOptions.OnlyOnRanToCompletion);
// Task taskForMethod4 starts after taskForMethod3
Task taskForMethod4 = taskForMethod3.ContinueWith(ExecuteMethodFour,
TaskContinuationOptions.OnlyOnRanToCompletion);
```

Using the async and await Keywords

The `async` and `await` keywords make the TAP pattern very flexible. Since the beginning of this chapter, I used two methods. The first method is a long-running method that takes more time to complete than the second method. In the upcoming examples, I continue the case studies with similar methods. For simplicity, let's call them `Method1()` and `Method2()`, respectively.

Initially, I used a nonlambda version, but in the analysis section, I *used* the lambda expression variant of the code. First, let's look at Method1() again.

```
private static void Method1()
{
    Console.WriteLine("Method1 has started.");
    Console.WriteLine("Inside Method1(),Thread id {0} .", Thread.
    CurrentThread.ManagedThreadId);
    // Some big task
    Thread.Sleep(1000);
    Console.WriteLine("Method1 has completed its job now.");
}
```

When you use lambda expression and use the async/await pair, your code may look like the following.

```
// Using lambda expression
private static async Task Method1()
{
    await Task.Run(() =>
    {
        Console.WriteLine("Method1 has started.");
        Console.WriteLine("Inside Method1(),Thread id {0} .", Thread.
        CurrentThread.ManagedThreadId);
        // Some big task
        Thread.Sleep(1000);
        Console.WriteLine("Method1 has completed its job now.");
    }
    );
}
```

Have you noticed an interesting fact? The method bodies of the synchronous version and the asynchronous version are very similar. But many of the earlier solutions to implement asynchronous programming were not like this. (They were complex too.)

So, what does await do? When you analyze the code, you find that once you get an await, the calling thread jumps out of the method and continue with something else.

In the upcoming demonstration, I used Task.Run, and it caused the asynchronous call to continue on a separate thread. *It does not mean that the continuation work should always be done on a new thread, because sometimes you aren't worried about different threads; for example, when your call is waiting to establish a connection over a network to download something.*

Lastly, in the nonlambda version (demonstration 12), I used the following block of code.

```
private static async Task ExecuteTaskOne()
{
    await Task.Run(Method1);
}
```

And inside Main(), instead of calling Method1(), I used ExecuteTaskOne() to execute Method1() asynchronously. You can see that I passed the method name, Method1, inside the Run method. You can recognize that I used the shortest overloaded version of the Run method here. Since Method1 matches the signature of an Action delegate, you can pass this method name as an argument in the Run method of the Task class.

Demonstration 12

Here is the complete demonstration.

```
using System;
using System.Threading;
using System.Threading.Tasks;

namespace UsingAsyncAwait
{
    class Program
    {
        static void Main(string[] args)
        {
            Console.WriteLine("***Exploring task-based asynchronous
            pattern(TAP) using async and await.****");
            Console.WriteLine("Inside Main().Thread ID:{0}", Thread.
            CurrentThread.ManagedThreadId);
```

```csharp
            /*
             This call is not awaited.So,the current method
             continues before the call is completed.
             i.e., following async call is not awaited.
            */
            ExecuteTaskOne();
            Method2();
            Console.ReadKey();
        }

        private static async Task ExecuteTaskOne()
        {
            await Task.Run(Method1);
        }
        private static void Method1()
        {
            Console.WriteLine("Method1() has started.");
            Console.WriteLine("Inside Method1(),Thread id {0} .", Thread.
            CurrentThread.ManagedThreadId);
            // Some big task
            Thread.Sleep(1000);
            Console.WriteLine("Method1() has completed its job now.");
        }

        private static void Method2()
        {
            Console.WriteLine("Method2() has started.");
            Console.WriteLine("Inside Method2(),Thread id {0} .", Thread.
            CurrentThread.ManagedThreadId);
            //Some small task
            Thread.Sleep(100);
            Console.WriteLine("Method2() is completed.");
        }
    }
}
```

Note I recommend that you execute the task-based asynchronous programs in the latest editions of Visual Studio 2019 to avoid some misbehaviors, which were seen in older versions of Visual Studio.

Output

The following is a possible output.

```
***Exploring task-based asynchronous pattern(TAP) using async and
await.****
Inside Main().Thread ID:1
Method1() has started.
Inside Method1(),Thread id 4 .
Method2() has started.
Inside Method2(),Thread id 1 .
Method2() is completed.
Method1() has completed its job now.
```

Analysis

In the previous output, you can see that Method1() was invoked earlier, but Method2()'s execution was not blocked due to that. Please note that this output may vary. So, in some cases, you may also see that Method2() starts before Method1(). So, if you want Method1() to start first, you can put a small Sleep() before the Method2() execution. You can see that Method2() ran inside the main thread, whereas Method1() executed in a different thread.

If you prefer to use lambda expressions, you could replace the following code segment

```
private static async Task ExecuteTaskOne()
{
        await Task.Run(Method1);
}

private static void Method1()
{
        Console.WriteLine("Method1() has started.");
```

```
    Console.WriteLine("Inside Method1(),Thread id {0} .", Thread.
    CurrentThread.ManagedThreadId);
    // Some big task
    Thread.Sleep(1000);
    Console.WriteLine("Method1() has completed its job now.");
}
```

with this one.

```
// Using lambda expression
private static async Task ExecuteMethod1()
{
    await Task.Run(() =>
    {
        Console.WriteLine("Method1() has started.");
        Console.WriteLine("Inside Method1(),Thread id {0} .", Thread.
        CurrentThread.ManagedThreadId);
        // Some big task
        Thread.Sleep(1000);
        Console.WriteLine("Method1() has completed its job now.");
    }
    );
}
```

Now in the previous demonstration, instead of calling ExecuteTaskOne(), you can directly call the ExecuteMethod1() method to get a similar output.

Note   In the previous example, you see a warning message for the following line: ExecuteMethod1(); which tells the following:

Warning CS4014 Because this call is not awaited, execution of the current method continues before the call is completed. Consider applying the 'await' operator to the result of the call.

If you hover your mouse on this, you get two suggestions: One of these suggestion tells you to apply discard as follows.

```
_ = ExecuteMethod1(); // applying discard
```

Note   The discards have been supported since C# 7.0. These are temporary, dummy, and unused variables in an application. Since these variables may not be on allocated storage, they can reduce memory allocations. These variables can enhance better readability and maintainability. You use an underscore (_) to indicate a discard variable in your application.

But if you follow the second suggestion and insert await before the line, like in the following.

```
await ExecuteMethod1();
```

The compiler raises another error that states the following.

```
Error CS4033 The 'await' operator can only be used within an async method.
Consider marking this method with the 'async' modifier and changing its
return type to 'Task'.
```

To remove this error, you need to make the containing async method (i.e., now you start with the following line.

```
static async Task Main(string[] args)
```

After applying async/await pair, the Main() method may look like the following.

```
class Program
{
    // static void Main(string[] args)
    static async Task Main(string[] args)
    {
        Console.WriteLine("***Exploring task-based asynchronous
        pattern(TAP) using async and await.****");
        Console.WriteLine("Inside Main().Thread ID:{0}", Thread.
        CurrentThread.ManagedThreadId);
        await ExecuteMethod1();
        // remaining code
```

This overall discussion is made to remind you that you should apply async/await together and place them properly.

I finish the chapter with one final demonstration, and this time, I slightly modify the calling sequence of the application. Now I introduce another method called Method3(), which is similar to Method2(). This newly added method can be called from ExecuteTaskOne(), which has the following structure.

```
private static async Task ExecuteTaskOne()
{
        Console.WriteLine("Inside ExecuteTaskOne(), prior to await()
        call.");
        int value=await Task.Run(Method1);
        Console.WriteLine("ExecuteTaskOne(), after await() call.");
        // Method3 will be called if Method1 executes successfully
        if (value = = 0)
        {
            Method3();
        }
}
```

Take a look at the previous segment of code. It simply says that I want to grab the return value from Method1(), and based on that value, I decide whether I call Method3() or not. So, this time, Method1()'s return type is not void; instead, it is returning an int (0 for successful completion, otherwise -1), and this method is restructured with a try-catch block like the following.

```
private static int Method1()
{
    int flag = 0;
    try
    {
            Console.WriteLine("Method1() has started.");
            Console.WriteLine("Inside Method1(),Thread id {0} .", Thread.
            CurrentThread.ManagedThreadId);
            // Some big task
            Thread.Sleep(1000);
            Console.WriteLine("Method1() has completed its job now.");
    }
```

```
catch (Exception e)
{
        Console.WriteLine("Caught Exception {0}", e);
        flag = -1;
}
return flag;
}
```

Now go through the following example.

Demonstration 13

Here is the complete demonstration.

```
using System;
using System.Threading;
using System.Threading.Tasks;

namespace AsyncAwaitAlternateDemonstration
{
    class Program
    {
        static void Main(string[] args)
        {
            Console.WriteLine("***Exploring task-based asynchronous
            pattern(TAP) using async and await.****");
            Console.WriteLine("***This is a modified example with three
            methods.***");
            Console.WriteLine("Inside Main().Thread ID:{0}", Thread.
            CurrentThread.ManagedThreadId);
            /*
             This call is not awaited.So,the current method
             continues before the call is completed.
             i.e., following async call is not awaited.
             */
```

```
    _ = ExecuteTaskOne();
    Method2();
    Console.ReadKey();
}

private static async Task ExecuteTaskOne()
{
    Console.WriteLine("Inside ExecuteTaskOne(), prior to await()
    call.");
    int value = await Task.Run(Method1);
    Console.WriteLine("Inside ExecuteTaskOne(), after await()
    call.");
    /*
    Method3() will be called if Method1()
    executes successfully(i.e. if it returns 0)
    */
    if (value == 0)
    {
        Method3();
    }
}

private static int Method1()
{
    int flag = 0;
    try
    {
        Console.WriteLine("Method1() has started.");
        Console.WriteLine("Inside Method1(),Thread id {0} .",
        Thread.CurrentThread.ManagedThreadId);
        //Some big task
        Thread.Sleep(3000);
        Console.WriteLine("Method1() has completed its job now.");
    }
    catch (Exception e)
    {
        Console.WriteLine("Caught Exception {0}", e);
```

```
                flag = -1;
            }
            return flag;
        }
        private static void Method2()
        {
            Console.WriteLine("Method2() has started.");
            Console.WriteLine("Inside Method2(),Thread id {0} .", Thread.
            CurrentThread.ManagedThreadId);
            Thread.Sleep(100);
            Console.WriteLine("Method2() is completed.");
        }
        private static void Method3()
        {
            Console.WriteLine("Method3() has started.");
            Console.WriteLine("Inside Method3(),Thread id {0} .", Thread.
            CurrentThread.ManagedThreadId);
            Thread.Sleep(100);
            Console.WriteLine("Method3() is completed.");

        }
    }
}
```

Output

The following is a possible output.

```
***Exploring task-based asynchronous pattern(TAP) using async and
await.****
***This is a modified example with three methods.***
Inside Main().Thread ID:1
Inside ExecuteTaskOne(), prior to await() call.
Method1() has started.
Inside Method1(),Thread id 4 .
Method2() has started.
Inside Method2(),Thread id 1 .
```

```
Method2() is completed.
Method1() has completed its job now.
Inside ExecuteTaskOne(), after await() call.
Method3() has started.
Inside Method3(),Thread id 4 .
Method3() is completed.
```

Analysis

Look at the output closely. You can see that Method3() needed to wait for Method1()'s completion, but Method2() could finish its execution before Method1() ends its execution. Here Method3() can continue if the returned value from Method1() is 0 only (if there is any exception raised inside Method1(), I set the flag value to –1). So, this scenario is similar to the ContinueWith() method in demonstration 11.

POINT TO NOTE

In demonstration 13, notice the following line of code inside ExecuteTaskOne().

```
int value=await Task.Run(Method1);
```

It simply divides the code segment into two parts: *prior call to await* and *post call to await*. This syntax is like any synchronous call, but by using await (inside an async method), you apply a suspension point and use the power of asynchronous programming.

I finish this chapter with some interesting notes from Microsoft. They can be handy when you further explore async/await keywords. Remember the following points.

- The await operator cannot be present in the body of a lock statement.

- You may see multiple await operators inside the body of an async method. But if it is not there, this does not raise any compile-time error. Instead, you get a warning, and the method executes synchronously. So, you may notice the following warning in a similar context: Warning CS1998 This async method lacks 'await' operators and will run synchronously. Consider using the 'await' operator to await non-blocking API calls, or 'await Task.Run(...)' to do CPU-bound work on a background thread.

A big chapter! Hopefully, I was able to demystify the different patterns in asynchronous programming. Although the IAsyncResult pattern and event-based asynchrony are not recommended in the upcoming chapters, I discussed them in this chapter because they help you understand legacy code, they show you the evolution of asynchronous programming. You may find them useful in the future.

This is the end of my discussions on patterns. I hope that you enjoyed learning these patterns. Now you are ready to jump into the vast ocean of programming using various patterns. Let's explore the remaining corner cases, which can't be mastered without practice. So, keep coding.

PART III

Final Thoughts on Design Patterns

CHAPTER 28

Criticisms of Design Patterns

Design patterns let you benefit from other people's experiences, which is often called *experience reuse*. You learn how they solved problems, how they tried to adopt new behaviors in their systems, and so on. A pattern may not perfectly fit into your work, but if you concentrate on the best practices as well as the problems of a pattern at the beginning, you are more likely to make a better application. This is why I will now discuss design pattern criticisms. Knowing about them can offer you some real value. If you think critically about patterns before you design your software, you can predict your return on investment to some degree. Let's go through the following points that are often raised by some developers:

- The concept of patterns came through Christopher Alexander. He was an architect, but not a computer programmer. He considered the domain that did not change a lot over the years (compared to the software industry). On the contrary, the software industry is always changing, and the changes to software development are much faster than any other domain. This is why critics often say that you cannot start from a domain (of buildings and towns) that Christopher Alexander considered.

- The way you wrote a program in the early days of programming compared to today is very different. Currently you enjoy more facilities compared to early days of programming (e.g., bigger storage, super-fast computing capabilities etc). So, when you extract patterns based on old practices, you show additional respect to them.

© Vaskaran Sarcar 2020
V. Sarcar, *Design Patterns in C#*, https://doi.org/10.1007/978-1-4842-6062-3_28

- Many patterns are similar, and there are always pros and cons associated with each of the patterns. (I discussed them in the "Q&A Sessions" at the end of each chapter.) A pitfall in one case can be a real virtue in a different case.

- The pattern that is giving you satisfactory results today may be a big burden to you in the future due to continuous change in the software industry.

- It is very unlikely that the infinite number of requirements can be well designed with a finite number of design patterns.

- Designing software is an art. And there is no definition or criteria for the best art.

- Design patterns give you the idea but not the implementations (like libraries and frameworks). You know that each human mind is unique. So, each engineer may have his preferences for implementing a similar concept, and that can create chaos in a team if mindsets widely vary.

- Consider a simple example. Patterns encourage people to code to a supertype (abstract class/ interface). But for a simple application where you know that there are no upcoming changes, or the application is created for a demo purpose only, this idea may not make much sense to you.

- Similarly, in some smaller applications, you may find that enforcing the rules of design patterns is increasing your code size and maintenance costs.

- Erasing the old and adopting the new is not always easy. For example, when you first learned about inheritance, you were excited. You probably wanted to use it in many ways and were seeing only the benefits from the concept. But later, when you started experimenting with design patterns, you started learning that in many cases, compositions are preferred over inheritance. This shifting of programming mindsets is not easy.

- Design patterns are based on some of the key principles, and one of them is to *identify the code that may vary and then separate it from the rest of the code.* It sounds very good from a theoretical perspective. But in real-world implementations, who guarantees that your judgment is perfect? The software industry always changes, and it needs to adapt to new requirements/demands continuously.

- Many patterns are already integrated into modern-day languages. Instead of implementing a pattern from scratch, you can use the built-in support in the language constructs.

- Inappropriate use of patterns can lead to antipatterns (e.g., inappropriate use of the Mediator pattern can lead to the God Class antipattern). I provide an overview of antipatterns in Chapter 29.

- Many people believe that the concepts of design patterns simply indicate that a programming language may need some additional features. So, patterns have less significance with the increasing capability of modern-day programming languages. Wikipedia says that computer scientist Peter Norvig believes that 16 out of the 23 patterns in the GoF design patterns are simplified or eliminated via direct language support in Lisp or Dylan. You see similar thoughts at `https://en.wikipedia.org/wiki/Software_design_pattern`.

- The patterns I discuss in this book are solely based on object-oriented programming. The efficiency and applicability of these patterns are questionable in other domains.

- These patterns are not interchangeable.

- In the end, design patterns help you benefit from others' experiences. You get their thoughts; you come to know how they encountered the challenges, how they implemented new behaviors in their systems, and so forth. But if you dive deep down to the basic thought, you find that you start with the assumption that a beginner or relatively less experienced person cannot solve a problem better than his/her seniors. Sometimes, a relatively less experienced person has a better vision than his seniors, and he proves himself more effective.

Q&A Session

28.1 Is there any catalog for these patterns?

I started with the GoF's 23 design patterns and then discussed some more patterns in this book. The GoF's catalog is considered the most fundamental pattern catalog.

Many other catalogs focus on domains. The Portland Patterns Repository and The Hillside Group's website are well-known in this context. You can get valuable insights and thoughts from these resources. The Hillside Group website also features information on various conferences and workshops.

As a starting point, you can visit `https://wiki.c2.com/?PortlandPattern Repository` and `https://hillside.net/patterns/patterns-catalog`.

Note   At the time of this writing, the URLs mentioned in this book work fine, but they may change in the future.

28.2 Why are you silent about other patterns?

These are my personal beliefs.

- Computer science will keep growing, and you will keep getting new patterns.

- If you are not familiar with the fundamental patterns, you cannot evaluate the true needs of the remaining or upcoming patterns. For example, if you know MVC well, you can see how it is different from model-view-presenter (MVP) and understand why MVP is needed.

- This book is already big. A more detailed discussion of each pattern would require many more pages, which would make the size of this book too big to digest.

So, in this book, I focused on fundamental patterns that are still relevant in today's programming world.

28.3 I often see the word *force* with the description of design patterns. What does it mean?

It is the criteria based on which developers justify their developments. Broadly, your target and current constraints are two important parts of your force. Therefore, when you develop your application, you can justify your development with these parts.

28.4 In various forums, I see that people are fighting about the pattern definition and say something like, "A pattern is a proven solution to a problem in a context." What does that mean?

This is a simple and easy-to-remember definition of what a pattern is. But simply breaking it down into three parts (problem, context, and solution) is not enough.

For example, you are on your way to the airport, and you are in a hurry. Suddenly, you realize that you left your boarding pass at home. Let's analyze the situation.

Problem: You need to reach the airport on time.

Context: You left your boarding pass at home.

The solution that may come to you is to turn back and rush home to get the boarding pass.

This solution may work once, but can you apply the same procedure repeatedly? You know the answer. It is not an intelligent solution because it depends on how much time you currently have to return home to get the boarding pass and then get to the airport. It also depends on the current traffic and many other factors. So, even if you're successful once, you want to prepare yourself for a better solution for a similar situation in the future.

Try to learn the meaning, intent, context, and so on, to understand a pattern clearly.

28.5 I am confused when I see similar UML diagrams for two different patterns. Also, I am further confused with the classification of the patterns in many cases.

This is perfectly natural. The more you read and analyze the implementations, and the more you try to understand the intent behind these designs, the distinctions among them will become clearer to you.

28.6 When should I consider writing a new pattern?

Writing a new pattern is not easy. You need to study and evaluate the available patterns. But if you do not find an existing pattern to serve your domain-specific needs, you may need to write your own pattern. It is best if your solution passes the **Rule of Three**, which says that to achieve a tag pattern, a solution needs to be successfully applied in a real-world solution at least three times. Once you have done this, you can let others know about it, participate in discussion forums, and get feedback from others. This activity can help both you and the development community.

CHAPTER 29

AntiPatterns

The discussion of design patterns cannot be completed without discussing antipatterns. The following chapter covers a brief overview of antipatterns. Let's start.

Overview

In real-world application development, sometimes you may follow some approaches which are very attractive at the beginning, but in the long run, they create problems. For example, you may try to get a quick fix to meet a delivery deadline. But if you are not aware of the potential pitfalls, you may need to pay a big penalty for those mistakes.

Antipatterns alert you about the common mistakes that can lead a problem to a bad solution, so that, you can take precautionary measures. The proverb "prevention is better than the cure" suits in this context.

POINTS TO REMEMBER

Antipatterns alert you to common mistakes by describing how attractive approaches can make your life difficult in the future. At the same time, they suggest alternate solutions that may seem tough or ugly at the beginning but ultimately help you build a better solution. In short, antipatterns identify problems with established practices, and they can map general situations to a specific class of highly productive solutions. They can also provide you better plans to reverse some bad practices to make those healthy solutions.

© Vaskaran Sarcar 2020
V. Sarcar, *Design Patterns in C#*, https://doi.org/10.1007/978-1-4842-6062-3_29

A Brief History of AntiPatterns

The original idea of design pattern came from building architect Christopher Alexander, a professor at Berkeley. He shared his ideas for the construction of buildings within the well-planned towns. Gradually, these concepts entered software development, and they gained popularity through leading-edge software developers like Ward Cunningham and Kent Beck. In 1994, the idea of design patterns entered the mainstream of object-oriented software development through an industry conference called Pattern Languages of Program Design (PLoP) on design patterns. The Hillside Group hosted it, and Jim Coplien's paper "A Development Process Generative Pattern Language" is a famous for its context. And with the launch of the classic textbook *Design Patterns: Elements of Reusable Object-Oriented Software* by the GoF, the ideas of design patterns became extremely popular.

Undoubtedly, these great ideas of design patterns helped (and are still helping) programmers to develop high-quality software. But in some cases, people started noticing the negative impacts also. Here is a common example. Many developers wanted to show their expertise without the true evaluation or consequences of these patterns in their specific domains. As an obvious side effect, patterns were implanted in the wrong context, produced low-quality software, and ultimately resulted in large penalties for the developers or their organizations.

So, the software industry needed to focus on the negative consequences of similar kinds of mistakes, and eventually, the idea of antipatterns evolved. Many experts started contributing to this field, but the first well-formed model came through Michael Akroyd's presentation titled "AntiPatterns: Vaccinations against Object Misuse." It was the antithesis of the GoF's design patterns.

The term *antipattern* became popular with the book *AntiPatterns: Refactoring Software, Architectures, and Projects in Crisis* by William Brown et al. (John Wiley & Sons, 1998). The following is from the book.

> *Because AntiPatterns have had so many contributors, it would be unfair to assign the original idea for AntiPatterns to a single source. Rather, AntiPatterns are a natural step in complementing the work of the design pattern movement and extending the design pattern model.*

Examples of AntiPatterns

These are some examples of the antipatterns and the concepts/mindsets behind them.

- **Over Use of Patterns** Developers may try to use patterns at any cost, regardless of whether it is appropriate or not.

- **God Class** A big object that tries to control almost everything with many unrelated methods. Inappropriate use of the Mediator pattern may end up as an antipattern.

- **Not Invented Here** I am a big company, and I want to build everything from scratch. Although there is already a library available developed by another company, I will not use that. I will make everything on my own, and once it is developed, I will use my brand value to announce, "Hey guys, the ultimate library has been launched for you."

- **Zero Means Null** As a common example, developers think that no one wants to be at latitude zero and longitude zero. Another common variation is seen when a programmer uses –1, 999, or anything like that to represent an inappropriate integer value. Another erroneous use case is when a user treats "09/09/9999" as a null date in an application. So, in the preceding cases, if the user needs to have the numbers –1 or 999, or the date "09/09/9999", he will not get it.

- **Golden Hammer** Mr. X believes that technology T is always best. So, if he needs to develop a new system (that demands new learning), he will prefer T even if it is inappropriate. He thinks, "I am quite busy. I do not need to learn any more technology if I can somehow manage with T."

- **Shoot the Messenger** I'm already under pressure, and the program deadline is approaching. The tester, John, always finds typical defects that are hard to fix. Also, John does not like me, so he likes to find defects in my code. So, at this stage, I do not want to involve him; he will find more defects, and I will miss the target deadline.

- **Swiss Army Knife** Demand for a product that can serve a customer's every need, like a drug that can cure all illnesses, a software that serves a wide range of customers with varying needs—it does not matter how complex the interface is.

- **Copy and Paste Programming** I need to solve a problem, but I already have a piece of code that deals with a similar situation. So, I can copy the old code that works, and then I modify it if required. But when you start from an existing copy, you essentially inherit all the potential bugs associated with it. Also, if the original code needs to be modified in the future, you need to implement the modification in multiple places. This approach also violates the *Don't Repeat Yourself* (DRY) principle.

- **Architects Don't Code** I am an architect. My time is valuable. I only show paths or give great lectures on coding. There are enough implementers who should implement my idea. *Architects Play Golf* is also a sister of this antipattern.

- **Hide and Hover** Do not expose all edit or delete links until the user hovers over the element.

- **Disguised Links and Ads** Fool your users and earn revenue when they click a link or an advertisement, although they cannot get what they want.

- **Management by Numbers** The greater the number of commits, the greater the number of lines of code, or the greater the amount of defect fixing are signs of a great developer.

Measuring programming progress by lines of code is like measuring aircraft building progress by weight.

—Bill Gates

POINTS TO NOTE

- Nowadays, you can learn about various antipatterns from different websites/sources; for example, `https://en.wikipedia.org/wiki/Anti-pattern`.

- You can also get a detailed list of the antipattern catalog at `http://wiki.c2.com/?AntiPatternsCatalog`.

- You may also notice that the concept of antipatterns is not limited to object-oriented programming.

Types of AntiPatterns

Antipatterns can belong to different categories. Even a typical antipattern can belong to more than one category. Here are some common classifications.

- **Architectural antipatterns** The Swiss Army Knife antipattern is an example in this category.

- **Development antipatterns** The God Class, Overuse of Patterns are examples in this category.

- **Management antipatterns** The Shoot the Messenger antipattern falls into this category.

- **Organizational antipatterns** The Architects Don't Code, Architects Play Golf belong in this category.

- **User Interface antipatterns** Examples include Disguised Links/Ads.

Note   Disguised links/Advertisements are also called Dark patterns.

Q&A Session

29.1 How are antipatterns related to design patterns?

When you use design patterns, you reuse the experiences of others who came before you. When you start blindly using those concepts for the sake of use only, you fall into the traps of *reuse of recurring solutions*. This can lead you to a bad situation later on, and then you discover that your return on investment (ROI) is decreasing, but maintenance costs are increasing. Simply put, the easy and attractive solutions (or patterns) may cause more problems for you in the future.

29.2 A design pattern may turn into an antipattern. Is this correct?

Yes, if you apply a design pattern in a wrong context that can cause more trouble than the problem it solves and eventually it will turn into an antipattern. So, before you start, understanding the nature and context of the problem is very important.

29.3 Antipatterns are related to software developers only. Is this correct?

No. The usefulness of an antipattern is not limited to developers. It may apply to others; for example, it is useful to managers and technical architects also.

29.4 Even if you do not get much benefit from antipatterns now, these can help you easily adapt new features with lower maintenance costs in the future. Is this correct?

Yes.

29.5 What are the probable causes of an antipattern?

They can come from various sources or mindsets. The following lists a few common examples of what someone might say (or think).

- "We need to deliver the product as soon as possible."

- "We have a very good relationship with the customer. So, at present, we do not need to analyze future impact."

- "I am an expert on reuse. I know design patterns very well."

- "We use the latest technologies and features to impress our customers. We do not need to worry about legacy systems."

- "More complicated code reflects my expertise in the subject."

29.6 Can you list some of the symptoms of antipatterns?

In object-oriented programming (OOP), the most common symptom is your system cannot easily adapt a new feature. Also, maintenance costs continuously increase. You may also notice that you have lost the power of key object-oriented features like inheritance, polymorphism, and so forth.

Apart from this, you may see the following symptoms.

- Use of global variables

- Code duplication

- Limited/no reuse of code

- One big class (God Class)

- A large number of parameterless methods etc.

29.7 What is the remedy if you detect an antipattern?

You may need to refactor your code and find a better solution. For example, here are some solutions to the following antipatterns.

- **Golden Hammer** Try to educate Mr. X through some proper training.

- **Zero Means Null** Use an additional boolean variable, which is more sensible to you to indicate the null value properly.

- **Management by Numbers** Numbers are good if you use them wisely. You cannot judge the ability of a programmer by the number of defects he fixes each week. Quality is also important. A typical example is that fixing a simple UI layout is much easier than fixing a critical memory leak in the system. Consider another example. "A greater number of tests are passing" does not indicate that your system is more stable unless these tests exercise different code paths/ branches.

- **Shoot the Messenger** Welcome tester John and involve him immediately. Don't consider him your rival. You can properly analyze his findings and fix the real defects early to avoid last-minute surprises.

- **Copy and Paste programming** Instead of searching for a quick solution, you can refactor your code. You can also create a common place to maintain frequently used methods to avoid duplicates and to make maintenance easier.

- **Architects Don't Code** Involve architects in some parts of the implementation phase. This can help both the organization and the architect. It gives them a clearer picture of the true functionalities of the product. This process also helps them to value your efforts.

29.8 What do you mean by *refactoring*?

In the coding world, the term *refactoring* means improving the design of existing code without changing the external behavior of the system/application. This process helps you have more readable code. At the same time, this code should be more adaptable to new requirements (or change requests), and they should be more maintainable.

CHAPTER 30

FAQ

This chapter is a subset of the "Q&A Session" sections of all the chapters in this book. Many of these questions were not discussed in specific chapters because the related patterns were not covered yet. I highly recommend that in addition to the following Q&As, you go through all the "Q&A Session" sections in the book to better understand the patterns.

30.1 Which design pattern do you like the most?

It depends on many factors, such as the context, situation, demand, constraints, and so on. If you know about all the patterns, you will have more options to choose from.

30.2 Why should developers use design patterns?

A common answer is that they are reusable solutions for software design problems that repeatedly appear in real-world software development. But I mentioned it before (for example, in the Q&A session of Chapter 28), you need to analyze various aspects, such as the context and intent of the problem before you implement a pattern.

30.3 What is the difference between the Command and Memento patterns?

All actions are stored for the Command pattern, but the Memento pattern saves the state only on request. Additionally, the Command pattern can support undo operations for every action, but the Memento pattern does not need that. I strongly recommend you to visit the Q&A 19.4 from Chapter 19 to understand the difference clearly.

30.4 What is the difference between the Facade pattern and the Builder pattern?

The Facade pattern aims to make a specific portion of code easier to use. It abstracts details away from the developer.

The Builder pattern separates the construction of an object from its representation. In Chapter 3, the director is calling the same method, `Construct()` in demonstration 1 and `ConstructCar()` in demonstration 2, to create different types of vehicles. In other words, you can use the same construction process to create multiple types.

© Vaskaran Sarcar 2020
V. Sarcar, *Design Patterns in C#*, https://doi.org/10.1007/978-1-4842-6062-3_30

30.5 What is the difference between the Builder pattern and Strategy pattern? They have similar UML representations.

First, you must examine the intent. The Builder pattern falls into the category of creational patterns, and the Strategy pattern falls into the category of behavioral patterns. Their areas of focus are different. When you consider the Builder pattern, you can use the same construction process to create different types, when you use the Strategy pattern, you have the freedom to select an algorithm at runtime.

30.6 What is the difference between the Command pattern and the Interpreter pattern?

In the Command pattern, commands are objects. In the Interpreter pattern, the commands are sentences. In the Interpreter pattern, you can make your own rule for evaluation and build the syntax tree. For a simple grammar, it is fine, but it becomes tough to implement when your grammar is complex. It is because the cost of building an interpreter can be a big concern for you.

30.7 What is the difference between the Chain of Responsibility pattern and Observer pattern?

For the Observer pattern, all registered users are notified or get requests (for the change in the subject) in parallel. For the Chain of Responsibility pattern, you may not reach the end of the chain, so all users do not need to handle the same scenario. The request can be processed much earlier by some user who is placed at the beginning of the chain. I suggest that you refer to Q&A 14.4.

30.8 What is the difference between the Chain of Responsibility pattern and Decorator pattern?

They are not the same at all, but you may think that they are similar in their structures. Like FAQ 30.7, in the Chain of Responsibility pattern, in general, only one class handles a request, but in the Decorator pattern, all classes handle a request. You must remember that decorators are effective in the context of adding and removing responsibilities only. If you can combine the Decorator pattern with the single responsibility principle, you can add (or remove) a single responsibility at runtime.

30.9 What is the difference between the Mediator pattern and the Observer pattern?

The GoF says, "These are competing patterns. The difference between them is that Observer distributes communication by introducing observer and subject objects, whereas a mediator object encapsulates the communication between other objects."

Here I suggest you consider the examples of the Mediator pattern in Chapter 21. In demonstration 2, I explained that a sender could receive a message to the target receiver if he is online. I described how to restrict an outsider and promote security. But in the observer pattern, a subject/broadcaster normally does not care about its observer's state. It simply broadcast the messages.

The GoF book is telling that you may face fewer challenges when making reusable observers and subjects than when making reusable mediators, but regarding the flow of communication, Mediator scores higher than Observer.

30.10 Which one do you prefer, a singleton class or a static class?

It depends. First, you can create objects of a singleton class, which is not possible with a static class. So, the concepts of inheritance and polymorphism can be implemented with a singleton class. Also, some developers believe that mocking a static class (e.g., consider unit testing scenarios) in a real-world application is challenging.

30.11 How do you distinguish between proxies and adapters?

Proxies work on similar interfaces as their subjects. Adapters work on different interfaces (to the objects they adapt).

30.12 How are proxies different from decorators?

There are different types of proxies, and they vary by implementation. So, some of these implementations may be close to decorators. For example, a protection proxy might be implemented like a decorator. But you must remember that decorators focus on adding responsibilities, while proxies focus on controlling the access to an object.

30.13 How are mediators different from facades?

In general, both simplify a complex system. In a Mediator pattern, a two-way connection exists between a mediator and the internal subsystems. In contrast, in a Facade pattern, you generally provide a one-way connection (the subsystems do not know about facades).

30.14 Is there any relation between the Flyweight pattern and the State pattern?

The GoF book mentions that the Flyweight pattern can help you to decide when and how to share the state objects.

30.15 What are the similarities among the Simple Factory, Factory Method, and Abstract Factory design patterns?

All of them encapsulate object creation, which suggests that you code to the abstraction (interface) but not to the concrete classes. Simply put, each of these factories promotes loose coupling by reducing the dependencies on concrete classes.

30.16 What are the differences among the Simple Factory, Factory Method, and Abstract Factory design patterns?

This is an important question that you may face in various job interviews. First, refer to Q&A 5.3 in Chapter 5, and if needed, go through all the Q&A sessions in Chapters 4 and 5.

30.17 How do you distinguish the Singleton pattern from the Factory Method pattern?

The Singleton pattern ensures that you get a unique instance each time. It also restricts the creation of additional instances.

But the Factory Method pattern does not say that you only get a unique instance. Most often, this pattern creates as many instances as you want, and the instances are not necessarily unique. These newly typed instances may implement a common base class. (Just remember that the Factory method lets a class defer instantiation to subclasses, according to the GoF definition.)

30.18 How does the Template Method pattern differ from the Strategy pattern?

In the Strategy pattern, you can vary the entire algorithm using delegation. On the other hand, using the Template Method pattern, you vary only certain steps in an algorithm using inheritance, but the overall flow of the algorithm is unchanged.

30.19 How do you distinguish the Visitor pattern from the Strategy pattern?

In the Strategy pattern, each subclass uses a different algorithm to solve a common problem. But in a Visitor design pattern, each of visitor subclasses may provide different functionalities from each other.

30.20 How null objects are different from proxies?

In general, proxies act on real objects at some point in time, and they may also provide some behavior. But a null object does not do any such operation.

30.21 How do you distinguish the Interpreter pattern from the Visitor pattern?

With the interpreter pattern, you represent simple grammar as an object structure, but in a Visitor pattern, you define some specific operations that you want to use on an object structure. In addition to this, an interpreter has direct access to the properties that are needed, but in a Visitor pattern, you need special functionalities (similar to an observer) to access them.

30.22 How do you distinguish the Flyweight pattern from the Object Pool pattern?

I did not discuss the Object Pool pattern in this book. But if you know the Object Pool pattern already, you notice that in the Flyweight pattern, flyweights can have intrinsic and extrinsic states. So, if a flyweight has both states, its states are divided, and the client needs to pass part of the state to it. Also, in general, the client does not change the intrinsic state because it is shared.

Object Pool does not store any part of the state outside; all state information is stored/encapsulated inside the pooled object. Also, clients can change the state of a pooled object.

30.23 How are libraries or frameworks similar to and different from design patterns?

They are not design patterns. They provide the implementations which you can use directly in your application. But they can use the concept of the patterns in those implementations.

30.24 What is a callback method?

It is a method that can be invoked after you perform some specific operations. You'll often see the usage of this kind of method in asynchronous programming, and it can be useful when you do not know the exact finishing time of prior operations, but you want to start some specific task once the prior task is over. You should refer to demonstration 7 in Chapter 27 to understand it better.

A Brief Overview of GoF Design Patterns

We all have unique thought processes. So, in the early days of software development, engineers faced a common problem—there was no standard to instruct them on how to design their applications. Each team followed its own style, and when a new member (experienced or inexperienced) joined an existing team, understanding the architecture was a gigantic task. Senior or experienced members of the team would need to explain the advantages of the existing architecture and why alternative designs were not considered. The experienced developer also would know how to reduce future efforts by simply reusing the concepts already in place. Design patterns address this kind of issue and provide a common platform for all developers. You can think of them as the recorded experience of experts in the field. Patterns were intended to be applied in object-oriented designs with the intention of reuse.

In 1994, Erich Gamma, Richard Helm, Ralph Johnson, and John Vlissides published the book *Design Patterns: Elements of Reusable Object-Oriented Software* (Addison-Wesley, 1994). In this book, they introduced the concept of design patterns in software development. These authors became known as the Gang of Four. I refer to them as the **GoF** throughout this book. The GoF described 23 patterns that were developed by the common experiences of software developers over time. Nowadays, when a new member joins a development team, the developer is expected to know about the design patterns, and then the developer learns about the existing architecture. This approach allows a developer to actively participate in the development process within a short period of time.

The first concept of a real-life design pattern came from the building architect Christopher Alexander. During his lifetime, he discovered that many of the problems he faced were similar. So, he tried to address those issues with similar types of solutions.

Each pattern describes a problem, which occurs over and over again in our environment, and then describes the core of the solution to that problem, in such a way that you can use this solution a million times over, without ever doing it the same way twice.

—*Christopher Alexander*

The software engineering community started believing that though these patterns were described for buildings and towns, the same concepts can be applied to patterns in object-oriented design. So, they felt that we could substitute the original concepts of walls and doors with objects and interfaces. The common thing in both fields is that, at their cores, patterns are solutions to common problems.

It is important to note that the GoF discussed the original concepts of design patterns in the context of C++. But C# 1.0 was released in 2002, and then it went through various changes. It grew rapidly and secured its rank in the world's top programming languages within a short time, and in today's market, it is always in high demand. At the time of this writing, C# 8.0 is available with Visual Studio 2019. The concepts of design patterns are universal. The book is written in C#, but if you are familiar with any other popular programming languages such as Java, C++, and so on, you can relate because I primarily focus on the design patterns and not on the latest features of C#. I purposely chose simple examples to help you understand these concepts easily. Exercising these fundamental concepts of design patterns using C# always make you a better programmer and help you to reveal an upgraded version of you. The following are some important points to remember.

- A design pattern describes a general reusable solution to software design problems. When developing a software application, you may encounter these problems frequently. The basic idea is that you can solve similar kinds of problems with similar kinds of solutions. And these solutions were tested over a long period of time.

- Patterns provide you a template of how to solve a problem and can be used in many different situations. At the same time, they help you to get the best possible design much faster.

- Patterns are descriptions of how to create objects and classes and customize them to solve a general design problem in a particular context.

The GoF discussed 23 design patterns. Each of these patterns focuses on object-oriented design. Each pattern can also describe the consequences and trade-offs of use. The GoF categorized these 23 patterns based on their purposes, as shown next.

A. **Creational Patterns**

These patterns abstract the instantiation process. You make the systems independent from how their objects are composed, created, and represented. In these patterns, you should have a basic concern: "Where should I place the new keyword in my application?" This decision can determine the degree of coupling of your classes. The following five patterns belong in this category.

- Singleton pattern

- Prototype pattern

- Builder pattern

- Factory Method pattern

- Abstract Factory pattern

B. **Structural Patterns**

Here you focus on how classes and objects can be composed to form a relatively large structure. They generally use inheritance or composition to group different interfaces or implementations. Your choice of composition over inheritance (and vice versa) can affect the flexibility of your software. The following seven patterns fall into this category.

- Proxy pattern

- Decorator pattern

- Adapter pattern

- Facade pattern

- Flyweight pattern

- Composite pattern

- Bridge pattern

617

C. **Behavioral Patterns**

Here you concentrate on algorithms and the assignment of responsibilities among objects. You also need to focus on the communication between them and how the objects are interconnected. The following 11 patterns fall into this category.

- Visitor pattern

- Observer pattern

- Strategy pattern

- Template Method pattern

- Command pattern

- Iterator pattern

- Memento pattern

- State pattern

- Mediator pattern

- Chain of Responsibility pattern

- Interpreter pattern

The GoF made another classification based on scope, namely whether the pattern primarily focuses on the classes or its objects. Class patterns deal with classes and subclasses. They use inheritance mechanisms, so, these are static and fixed at compile time. Object patterns deal with objects that can change at run time. So, object patterns are dynamic. Factory Method pattern, Interpreter pattern, and Template Method pattern can be classified as class patterns. Remaining patterns of the GoF can fall into object patterns. It is interesting to note that depending on the implementation, an Adapter pattern can fall in both category.

Note   In this book, each chapter is self-contained, and you can start with any pattern you like following the guidelines given at the beginning of the book. I use simple examples so that you can pick up the basic ideas quickly. But you must read, digest, and practice, and try to link to other problems and keep coding. This process will help you to master the subject quickly.

Q&A Session

A.1 What are the differences between class patterns and object patterns?

In general, class patterns focus on static relationships, but object patterns can focus on dynamic relationships. Class patterns focus on classes and subclasses, and object patterns focus on an object's relationships.

Table A-1 shows the summarized content that was discussed in the GoF's famous book.

Table A-1. *Class Patterns vs Object Patterns*

	Class Patterns	Object patterns
Creational	Can defer object creation to its subclasses	Can defer object creation to another object
Structural	Focuses on the composition of classes (primarily uses the concept of inheritance)	Focuses on the composition of objects
Behavioral	Describes algorithms and execution flows; uses inheritance mechanism	Describes how different objects work together to complete a task

A.2 Can I combine two or more patterns in an application?

Yes. In real-world scenarios, this type of activity is common.

A.3 Do these patterns depend on a particular programming language?

Programming languages can play an important role. But the basic ideas are the same, patterns are just like templates, and they give you an idea in advance of how you can solve a problem. In this book, I primarily focused on object-oriented programming with the concept of reuse. But instead of any object-oriented programming language, suppose you have chosen some other language like C. In that case, you may need to think about the core object-oriented principles such as inheritance, polymorphism, encapsulation, abstraction, and so on, and how to implement them. So, the choice of language is always important because it may have some specialized features that can make your life easier.

A.4 Should I consider the common data structures like arrays, linked lists also as different design patterns?

The GoF excludes those saying that *they are not complex, domain-specific designs for an entire application or subsystem.* They can be encoded in classes and reused as-is. So, they are not your concern in this book.

A.5 If no particular pattern is 100% suitable for my problem, how should I proceed?

An infinite number of problems cannot be solved with a finite number of patterns for sure. But if you know these common patterns and their trade-offs, you can pick a close match. Lastly, no one prevents you from using your own pattern for your own problem. But you must tackle the risk, and you need to think about your return on investment.

A.6 Do you have any general advice before I jump into the topics?

I always follow the footsteps of my seniors and teachers who are experts in this field. And here are some of their general suggestions.

- Program to a supertype (Abstract class/Interface), not an implementation.

- Prefer composition over inheritance in most cases.

- Try to make a loosely coupled system.

- Segregate the code that is likely to vary from the rest of your code.

- Encapsulate what varies.

A.7 How do I use this book effectively?

This book focuses on commonly used design patterns. Most likely, you will face them very often in your everyday life. But the world is always changing, and new patterns keep evolving. To understand the necessity of a new pattern, you may also need to understand why an old/existing pattern is not enough to fulfill the requirement. You may consider this book as an attempt to make a solid foundation with design patterns so that you can move smoothly in your professional life, and you can adapt to the upcoming changes easily.

APPENDIX B

Useful Resources

This following is a list of useful resources. Many of them use a different programming language, but you will benefit from reading these great books.

- *Design Patterns: Elements of Reusable Object-Oriented Software* by Erich Gamma et al. (Addison-Wesley, 1995)

- *Head First Design Patterns* by Eric Freeman and Elisabeth Robson (O'Reilly, 2004)

- *Java Design Patterns* by Vaskaran Sarcar (Apress, 2018)

- *Design Patterns for Dummies* by Steve Holzner (Wiley Publishing, Inc., 2006)

- *C# Design Pattern Essentials* by Tony Bevis (Ability First Limited, 2012)

- *Design Patterns in C#* by Jean Paul (Kindle edition, 2012)

The following are helpful online resources/websites.

- http://sourcemaking.com/design_patterns

- https://en.wikipedia.org/wiki/Software_design_pattern

- www.dofactory.com

- www.c-sharpcorner.com

- www.dotnet-tricks.com

- www.codeproject.com

- www.youtube.com/watch?v=ffQZIGTTM48&list=PL8C53D99AB AD3F4C8

© Vaskaran Sarcar 2020
V. Sarcar, *Design Patterns in C#*, https://doi.org/10.1007/978-1-4842-6062-3

- www.tutorialspoint.com
- www.dotnetexamples.com
- https://docs.microsoft.com/en-us/
- http://wiki.c2.com/?AntiPatternsCatalog
- http://hillside.net

APPENDIX C

The Road Ahead

Congratulations! You have reached the end of this journey. Anyone can start a journey, but only a few can complete it with care. So, you are among the minority who possess the extraordinary capability to cover the distance successfully. I hope that you have enjoyed your learning experience. If you continue to think about the discussions, examples, implementations, and the Q&A Sessions in this book, you will have more clarity, you will feel more confident about the content, and you will remake yourself as a programmer.

Truly, a more detailed discussion on any design pattern would require this book to be too big to digest. So, what is next? You should not forget that *learning is a continuous process*. This book attempts to encourage in-depth learning of its core concepts.

I believe that only learning and thinking by yourself is not enough. I suggest you participate in open forums and join discussion groups to get more clarity on this subject. This process will not only help you; it will help others also.

Lastly, I have a request. You can always point out the areas for improvement, but at the same time, please let me know what you liked about this book too. In general, it is always easy to criticize, but an artistic view and an open mind are required to discover the true efforts that are associated with any work.

Thank you, and happy coding!

© Vaskaran Sarcar 2020
V. Sarcar, *Design Patterns in C#*, https://doi.org/10.1007/978-1-4842-6062-3

APPENDIX D

Important Updates in the Second Edition

This second edition offers descriptive class diagrams and more code explanations in every chapter. Table D-1 lists the most important updates in this edition.

Table D-1. *The Most Important Updates in This Edition*

Pattern Name	Key Update (or Inclusion)
Singleton	Additional implementation using a single lock, Lazy<T>.
Prototype	Additional implementation for shallow vs. deep copy.
Builder	Additional implementation using method chaining.
Factory Method	Shorter and concise implementation; one improved version is added (using method parameters).
Abstract Factory	Implementation fine-tuned and modified.
Proxy	Additional code explanation with Q&A is added.
Decorator	Implementation modified with more code explanation.
Adapter	Implementation fine-tuned; a complete example of class adapter is added.
Facade	Implementation made shorter and fine-tuned with additional explanations.
Flyweight	Implementation modified with extrinsic and intrinsic states. A factory class is implemented as a singleton to show an alternative design of this pattern.

(continued)

© Vaskaran Sarcar 2020
V. Sarcar, *Design Patterns in C#*, https://doi.org/10.1007/978-1-4842-6062-3

Table D-1. (*continued*)

Pattern Name	Key Update (or Inclusion)
Composite	Implementation fine-tuned with additional property (designation) and more code explanation.
Bridge	An additional implementation is added.
Visitor	Replaced the first implementation with a better one (extended in the Q&A session), and following the same design, fine-tuned the second implementation using both the Visitor and the Composite patterns.
Observer	Implementation fine-tuned; Now you see multiple celebrities with multiple observers.
Strategy	Better example provided; Q&A session is enhanced.
Template Method	Implementation fine-tuned with more Q&A.
Command	Old programs are replaced with new programs; additional explanation for undo, logging, and so forth are included.
Iterator	An additional program using C#'s built-in support for iterators is included.
Memento	One new implementation using nested class is included. Q&A session is enhanced.
State	More Q&A and explanation are added.
Mediator	Minor modification to the programs in previous edition of the book. Now these programs have both send and receive logic. Additional explanations are added.
Chain of Responsibility	Old program is modified. More code explanation with a real-life example is added.
Interpreter Pattern	One new implementation is added in this chapter. First demo is a fine-tuned version from previous edition of the book.
Simple Factory	Old program is replaced with a shorter and more concise implementation.
Null Object Pattern	More explanation (including null conditional operator) is added. Q&A session is enhanced.

(*continued*)

Table D-1. (*continued*)

Pattern Name	Key Update (or Inclusion)
MVC	The Winform application is replaced with a console application.
Asynchronous Programming	This is a new chapter in this book.
Criticism to Design Patterns	More information is added.
Antipatterns	Enhanced with history, types, and examples of antipatterns.
FAQ	Fine-tuned with additional questions and answers.

Index

A

AboutMe() method, 84, 90, 145, 147, 155, 159, 181

AboutTriangle() method, 146, 156, 160

Abstract keyword, 92

Abstract class, 69

Abstract creator class, 81, 82

AbstractDecorator class, 130, 141

AbstractExpression, 439

Abstract Factory pattern, 612
  challenges, 107
  concept, 97, 98
  vs. factory method pattern, 108
  factory of factories, 97
  GoF definition, 97
  IAnimalFactory, 99
  IDog and ITiger interfaces, 107
  implementation
    class diagram, 101
    demonstration, 102–106
    solution explorer view, 102
  real-world and computer-world
    example, 98
  vs. simple factory pattern, 107–109
  structure, 98
  WildAnimalFactory, 99

Abstract prototype, 27

Action delegate, 568

Adaptee interface method, 160

Adapter pattern

concept, 143

drawbacks, 161

GoF definition, 143

implementation
  class adapter, demo, 155–159
  class diagram, 148
  demonstration, 150–153
  IRectangle interface, 145
  IRectangle methods, 147
  Main() method, 153
  Rectangle hierarchy, 146
  solution explorer view, 148

real-world and computer-world
  example, 143–145

Adapters, 611

AddHeadlights(), 59

Aggregate, 338

AnimalFactory, 82, 85

Antipatterns
  causes, 606
  concepts, 603, 604
  design pattern, 606
  examples, 603
  history, 602
  overview, 601
  real-world application development, 601
  solutions, 607
  symptoms, 607
  types, 605

Architectural antipatterns, 605

© Vaskaran Sarcar 2020

V. Sarcar, *Design Patterns in C#*, https://doi.org/10.1007/978-1-4842-6062-3

C

T

U

Printed in the United States
By Bookmasters